Theological Education by Extension

Leadership Education for the Church

by

Linda Cannell

EDCOT® Press
MorgenBooks

Theological Education Matters
© 2006 Linda Cannell. All rights reserved.

Bibliographic Citation
Cannell, Linda. 2006. *Theological Education Matters: Leadership Education for the Church*. Newburgh, IN: EDCOT Press.

Notice of Rights
All rights reserved. No part of this book may be reproduced or transmitted in any form or by any means, electronic or mechanical, including photocopying, recording, or by any information storage or retrieval system, without the prior written permission from the author, except for inclusion of brief quotations in a review.

Notice of Liability
Although the author and publisher have made every effort to ensure the accuracy and completeness of information contained in this book, the author and publisher assume no responsibility for errors, inaccuracies, omissions, or any inconsistencies herein. No liability is assumed for incidental or consequential damages in connection with or arising out of the use of the information contained herein. All slights of people, places, or organizations are unintentional.

Trademarks
Throughout this book, trademarks may be used. Rather than put a trademark symbol in every occurrence of a trademarked name, the author and publisher state that the names are used in an editorial fashion only and to the benefit of the trademark owner with no intention of infringement of the trademark. Use of a term in the book should not be regarded as affecting the validity of any trademark or service mark.

Scripture quotations marked (NRSV) are taken from the New Revised Standard Version of the Bible, copyright 1989 by the Division of Christian Education of the National Council of the Churches of Christ in the USA. Used by permission. All rights reserved.

Printed in the United States of America
Fourth printing 2008

17 16 15 14 13 12 11 10 09 08 / 04 05 06 07 08 09 10 11 12 13 14

ePrint by EDCOT® Press for MorgenBooks
Paperback and Hardcover by BookSurge Publishing for EDCOT® Press

Cover by Wayne Kijanowski
Edited by Ruth Goring
Layout by Mark Simpson

www.edcotpress.com
www.morgenbooks.org
www.lulu.com
www.booksurge.com

Contents

Acknowledgments 8

Foreword by Ted Ward 9

Introduction 17

Emerging Trends in Theological Education:
An Interview 28

PART I — A THREAT MATRIX FOR THEOLOGICAL EDUCATION: SPECIAL PROBLEMS FOR THE CHURCH

CHAPTER 1
Perspectives on Contemporary
Theological Education 35
    Farley on *Theologia* and the Clerical Paradigm 37
    "The Delicate Fabric of Informed Wisdom" 40

CHAPTER 2
Persisting Factors That Affect the Future of
Theological Education 44
    Factor 1: The Rise of Institutions 44
    Factor 2: The Rise of Academic Theology 58
    Factor 3: The Rise of Professionalism in Higher Education 77
    Factor 4: The Disposition of the Soul toward God 86

CHAPTER 3
A Threat Matrix: Challenges Confronting the
Seminary and the Church 102
    Implications from Four Interdependent Processes
        from the History of Higher Education 102
    Toward a New Matrix for 21st Century Theological Education 113
    Funding the Future of Theological Education 122

Part II — Historical Backgrounds

Chapter 4
The Development of Institutions of Theological Education 126
- The Monasteries and the Cathedral School 126
- The Scholastic Universities 128
- Patterns of Education during the Renaissance and Reformation Eras 130
- The Idea for a New University in Berlin 134
- Educational Institutions in North America 136
- The Development of Universities and University Divinity Schools in North America 145
- Surveys of Theological Education, 1924–1956 150
- The Final Surveys of the Twentieth Century 158

Chapter 5
The Shaping of Academic Theology 164
- Scholastic Theology and the Universities 165
- The New Universities of the Renaissance and Reformation 171
- Schleiermacher and the Founding of the University of Berlin 174
- Theology and Education in Colonial America 177
- The Compartmentalization of Academic Theology 184

Chapter 6
The Emergence of Professionalism in Theological Education 188
- Emergence of the German Research Model for Professional Preparation 191
- The Flexner Report 199
- The Growth of Professionalism in Theological Education 201
- Challenges to Professionalism 204
- Expansion of University-Based Professional Education 207
- The Seminary and Professional Education 211

Chapter 7
***Theologia* and the Desire to Know God** 213

The Meaning of Theology in the Early Church 213
Evagrius's Influence on the Meaning of *Theologia* 216
The Development of *Theologia* and Spirituality
    in Western Mystical Theology 221
The Brethren and Sisters of the Common Life 227
Seventeenth-Century Pietism 231
Schleiermacher and Pietistic Influence in the
    German University 234
Toward a Holistic Understanding of Reason and Spirituality 236

PART III — IMPLICATIONS FOR 21ST CENTURY INTERNATIONAL THEOLOGICAL EDUCATION

CHAPTER 8
Recovering a Focus on the Church 238
The Church as a Theological Community 244
The Church as a Sociological Community 248
Theological Education and Leadership Development 250
Toward a More Appropriate Approach to
    Leadership Development 252
Effects of the Professional Model of Ministry on the Church 254
Emerging Initiatives in Theological Education Related
    to the Church 256
A Congregational Paradigm: A Dilemma for
    Theological Education 261
Recovering the Focus on the Church 268

CHAPTER 9
**Toward a "Learning Century" for
Theological Education** 270
Factor 1: Learning—A Holistic Process of Development 271
Factor 2: Reconceiving Practice to Put Theory in
    Proper Perspective 278
Factor 3: The Community as the Proper Context
    for Learning 289
Factor 4: The Lifelong Learner—A Spiritual Vision
    for Theological Education 302

CHAPTER 10
**Toward an International 21ˢᵗ Century
Theological Education**.. 306
    Perspectives on the Nature of Theological Dialogue.......... 308
    Theological Education and the Growing
        International Church... 311
    International Theological Education..................................... 314

CONCLUSION
What *Does* It Mean to Be Theologically Educated?................. 317
    "I Skate Where the Puck Will Be, Not Where It Is"............ 319
    Becoming Theologically Educated... 324

References.. 327

Index 364

Acknowledgments

I am indebted to generations of colleagues and companion learners in the PhD in Educational Studies program at Trinity Evangelical Divinity School who stimulated and enlarged my perspectives.

Several close friends have been part of the journey that has resulted in this book. Ted Ward has been the "iron that sharpened iron" over the many years of our friendship. His contribution to my life cannot be measured. Walt Liefeld is one of the best examples I know of the integration of ministry and scholarship. LeRoy Ford, in the formative years of my own education, showed me that it was possible to make a difference in higher education. I am also grateful for Perry and Sandy Downs whose friendship and care kept me going.

My thanks to copy editor, Ruth Goring, for her careful work with the manuscript; and to Mark Simpson whose technological savvy made the publication of this manuscript possible.

Foreword

The Anomaly of Theological Education: Institutions Serving an Institution

The church is more than an organization. It is a body of people; biblically it is identified as "the body of Christ." It is a community of faith, a collective of those committed to a belief. But the church is often mistaken as an organization, and as such, it is assumed to be represented by one or more institutions of education, especially because it is associated with training academies of many sorts: Bible schools, ministerial seminaries, theological schools, divinity schools. Whether such schools are *served by* the church or are intended *to serve* the church is one of the most confused issues in all of professional education. Exploring this issue and identifying the historical and philosophical roots of its confusion are the driving motives that have led Linda Cannell to write this book.

Although the church can be classified sociologically as an institution, it is more metaphysical than this term suggests. Biblically, the church is identified with the qualities of personhood as "the bride of Christ." This metaphor's distance from the realm of organizational structures and management is dramatic and surely intentional. The special relationship of Christ and his followers is identified in the vocabulary of relationships. The intimacy of this relationship is revealed in its special form of affiliation. The church is a family, not merely a membership organization.

The church functions within two domains: the physical universe of human relationships and the spiritual realm of eternal and transcendent truth. Great care is required to reconcile the ways and means of the differing value systems of these two domains. The difficulties in maintaining such reconciliation are especially evident in matters of leadership and in the ways and means of developing leaders.

Dealing with the physical universe requires accepting the importance of information. Those who lead—whether at the level of supervision and management or at the level of planning and evaluative judgment—must know the basic stuff of the job. They must be prepared through appropriate modes of experience so that they know the skills, understandings, and roles needed to fulfill the job. They also must be carefully oriented to the social and emotional context of the job—inspired and motivated to fulfill their appointed role in the organization, to represent faithfully the ethos of its purposes.

Whether this need to know is a matter of memorizing facts or of developing complex reasoning and spiritual maturity in order to make appropriate choices and judgments (some of us believe the latter is the preferred outcome), it seems to call for some kind of educational intervention. Leaders of the church must *know*, they must *do*, and they must *become* in order to be exemplars of the values, style, and social-emotional orientation demanded for the tasks, management, and purpose-fulfillment of the organization.

Thinking of job requirements and necessary competencies in terms of learning tasks, however, leads to several dangerous habits. First, it leads to the presumption that skills and knowledge are the only sorts of qualifications that are important to establish qualifications. (What about character traits and moral judgment?) Second, it exalts the qualities of a person that can be assessed through objective testing. Testing objectively justifies a piecework mode of teaching that dehumanizes our development and growth processes. (Is it enough to assess the stuff on information shelves and to come up with scores for the skills that a person possesses?) Third, it overlooks the human quality of interrelationship. A person is not simply the sum of what is remembered and what can be done with that information. (Do fragmented facts and catalogs of information add up to a fair representation of one's personality, style, sensitivities, and being, a true assessment of the person?)

Such a tendency to oversimplify, to dry out, and to objectify in cold and inhuman representations leads educators today to warn against excesses of the objective testing movement. The resultant conflict in this domain is just the tip of the iceberg of the current dissonance between school and church.

The Question of Values

Institutions of one sort can effectively serve institutions of another sort if their values are consistent. When any institution, the church, for example, is served by another institution, a school, for example, the similarity of their purposes and values will determine the worth of the service. If the purposes and values are different on any significant issue, the service will be weakened, quite possibly invalidated. In the business and financial world, banking institutions can serve business institutions well because banks and mercantile institutions share the same competitive values and profit-making purposes.

On the other hand, the likelihood of conflicting purposes when medical and pastoral personnel are called upon to serve military purposes is accommodated by setting them apart as noncombatants; this status is formally recognized by the Geneva Convention. These humanitarian specialists are dedicated to different purposes from those of soldiers and military commanders: *saving lives*, a high value of most religions, stands in contrast with *ending lives*, which is the immediate purpose of modern warfare.

Conflicts between the fulfillment of higher moral values and the possibility of doing possible damage to those values is a matter of concern to most honorable institutions and organizations. For this reason, most universities are constantly on guard lest their research facilities be used for immoral or dishonest purposes.

My attempt to connect issues of selection and training of pastors to matters of warfare and immorality may seem strained. But to the extent that theology (the study of basic sources in religion) involves one institution (the church) entrusting itself to another institution, schooling, to be the developer of its leaders, the parallels are clear. Perhaps it should be stated more boldly: *the church has not consistently been well served by the schools and school-like institutions to which it has delegated the responsibility to prepare its own leaders.*

Theological Education Matters aims to get to the bottom of this failure. It reveals the breadth of the issues—not only in terms of the diversity of curricula but in terms of the forms and symbols theological institutions represent and provide as they attempt to deliver the appropriate services.

The church, as understood by Christians, is itself an odd case among the religious institutions of human societies. The church of Jesus Christ is far more than a New Testament manifestation of the synagogue of the Old Testament. It is far more than a temple or place of worship (a mosque, for example). Yes, *church* (Gr. *ekklesia*) occasionally denotes a place of worship, but more often—and more substantially—the term denotes an assembly of followers of Christ, whether in a place or on the move. Always the distinction is illustrative of a common commitment to God through the crucifixion, death, burial, and resurrection of this glorified and ascended person, Emmanuel, God with us.

The purpose of this body of people, the family of God, whether in whole or in a specific place, is always the same: to perpetuate Christ's call to humankind. *Repent and be baptized.* It is not an organization, surely not a club or a collective of delegates to a meritorious organization. The distinctives of the life and motives of Jesus were intensely personal: truth, hope, compassion, faith, forgiveness, gentleness, and mercy. These values difficult to embody; even those who are sincerely committed to Christ find themselves engaged in a lifetime challenge and inspiration. A common trait of Christians is that they accept the futility of self-improvement toward the goal of becoming Christlike and give themselves over to the grace of God and the work of the Holy Spirit.

Who Chooses the Leaders?

Leadership of this assembly, the church, was not left to chance. It was charged to carry out its purposes under the guidance of the Holy Spirit as leaders were identified, equipped, and gifted specifically for the offices and services of the church. This process borders on the mystical, although deliberate decisions and choices are illustrated in numerous biblical examples.

Selecting and preparing leaders to enable the church to carry out its ministry, as established by Christ and the apostles, is a responsibility charged to the church. Nowhere in Scripture is this task assigned to another agency or institution. Thus each theological school must accept its accountability to the church, lest it become a potential source of dissonance. All churches and organizations of churches do not see this matter alike. Various arrangements are made to assign the labors and responsibilities of educational tasks. Some scholars underestimate the importance of harmony on these matters. Others are intolerant in their insistence on assigning *sole* authority to the local church or to the institutions of the denominational affiliation.

For some, it is a matter of convenience and management: the special work of preparing and certifying pastoral leaders is a service *to* the church, not primarily a responsibility *of* the church. Such a view allows that the tasks of selecting and preparing leaders can be delegated to specialized institutions of pastoral education and training—schools. This reasoning has long-standing acceptance and support, although it seems inconsistent with

New Testament teachings and practices. In recent years, as schooling has become more concerned with technology than with philosophy and history, important questions are being raised about its appropriate role within the church.

Theological Education Matters explores the beliefs, traditions, and history of these conflicting views of leadership and its development within and among churches. Because of the worldwide growth of the Christian church and the diversities and dissonances arising in various cultural situations in which the church is emerging, understanding the shapes, forms, and diverse formation of church leadership requires careful examination and reflection.

Schools for Developing Leaders

Three factors are linked to the presumption that the church needs schools.

1. Christians Identify Themselves as the People of the Book

While this self-description is not absolutely unique to Christianity, it would be hard to find a more likely claim by a more self-aware group. In Old Testament Judaism, tracking God's dealings with his people, in an era much less familiar with writing, God provides Moses with carvings in stone to explicate his law to his people. In modern times there has been an unbroken chain of expository writings that document God's guiding hand in human history. The Christians' great book, the Bible, has served to stimulate and initiate the creative spirit of missionaries and inventors. "Bringing the Word" requires two things: a bringer and the book. *Bringers* are first identified in the Old Testament as prophets, and their role is fulfilled in the New Testament as "Apostles." This book, the Bible, has been the focus and the calling of uncounted generations of scribes, translators, and copyists.

This emphasis on the book may have led to a fundamental distortion within Christian doctrine and practice. The preoccupation with the written text has led to a perpetual discourse about textual accuracy. The concern itself illustrates the dilemma: either the text is an accurate representation of the truth or it is not. Indeed, but the issue is in the meaning of "representation of the truth." When loyalty to the text is exaggerated beyond the truth itself, we become vulnerable to bibliolatry. In defense of the Bible's presumed inherent linguistic precision, all sorts of campaigns are mounted in which the issue becomes accuracy of translation rather than a search for inherent evidences of *God's* consistency. It is quite a leap to think of a printed book as Word in the same way we think of the divine Person as Word. The apostle John speaks of the latter when he says of Christ, "In the beginning was the Word, and the Word was with God, and the Word was God. He was in the beginning with God.... The Word became flesh and lived among us, and we have seen his glory, the glory as of a father's only son, full of grace and truth" (John 1:1–2, 14). The cause of Christ would be better served by book-centered scholarship if it were fulfilled in light of the teachings of the Epistle of James (e.g., James 1:22, 27; 2:14, 18, 26; 3:13; 4:17).

2. Loyalty to a School Fulfills the Human Pride in Affiliation

Human cultures generally discriminate between appropriate and inappropriate ways to identify oneself as an affiliate of a religion. Christians, especially, are sensitive to displays of pride and superiority in the name of Christ. It is assumed to be more seemly to take pride in the schools that have been instrumental in one's religious development and to substitute glorification of the academic realm for glorification of the religion. Thus symbols of academic achievement are deemed acceptable where symbols of spiritual development would be inappropriate.

The prestige of an outstanding theological seminary or university is marketable; it has value in establishing the worth of the degrees that the institution grants. By no means is this a recent phenomenon. To have studied with the "right" mentor and to have partaken of the intellectual aura of a "great" scholarly community have apparently been venerated since earliest times. Today, however, competition is exaggerated beyond a school's claim of excellence, and excellence is converted to values of the marketplace. To be "the best" has worth on the secular balance sheet, and to have degrees from the best schools increases one's prospects for a large salary.

In many ways, academic experiences can shape the student's philosophical and moral character. For those who understand this, there is more than a touch of sadness when we consider the sorts of schools students tend to prefer. Respect for biblical authority maintained by a school commonly seems far less important than prestigious reputation and the pragmatic value a school provides by sending its graduates on to even more prestigious institutions. Those of us engaged in international education have seen many sincere international Christians put such an institution as Harvard Divinity School at the top of their list simply because of the reputation of Harvard University.

The secularizing tendencies in the church and its leadership spread steadily into all sorts of matters. Preference for academic excellence over spiritual depth is surely among the most serious of these. Closely related, the preference for "book learning" over experience and application leads a person (or a congregation) into habits of personal isolation and disdain for practical applications of truth.

Accreditation is assumed to provide safeguards against deviations from purpose and from excellence. Modern accreditation has a strangely mixed parentage. Among its more admirable intentions is the sustaining of academic quality through standardization of courses and degrees. In its earliest days, American-style accreditation emerged from the complaints of registrars in frontier universities that they needed protection from increasing numbers of poorly educated rural high school graduates. Accreditation was originally more concerned with the quality of applicants than the quality of the institution.

As often happens despite best intentions, the methods employed for judging quality and making preferential choices have led to a contradictory extreme: the most apparent consequence of accreditation has become the suppression of innovation in favor of maintaining the status quo, no matter how antiquated or ill-advised. Commonly, the very exalting of excellence is itself over structured in such a way as to suppress any changes that would make an institution unique. Thus a vicious circle results in which the quest for excellence is discouraged.

3. *The Human Thirst for Learning Seems More Manageable and Easier to Fulfill When It is Regimented*

Church architecture reflects the Roman lecture hall and the Greek amphitheater rather than honoring Jesus' own fondness for seated circles of people, as in the synagogues of his day. We learn to think of church as a big space where all but one or two people sit staring forward in rapt attention as one person interprets a text and promulgates conclusions.

Rarely do we see the preaching and teaching style of Jesus practiced by leaders in the church. For example, Jesus *stood* respectfully while reading the text of scripture but *sat* among the other worshipers to engage in discussion of the text (see Luke 4:16–21). It would not be wise to make such a detail a core value, but neither should it be overlooked. Walking together, eating together, and sitting together, always accompanied by talking together in a dialogic manner, are not the images that first come to mind when Jesus is identified as a great teacher or preacher. But details within the Gospel descriptions of Jesus' interactions with his followers, along with evidences of his tendency to invite himself into social situations with others, suggest a persistent habit—indeed a remarkable style—not just several coincidences. Jesus emerges as an artist—a skillful, warm, compassionate specialist in adult education. The twin maxims that are attributed occasionally to my own style and habits as a facilitator of learning are not mine; I learned them from Jesus: *Learning is lifelong. Learning is collaborative.*

When teaching is scheduled, boxed, structured, "presented," and over organized, it is reduced to a *thing*. Teaching must struggle to free itself from such habits, customs, and limitations so that learning may occur. Learning, at its finest, is a lively encounter with some intriguing aspect of life. Thus learning is the extending of one's thoughts and understandings to encounter, discover, and blend one's past with the unfolding present, thus enabling an active involvement in the shaping of a creative future.

This sort of learning is not a mechanical response to managed and manipulated stimuli. It is not simply arrangements of habit displayed in sequences that satisfy curricular inquiries. Learning is not only responses to questions; it is creation and appreciation of questions. Valuing the human thirst for learning, I have come to reject any manageable, regimented, easy-to-fulfill series of lonely learning tasks. Learning works best when it occurs as part of a community's experience. I learned this from Jesus: *Learning is a lifelong engagement that is collaborative.*

Thirst for learning is an important trait of human beings. It should be encouraged and nurtured. Within the teaching-learning ministries of the church, our task is to facilitate—to help it happen. To stimulate and challenge. To nurture and encourage. To be resonant chambers that enable the strings of the discoverer's violin to transform from squeaks and scrapes into an unfolding promise of heavenly melody. The work of Jesus Christ in this troubled world needs disciples who are motivated to serve the church in collaborations that fulfill his purposes. Thus the church may become an institution served by other institutions, allied in God's purposes.

Ted Ward
Professor Emeritus of Education and International Studies
Trinity Evangelical Divinity School
Michigan State University

Introduction

In 1994, "Jeffery Sachs, an American economist and an advisor to several reforming governments, [argued] that the communist economies ran into three simultaneous crises: they were doing the wrong things, they were doing them badly, and they ran out of money" (*After Communism*, 1994, 23). History may show that theological institutions ran into their own set of crises at the beginning of the twenty-first century: they were trying to do the right things, they missed the warning signals, and they ran out of money.[1]

The flurry of literature on the crises afflicting theological education seems to have abated somewhat, but concerns about the future of institutionalized theological education linger. Some efforts to deal with these concerns simply recycle existing conditions. It is likely that the more effective efforts will be international in scope, learning focused, deeply concerned about theological education in relation to a biblical ecclesiology, committed to service within society, and increasingly decentralized in structure and affiliations. Credentialing and accreditation that have tended to limit development in theological education are today, especially in North America, less determinative and more supportive of change. Efforts to assist productive relationships between nondegree, noncredentialed initiatives and formal or conventional theological education are emerging in different countries. Correspondingly, some accrediting agencies are less preoccupied with counting, checklists, and control and more concerned about encouraging member institutions to clarify outcomes, values, and institutional culture and to identify appropriate practices in relation to these.

---

[1] This malaise is not unique to theological schools and seems to be a persisting concern in higher education. In 1997, Madeleine Green and Fred Hayward described secular higher education as being in a period of unprecedented change. Indicators of such change were felt needs for increased access and internationalization, declining resources, public doubt about its usefulness, too many graduates for too few jobs, graduates ill-equipped for the jobs that do exist, and a quest to effectively incorporate technology. "Making good judgments about what needs to be preserved, what might be altered, and what should be totally redesigned are the difficult issues that institutions face" (In Green 1997, 4).

The final report on redeveloped standards for the Association of Theological Schools (ATS),[2] for example, states: "Theological schools are communities of faith and learning guided by a theological vision.... Their educational programs should continue the heritage of theological scholarship, attend to the religious constituencies served, and respond to the global context of religious service and theological education" (Standards of Accreditation 1996, 23). According to the new standards, "a theological school is a community of faith and learning that cultivates habits of theological reflection, nurtures wise and skilled ministerial practice, and contributes to the formation of spiritual awareness and moral sensitivity. Within this context, the task of theological scholarship is central. It includes the interrelated activities of learning, teaching, and research" (Standards of Accreditation 1996, 25).

However, concerns about the state of theological education persist: the curriculum is specialized and fragmented, thus hindering the equipping of leaders; a coherent purpose and compelling vision for theological education are lacking; the effort historically to integrate the curriculum around theology has been lost; theology itself is undefined, fragmented, rationalized, and specialized; theory and practice are in perpetual tension; and education is not sufficiently concerned with learning. Early critiques generally assumed that institutions of theological education would continue, but would be reformed over time. More recently, the suspicion is emerging that institutions of theological education as we know them—the seminary in particular—may not be necessary at all. Cynical critics ask, what is the point of a seminary education that requires more time than people are willing to give, more money than people are able to pay, more disconnection from family and career than people are willing to tolerate, and that seems to be less than effective in equipping women and men for leadership and ministry?

For many years, institutional theological education functioned as an industry concerned about the economics of human and knowledge products from schools that were more like factories than centers of learning. Today many churches, frustrated with the graduates of theological schools, are challenging existing systems and joining their efforts to find new models. Schools, worried about economic survival, seek to retain current church

---

[2]ATS accredits theological seminaries in the United States and Canada.

constituencies while attracting new markets. Many schools, desiring to meet what are perceived as current needs of the church and society, have spawned a variety of emphases and new degree programs, formed partnerships, and established institutes to do what the traditional curriculum seems unable to do. Unfortunately, simply adding more courses, designing new programs, and finding more money are not sufficient responses to the problems. In spite of these efforts, many graduates still struggle in ministry, many schools are still worried they may not survive, and many churches continue to experiment with alternatives.

The vultures are not circling—yet. But the persisting criticisms and the reality that change in higher education tends to move at a glacial pace increase the probability that initiatives rapidly coming to maturity will supplant or forever change theological education as we know it. Church-based theological education, e-learning, seminars offered by multi-campus churches in subject matters long part of the traditional seminary curriculum, institutes established in relation to schools but not organically linked to them, centers on the traditional campus offering new programs that parallel or supplant a hopelessly mired curriculum, an emphasis on theological education for the whole people of God, and redefined roles of faculty and academic leadership are among the developments that are assuming greater significance. However, if we do not make some attempt to understand at a deeper level the complex matrix of issues that affect theological education, even these initiatives will fall far short of what is needed.

The literature on theological education has focused in recent years on Roman Catholic and mainline Protestant schools. Though "mainline," "evangelical," and "liberal" as categories to describe schools are less useful today, the literature presumes that "Protestant mainline" and "Protestant evangelical" demarcate two different clusters of schools. This clustering also reflects how the membership of ATS is described. To date, concern about the state of Protestant theological education has been addressed by those identified with mainline schools and churches. Dan Aleshire, executive director of ATS, suggests that there are particular threats confronting evangelical seminaries that have yet to be addressed adequately.[3]

---

[3]From a personal conversation.

- Since many evangelical seminaries tend to be overly tuition driven and limited in endowment, they are especially vulnerable to economic downturns and international crises that affect immigration policies and hence limit applications. Without an adequate funding legacy, evangelical seminaries may not be able to afford current models of institutionalized theological education. For example, data gathered by ATS indicates that the number of full-time faculty members is in decline, largely for economic reasons.

- As evangelical institutions undergo financial stress, relationships between schools and denominations will grow increasingly tense and perhaps tenuous.

- Evangelical schools proliferated over the past five decades. The evangelical constituency cannot support (and may not need) the number of evangelical schools that currently exist in North America. Since too many schools are competing for a relatively small market share, it is inevitable that some will go out of existence. Aleshire believes that this threat is not as immediate as the financial threat; however, economic wisdom would discourage a comparable proliferation in the next twenty years.

- The proliferation of Ph.D. programs in seminaries in North America and around the world is evidence of a desire to advance evangelical scholarship. However, in many cases the faculty, support services, and financial resources are not available to sustain academic research doctoral programs at acceptable levels of quality.

- Issues related to the nature of teaching and learning command increased attention. Existing patterns of education and academic life will not be as tolerable for the older learner in graduate school—especially those who are second-career students.

- Churches are pressuring seminaries to better equip men and women for ministry in the church and society—sometimes ill-advisedly. Evangelical seminaries need to listen to the church while at the same time functioning as the church's best critic.

Full answers to these concerns and others will require more attention than this book can provide, of course. My observations about issues that affect the future of theological education will be influenced by my experience as a faculty member in evangelical seminaries.[4] For example, to critique a tendency of theological education to educate men and women for a church that no longer exists makes less sense for mainline seminaries. Similarly, the trend toward an alternately credentialed clergy is a much greater threat to evangelical schools. Though some evangelical seminaries are denominationally connected, the idea that a seminary could exist apart from a denominational context would seem a foreign concept to many mainline schools. Stereotyping and areas of genuine difference in theological and sociological perspectives exist on each side of the Protestant mainline and evangelical divide. When the dust clears, though, the statements of mission and the structures of theological institutions tend to be similar, and concerns for what constitutes theological education are equally great. In reality, this book would not have been possible without my interactions across the years with colleagues in institutions that represent the broad range of Protestant and Roman Catholic traditions.

An evolution of questions stimulated by various experiences prompted the writing of this book. After a few years of teaching in a seminary in Canada and realizing that its graduates were not surviving well in churches, I resigned and started a consulting ministry to serve particularly the smaller churches in Canada. As I recognized the deep problems of the church, the question became, what is the nature of the church as God sees it, and what if any relationship must therefore exist between the church and theological education? After ten years I responded to the encouragement of Ted Ward and accepted an invitation to join the faculty at Trinity Evangelical Divinity School in Chicago. There I was once again confronted with the frustrations of working in an academic environment. The question then became, what is the nature and purpose of theological education? At that time several books on problems in theological education had appeared, most notably *Theologia* by Edward Farley. My reading was informative but still not satisfying.

About this time, Rich Mouw, president of Fuller Seminary, secured a grant to gather faculty representing different disciplines in evangelical seminaries to form a community of discourse around the question "What are the aims and purposes of theological education?" I was invited to join this

---

[4]My church affiliations, however, are more traditionally mainline.

group partway into the process and met with its members for several years. Among other considerations, the problems created by the conventional fourfold model of the theological curriculum were discussed, and Friedrich Schleiermacher's legacy was said to have contributed to these problems. Wondering to what extent Schleiermacher and the German university model were actually to blame, I sketched out an article to explore Schleiermacher's vision. This quickly grew into a monograph when I began to wonder if the central problem in theological education *was*, in fact, the distortion of theology or the loss of a theological center. Then a larger manuscript emerged as research into Schleiermacher's vision and the changes in theological method led to further research on when (and why) theology and spirituality ceased to be understood as of one essence. This search led to inquiry into the rise of academic theology and the effects of institutionalization and rationalization on views regarding the nature of knowledge. The question of how these factors contributed to the apparent compartmentalization of reason and spirituality in theological education led me to wonder, would rationalism and spirituality have a different character and relationship today if Eastern and Western mysticism had managed to sustain a productive tension beyond the eleventh century and into the thirteenth century, when Scholasticism dominated the universities?

Finally, deep concern for the future of theological education and the seeming impossibility of breaking out of centuries-old patterns led to a more comprehensive reading of the history of higher education from the patristic era to the present. This survey prompted a realization that the literature tends to critique theological education in relation to one dominant factor or in relation to two or three factors *treated separately* (e.g., the functionalization of theology, the need for in-ministry education, specialization of the curriculum, the need for spiritual formation, poor educational design, and so on). I became convinced that concerns about theological education need to be understood in relation to a matrix of factors that *together* contribute to the problems that beset contemporary theological education.

To describe a matrix and its effects well would require a book that is more like a hologram. Since writing a hologram is impossible, the chapters that follow attempt to show how a cluster of factors has actually become a threat matrix for theological education and, consequently, the church. A brief revisiting of the contemporary literature and a more extensive historical background section provide both context and support for the designation of factors that constitute the matrix.

Obviously any book provides only a snapshot of reality. In the chapters that follow, persons with more expertise than I in certain areas will recognize gaps. This is to be expected. Still, I hope that the central intent, to describe a matrix of influences, has been fulfilled.

Excerpts from an interview between the editor of the *Wilberforce Forum* and me are included as a simple introduction to particular issues that concern many of us involved in theological education. Chapter 1 briefly synthesizes critiques of theological education found in readily available literature and highlights two questions: (1) To what extent do a distortion of theology and the consequent focus of theological education on developing the functions of ministry (the clerical paradigm) constitute a sufficient analysis of that which troubles theological education? (2) To what extent has wisdom—typically embedded in theology—as the solution to contemporary problems been sufficiently clarified to be of use to twenty-first-century international theological education? Chapter 2 discusses four major factors distilled from the literature and the long history of higher education and suggests that these factors make up a complex matrix that troubles theological education. Chapter 3 warns that taken together, these factors form a threat matrix that continues to affect theological education and the accomplishment of the mission of the church in the world.

Chapters 4–7 provide historical background related to the synthesis offered in chapter 1 and the factors discussed in chapters 2 and 3. From the patristic period through much of the twentieth century, questions of theological education—perspectives on the purpose of theological education; questions about the nature and purpose of theology; distinctions between professional and practical, theory and practice; the development and relationship of the disciplines; perspectives on education and the consequent shape of the curriculum—were wrestled with against a backdrop of continuing questions regarding the relationship of piety and intellect; the meaning and purpose of theology, society, and culture; and the identity of the people of God.

The history of higher education and the more recent history of theological education testify to the fact that perspectives and practices do change. Frustration and changing contexts do stimulate new vision and experimentation. The "schooling" metaphor, though persistent, has never been accepted as the sole model for education, and differing perspectives on the nature and purpose of theology have existed throughout history. Curricular forms have never been constant. We are not required to repeat or replicate history, but patterns evident in the long history of higher education should not be ignored as theological education struggles to find its way in the twenty-first century.

The final section, chapters 8–10, presents implications for seminaries seeking to renew their identity and purpose in the twenty-first century: What are the issues at stake for theological education to recover a focus on the church? How necessary is it that theological education be characterized by *praxis* and holism rather than by persisting polarities such as theory and practice? Can the seminary today *recover* holism and *praxis* within current structures and educational processes? To what extent can the seminary in the twenty-first century resolve the perceived tension between instruction and learning? How will the West respond to the fact that theological education is now international and increasingly decentralized? To what extent will the practices of theological education in its varied forms and contexts in many countries collaborate to serve the church and society?

In this postmissionary,[5] postconservative,[6] postmodern, post-postmodern,[7] post–rigidly structured institutional era, seminaries that see their role as preparing and sending people to do things for, or to, others will never pierce the myth that they bear sole responsibility to produce a sufficient number of leaders for the church. Seminaries whose modes of educa-

---

[5]Charles Van Engen asserts that one of the last vestiges of missionary colonialism today is theological education. Missionaries created Bible institutes and seminaries that are exact replicas of those they knew so well (Van Engen 1994, 15). It appears that theological education is entering a postmissionary era as nationals (many with degrees earned in North America and Europe) assume leadership. These nationals are thinking outside the inherited formal structures of education and joining networks of professionals who support one another's growth in administrative and teaching capacity.

[6]Kevin Vanhoozer describes himself as a postpropositionalist theologian who begins with Scripture as truthful special revelation but who does not conceive of truth or revelation as narrowly propositional. "Biblical authority is not simply a matter of its conveying information" (Vanhoozer 2000, 75).

[7]See Robert Greer (2003). "In this book, I will give voice to a number of theologians who are in hot pursuit of an epistemology with which to repudiate both modernism and postmodernism. Collectively, their voices are giving shape to a new paradigmatic structure from which to philosophize and theologize. I call this newly forming paradigm post-postmodernism" (Greer 2003, 22).

tion are out of step with the holistic capacities of human beings will become increasingly minor players in efforts to help Christians deepen their biblical understanding, develop mature practices of faith, and grow in wisdom. Seminaries that ignore the fact that their context is unavoidably international and vastly interconnected will never examine institutional dynamics and structures that obscure the realities of cultural engagement and that shield faculty and students from the need to examine how they listen to and interact with others different from themselves. In chapters 8–10, the institutional forms of theological education are deemphasized and hope emerges for international, learning-focused, more flexible, less institution-bound communities determined to serve the church in its fundamental mission of reconciliation and leading men and women toward the knowledge of God.

The conclusion reiterates that this book does not propose doing away with the academy *per se* but points out that serious flaws embedded in the very life and structure of the university were copied, unwittingly in many cases, by divinity schools and seminaries. The question of whether society and the church need universities, divinity schools, and seminaries will not be answered by this book. The more pressing questions relate to what institutions of higher learning have become and what alternatives are possible for leadership development and theological education for the whole people of God.

You have already read the *Foreword*. My reasons for inviting Ted Ward to write it are important at this point. Ted has spent all of his career in formal education at the University of Florida, Michigan State University (MSU), and Trinity Evangelical Divinity School (TEDS). His affiliation with two Land Grant universities reflects his lifelong commitment to education as service and as a lifelong discipline. However, Ted has also spent his career warning of the limitations of schooling and championing nonformal modes of education. He is considered by many to be one of the more important and influential educators of the twentieth century. Graduates of the Ph.D. programs he directed are scattered throughout the world, serving in numerous organizations as faculty members, presidents, deans, and provosts, as relief and development specialists, parachurch leaders, congregational leaders, mission leaders, and corporate executives. In retirement, Ted continues to influence education and leadership development in his capacity as senior adviser for leadership development with the Maclellan Foundation. I invited Ted to write the Foreword because he embodies several commitments that I believe are important as we struggle to find solutions to besetting problems in theological education.

From childhood, Ted determined that a primary characteristic of his life would be to make a difference. Early in his university career, he made a difference by pioneering new models of teacher education in Florida and Michigan. While at Michigan State University, he was on call with the U.S. Agency for International Development to go anywhere in the world where there was need on seventy-two hours' notice. For the tangible differences he made in less privileged countries he was given the *Dag Hammarskjöld Citation for Service in Developing Nations*, Uppsala, Sweden (1975) (he was the first American to be so honored), and later the Faculty and Alumni Award for Service, College of Education, Michigan State University (1986). His commitment to the health of family life resulted in an invitation to serve as consultant on moral values and family for the White House and the U.S. Congress, 1984–1987. On his overseas tours, in his spare time, he consulted with mission agencies and Christian leadership development initiatives to help them think through their particular responsibilities in the service of the church. His consultancies with Christian organizations, government agencies, and corporations are too numerous to mention here.

Important to this book, and the primary reason for asking Ted to write the Foreword, is that his commitment to service—to making a difference—is under girded by three primary educational values:

1. *Learning is collaborative and lifelong.* For example, his overseas contracts included stipulations that the relationship be collaborative and that he expected to learn from the situation. Nearly all his students can attest to the value of the learning communities that emerged in doctoral programs at MSU and TEDS.

2. *Development is a chief outcome of any educational endeavor.* For Ted this has meant investment in the personal and professional development of individuals, active response to injustice, effort to help communities develop in ways appropriate to their culture, and both the challenging and the recrafting of educational structures to reflect what most educators claim is their purpose—development!

3. *The necessity of research.* Little progress is made in any endeavor without carefully designed research. The habit of inquiry into truth, the intentional seeking for truth, is a hallmark of the doctoral programs Ted de-

veloped. Most of his students came to understand the importance of his insistence that even theology must be marked by openness to critique and inquiry.

That Ted has done all of this while involved in formal higher education marks him as someone who has not utterly dismissed the academy. However, he continues to call the academy to the purposes it espouses but often has failed to demonstrate.

Finally, Ted is a musician. Though his once considerable instrumental skills have diminished, and though he no longer conducts large choirs, he remains musically literate and has strong convictions about the place of music and the arts in society and in the Christian life. The capacity that is important in relation to this book is that his musicianship strengthened his ability to see patterns, to think in whole phrases, to hear the holism of things. Several years ago, some of Ted's former students prepared a *festschrift* to reflect what they had learned from him and what they felt were his most enduring contributions to education. The choice of title, *With an Eye on the Future* (Monrovia, California: MARC, 1996), was a deliberate recognition of Ted's capacity to see patterns and to propose implications for the future. That many of his collected writings and speeches across more than thirty years read like today's newspaper testifies to this ability and discipline.

We are in a time when the ability to discern implications for the future of theological education is essential. The need to see situations through fresh lenses is both mandatory and possible as leaders from different cultures and organizations come into conversation. Many colleagues and generations of doctoral participants have informed the themes in this book. However, in the task of discerning implications and alternatives, Ted Ward is still one of my most valued dialogue partners.

Emerging Trends in Theological Education: An Interview[1]

WF: *Linda, we met in Knoxville at our consortium meeting, where we discussed ongoing issues and emerging trends in the development of theological education. How long have you been involved in theological education, and how did you get started?*

LC: Through the 1970s and 80s I worked with Canadian churches and theological institutions. With many at that time I developed a growing unease about the effectiveness of churches and theological institutions. In 1990, I accepted the invitation to join the faculty of Trinity Evangelical Divinity School, primarily to work with Ted Ward. Through the years of our friendship, and in interaction with leaders from many countries and organizations, my early, admittedly more radically stated concerns have developed into more useful categories. In other words, the issues have become more clearly defined.

The solutions? Well, aren't we all still working at that? Today I find myself among a growing number of men and women from churches and theological institutions who share a common concern for the development and reform of the church and theological education.

WF: *From our interaction in Knoxville, it was apparent that theological education, for you, means something more than an institution or a school.*

LC: Yes, our habit of equating theological education almost exclusively with what happens in school buildings and classrooms has hurt the church worldwide. Today, the efforts to watch are the nonformal or nontraditional sectors in every country. These initiatives are often more holistic and therefore more productive in helping men and women develop biblical and theological understanding, competency in ministry, growth in spiritual maturity and interpersonal responsibility. Significantly, most of these initiatives are grounded in the

---

[1] This interview was conducted by the Wilberforce Forum. It is excerpted with permission from Linda Cannell, "Emerging Trends in Theological Education," Theological Educators Bulletin, no. 3, Fall 2003.

church. And I would agree that without a serious ecclesiology, formed and reformed through dialogue and relationship across culture, social, and gender boundaries, the Christian community will *never* have the sort of education that is required to develop us all for our "reasonable service" in the world. We will persist in building schools engaged in seemingly endless turf wars about what to do with the theological curriculum!

I remember Ted saying that the church has given away two of its central responsibilities: education and mission. It has entrusted these vital responsibilities to organizations that have developed institutional forms that may or may not be consistent with God's purposes for the church in the world.

WF: *Do you believe, then, that the church is the more appropriate context for theological education?*

LC: The church is the more appropriate *focus* for theological education, whether it takes place in church buildings, in seminaries, in homes, or under a tree. Over the years, three principles have become important for me: the church is central to what God is doing in the world; neither the church nor theological education should be understood as synonymous with the institutions we have created to house the church and to give shape to its responsibilities; and leaders *among* the people of God help churched people understand their identity. They stimulate worship and ways of being in a faith community that reflect and honor that identity, and they assist in developing the people of God for their service as the priesthood of all believers.

However, these principles have to be worked out against the reality that the history of the church has been a long struggle with issues of human ambition, organizational inadequacy, interpersonal conflict, immature relationships, and so on. Ted's observation that the institutional church is like a leaky boat and that we will spend all of our lives bailing is apt! . . .

WF: *One of the concerns of theological education among evangelicals has been the largely "academic" model in which learning is often equated with passing tests, writing papers, and taking courses. To what extent can these purposes and tasks be fulfilled in the academic or university model?*

LC: That's an interesting question. I would say that because we have begun with the premise that theological education takes place primarily or only in schools, we spend far too much time agonizing over what should be the purposes and tasks of theological education. I am concerned that we are laboring so hard to focus our purpose and tasks, or to return to some idealized form of something we can only imagine, that we are in danger of paralyzing ourselves. If we broadened our view of what the tasks really are and where and how these are accomplished, we wouldn't be as stuck in the "academic" model as we are today—or as defensive or protective when it is challenged. The academic model is appropriate but not necessarily for all the purposes or tasks that we have assigned to it by default.

Actually, I'm not convinced that descriptors such as *academic, professional, formal, nonformal,* and so on are helpful today. When we use these labels, the tendency is to get polarized around what we envision as *the* academically credible method. I remember hearing a prominent evangelical theologian say of an eminent educator, "Oh, he's just about methods." The reality is that all of us are about methods—no matter our discipline—and that many of the same methods can be applied to the descriptors we use today for education (*academic, professional,* and so on). I would rather we thought together about such questions as, What is the nature of learning? What are the social contexts and realities within which learning takes place? How is learning assessed? What institutional forms and attitudes are most appropriate for the learning task? As we become more comfortable envisioning a number of related tasks and formats for theological education, the protectiveness that some feel for the stereotypical academic model should go away—I hope.

WF: *In relation to this, would you agree with those who suggest that the curriculum should be more of an integration of disciplines than what is now described as separate "silos," each containing its own substance and never connecting?*

LC: Talk of integrating disciplines has a long history. Some in evangelical circles fear that integration will lead to relativism or to acceptance of all perspectives with no closure around what they see as truth. However, the fears are probably groundless, since by pursuing integration we may be pursuing a dream or going at it the wrong way around anyway. If we accept the definition of a discipline as that which has its own subject matter, its own questions, and its own methodology, then integration is not going to be a simple matter. Nor will it be accomplished by simply putting faculty from different disciplines together in a classroom....

WF: *Are you questioning the validity of organizing the theological curriculum around disciplines—or almost exclusively around disciplines?*

LC: Rick Dunn, a member of the Knoxville Consortium, describes theological education as an ecology as opposed to silos. In other words, what if we envisioned theological education as a synergy of several elements: the church, the academy, nontraditional learning, participating organizations in society, an individual's vocational experience, and so on? This would leave the way open for two critical changes in the way we envision theological education. First, we could accept a number of varying purposes for theological education, drawing the rationale for these purposes from the gifts given by the Holy Spirit to people for the sake of the church and seeing them developed through any number of learning processes in any number of contexts. Second, we could envision defining issues and problems affecting Christianity in our world and create learning experiences where those who have spent a lifetime in disciplined study could productively bring insights from their pursuit of knowledge to bear on these problems.

Students in such experiences would be confronted with the claims of a discipline and its subject matter much more effectively and more productively than at present, where information is lost as soon as the exam is over! I am not the only faculty member who hears over and over again the lament of graduates, "I wish I had paid more attention to *that*." Or, "Most of what I 'learned' has little relevance in my cultural context." Clearly, intellectual and personal categories and capabilities are shaped in current academic contexts, but not as responsibly or effectively as they could be....

WF: *Are you observing changes in the way theological schools are organizing their curricula?*

LC: Curricular reform in higher education typically proceeds at a pace too glacial to be of much impact and is too often derailed by faculty, administrative, and constituency interests. We are long past the day when a seminary can do all that's expected of it. The curriculum is glutted with programs, littered with degrees, stuck in an instructional paradigm. It is likely that the pressure from congregations and society and developments in distance learning will force major changes such as a shift from an instructional paradigm to a learning paradigm, a recognition that learning is lifelong, and an internationalization of the curriculum. When this happens, I think we will see some constructive models emerging in theological education. But to answer your question: Yes, some schools are experimenting with curricular reform....

WF: *Is anything changing in that other problematic area of curriculum development, credentialing—I mean, grades, degrees and so forth?*

LC: I do wonder how much longer the perceived need for a degree and institutional credentialing will attract and hold students. Unfortunately, many students and faculty still look to the grade as the measure of their learning and teaching and see the credential as necessary. Information about assessment abounds but is not taken seriously enough in theological institutions. In some places, portfolio assessment and problem-based learning are being used with great effectiveness; but these initiatives, long part of education generally, are not common in theological education.

WF: *Take a moment to speak to the fact that theological institutions are increasingly concerned about the spiritual formation of students.*

LC: Pardon the cynicism, but Protestant evangelical seminaries tend to respond to this issue by adding a course to the curriculum. In some instances, even the addition of a course is resisted because, after all, how does one grade prayer? The "forming" language, especially where it is translated into a course or a slogan, is problematic for me.

The ATS Standards for North American seminaries define theological institutions as "communities of faith and learning." Can we reasonably expect that such communities will develop spiritually through courses if institutional dynamics, attitudes, and practices counter what we say? How about the way we deal with those issues that divide us—academic versus professional, men versus women, different theological perspectives, different views on leadership and ministry, and so on? These are the arenas where spirituality is challenged and matured. Let's not talk about adding a spiritual formation emphasis to the curriculum, or writing it up as a slogan, until we have examined how we treat one another and deal with those issues that divide us.

WF: *What are the two or three most encouraging trends in theological education that you are observing?*

LC: I would say that the increasing efforts toward more holistic models of theological education represent an encouraging trend. This holism can be described as learning experiences that take account of more than the cognitive—or even the practical—or as the effort to build consortia comprised of different organizations....

The increasing resistance of international leaders and scholars to simply continuing patterns from the West is encouraging wherever I see it in the world. At first, it was resistance to anything Western, while Westerners felt that they had nothing more to contribute. Now it seems that there are increasing attempts to form international *partnerships* where we can learn *from one another* across international and cultural boundaries....

WF: *What advice would you give to churches—such as those in our consortium here in Knoxville—who want to provide a level of theological education to the people in their community?*

LC: My concerns for any group of people or institutions who get together to offer something to others are twofold. First, we fail to involve the people we purport to serve in the process and gradually fall into a mode where we see ourselves teaching *them*. Second, the dangers that threaten the seminary will also infect churches that are concerned about "theological education for the whole people of God."

If churches believe that offering theological education to laity and leaders is simply a matter of transferring the theological curriculum to churches, the same fragmentation and isolation of subjects, and people, will result. Similarly, if churches do not think through what it means to nurture learning communities, then we will soon be reading books about the crises and failures in church-based theological education!

PART I

A Threat Matrix for Theological Education: Special Problems for the Church

Chapter 1

Perspectives on Contemporary Theological Education

We're lost, but we're making good time.—Yogi Berra

Robert Banks has provided one of the better reviews of the literature dealing with contemporary theological education (see pt. 1, "Reassessing Theological Education," in Banks 1999). In brief, concerns addressed in the literature about the future of theological education seem to revolve around three interrelated issues. First, some believe that the meaning of theology has been distorted—that the unifying principle in theological education has been lost. The second issue is related to the first: the seminary's curriculum, without an adequate definition of the nature and purpose of theology, devolves into a collection of specialized subjects. The third issue derives from specialization: a fragmented curriculum, organized generally into theory and practice divisions, leads to a distorted understanding of that which theological education addresses.

Taken together, these issues point to a theological education curriculum characterized by minimal integration among the disciplines and a tendency to functionalism. Banks is dissatisfied with the various proposals for change in light of these critiques, because for the most part they retain a cognitive orientation. Banks' alternative is not foreign to the literature, but he gives it considerably more attention and a well-developed biblical context—the missional model. He writes, "By mission I mean not just 'mission-oriented,' but an education undertaken with a view to what God is doing in the world, considered from a global perspective.... By 'missional,' I mean theological education that is wholly or partly field based, and that involves some measure of doing what is being studied" (Banks 1999, 142). Banks adds that the 'missional' model of theological education places the main emphasis on theological *mission*, on hands-on *partnership* in ministry based on interpreting the tradition and reflecting on practice with a strong spiritual and communal dimension. On this view theological education is primarily though not exclusively concerned with actual *service*—informed and transforming—of the *kingdom* and therefore primarily focuses on acquiring cognitive, spiritual-moral, and practical *obedience*. (ibid., 144)

Similarly, the literature presents various perspectives as to the purpose of theological education. Clearly, the purpose that is foremost in a seminary will shape the nature and content of the curriculum and the relationships among the institution, the church, and society. Since the 1980s, the nature and purpose of theological education has been described in various ways (see Farley 1983a; Hopewell 1984; Hough and Cobb 1985; Wood 1985b; Gustafson 1988; M. Stackhouse 1988; Dykstra 1991b; Wheeler and Farley 1991; Kelsey 1992, 1993; Banks 1999, among others). A brief description of these perspectives follows:

- Theological education deals with knowledge. In some instances, knowledge is seen as an objective body of information, doctrine, and/or the Christian tradition transmitted to students. In other instances, knowledge is synonymous with wisdom, e.g., Farley's *habitus* or Wood's interplay between vision and discernment. Fostering the capacity of theological reflection is considered an important part of an educational process that links knowledge and wisdom.

- Theological education is concerned with the professional development of leaders for the church, with an emphasis on the functions and skills of ministry. Typically, the movement of the curriculum is from theory to practice. This linearity assumes that the theoretical disciplines are somehow the theory for the applied or practical disciplines. Legitimate questions relate to how the theoretical disciplines could be an adequate theory without reflexive input from the applied disciplines, or how a series of fragmented theoretical disciplines could provide a coherent theory for the practical disciplines.

- The reflective judgment literature and those concerned about *praxis* assert that theological education is a reflection on the practice of ministry while one is involved in that ministry. The assumption of a theory-to-practice linearity is replaced with the assumption that practice can also influence theory.

- More recently for Protestant schools, spiritual development, which is sometimes coupled with the term *character formation*, is accepted as one of the necessary outcomes of the seminary curriculum and institutional life.

- Finally, and not as frequent in evangelical theological education, is the view that theological education is the shaping of students' capacities to hear another's experience and to respond with acts of justice.

Farley on Theologia and the Clerical Paradigm

Arguably, one of the most influential books related to concerns about theological education is Edward Farley's *Theologia* (1983). By describing the problem in terms of the definition and role of theology, Farley shaped the ways in which theological faculty and administrators, in particular, view theological education and its perceived problems. Theology is ambiguous, argues Farley, because the term refers to two different *premodern genres*.

> First, theology is a term for an actual, individual cognition of God and things related to God, a cognition which in most treatments attends faith and has eternal happiness as its final goal. Second, theology is a term for a discipline, a self-conscious scholarly enterprise of understanding. In the former sense theology is a habit (*habitus*) of the human soul. In the latter it is a discipline, usually occurring in some sort of pedagogical setting. (Farley 1983a, 31)

Farley defines *theologia* as "a state and disposition of the soul which has the character of knowledge" and adds that the dominant understanding from the most relevant period for his purposes, the twelfth to seventeenth centuries, was that "theology is a *practical*, not theoretical, habit having the primary character of wisdom" (ibid., 35 emphasis in text). In time, this meaning was distorted, as theology became a specialized preoccupation of the schools oriented toward training and skills. It evolved into separate disciplines, creating the fragmentation that, according to Farley, has had devastating effects on theological education. One might argue, following

Farley, that theological education has lost its soul. "The most recent generation in America appears to have a primarily institutional/administrative view of the tasks of ministry," and wisdom has become a technology (ibid., 43).

> *Theologia* no longer forms part of a theological school's conception of its course of study, and the result is a loss of unifying subject matter and criteria for the various catalogue areas. This absence of criteria and subject matter tends to rob the catalogue areas of their potentialities to be theological disciplines and turns them over to the control of their auxiliary sciences. As a result, theological education becomes an amalgam of academic specialization and culture adaptation. (ibid., 151)

Given that the critiques of contemporary theological education can be seen as a series of footnotes to Farley, his perspectives should be taken seriously *and* questioned. His assertion that theology has become distorted and that theological education has suffered as a result is no doubt valid. Admittedly, theological focus does shape curriculum and outcomes. For example, if theology is understood as a series of propositions organized in specialized courses, then professionalism, scholarly specialization, and linearity in the curriculum are not surprising. If theology embraces spirituality and justice, curricular emphases on spiritual formation and social engagement could be the logical result. If theology is concerned with meaning and seen as ineffectual without engagement with social, personal, and cultural realities, curricular processes of theological reflection, *praxis*, and integration are consistent. But is the loss of a unified theological vision the *essential* problem and sufficient description of what troubles theological education? The confusion related to theology and its role in theological education may actually suggest that there is a larger, more complex set of factors at work. Farley himself opens the door for this consideration by suggesting that "the reason the standard criticisms of theological education do not amount to a call for reform is that their focus is more on the symptoms than on the disease itself" (ibid., 4).

Farley's corollary concern about a clerical paradigm may not be as immediately problematic for the seminary as it is for the church. In other words, men and women who pursue a pastoral degree could become less concerned about its adequacy in shaping pastoral skills, knowing that leadership development is being offered increasingly by larger churches.[1] Therefore, the concerns that Farley addresses about the clerical paradigm may actually become more relevant for church-based pastoral conferences. In the United States, churches and entrepreneurial efforts, often sponsored by prominent lay leaders, provide seminars and support services for ministers, partly to address the problems that they perceive seminaries are ineffective in addressing. Significantly, institutes and training centers are developing *outside of* theological schools to train competent leaders. Or seminaries are *coming alongside* larger churches and depending on them to offer pastoral leadership training. In North America, church-based conferences are probably more likely than seminaries to be caught in a clerical paradigm, emphasizing leadership functions and organizational technique. Even though most seminaries would admit that they have contributed to the perceived limitations on the capacities of leaders, it is a mistake to assume that the seminary is solely at fault for impoverished leadership and dysfunctional churches.

If churches believe that a certain type of leader is necessary, they will demand that seminaries produce this leader. If seminaries are unable to produce the type of leader they want, churches will look to conferences and borrow familiar images from the marketplace. In many instances, these borrowed images will fail the church. When churches yield to popular pressure and uncritically adopt certain understandings of an effective leader, or certain ideas of what makes a successful church, who or what will help them evaluate the appropriateness of these images? Though some would welcome the demise of the North American seminary as we know it, the loss of *any* suitable framework for a community of scholars would be disastrous for the church. Clearly, though, the seminary has not presented itself as an effective community of scholars who with humility assist congregations to understand their identity and purpose as the people of God, who participate in a shared journey toward spiritual growth and understanding, and who are learning how to engage contemporary issues *with* members of congregations and society.

---

[1]While in Malaysia, I was interested to learn of seminaries' developing institutes for training the laity and churches' offering institutes for pastoral development! International Ph.D. students at TEDS tell me that this pattern is not unique to Malaysia.

Communities concerned about learning, development, and service encourage and enable the interaction of scholars with the larger community of faith and the world. Authentic communities resist the besetting sins of higher education—pride, power, arrogance, elitism—that hinder engagement with people who are searching for understanding, whose perspectives need to be challenged, and who themselves have something to contribute to the continued formation of the faculty-scholar. The academics' temptation to give the final answer, and to create controlled settings where such answers can be given, is often counterproductive. Questions must be heard. Presuppositions, perspectives, and practices must be assessed, and criteria for this assessment are drawn from interacting disciplines of knowledge, the wisdom of experience, and reasonable discourse among members of communities of faith and learning.

"The Delicate Fabric of Informed Wisdom"

Farley organizes his solution to the problems of theological education around at least three propositions. First, *theologia*, a *habitus*, "a cognitive disposition and orientation of the soul, a knowledge of God and what God reveals," is the central outcome of theological education (Farley 1983a, 35). He asserts, "The education whose center is *theologia* is an ecclesial counterpart to *paideia*, focusing as it does, not on *areté*, but on a sapiential knowledge engendered by grace and divine self-disclosure" (ibid., 153). Second, a distinction between theology as a course of study and theology as understanding is mandated before theological education can be reformed. "Theology in its primary meaning and as we are using it is a personal and existential wisdom or understanding. As such it is not tied to any specific course of studies such as clergy education. As such it sets its own requirements for studies, knowledge, and disciplines depending on the context" (ibid.). Third, *theologia* is not to be equated with piety. Farley suggests that efforts to restore piety through the activities of formation or spirituality are so far not credible in Protestant theological education. By seeking to spiritualize the "school's life and ethos but not its course of studies, the formation movement perpetuates the inherited separation of piety and intellect" (ibid., 160–61). Contemporary efforts at formation and spirituality seem to have little to do with *theologia* or "faith's sapiential knowledge." That is, following Farley, *theologia* is a more appropriate corrective and pathway to wisdom because it incorporates the discipline of scholarly reflection and reflection on concrete situations. In effect, theology is "evoked by faith's attempt to live faithfully in its situations" (ibid., 169).

Kevin Vanhoozer agrees that theology aims at the knowledge of God and is contextual.[2] Neither *theoria*, which is a knowledge of true propositions, nor *techem*, which is a result of instrumental reasoning, is an appropriate descriptor for theological interpretation. A third way of reason is needed which allows for the general principle *and* a clear understanding of a situation or context. This third way Vanhoozer describes as *phronesis*, "the ability to exercise good judgment in specific contexts. In short, it is wisdom: the ability (which includes knowing but is not limited to knowing) to say or do the right thing in a specific situation" (Vanhoozer 2000, 81–82). Both Farley and Vanhoozer view wisdom as an exercise of reasoned faith in context. Vanhoozer adds the need for a canonically situated reason, viewed from an evangelical but postconservative perspective. "What is postconservative about the present proposal…is its claim that the practices that teach us to respond, and correspond, to God rightly are *canonical* practices: the sum total of the diverse communicative practices that make up the biblical text. My thesis is that theological wisdom and understanding are formed through an apprenticeship to the biblical texts" (ibid., 82).

The outcome of this apprenticeship is not a set of logically ordered propositions (*theoria*) that simply need to be applied or called upon as proof texts; nor is it functional knowledge or skills (*techem*). The qualities required and shaped in this apprenticeship are reliable reasoning, intellectual and spiritual virtue (because interpretation is fallible), and humility. The result of an apprenticeship to the biblical texts should be judgment, deliberation, consideration or other higher order capacity.

Walter Liefeld has described these qualities as wisdom that is not merely knowledge or practical application. Together they comprise a delicate fabric of informed wisdom woven of the multiple strands of our understanding of God and "not from a monolithic block of some theological, curricular, or ecclesiastical matter." This wisdom is informed by all that we learn about God and the Scripture and from courses and other forms of

---

[2]Vanhoozer describes evangelical theology as a drama, a unifying narrative, integrating covenant and canon. He describes his approach to theology as "canonical-linguistic," which is "my shorthand…for postpropositional, pluralistic, phronetic, Protestant, and postfoundational" (Vanhoozer 2000, 75).

training one receives. Finally, it is delicate, in that it can be "torn by selfish motives, heresy, temptation, and personal attack; and frayed at the edges by the ruinous effect of parish and community duties. Its delicate colors can be faded under the light of a harsh environment and criticism. Its more bold colors can run and be blurred by peer pressure, public opinion and compromise."[3]

Paul Wilkes adds a further dimension: the goal for seminary education should be oriented around the construction of a moral, ethical, inner spirituality in ministers that, in some ineffable way, inspires those to whom they minister. Wisdom, in other words, has the quality of *calling others to do what is right*.

> If they are to succeed, this generation of seminarians must, of course, be educationally and spiritually sound, politically aware, as conversant with demography as they are with morality. They must be sensitive to race, ethnicity, gender, and sexuality, but they must not drive us up still another wall with their convictions.... When our future clerics speak we want to hear powerful yet measured voices bringing out the moral dimension of life.... In the end, I think, we are looking for those who will help us find that voice deep within us which is not our own, but calls us to do what is right. (Wilkes 1990, 88)

The consensus of the contemporary literature is that theological education is in crisis. The analysis of the problem is that seminaries have failed to produce the desired product, a skilled leader, or that the purpose of theology is not understood and therefore the theological curriculum is in disarray. The representative perspectives from Farley, Vanhoozer, Liefeld, and Wilkes suggest that theological education is ineffectual if all that is produced is knowledge of a set of propositions, polished skills, or a well-stocked mind.

Most faculty know that leaders will be required to make decisions that defy textbook answers and require more skill than can be practiced in limited field-education experiences. However, wisdom, spirituality, and in-

---

[3] Walter Liefeld, unpublished written comment.

formed judgment are not likely products of progress through the typical theological curriculum. These qualities are difficult to assess, cannot be taught, though they can be learned, and are seldom prized by theological students endeavoring to complete requirements for a degree.

Wisdom, fostered by development of the capacities of theological judgment, reflective practice, spiritual discernment, and inquiry, is an appropriate quest for theological education. That quest is failing. However, the reason for the failure is not found simply in the loss of theology, loss of theological unity, or the distortions created by an inadequately conceived theology. The history of higher education suggests four major factors that have persisted to the present. The burden of chapters 2 and 3 is the extent to which these factors have created a threat matrix—that is, an environment that can lead to no productive future for theological education.

CHAPTER 2

Persisting Factors That Affect the Future of Theological Education

The saga of efforts to reform higher education often seems like a Russian novel: long, tedious, and everyone dies in the end.—Mark Yudof, Chancellor of University of Texas System

The tendency in the literature is to attribute theological education's troubles to isolated issues. Because of this tendency, factions can develop among faculty, administrators, church leaders, and concerned laity, with each faction owning a problem and proposing its own solution to it. This chapter proposes that important questions related to theological education and the mission of the church in the world have been obscured by four key factors, rooted in the long history of higher education, that have *worked together* to profoundly affect the academy and the church: the rise of institutions, the rise of academic theology and academic rationalism, the rise of professionalism, and ways in which the church and the academy have understood the desire to know God.[1]

Factor 1: The Rise of Institutions

How institutionalism influenced understanding of the nature of knowledge and perceptions of the role of theology

(For background, see Chapter 4, "The Development of Institutions of Theological Education.")

---

[1] These factors are best understood against the historical background presented in chapters 4–7. However, after reading chapters 2 and 3, you may wish to proceed directly to chapters 8–10, which deal with issues in international theological education in the twenty-first century, and return to Chapters 4–7 at a later time.

Observing that institutions are a product of the past 200 years and therefore relatively new, Robert Greenleaf warns that the United States has "not yet explicitly faced the question of what kind of institution-bound society will serve us best. We have simply improvised from our 200-year-old seminal thinking about a nation of persons. And one of the results, at this point, is a society that does not have a hopeful outlook" (Greenleaf 1996a, 192).

Institutions in the latter part of the twentieth century rushed to reinvent, reenvision, restructure, and renew themselves. Total quality management, the learning organization, and the metamodel are among the several initiatives designed to make institutions more effective. In most of these initiatives, people are described as central to change in institutional ethos and behavior, but the institution is still at the heart of the concern. We want effective organizations, excellent schools, successful corporations, and large churches. Believing that effectiveness is important, organizational leaders direct human talent into the care of the system; considerable effort is expended in determining how to make the institution more effective; much time is spent anguishing over matters that appear to be the chief factors threatening the success or survival of an institution; creativity is too often diluted in the forming of strategic alliances to make institutions more powerful.

So pervasive and powerful have institutions become that few question their legitimacy. The health of societies is perceived as directly related to the health of institutions. Indeed, one could argue that society *is* its institutions. However, as Greenleaf observes, corporations "get their legal status from the willingness of the courts to construe them as persons" (Greenleaf 1996a, 192). It is this identification of institutions as persons that signals the implicit warning in Greenleaf's observation: institutions are *not* people. It is the people who serve and who are served by institutions that are the critical factor in the health and effectiveness of any endeavor. The arrangements, the relationships, of people are not just means to get a job done. People are not just the servants of institutional effectiveness. People, in communities, serve a purpose larger than themselves, and ideally that purpose is expressed in and through values, procedures, and activities reflected in the institutions that develop in complex societies to serve the society's needs and purpose. However, because the effort and time required to create a community that will sustain and energize the mission of an institution are considerable, institutions tend to be sustained by technique, science, technology, and arrangements of power.

Institutions are a necessary part of a complex society; they provide much of the society's care and support for its citizens. When they function well, they stabilize society and provide energy and structures for prosperity and justice. Unfortunately, as the exposure of corruption in corporations suggests, human greed and the quest for status and position can corrupt any good. The capacity of institutions to tolerate incompetency, to ignore or rationalize away the voice of the community, to favor those who contribute to the maintenance of the institution, or to consciously or unconsciously affirm that the full development of human beings is secondary to the success of the institution is equally destructive.

Ted Ward asserts that the task for the twenty-first century is not to determine how one institution will relate to another institution, or even how institutions will find new and better ways to be successful, but rather how institutions, understood as relationships among people, will collaborate to respond effectively to human need and assume responsibility for the development of human beings.[2] Implicit in his comment is an underlying passion for the empowerment of communities of people who act justly, who serve with integrity, and who see development toward maturity as more important than success or efficiency.

The danger that confronts us in the twenty-first century is that society will be defined by its institutions, leading to the depersonalization of the individual and the weakening of community life. As Greenleaf suggests, the Christian community should lead the way in exemplifying values that form healthy communities. However, the danger is equally great that the church will be defined by its institutional expression and that leadership will be defined in relation to the skills required to make the institution successful. Inevitably, the educational processes needed to serve the institutional church and extend its mission in the world will then be defined by schooling institutions, whether in church-based or academic arrangements. If these institutions are driven by a demand for leaders who can in turn create successful institutions, or by the quest for academic superiority, they will lose their prophetic and serving character. Unevaluated and unchecked, these

---

[2] Personal conversation with Ted Ward.

outcomes will lead ultimately to competition, professional elitism, academic arrogance, and a renewed cycle of institutional ineffectiveness.

Institutions are not neutral, valueless, inert entities. In ways that are almost mystical, an institution takes on power, energy, and self-serving forms of behavior that can be quite different from the values and character of the majority of individuals who make up that institution. Witness how long it takes for the people within an organization to name problematic values and processes and to mobilize the will and resources to act. Institutional dynamics tend to create the impression that problems are perceived by one person only, that this perception is incorrect, that nothing can be done about the problem anyway, and that any criticism implies disrespect or disobedience, leading to punishment or ostracism. In many instances, communication channels allow one or a small number of voices to speak for the larger group. In most cases, procedures that would help the group assess the validity of these voices are lacking, or "groupthink" is too pervasive to allow the larger group to discern if those voices are wise or spurious and to respond accordingly. Church business meetings, and faculty meetings, are sometimes a case in point.

Clearly a different view of institutions is needed for the twenty-first century. Greenleaf offers a surprising yet reasonable proposal, observing that a theology of institutions is needed to guide future development.

> If one views all institutions as intricate webs of fellow humans groping for meaning, order, and light, then the essential problem of all institutions is (and has always been) theological. This assumption places seminaries at the top of the hierarchy, even though others may not readily accept or understand this position.... I see the role of seminaries as pivotal and crucial to the quality of the total society. (Greenleaf 1996c, 203)

He asserts that the root problem that underlies all social ills is the failure of religious leadership and that the source of this failure is the marginalization of seminaries from the realities of an "institution-bound society." Concerned that the institutions that support societal functions and values have lost their center, Greenleaf laments that seminaries have "not produced a persuasive theology of institutions. Consequently, pastors have not been prepared who will mediate that theology, through churches, to those who are in a position to lead or influence the character of our many institutions" (Greenleaf 1996a, 180). He adds that the adequacy of the theology of institutions rests on the extent to which it generates "a sufficient moral imperative as a moving force in the persons of trustees and directors of institutions of all sorts" to take and sustain initiatives that result in their institutions becoming more serving than they are now (ibid., 196–97).

Greenleaf offers a hierarchy of institutions that, if properly integrated and functioning, will contribute to the health of a society. He warns that this hierarchy will appear odd, and it does in spots, but it is intriguing.

> In the base group are the legions of "operating" institutions, such as schools, governments, labor unions, businesses, hospitals, social agencies, communities, and families. At the next level one might put churches and universities. They stand somewhat apart because of their role as the "glue" of society, shaping and transmitting the culture and clarifying values. At the top level are two institutions that are distinguished from the others because of their unique opportunity to harbor prophetic voices that give vision and hope, and that have perhaps the widest scope of all to be and do as they think they should. These are theological seminaries and uncommitted, trusteed resources such as foundations. The utility of such a hierarchical view of institutions may be that, when there is faltering at the lower levels, one is reminded to ask where the higher level institutions failed in serving those at the lower levels. (Greenleaf 1996c, 203)

Though Greenleaf's enthusiasm for the contribution of seminaries is compelling, the possibility that seminaries as we know them could fulfill this role in society is overstated.

Elizabeth Lynn and Barbara Wheeler (1999) offer the disturbing analysis that theological schools are virtually unknown in public society and therefore have little influence on it.[3] They admit that their study was a probe: they identified four American cities with different kinds of semina-

---

[3] See also Jones, Greenman, and Pohl (2000) on the public character of theological education.

ries present (Catholic, mainline, evangelical Protestant, and a university divinity school). The cities varied in size, economic prosperity, and religious climate. Under the auspices of the Auburn Institute, Lynn and Wheeler conducted interviews with 254 people, individually and in groups. The interviewees included church executives; business and nonprofit leaders; government officials; presidents and trustees of colleges, universities, and seminaries; student affairs representatives; local clergy; community activists and volunteers; church laity; and the local religion reporter (Lynn and Wheeler 1999, 3). The findings revealed that the seminaries were typically unknown to all in a community save the insiders in the religious tradition of each. In general, the seminaries were not viewed as vital to local society and civic affairs. The fallout from this invisibility, Lynn and Wheeler conclude, is that the religious leaders seminaries train are also absent from community life. Other findings suggest that seminaries are missing the mark in terms of instruction: method and content are unrelated to real issues. Communication skills, reflection on life experience, and interpersonal competency are lacking in curricular outcomes.

Questions were also asked about whether and how much seminaries *should* get involved in political and social affairs. Should they remain detached in order to foster an almost monastic climate for spiritual nurture? Commenting on this study, Richard Mouw notes, "The underlying question, of course, is the role of the seminary *as seminary* in addressing issues of public life" (Mouw 1999, 18). If the seminary is deeply invested in social causes, it could foster social activists (for the Right or the Left) who are poorly equipped for evangelism and pastoral care. It could be argued that it is not fundamentally the seminary's business, nor is the seminary competent, to influence the civic culture in which it is located. However, Mouw also argues that if God issues a mandate that Christians must be involved in the public arena, then our response must be to obey. Examples of injustice and impoverished morality are common in the communities where any seminary is located. "How can we *not* address those topics directly as a seminary community?" He adds, "And let us examine ourselves to be sure that the approaches we claim to be adopting have some match with the problems we claim to be addressing" (ibid., 19).

Barbara Wheeler, in a separate piece (1999), observes that a tendency to spectatorism is not unique to religion or seminaries. Similar concerns have been raised in connection with higher education and public life as a whole. Further, the best response is not to introduce yet more programming in seminaries to address yet another need, thus contributing to the out-of-control program sprawl in the theological curriculum. As Wheeler suggests, perhaps the current task is for seminaries to establish relationships in a community and for clergy and other religious leaders who have been shaped by these seminaries to preach and teach in such compelling ways that a community is drawn to their witness. Citing Jeremiah 29:7 ("But seek the welfare of the city where I have sent you into exile, and pray to the Lord on its behalf, for in its welfare you will find your welfare.") Wheeler notes, "If we make progress on the tough question of why our institutions and their graduates should and how they can more powerfully tell and show the public, the people, what God intends for the world, we will greatly benefit the core mission of theological education as well as the wider cause it serves" (Wheeler 1999, 23).

Institutionalism and the Nature of Knowledge

Dallas Willard once said that because the knowledge project is so vast and cannot be completed in one lifetime, it inevitably generates institutions (Willard 2000a). Because knowledge tends to be understood as a body of content, the institutions take on a form that seems to fit what people believe about how that knowledge is kept, enlarged upon, and communicated. The role of academic institutions is commonly understood to be supporting the creation of new knowledge while serving as the guardians of "old knowledge." Scholars and researchers brought together to fulfill this role are supported by increasingly complex institutional structures. Students join the academic community presumably to contribute to the shaping of knowledge and to assume responsibility, *upon graduation*, for responsible action in relation to knowledge. Institutions seen as successful tend to take on a life of their own and persist from generation to generation. The character and structure of these institutions shape faculty and administrators' understanding of the nature of knowledge just as much as their convictions about the nature of knowledge shape the character and structure of the institutions. Education and learning are often held hostage in this interplay.

Inevitably, concern for grades, outside responsibilities, and focus on completing coursework for a degree almost overwhelm whatever desire students may have had to learn and to act in relation to learning. The president, who is now the president of an institution rather than head of the faculty, is removed from matters vital to the *educational* tasks of the institution.[4] Further, in many theological institutions the preferred academic dean is an academic, a designation that *may* have little correlation with the individual's capacities as an educator and leader within a highly complex, unusually structured academic organization.[5] Robert Maynard Hutchins's remark that a university is a collection of faculties and departments held together by a central heating system is not too far off the mark.

In certain respects, faculty can be described as independent contractors and the institution as a base from which they pursue their professional activities. The nature of academic institutions also allows faculty to create their own personal enterprises. Institutes, not-for-profit companies, and other ventures seem to be developing at an unprecedented rate alongside the traditional curriculum in seminaries—often created by faculty members. Perhaps these ventures at the fringes of theological education are, in fact, the shape of the future.

It is not surprising that institutions of higher education are notoriously incoherent in their structures and modes of operation. Educational administrators, especially in seminaries, often come to the task from the ranks of faculty or from pastorates. Few have specialized training and experience as leaders of educational institutions. Institutional factors such as the specialization of disciplines, the independence and special interests of faculty, multiple demands from multiple constituencies, and the need to be part of a global society create a confusion of dynamics that often frustrates and sometimes paralyzes administrators with limited expertise. Inevitably, administrators discover that change in academic institutions proceeds glacially

---

[4]This shift in responsibility took place during the era of the surveys of theological education described later in this document.

[5]James Martin and James Samels note that the first dean in American higher education was appointed in 1870 by Charles Eliot, president of Harvard University (Martin and Samels 1997a, 3). In 1960, one-third of 166 deans surveyed "rated formal training 'desirable,' 36 percent had stopped teaching, and 71 percent had no experience when they were appointed" (ibid., 5). In 1989, 62 percent of senior administrators "viewed a doctorate in higher education as 'less preferable' than the traditional doctorate in an academic discipline for the academic affairs position" (ibid., 6). With the nature of academic leadership identified as the most pressing concern today, such a lack of experience and training could seriously limit the effectiveness of academic deans and provosts.

and that books on corporate management and leadership are only minimally helpful. In seminaries, many of the differences in perspective among faculty are couched in the language of belief or orthodoxy—differences that therefore become difficult if not impossible to reconcile. In time, institutional survival and growth become more important than learning and human development. Consequently, the institution becomes larger and more powerful than the individuals within it. Caught in a cycle of self-perpetuation, academic institutions can fail in their most important tasks: coming to terms with the meaning of knowledge, how best to foster its development in communities of learning, and how to stimulate responsible action, character development, and spiritual values that permeate all of life.

Admittedly, in many if not most institutions there are faculty who facilitate transformative learning and foster habits of lifelong learning. However, they do this often in spite of institutional structures rather than because of them. Processes of evaluation and development in many institutions remain frustrating exercises. Theoretically, the process of accreditation should provide a level of discourse that can move institutions out of unproductive patterns, and such movement should then affect the ways the academy fulfills its educational responsibilities. However, accrediting associations are typically concerned with the organizational and program structures of institutions and not with how knowledge is understood and fostered. Concern for the quality of teaching and learning is not absent, but generally notations are given to warn an institution about *organizational and/or program* matters that fall short of accreditation standards. As theological institutions become more concerned about maintaining or securing accreditation status, accrediting bodies may be seen not as agencies of peer review that provide opportunity for the institution to evaluate itself but rather as licensing bodies. This subtle change in perception can lead committee members responsible for preparation of accreditation review documents to do whatever is necessary to ensure that "our license" is renewed for another period of years. In addition, the usefulness of the accrediting process can be hindered if a visiting team is not skilled at in-depth interviewing. To exacerbate the problem, limited time on site diminishes the possibility that critical institutional culture matters will be discerned by the visiting team.

In the case of the Association of Theological Schools (ATS), the body that accredits North American seminaries, the Redeveloped Accrediting

Standards (1996) do provide some space for development and experimentation in areas that affect learning and human development. Further, the program division of ATS offers workshops and supports networking opportunities for president, deans, and new faculty. Funding is also being offered from foundations for long-term discourse among theological faculty. Assessment, however, remains a critical issue. How do external reviewers assess standards that are not primarily quantitative in nature?

The challenge for future development is not a lack of people with an educational vision. The challenge for the future is twofold: the lack of a coherent frame of reference and criteria against which to assess the validity of vision, and the lack of administrators and faculty who understand the complexity of the educational process in relation to how knowledge is generated, examined, and communicated. The assumption that the way to do theological education is to build a school is a seriously limiting assumption. Institutionalism has contributed to a view of knowledge as information to be stored and transmitted to the next generation of guardians and a view of learning as a function of schooling, not life.

When seminaries were created, the power of the university model was such that organizational and curricular structures were carried over into the seminary with little change. John Cobb, for one, is willing to examine different institutional arrangements in relation to disciplines of knowledge. His disclaimer that he is not calling for the abandonment of disciplines and specializations altogether is probably wise at this point in the dialogue. However, note his opposition to perpetuating particular structures in relation to these disciplines.

> The rejection of the disciplinary organization of knowledge must not mean that individuals cease making concentrated efforts to understand particular topics! It should mean, however, that reflection on these topics will be ordered to larger purposes and sensitive to their interrelatedness with many other topics.... [T]he academic disciplines still play a role. They are powerful ways of gaining information. My strong opposition is to their constituting the organizing principle of knowledge and of the university. (Cobb 1991, 255–56)

Formal Institutions and Nonformal Initiatives

Before different arrangements of the disciplines can be considered, the institutionalization of education needs to be revisited. Because formal schooling is considered synonymous with education, institutions that purport to provide education look like schools. Reform initiatives often fail to take account of how formal schooling and nonformal education initiatives can interrelate, and thus such initiatives tend to polarize formal and nonformal modes. Debates over whether education should be formal or nonformal are generally irrelevant and unproductive. Typically, the debate assumes that the formal mode of education is concerned with knowledge and theory and is therefore superior, whereas the nonformal mode deals with training and technique and is therefore inferior. Formal education is considered more effective in producing people who are inventive, because they can think and work in relation to precedents from established theory and bodies of knowledge. On the other hand, nonformal education is assumed to be preoccupied with skill development or training in repeatable behaviors, not with invention or creativity. Ward asserts that when the debates about education devolve to questions about mode and method, comparisons are made between formal education *at its best and narrowly defined* and nonformal education *at its worst and poorly defined.*

Clearly, an educated person is greater than the institutions and procedures of either formal or nonformal education. If an educated person is defined simply in terms of how much information she possesses or how well he can perform a task, then either mode can be utilized. If the educated person is defined as one who is able to make connections, a conceptualizer, a creator, someone who is able to organize knowledge in relation to action, these qualities can be developed in either mode—at its best.

At least one reason for the seemingly intractable polarization created when modes or methods become the focus of the debate is the tendency to assume that for education to be effective it must be connected with a school. As institutions of education have evolved over several hundred years, corresponding tendencies to equate teaching with learning, degrees with understanding, testing with competency, and position with power have also evolved. Why is it that many faculty believe they are educators simply because they have been awarded a Ph.D. in a particular discipline, are resident in an educational institution, and have been given a contract to teach a certain number of courses? Is an educator, then, someone who has taken

education vs teaching

courses in education or someone who has a doctorate in education? Not necessarily. The reality is that connections between courses of study and practices of teaching and learning are <u>tenuous at best.</u>

Further, why are faculty contracts most often written in relation to a fixed number of academic credit hours to be taught rather than in terms of responsibilities that define competency in teaching and learning? Why do some students feel better in classes where they get lots of notes? Why do some resist being asked to do more than what is normative in school—sitting in lectures, reading books and writing book reports, writing term papers, working on projects, and taking tests? <u>Why is teaching assumed to be acceptable and learning less than acceptable?</u>

Is schooling an aberration? Is it significant that Jesus never founded a school or created a three-year degree program for his disciples, even though schools existed at the time? Why do we assume that what we do in three years of formal instruction in seminaries is in some way more appropriate than what Jesus did in three years on the road, in villages, and through discourse coupled with reflection on real experience? Unfortunately, the debate persists and is increasingly tiresome and destructive to education. It seems that academia is engaged in a never-ending mental blood sport between those whose educational philosophy is stereotyped as "traditional" and those whose educational philosophy is stereotyped as "progressive." Even though debates about modes or methods do not address the central issue, they have a long history. The persisting belief that more interesting methods and more creative degree programs will fix education continues to deflect substantive thought about the effect of institutionalized education on learning and service.

Institutions are created by people to serve a particular need, to reflect a particular belief, or to address a particular set of circumstances. Institutions consist of patterns of behavior that are allowed to endure over time. Significantly, as Greenleaf suggests, institutions *as we know them today* are a recent invention. Likewise, educational institutions as we know them today are a recent invention. Interestingly, for most of history, as the inexorable development of institutions proceeded, nonformal education was not in itself the corrective to problems that emerged in formal education. Rather, the source of correctives came most often through men and women in the church concerned about spirituality and the mission of the church in the world. The belief that one mode of education is the corrective for another mode has created many stereotypes about formal and nonformal modes and has fueled unproductive educational polarities.

The Search for the Proper Context of Theological Education

Debates about the nature of theological education and its location obscure deeper questions about its ultimate purpose. Since God affirms the utterly unique role of the church in the world, it follows that Christians should be responsible participants in matters that affect individuals and societies. The majority of those who attempt to apply their theological education begin where the mission of the church begins—with the problems of the human condition. In this view, theological education restricted to the academy, or formal schooling, is not adequate. Should theological education, then, view itself as the church's school, where instruction directly concerns the mission of the church? Cobb asserts that "the theological seminary as the church's school should accept a responsibility for theological leadership in the struggles within the church. If professors positioned in academic disciplines cannot, or will not do this, then the church needs to find ways to support others, not so positioned, who will, even if this means a reduction in faculty in the academic disciplines" (Cobb 1996, 199–200). However, a seminary that has borrowed its curriculum models and institutional structures from the university seems unable to relate effectively to the church.

Currently seminaries are restructuring themselves as universities.[6] Inevitably, the question will be asked if this restructured seminary is in fact able to function as a university, and if it will be any more able to serve the church. If theological education is to survive in a university structure, then it would seem that the (Christian) university must actively seek relationship and conversation with the church—if for no other reason than to be reminded of the values of the gospel that can get lost in the academy. However, academics often perceive the modern church as dysfunctional, confused, at the margins of society, and lacking in spiritual character. Similarly, church

---

[6]Interestingly, the Protestant seminary was born in North America in the 1800s as a reaction to the university. However, when the seminary was established, it borrowed the structures and practices of the university. The criticism that the seminary established itself not on biblical models but on models often foreign to the gospel is not to be dismissed lightly.

leaders are often reluctant to interact with the academy because of perceptions that its language is too esoteric, offering a scaffolding of answers often unrelated to real and increasingly complex problems.

Should theological education move to the church, so that the disciplines are developed in light of God's purposes for his church and addressed in communities of the faithful, and so that the knowledge *and* action of communities of the faithful can be informed by scholars who are participants in the church and in society?

Clearly, a viable community of scholarly inquiry and research located in the church, the seminary, and/or the university could be an essential resource for people seeking to integrate Christian faith with issues in their life and their profession and in relation to the real problems of society. However, arguments over the whether the church, the seminary, or the university is the proper context for theological education miss an important point. Theological education cannot be contained in one institution. Nor can it be defined by one mode of education (formal or nonformal). The real issues are not the survival of existing seminaries, the return to a university structure, the relocation of theological education to the church, or the formation of new institutions. New or reconfigured institutional forms and programs, along with infusions of capital, will not by themselves solve the problems that currently trouble theological institutions.

A more productive way of thinking about theological education is stimulated by Miroslav Volf's discussion about the place of theology. Volf suggests that because contemporary society is differentiated into several subsystems and is characterized by cultural plurality, it rejects any central, unifying structure of values or religious doctrines that once held it together, or gave the appearance of holding it together. Christian faith, he continues, cannot locate itself at the center of society, because a differentiated society resists orientation around a center.

> Social marginality is not to be bemoaned, but celebrated—not as a ghetto protected from the rest of the culture by a high wall of private communal language and practices, but as a place from which the church can, speaking its own proper language, address public issues, and holding fast to its own proper practices, initiate authentic transformations in its social environment. (Volf 1996b, 111)

In a diverse world, Volf asserts that the more rigid, rigorous theologies that seek stability and system are of little use. Anticipating objection, he asks, "Does theology so conceived forfeit its universal claim? To the contrary: It is *because* 'Jesus Christ is the same yesterday and today and forever,' it is *because* Christian faith is for all times and all places, that our theologies need to be nonsystemic, contextual, and flexible" (ibid., 112 emphasis in text). Citing Jürgen Moltman's address to the American Academy of Religion in 1994, Volf affirms Moltman's vision that theology must be for the world. God's delight and God's pain cannot be contained within the walls of ecclesial communities and universities; neither can theology "just feed the pious souls in the church nor just delight the inquisitive minds in the academy. Beyond the church, beyond the academy, the horizon of theology is the world as the place of the coming reign of God. For the sake of the future of the world, that object of God's pain and God's delight, theology must be a public endeavor" (ibid.).

One can easily draw a parallel between the place of theology as Volf sees it and the role of theological education. When the future of theological education is presented merely as a choice among institutions, God's ultimate concern is for the world is obscured. Multiple, interacting learning environments are needed to allow academic specialists, students, members of congregations, and interested members of society to engage authentic problems. Again, the solution to the problems that beset theological education is *not* to be found in a change of mode, from formal to nonformal. Rather, at least a partial solution is to be found in a more thorough understanding of the nature of learning in *each* mode and an appreciation of how formal and nonformal modes of education can work together as a complex network of experiences, processes, and relationships. The default preoccupation with building institutions, developing organizations, creating systems of control, and equating achievement with degrees, awards, grades, and particular forms of dress perverts the natural (and necessary) connections between formal and nonformal modes and blunts the contributions of education to the fostering of lifelong learning, spirituality, and service.

This leads to a discussion of a second factor, the rise of academic theology. Note that this factor follows from and is integrally related to the rise of institutionalism.

Factor 2: The Rise of Academic Theology
How academic rationalism has shaped perceptions of the purpose of knowledge and the nature of education

(For background see Chapter 5, "The Shaping of Academic Theology.")

Certain trends in academic theology are evident across time: the creation of separate categories for theoretical and practical knowledge, the movement of theology from the center of the curriculum to the margins, the transition from questions of doctrine open to debate to issues of dogma settled by an authoritative church and vice versa, the transition from spiritual theology to philosophical rationalism, and so on. Over time, the university structure reinforced a rationalistic orientation to knowledge with distinct disciplines. Studies within these disciplines are now at best parallel to, at worst isolated from, studies in other disciplines.[7] In the late twentieth century the effects of these trends on the university became the subject of numerous books, articles, and conferences. When the seminary separated from the university, it retained its academic and institutional structures. Inevitably, many of the same concerns about the university are to be found in the literature on concerns about seminary education. The extent to which university theology has shaped theology in the seminary is a serious consideration. Inevitably the seminary, structured as it is on the university model, will be affected as the role of theology in the university is assessed. Therefore, consideration of the rise of academic theology and contemporary challenges for theology in relation to the university may be suggestive of future patterns in theological education.

Theology in the Context of the University
Philip Sheldrake notes that the precise date when a rational or scientific theology emerged in the West is impossible to determine. However, from

---

[7]The problem is not with disciplines *per se* but with persisting specialization and fragmentation within and among disciplines. Disciplines serve as a framework for teaching and research. A discipline is characterized by a more or less well structured theoretical framework and a particular methodology for continued inquiry. However, with increasing specialization and fragmentation, Janet Donald proposes "that it may no longer make sense to think of discipline as a unitary and coherent domain but rather as a family that provides local metaphors or models" (Donald 1997, 30).

about 1100 onward, scholars defined theological understanding increasingly as a task of intellectual speculation. Scripture and patristic writing began to be treated as propositions subject to the rules of Aristotelian logic.

> The centres of theological inquiry increasingly moved during the twelfth century from the monasteries to new cathedral 'schools' that eventually gave birth to the great European universities.... The theological enterprise was no longer to be focused in centres that were explicitly dedicated to a religious way of life. The new scholarship in the narrow sense created centres that existed primarily to foster teaching and learning. The new theology gradually gave birth not only to distinctions between disciplines such as biblical theology, doctrinal theology and moral theology, it also produced a belief that the discipline of mind could be separated from the discipline of an orderly lifestyle or *ascesis*.... (Sheldrake 1998, 39–40)

In the nineteenth century, in order to make theology a university-acceptable discipline, Friedrich Schleiermacher recast it as a "positive science" related to the development of the church's leadership. By the late nineteenth century, theology had become an encyclopedia of several disciplines with tenuous linkages to certain practical fields. Ironically, though one of the major tasks of theology was to inform the church's leadership, the contemporary church seems to have lost interest in theology. Cobb reflects that the growing lack of interest in theology by church members is

> partly the church's fault and partly the fault of practitioners of the discipline. The church all too easily gets lost in the weekly routines and forgets that these are all for the sake of a faith whose intellectually responsible continuance in the world is precarious.... On the other hand, much of the fault lies with the professional theologians. The connection between their research and the real need to maintain a credible theology is often obscure. The more fully theology becomes a discipline in the standard academic sense, or worse, a set of disciplines, the less direct is the concern

of most practitioners to provide thoughtful Christians with an intellectually responsible theology. (Cobb 1996, 197–98)

As the disciplines of academic theology were consolidated, theological specialists trained in the academy were increasingly ill equipped to relate theology to the pressing concerns of congregations and society. Inevitably, faculty in the institutional culture of the academy tended to regard engagement with these issues as matters beyond their own specialized theological activity. Jeffrey Stout maintains that one result of this situation is that "academic theology seems to have lost its voice, its ability to command attention as a distinctive contributor to public discourse in our culture" (Stout 1988, 163). Almost a decade later, Volf affirms that the church's loss of interest in academic theology is disturbing. Scholars write for students and other scholars, while "the ear of church folk is tuned in elsewhere.... Like the street-corner preachers of yesterday, [theologians] find themselves talking to a crowd too hurried to honor them with more than a fleeting glance" (Volf 1996, 98). Cobb warns: "The farther the theological disciplines go in this direction, the less reason there will be for their continuance" (Cobb 1996, 198).

The specialization of theology has contributed to what may be a more pressing problem. A more reasoned academic theology was seen as a corrective to undue reliance on human experience and intuitive spirituality. The assumption that academic theology "is the theory of Christian belief" fostered the corollary assumption that theology "is to be understood, internalized, and acted upon in a purely cognitive procedure of assent and decision-making" (Charry 1997, 240). Unfortunately, in approaching theology as a process of disciplined, analytic rationality, i.e., as an exercise of mind and language, the less precise understanding of theology as that which is derived from the desire to know God and the need to relate faith to all of life retreated to the margins of the academy. Interestingly, Ellen Charry, commenting on the purpose of her book, writes, "Although I started this project as an exercise in historical theology, a constructive thesis emerged: when Christian doctrines assert truth about God, the world, and ourselves, it is a truth that seeks to influence us. As I worked through the texts, the divisions of the modern theological curriculum began making less and less sense to me" (ibid., viii).

Increasingly, faculty and church leaders are concerned that a fragmented theological curriculum has helped to weaken the connections between belief and practice, piety and reason, knowledge and virtue. Contemporary theological educators from different disciplines, perceiving that how theology is understood affects the structures and practices of theological education (and vice versa), are challenging the perception that the primary task of theology is to understand itself intellectually. Renewed concern for the virtue-shaping function of theology and the role of theology in the transformation of the church and society is gradually refocusing attention on the relationship of theology to the essential practices of the faith community: prayer, learning, service, and worship. David Kelsey affirms that theological inquiry into the nature of Christian witness is not just *applied to* Christian activity but is part of that activity. Further, theological inquiry is a public activity composed of three dimensions, which he illustrates by three questions: Is the witness genuinely Christian (historical theology)? Is it true (philosophical theology)? Is it enacted appropriately to its context (practical theology)? To see the first as simply the theory for the third, the practice, is inadequate. All three dimensions are at the same time practical and theoretical (Kelsey 1993, 203–8).

Decisions about the nature of knowledge in relation to practices and virtue are influenced still by two dominant epistemologies or cultures that form the backdrop for the polarities that will become increasingly problematic in the quest to understand the role of academic theology and the place of academic rationalism.

The Legacy of Greek and Hebrew Epistemologies: A Tale of Two Cultures

A persisting debate in higher education relates to the origins of what is perceived as the dominant educational culture, structures, and practices. "Greek" modes of education and "Hebrew" modes of education are often used as the discriminating categories of origin. Though a purely "Greek" mode or "Hebrew" mode of education is unlikely, educators routinely appeal to the two modes in their criticisms and characterizations of education. Strangely, the assumption that two distinct modes exist arouses strong emotion and the tendency to stereotype faculty who hold, or who are perceived to hold, to one or the other perspective. Typically, faculty who represent these different perspectives can be found in the same educational institution. The structure of disciplines and departments that has evolved over time, and that is now extensively criticized in the literature on higher education, tends to isolate these faculty from one another; and disparaging attitudes, however civilly expressed, or stereotypes about other disciplines, often hinder substantive interaction. Those who believe that educational institutions need to bring together the best minds who will *through the impartation of disciplines of knowledge* inspire another generation to high scholarship, exemplary service, and good character seem forever alienated from those who believe that the fundamental task of education is to shape character, conceptual capacities, and service through *theoretical knowledge critiqued by reflection on responsible experience.*

Christian educators may be uniquely suited to shift the debate from the level of personal opinion and prejudice to a thoughtful consideration of the legacy of Hebrew and Greek epistemologies. As scholars examine these epistemologies, it becomes apparent that there is, in fact, a difference and that formal education in the West has been shaped almost exclusively by Greek epistemology. Efforts to describe the differences in these views of the nature of knowledge are suggestive that for Christians, in particular, something important was lost when one view of knowledge became dominant and when the implications of the struggle of Hebrew and Greek philosophies to coexist were not examined carefully enough in relation to education.

Greek and Hebrew epistemologies. Theologians and educators have long reflected on the differences between Hebrew and Greek thought forms. It is beyond the scope of this book to present the extensive details of perspectives on Hebrew and Greek thought, from ancient theologians to those who more recently have tried to either synthesize or claim irreconcilable differences between the two modes. However, it seems that since the suggestion was made that Hebrew and Greek modes are in opposition, the two modes have become polarities in *educational* debate. The Greek influence is assumed to be dominant in Western higher education. When suggestions are made that the educational implications of Hebrew thought forms should be considered, any effort to find a productive relationship between the modes is lost in an often compensatory response to preserve academic rigor, the structure of disciplines, or the hegemony of rational discourse. This response results in a further, often equally heated tendency to argue against the harmful effects of the Greek influence.

My discussion here proceeds from two assumptions: (1) Presumptions and stereotypes that have emerged from legitimate considerations of differences between the two cultures of thought hinder renewal in higher education. (2) A way forward will not be found until faculty who tend toward one or the other pole realize that it is the *relationship* between the modes of thought more than the differences that is important for the future of educational culture, structure, and practice. Indeed, in a world where cultural factors are important, higher education cannot be stuck in this persisting polarity. Conceivably, the future of theological education depends on a more willing exploration of a relationship between Greek and Hebrew modes of thought. *This exploration could guide further efforts to explore the contributions of other cultures to educational culture, structure, and practices.*

Tom Bloomer, in a review of literature on the subject (1997), argues that two distinct Greek and Hebrew worldviews existed in New Testament times. The Greeks probed the realm of ideas searching for wisdom, the Good, the Ideal. Their passion for knowledge made them teachers. "The Greeks...cared not so much for power (as the Romans did), but for influence. They taught the nations, including the Romans, their language, their reasoning...and how to see" (Bloomer 1997, 41). The Hebrews were concerned with knowledge, but knowledge expressed as righteousness, the doing of God's will. Knowledge and right actions could not exist without the other.

Robert Dentan was careful to note that while the terms *religion* and *theology* did not exist in early Hebrew thought—largely because there was no need for "technical words and precise definitions that are so essential for logical thinking in a scientific age"—the terms did enter the language at a later stage. Similarly, though Hebrew thought presumes that the whole is greater than the sum of its parts, that all of life is religious, and that thinking is synthetic rather than analytic, "even the Old Testament exhibits signs of an awakening tendency toward logical thought, especially in the Wisdom literature" (Dentan 1968, 34). Having said this, Dentan argued that two phrases define the Hebrew conception of knowledge: "the fear of God" and "the knowledge of God" (ibid., 34–36).

Significantly, Plato would not have taken exception to Dentan's observation that, though the verb *yada* (to know) refers to intellectual activity, it has a range of meanings far beyond the common English understanding of knowing.

> There is no special faculty of the intellect or reason in Hebrew psychology. The word most commonly used for 'mind' in Hebrew is simply the common word for 'heart'...The heart is regarded as the seat of the intellect, but it is also regarded as the seat of the will and the emotions as well.... (ibid., 37)

Clearly, "knowledge of God" refers not just to accurate theological information about God but to a much more intimate encounter, one that obligates ethical behavior. "In ancient Israel, knowledge that did not issue in appropriate action was not true knowledge at all; genuine knowledge involved the whole of a man's [sic] personality" (ibid., 40).[8] The necessary and vital inseparability of knowledge and ethical behavior is revealed in Scripture through its effects on human relationships.

The nature of relationships in educational settings is particularly telling. Abuse of authority, elitism, and arrogance are the besetting sins of excessive rationalism in education. Ward, concerned about the persisting effects of the infiltration of Greek epistemology into education—in spite of Jesus' and Paul's warnings against it[9]—characterizes the Greek legacy in four areas: hierarchy, social distance and the artifacts (e.g., lecterns, "robes for the elite") that reinforce assumptions about the nature of the teacher-to-student relationship, one-way communication from the knowledgeable authority to those who need to hear that knowledge, and the use of education to gain social privilege (Ward 1996, 39–40).

Bloomer offers that the Greeks' emphasis on intellectual precision in knowing was likely an attempt to counter the intellectual decadence of the time and to seek through pure thought to know the good. "But because of basic Greek epistemology, there was [never] the direct link between truth and its practice that the Hebrews had grasped" (Bloomer 1997, 41–42). Unfortunately, the notion that if one knows the good he or she will do the good persists in much of Christian education today. Marvin Wilson argues that "in the Western world knowledge has often been limited in definition, confined to abstract concepts or theoretical principles. But in Hebrew

---

[8] Dentan cites the powerful passage in Jeremiah 22:15–17 concerning what God values as true knowledge.

[9] See Matthew 23; 20:20–28; John 13:1–20. Also see below on E. A. Judge's depiction of Paul's criticism of the practices of the professional scholar.

thought to 'know' something was to experience it, rather than merely to intellectualize it" (Wilson 1989, 287).

The "grand project" of the academy—the organization and dissemination of knowledge—is such a powerful tradition that anyone committed to it is virtually unable to hear words such as *experience* and *praxis* without automatically assuming that the speaker is disparaging intellectual activity or reasoned discourse. The Bible never disparages idea, thought, or intellectual engagement; however, intellectualism without obedience, knowing without appropriate response, is severely judged by God. At its best, instruction in the Jewish world was a blend of the careful articulation of the Law and opportunities for interaction, *always in the context of real life*. Instruction as an exclusively cognitive, monological transmission of information conducted in formal schools where the teacher is revered as the expert and where interaction and questioning is not typical, and sometimes discouraged, was foreign to Jewish education. William Barclay describes education in the synagogue as "not primarily speculative wisdom and knowledge; it was not primarily intellectual or academic" (Barclay 1959, 25). Andrew Clarke observes that an earlier consensus that the synagogue was primarily a religious center has given way before the realization that "in the first century, both in the rural and urban settings, the overlap between religious and social domains of life was considerable" (Clarke 2000, 120). The synagogue was a community center serving religious, social, civic, and educational functions.[10] Education was heavily value laden and related to what the Law actually meant in all of life. That it is difficult to carry out such education through cognitive transmission of information alone is reinforced by Rabbi Israel Goldman's descriptions of the synagogue.

Goldman introduces his section on the synagogue with a statement about the unique nature of Jewish education. He argues that the ideal of Jewish education—to enlighten and inform the mind of every Jew at every stage of life—was unique among the peoples of the world. Most ancient cultures scrupulously kept religious knowledge secret, guarded by a priestly class. "Jewish life is, therefore, unique from the very dawn of its history in that the revelations of God, as contained in the Sacred Scriptures, were

---

[10] See Clarke (2000, 103–41) for a more complete description of the synagogue, its purpose, and its leadership.

made the possession of the whole people, whose duty it was for the sake of their own well-being and for the sake of the welfare of the nation, to study it the whole of their lives" (Goldman 1975, 7). When the synagogue appeared as a place of instruction, it was to be a place where the people would learn to know in a full and complete sense. Without knowledge, the Jew could not possibly hope to live the good life. The synagogue was therefore not only a place of prayer but also a house of instruction. The Pharisees initially emerged to renew the study of the Torah (probably during the exile), for without knowledge the Jews would not be a people. Unfortunately, as the Pharisees tried to keep and transmit knowledge as a thing unto itself, they separated knowing from spirit and truth, and eventually they came under the condemnation of the very Son of God.[11]

Study in Judaism was considered an act of worship. "This conception of individual and collective study as a form of divine service has persisted, inspiring Jews through the ages to become lifelong learners in order to more adequately commune with God" (Goldman 1975, 31). The study of Torah was always to lead to action, to the practice of the will of God, to doing good. The rabbis saw that the rewards of study were a deeper and stronger spiritual life (ibid., 47). Certainly in Judaism one can find evidence of rote learning and direct instruction. However, there is also evidence that the people were not simply passive recipients of another's instruction. They were to revere the Law, incorporate it actively into their lives, meditate on it every day to deepen understanding of its meaning (which implies active reflection), and make it their guide for life.

Clearly, educational practice in the West is weighted toward rationalism and cognitive mastery, which are seen as characteristic of Greek forms of thought. The Greeks introduced the capacity to stand apart from ideas and think about them. The precision and rigor of thought that they sought, along with their efforts to enlighten the *polis* through ideas and the imitation of heroes, have enriched education and Western culture. However, if Athens is the prototypical case study for the best the Greek forms of thought can produce, it also demonstrates the vulnerabilities inherent in

---

[11]Several passages highlight this condemnation, including Matthew 7:24–29; 12:1–8; 15:1–20; 16:1–12.

class elitism, abstracted knowledge, and the breakdown of a holistic social system designed to educate the young.

If Hebrew epistemology is characterized by a holism of knowing and responsible action, then the reason for Jesus' rebuke of the Pharisees for divorcing truth from practice is clear and suggests implications for educational practice. Bloomer notes that "Jesus also joins truth with its practice in the parable of the house foundations (Matthew 7:24–27): the one who built his [*sic*] house upon the sand was not the one who did not listen to the words of Jesus; but rather the one who listened, but did not *do* His words. It is clear that for Jesus, as well as for James and Paul, truth divorced from practice was not only meaningless but dangerous" (Bloomer 1997, 44–45).

The imbalance arising from knowledge acquisition and inquiry without a corresponding and intentionally encouraged commitment to responsible practice, or from experiential learning that fails to consider insights from relevant knowledge seriously, can only hinder efforts to think freshly about the future of theological education. Paulo Freire argues that word and *praxis* exist in the same moment—that the authentic word requires both action and reflection (Freire 1994). In this spirit, Ward's aphorism "To know and not to do is not to know" and Calvin Chong's addition "To do and not to know is also not to know,"[12] taken together, reflect Hebrew *with* Greek perspectives.

The Apostle Paul and the Greeks. Though separating Hebrew and Greek epistemologies altogether is problematic, we do need to acknowledge the effects of the polarities that result when Hebrew and Greek are taken as *types* of education today. Judge alludes to the clash between the posturing and arrogance of the Greek philosophers and teachers and the Christ-centered values in Paul's letters. He observes that schooling is not emphasized in the New Testament. Some ministries (e.g., teaching) are described in educational terms, but these descriptions cannot be used to support a notion of education as schooling. In fact, the *form* of education is of little concern in the New Testament (Judge 1983b, 7). Judge suggests that the Greeks had, by the time of the New Testament, practiced education for centuries in essentially the ways that are common today. He illustrates how Paul criticized Greek forms of schooling and perceptions of the nature of

---

[12]From a personal conversation with this Singaporean educator.

knowledge and how he tried to emphasize and model a different value system. Paul took commonly understood Greek terms and gave them different meanings in order to erase cultural boundaries. Phrases such as "Greeks and barbarians," "the wise and the foolish" (Rom. 1:14), were used in his culture to distinguish between those who shared the Greek *paideia* and those who did not speak Greek, between those who were educated and those who were not. Therefore, when Paul wrote, "I am a debtor both to Greeks and to barbarians, both to the wise and to the foolish," his readers would have understood his contrast between Greek educational values centered on wholly rational and humanistic endeavor and Christian values as articulated in the New Testament.

Judge notes that Paul also took commonly understood educational terms and gave them new meaning: wisdom (*sophia*), reason (*logos*), knowledge (*gnosis*). He asserted that the way to wisdom and knowledge hidden in Christ (the *Logos*) is through hearts knit together in love (Col. 2:2). Again, his readers and hearers would understand the contrast, for it was common knowledge that for the Greeks the way to wisdom was intellectual inquiry and contemplation. When Paul used educational terms such as "arguments" and "philosophy," he inserted the descriptors "fine-sounding...hollow and deceptive" (Col. 2:4, 8 NIV). These educational terms marked the two divisions of Greek education at the time: rhetoric and philosophical inquiry. In light of this, Judge suggests that Paul was promoting a new kind of educational goal for adults and that this often brought him into conflict in the churches influenced by Greek culture (Judge 1983b, 9–11). For example, in 2 Corinthians 2–3, Paul says that he and his companions are not "peddlers of the word." Paul refused to accept payment from the Corinthian church even though he accepted it from others. If he took payment in Corinth, he would be expected to perform in much the same way as did the professional teachers of Greek culture. Paul refused to adopt that style of rhetoric or to recommend himself as a professional teacher. In fact, while the teachers of his day boasted of their credentials, Paul boasted of his weakness. He made the point in a variety of ways that the teaching ministry was not an art form or a professional skill for self-display but a sharing of the knowledge of God that transforms one's thinking and lifestyle (ibid., 12–14). Paul challenged the ends of Greek rhetoric—manipulative persuasion—by advocating a new Christian rhetoric, obligating the hearer, respecting the hearer, faithfulness to the truth, and humility.

> The value-system upon which Greek education had been built up is deliberately overthrown.... [H]e deliberately tore down the structure of privilege with which his followers wished to surround him. In its place he set out a fundamentally new pattern of human relations in which each is endowed by God with gifts to contribute to the upbuilding of the others. (ibid., 14)

Conflicts concerning the roles of the intellect, feelings, and experience persist to the present in academia. In spite of a commonsense awareness that the three cannot be separated, university education, and theological schooling that is patterned after the conventional university, seems unable to maintain any sort of productive coherence. The literature on theological education attests that an increasing number of faculty, administrators, church leaders, and laity view efforts to under gird the multiple purposes of the seminary (professional development, personal and spiritual formation, engagement with culture, cultivation of a Christian mind) with a rationalistic view of knowledge in what is essentially a university structure as a failing enterprise. The array of voices critiquing higher education today is almost without precedent. The literature is replete with calls for alternatives to theological institutions as we know them.

In spite of centuries of exposure to the Bible and Christian theology, it was Greek epistemology that shaped Enlightenment rationalism and, in turn, the institutionalization and rationalization of knowledge in the West. The effects of this rationalization and institutionalization on theological education are pervasive and problematic. Curriculum and course structures tend to emphasize parts over the whole. The object of study is often more important than the relationships that are inherent in a holistic view of knowledge: relationships of ideas, relationships of ideas and action, relationships among those who make up the learning community. Individualism tends to be valued over community, competitiveness is often unchallenged, the importance of context and experience is underestimated, and the teacher-as-expert to student-as-passive-recipient hierarchy is accepted as the norm.

In recent years, the hegemony of rationalism in education is being challenged by research into the nature of Eastern and Western epistemologies—reinforcing the need for attention to the points at which the two great streams of thought can be reconciled. Kaiping Peng and Richard Nisbett (1999), Paul Hiebert (1985, 1999), and Kaiping Nisbett, Richard Peng, Incheol Choi, and Ara Norenzayan (2001) argue convincingly for the need to acknowledge the validity of *both* analytical and dialectical modes of thought and to create social and educational systems based on holistic thinking and development rather than on artificial distinctions such as process-content and theory-practice. One could argue that as the cultures of the world impinge on one another, it will be variations in thought forms rather than a Greek-versus-Hebrew dichotomy that will be of most value to renewal in higher education.

In Search of a Role for Academic Theology

As the legacy of Greek and Hebrew epistemologies is considered, it is inevitable that the hegemony of academic rationalism in the West will be questioned. What then will become of the role of academic theology in the university, and by extension the seminary, if different cultures of thought become important in the development of educational practice?

Nicholas Wolterstorff defines theology as sustained reflection about God in response to questions felt by the community of faith. The travail of theology in the academy is to be found in the expressed concern that theology "displays less and less the stamp of Christian conviction, and proves less and less useful for the life of the church" (Wolterstorff 1996, 37). However, does the recovery of theology by the church require that Christian theology once again find a place in the university? Wolterstorff maintains that it was precisely the attempt to make theology university-acceptable that stripped it of its uniqueness and meaning (ibid., 40). Therefore, he asserts, academic theology has little evidence of Christian conviction and is currently of little use to the church.[13]

In the midst of criticisms that the American university has no spiritual center and is no longer able to serve the church, George Marsden argues that American higher education should allow discussion of the relationship of faith to learning. Is this merely the reintroduction of the largely ineffective cognitive exercises that attempted to integrate faith and learning? Marsden allows that Christians have oversimplified the faith-and-learning

---

[13]See also a more recent collection of Wolterstorff's work that continues his reflection on concerns cited in this section: Wolterstorff 2004.

issue by simply applying a Christian principle or fact to an area of knowledge without much thought about how one affects the other. Because faith-and-learning issues were for the most part discussed in Christian enclaves insulated from engagement with the larger world of scholarship, the effort reflected, and perhaps contributed to, the trivialization of religion in society and in the university. Marsden, seeming to recognize this, takes the bold step of "advocating the opening of the academic mainstream to scholarship that relates one's belief in God to what else one thinks about" (Marsden 1997, 4). Though in the nineteenth and early twentieth centuries North American culture was strongly influenced by Christian values and many of the presidents of universities stressed moral ideals that were grounded in Christianity,[14] by the late 1900s university culture had changed to such an extent that little room was allowed for religious perspectives. Consequently, Christian universities and seminaries were developed as contexts for theological inquiry. Marsden clearly feels the time has come to reconsider theology's place; he muses on the difference a Christian perspective could make in scholarly activity in the university.

Wolterstorff (1995, 1996) and Stephen Toulmin (1990) make a similar case in relation to theology. Their perspectives are relevant in that the university, which once allowed no diversity, in a postmodern era is embracing all manner of human experience. Wolterstorff asks if theology is needed as a renewed method and content to guide thinking in these new areas of thought and research. Toulmin asks how the central intellectual concerns of theology connect with those of other disciplines in the university (Toulmin 1990, 51). For instance, what are the enduring and human questions in any discipline? Does theology have anything to say to these? As Toulmin observes, "The central, distinctive concern of theology is precisely with the *interrelatedness* of things that, for 350 years, the Academy has preferred to keep separate" (ibid., 64). In curriculum development, it may be possible to conceive of what Toulmin terms *transdisciplinary dialogue* rather than integration; and it may be possible for theology to play a role in such dialogue. In his view, *theology* is not

---

[14]See Marsden 1997, 15–18.

the name of a separate discipline, which exists alongside, and on a similar basis to, other academic disciplines.... Rather, issues of theology exist, and arise, *at the base of* all abstract academic disciplines equally. Just as problems in the physical theory of relativity can be discussed *philosophically*—note the adverbial form—so, too, problems in ecology and psychoanalysis can be discussed *theologically*: i.e., with an eye to their implications for religious life and experience. (ibid., 60–61)

A shift from defining theology as an abstract, rationalistic enterprise to that which was characteristic of theology throughout most of the history of Christianity is apparent in contemporary literature on the university, theological institutions, the church, and developments in theological method. The breadth of scope of this discussion is significant. Much of the literature attests that historically, in the church and in the university, theology was bound up with spirituality and was meaningful only when related to the practices of the church and human experience. The rationalistic trend in academic theology was, perhaps, inevitable and not necessarily invalid. However, the literature attests that the extent of the abstraction and rationalism in theology is being assessed and that spirituality and relationship to the practices of the church and human experience are being reintegrated into theological method.[15] At this point, the stage is set for a consideration of how theology developed in relation to the university and what it has become in relation to formal education institutions: university (Christian or not) and seminary.

The Reemergence of Theology in the University

In 1954, Nels Ferré proposed that the Christian worldview could be the new unifying center for the university (Ferré 1954, 237–42). In 1960, H. Richard Niebuhr, acknowledging the mutuality of universities, churches, and states, argued for the logical consistency that "intellectual activities are carried on in constant interaction with civil and moral activities and with the religious exercise of proclamation, prayer, and confession.... It is a poor

---

[15]"Practices" should not be understood as activities or programs. The practices of the church are those that are essential to its identity and purpose as the people of God.

theology that makes human reason the image and representative of God, but the theology that puts feeling, albeit a religious feeling, or moral will, above reason in the service and similitude of God is no less idolatrous" (Niebuhr 1960, 97). He asserted that theology is a servant of the church and, because it is also a servant of the truth, it "takes its place in the university alongside other inquiries, never separated from them, never dependent upon them, never isolating itself with them from the totality of the common life which is the universe" (ibid., 99).

Toulmin, Wolterstorff, Marsden, and Volf are among a number of contemporary university-based historians, philosophers, and theologians who propose that there has been a shift from philosophical and theological rationalism to a concern for the role of theology in human experience. On this basis, the legacy of rationalism in theology and philosophy from the seventeenth century through the positivism of the twentieth century can be challenged because of a return to "a *practical* conception of theology where the demand for rational 'proofs' no longer obscures the fact that doctrine has been rooted historically in human practice" (Toulmin 1990, 59–60 emphasis in text). For Toulmin, the

> shift is no ground for 'theoretical despair': still less does it imply 'nihilism.' Readers nostalgic for Cartesian foundationalism may greet its abandonment with a sense of loss, and rationalize it by talking of Absurdity. But rationalism relied from the start on a misconceived, quasi-Euclidean model of academic disciplines, and in setting it aside in the late twentieth century, we do not lose anything. Rather, we acknowledge that, in this respect, seventeenth century 'foundationalism' (both philosophical and theological) led into a *cul de sac* from which we are lucky to escape. (ibid., 60–61)

Toulmin does not suggest that all theological content be abandoned. He maintains that transdisciplinary dialogue will be effective only to the degree that theological *content* is preserved. However, he does not support the status quo in relation to the teaching of this content. The central ideas must be taught—but taught in relation to their practical effect, which "has implications for *how* theology is taught in the contemporary university"(ibid., 64). If academic theology is ever able to recover its historic position as a servant to the church and society, Toulmin concludes that "on more and more levels, any exclusive preoccupation with the ramifications of separate disciplines appears pointless and partial. In particular, if we explore the underlying presuppositions of different disciplines, and the assumptions involved in separating them, we are increasingly led into a *transdisciplinary* dialogue, of a kind to which theology has a distinctive contribution to make" (ibid., 62). Once theologians recognize that current human problems require input from overlapping disciplines, they can sit down with colleagues from different disciplines and participate as partners in the dialogue.

Wolterstorff addresses the role of theology in the university from a different direction. He notes that, historically, the "grand project" of the academy has been *scientia* and that the academy has tended to withdraw from issues of the everyday. Wolterstorff doesn't seem to take account of the service orientation of Land Grant universities, or the interventions of several of the larger universities (including Yale) in national and international affairs, and the benefits to society of certain research projects conducted by faculty in these universities. However, he may be referring to the tendency of universities not to take on, *as disciplinary concerns*, issues that affect particular groups in society. In any case, the crisis of the postmodern university is that it has to accept or reject all manner of new categories (e.g., feminism, masculinism, gay literary studies, liberation theology) as departments of study. In developing his distinction between the modern university[16] and the postmodern university, Wolterstorff argues that the medievalists understood theology to be grounded in the Christian Scriptures and inserted arguments from other sources into the Scriptural foundation—but these arguments were understood as inserted. In the contemporary university, theology has become *subject* to human concerns. Once claims from Christian theology are seen as suspect in relation to the human matters (e.g., can theology really claim that God was revealed uniquely to one Near Eastern

---

[16]The university that has emerged in the past twenty-five years is not, in Wolterstorff's judgment, to be confused with the "modern university." This university "emerged out of the universities of the Middle Ages and the Renaissance; and often the modern university continues its support of modes of learning no longer in fashion, on the ground that to abandon them would be for the university to repudiate an important part of its own tradition" (1996, 38).

ethnic group?), it loses its place in the university (Wolterstorff 1996, 40–41). As Wolterstorff points out, there is no rule that sustained reflection on God as the task of theology must take place in a university. However, contemporary universities are changing dramatically, and for Wolterstorff this changes the situation. Christian theology could once again thrive in the universities. But the threat is that more and more of these universities are "orienting themselves toward serving the professional and technological needs of modern society" (ibid., 44). Wolterstorff cites two hopeful signs: the breakdown of the notion that one can enter the university and have no concern for particular human issues, and the breakdown of the notion that some foundationalist logic is at the basis of true scientific knowledge. With these developments has come the collapse of the hierarchical system of the disciplines characteristic of the modern university. These developments are too recent, asserts Wolterstorff, for anyone to decide how the university is going to be affected. In such a climate, however, Christian theology could thrive. Since no one knows what an epistemology looks like that has rejected foundationalism yet resists sinking into relativism, it will be necessary for Christian theologians to enter the dialogue, even with those with whom they disagree (ibid., 45–46).

With a vision of the university as a community of scholars who withdraw from the current culture, some remain convinced that there is some store of objective, essential knowledge that must be studied in its own right and that principles derived from this study can be applied to issues in any age. For these, the crisis of the *modern* university is the tyranny of the immediate, the tyranny of special interests. Wolterstorff counters that it is misleading to think that one can enter the university and set aside one's beliefs and perceptions in order to do objective analysis. The assumption that the academy is isolated from the everyday, and that we, in the name of being objective, can set aside our prejudices as we enter into the academic world, is flawed. To learn is to confront the perspectives of others through genuine dialogue. However, to avoid constructing an academy characterized by only a "multiplicity of perspectival ghettoes," those with different "narrative identities" must share their different perspectives "so that all together we can arrive at a richer and more accurate understanding.... But that presupposes that the representatives of a particular perspective be willing both to share their insights with those outside and be willing to listen to their critique" (Wolterstorff 1995, 26–27).

Deep resentments, hostilities, and fears exist among those of differing positions. Wolterstorff calls for repentance and forgiveness from all sides and maintains that the grip of the "grand project" is loosening and should be loosened. Can the Christian scholar and theologian participate in the quest to find answers to humanity's most pressing problems without drawing unproductive lines?[17] Dallas Willard suggests that the university simply needs to recover that which it was for most of its history: a center for Christian theological inquiry. In a pluralistic age, the university will not become overtly Christian, and there are those who believe that the university is not the appropriate venue for religious studies of any kind (see Hart 1999). But as Willard observes, the belief that "God has nothing to do with the subject matter was a *decision* not a *discovery*" (Willard 2000a).

The contemporary university continues to struggle with its identity. Many admit that some kind of restructuring is needed. Should the curriculum be organized around themes or questions rather than around the less flexible disciplines? Should the service motif be expanded? Should the university become more deliberately a communal endeavour, as opposed to an isolated enclave of expert knowledge? The common criticism of the university is that it is no longer characterized by a unified vision. Can theology find a place in the university as a hyphenated discipline (e.g., theology-sociology)? In the nineteenth century, John Henry Newman suggested that intellectual fellowship is key to a university; the Western university is after all a guild, its craft scholarship. Newman maintained that the pursuit of knowledge in the university is a good in itself, regardless of any application to a profession. This assertion focuses a contemporary question: what is the proper application of scholarship, to train the mind, to prepare professionals who serve, or both? Needless to say, the answer to this question affects curricular decisions. If training the mind is the aim, what areas of knowledge are best suited to this task? If the central task of the university is to prepare professionals, is the emphasis on the learned professional or the competent practitioner? And what experiences and skills should be part of the curriculum? If *preparation* is the motive that drives professional programs, how is prior student experience assessed, what assessment procedures

---

[17]See Ward (1989).

are appropriate, what is the relationship of teaching and learning, and what is the role of the school in continuing education?

These questions are directly relevant to the development of the seminary, in that it incorporated the professional aspect of the divinity school while retaining the academic characteristics of the university. In an effort to understand further reasons for contemporary concerns about theological education, we must now consider the third factor.

Factor 3: The Rise of Professionalism in Higher Education
How professionalism has effected theological education and the church

(For background, see chapter 6, "The Emergence of Professionalism in Theological Education.")

One of the most persistent criticisms of contemporary theological education is that educational functionalism, or the clerical paradigm, has led to a curriculum organized around specializations intended to serve the profession of ministry. Two related concerns derive from this criticism: first, disciplines such as biblical studies and theology are diminished in such a curriculum, and second, when priority is given to the development of pastoral *functions* or leadership *skills*, ministry competency can actually suffer. Ministry practice requires much more than functional proficiency. Though most would acknowledge that theological education is almost hopelessly bound by an unproductive theory-and-practice dichotomy and would affirm that there are deficiencies in ministry competency, not all are agreed that professionalism *per se* is the causative factor.

The Seminary and Professional Education

Through the eighteenth and nineteenth centuries, seminary development was affected by the complex interplay of the demands of established churches for an educated clergy, the lingering effects of Colonial-era college ideals, concern that graduate education would lessen clergy effectiveness, the growth of the universities and their increasing distance from Christianity, and the influence of graduates from German universities. Early in the nineteenth century, theological education was still concerned to prepare persons for a revivalist ministry. It was more practical than intellectual and influenced more by Pietism than by the methods of scientific scholarship.

By the last half of the nineteenth century, many graduates of German universities returned to America and took teaching positions in the new seminaries. They brought the "new learning" to these schools, challenging traditional doctrines of the denominations and the ideals that had inspired college education. Paralleling a similar trend in the universities, seminaries began to incorporate increasing numbers of specialized, professional degree programs that were not always tied to theological inquiry or to ideals embodied in the colonial colleges.[18] The incorporation of German research methods and the emphasis on scientifically informed professionalism introduced into nineteenth-century Protestant theological education an element of confusion that continues to the present. Questions persist about the effectiveness of the German university's research model oriented toward professionalism, in relation to the English classical model oriented toward character, and in relation to the ideal of pious learning oriented to service.

William Rainey Harper, founding president of the University of Chicago, was not untypical of those who supported the university divinity school as the vehicle that would improve the ministerial profession.[19] He wrote of the seminaries: "An effort should be made to give the student that particular training that which will enable him to grow stronger in future years. It is an unfortunate fact that a large proportion of men who enter the ministry begin to lose intellect and strength from the moment they leave the seminary" (Harper 1899, 47). Harper criticized seminaries for their practice of focusing on one skill—the development of preaching. He argued that if the student did not have a broad background in "letters and sciences," the training cultivated a narrow and exclusive spirit. "In other words, the seminary is not a place in which men are to learn certain views, or to receive and adopt certain opinions. It is rather a place in which men shall be taught to think" (ibid.). After criticizing seminaries for focusing almost exclusively

---

[18] Initially, seminaries were schools for the study of theology and provided minimal training in practical skills. As the graduates of German schools returned to North America, except for a brief effort at Harvard, Andover Seminary was the first to embrace the German method (Goodwin 1989, 5). Princeton incorporated the German research model in the 1850s. James Bradley (1996) notes that initially the new learning was resisted because its critical, scientific method threatened the authority of the Scriptures and suited neither the spirit of pious learning nor the promotion of useful, practical theology.

[19] James Wind (1987) offers a compelling account of the vision and work of William Rainey Harper. See also Richard Storr (1966).

on preaching skills and for failing to understand that ministry had become a diverse and complex task, Harper concluded, "The day has come for a broadening of the meaning of the word minister, and for the cultivation of specialism in the ministry, as well as in medicine, in law, and in teaching" (ibid., 59).

Professional Ministry Education in the Twentieth Century

Though many founders of universities were sympathetic to religion and sought to advance Christianity in society, they did not see the university as a center for *theological* study and debate. The university could, however, provide a ministerial education equal in quality to that of other professions through its divinity school. "Offering avenues to the latest specialized, advanced learning as well as access to fast-breaking developments in professional training, universities were the appropriate places for training ministers who would serve an increasingly specialized, professionalized America" (Cherry 1995, 295).

There was little resistance to the professionalization of the curriculum from the churches that were themselves, by the early twentieth century, complex, specialized organizations. It was inevitable that the schools would be called upon to prepare ministry specialists for these churches. Though the possibility that specialization would fragment the curriculum seemed to concern the founders of the universities, they believed that their mission to serve the institutions of society would overcome the problems of fragmentation. Specialized ministerial education in the university divinity school would, they believed, unify society.[20]

As churches increased in complexity through the twentieth century, they began their gradual evolution into corporations managed by a CEO-style leader with special skills. The role of the minister as pastor and preacher did not disappear, but the relationship between the minister and the community was more often that of a specialist serving a particular sector of society. The curriculum of the schools was shaped by often-conflicting demands for education in pastoral and leadership skills and the traditional scholastic subjects. By this time, theology in the seminary had been shaped by more rational approaches to academic theology and diffused into specia-

---

[20]See Cherry 1995, 37–40.

lizations. Its development as a subject in the curriculum and increased isolation from the essential practices of the church rendered theology virtually impotent as a prophetic voice in the rush to congregational specialization.

Once churches felt the need for professionally trained leadership, the focus of the seminary changed. Through the twentieth century, theological education was tailored (consciously or unconsciously) to serve the church's felt need for specialized, professional leadership. In the 1970s, "liberating the laity" was a momentary theme in literature and conferences on church renewal, but the structures of the church were now so ingrained and the relationships of clergy and laity in relation to those structures so defined that only questions about the liberation of *structures* could make a difference.

It is still unclear whether the church has been well served by the inclusion of a substantial number of professional programs in the curriculum and by classification of the master of divinity degree as a professional degree. In reality, though the M.Div. is classified as a professional degree, in many seminaries it is treated as if it were a liberal arts degree. Assessment standards are not consistent with those expected of a professional program, admission requirements seldom assess the suitability of the applicant for the *profession*, and graduates are not expected to be accountable to professional standards or to undertake mandatory continuing education.

Does the seminary need to be a professional school, or would the church be better served by some productive relationship between the academy, a professional institute that connects the church and the academy, and required experiences in society and international contexts? Though professionalism is appropriate for the church and ministry, to copy definitions, standards, and educational practices from other professions may not be sufficient. In what ways would theological education for ministry be affected if the particular character of Christian ministry were taken seriously?

Professionalism: Definition and Critique

In 1956, Myron Lieberman identified eight factors characteristic of a profession: (1) a clearly defined social service, (2) the application of intellectual techniques to service activities, (3) specialized training over a long term, (4) autonomy for the individual and professional group, (5) acceptance of responsibility for one's professional judgments and activities, (6) priority given to service over economic gain, (7) a professional organization that maintains and evaluates standards for the profession, and (8) a code of ethics that is clarified when necessary by concrete cases (Lieberman 1956, 2–6). Generally, definitions of professionalism still include some notion of a membership of skilled men and women who hold themselves accountable to certain standards, who are committed to ongoing development, and who can be trusted to conduct their roles with competence. A profession is expected to serve society by practicing skills valued, or considered essential, by society. A professional is assumed to have expert knowledge and skills refined through an extended period of training and to use these skills ethically and honourably for the good of society rather than for economic gain. In most cases, the professional functions with autonomy and belongs to a professional association that takes responsibility for the development of standards considered appropriate to the profession. Standards of quality are maintained through a code of ethics, required professional development experiences, and regular evaluation (Wilshire 1990; Lieberman 1956; Cherry 1995).

Arthur Wilson, discussing the emergence of the adult education professional, observes that "there is a pervasive faith in American culture and professional life, running back before the Industrial Revolution, that scientific investigation will provide reliable solutions to the human and social problems that beset us" (Wilson 2001, 74). He notes that the ideology of professionalization as scientific, technical practice emerged more than a hundred years ago and has been the basis for graduate educational work since the 1930s—in spite of Eduard Lindeman's concern at the time about such a limited and potentially destructive identity.[21] Ultimately, the scientifically based technical approach to professionalism began to break down under the assaults of Donald Schön (1987), Ronald Cervero (1988) and Philip Nowlen (1988; see Wilson 2001, 76). The attempt to define professionalism operationally parallels concerns about clerical functionalism in theological education. The implication of such functionalism is that one believes one can fix the church, or grow the church, through the application of professional technique.

---

[21]See http://www.infed.org/thinkers/et-lind.htm for more on Lindeman's professional contribution. Last accessed in October 2005.

Critics of professional education and the ensuing professional associations asserted that the curriculum of the schools developed competencies that served a former era and that the standards were not sufficient to ensure that women and men could function in their work (Argyris and Schön 1974, 142–43; Light 1983, 346). Graduates of the professional schools were unable to learn adequately from one another, lacked the necessary skills for reflection on practice that could lead to productive change, communicated inexpertly with their clients, and tended to turn to how-to manuals when faced with a problem rather than reflecting on practice and interacting with their community. Professional associations were criticized for placing concerns for survival and prestige over service for the good of society. Further, professionals tended to remain inside their guild and would not feel it necessary to interact with areas of theory and practice outside it. Significantly, access to professional education and guild membership is also access to systems of power and control—abuses of which are not uncommon in all forms of leadership, including religious leadership. Expectations of power and control are directly related to the assumption that members of the profession control access to and production of professional knowledge, and thus "monopolize the market for their services...Producing a recognizable professional commodity means producing a professional trained in discipline-specific knowledge and skill who, as the only available purveyor can 'sell' that expertise in the professional marketplace" (Wilson 2001, 77).

Many in theological schools would take exception to these criticisms, believing them too harsh for the ministry profession. However, one of the current concerns in theological institutions is that the church is taking over the development of ministers. This is an implicit or explicit challenge to the academy's presumed right to control access to ministerial development and the knowledge of the profession.

If graduate education has little to contribute to the practice of ministry, as some claim, then the erosion of seminary programs should proceed. If the true development of the minister (broadly conceived) takes place through nonformal, lifelong learning, then professional programs in the seminary should be disbanded. However, it is unlikely that seminaries will abandon such programs. Rather than think of abandonment, think of timing. A recent denominational magazine featured testimonials from several pastors, bemoaning the fact that on graduation from seminary they were unprepared to do the work they were expected to do in the church. The implied criticism, of course, is that seminary education is not effective. Yet to what extent is any graduate of any profession able to conduct professional work immediately upon graduation? Most professional fields (medicine, law, engineering) have extensive periods of internship, residency, or apprenticeship before the initiate is deemed capable.

Perhaps the more appropriate way to think of the seminary's involvement in professional education is not as preparatory but as developmental. The curriculum is already hopelessly mired with courses. Reconfigure it to allow an appropriate sequence of courses while others are removed from the curriculum to become part of the graduates' lifelong learning experience. Professional education, except in ministerial education, presumes that the development of professional capacity extends over several years—it doesn't end once a degree is in hand. Further, one's continuance in the profession is contingent upon regular and continuing education throughout one's career in which the individual interacts with other professional fields and is guided in reflection on practice.

As seminaries and churches rethink the education of the minister, they also need to consider that the nature of leadership of congregations is fundamentally different from the professional notion of leadership. Having traced common elements in the definition of profession, David Kelsey proposes that church leadership is not consistent with many of the sociological characteristics of a profession. One of his more significant objections is consistent with a congregationally based understanding of leadership:[22] "Theologically, it is important to stress that it is the *entire congregation* that engages in ministry in the public worship of God. Various kinds of leadership in regard to that ministry are exercised by persons who stand in parity with everybody else so far as their shared ministry is concerned. Hence a profession's stress on 'autonomy' and its view of those served as 'clients' are both inappropriate in congregational leadership" (Kelsey 1992, 247, emphasis added).

---

[22]Students choose to go to seminary for three primary reasons: a call from God, opportunity for growth and study, and desire to serve. Students in Association of Theological Schools (ATS) member institutions tend to have made the decision to enter seminary at an older age than most students in other professional schools (Association of Theological Schools 2002–2003). This means that they enter their ministry career with potentially fewer years available for it.

Many, if not most, professional activities of clergy could also be carried out by laity. Is it, then, necessary for a layperson who is serious about ministry and spirituality to go to seminary and then into ministry? To what extent have criteria from operational notions of professional behavior been adopted uncritically in theological education?[23] How did the apostle Paul credential leaders in the church? What indicators satisfied Jesus that his disciples were becoming leaders?

The New Professionalism

Reflecting on the aftermath of the Enron scandal in America, William Sullivan concludes, "There has never been a time when the quality of professional education was more important, or more subject to question, than the present" (Sullivan 2005, 27). He asserts that the Enron crash and the crisis in the Catholic Church have exacerbated the public's loss of faith in the professions. In light of the public loss of faith in the professions and questions about the usefulness of the professional, Sullivan argues that renewal is necessary and that it must be stimulated by the professional schools (Sullivan 2005, 226). While he describes professional schools as the bridge between the academy and real-world practice, it is generally agreed that professional education at present is failing. Because of this concern, the Carnegie Foundation for the Advancement of Teaching has begun a study of professional programs including those designed to develop clergy, engineers, lawyers, nurses, and physicians (Chapman 2004, 11).

Perhaps Lieberman (1970) was right in his contention that society made the wrong choice in putting professionals in charge of essential societal functions. The assumption that the professional is morally and selflessly committed to the service of society, he argued, is false; further, the professional's primary allegiance is to the maintenance of the profession, and professional societies exist to protect the profession. Therefore, neither the professional nor the professional association is an appropriate source for

---

[23]Jackson Carroll (1985) notes that the image of the professional in the early nineteenth century was a gentleman with a liberal arts education buttressed by skills in a particular area. The skills were typically developed in an apprenticeship. As a more scientific or technical grounding was thought necessary, professionals came to be trained in schools designed for this purpose. One persistent question regarding professionalism is whether this move was necessary.

evaluation of the profession. In a similar way, one could argue that attempting to educate professional ministerial leadership using a curriculum limited by theory-practice divisions, and disposed to definitions of the profession that are neither adequately functionally nor theologically driven, fosters some of the problems that Lieberman cites. If professional-ism in Christian leadership is deemed insufficient, it follows that accreditation societies cannot be the only source for the assessment and accreditation of theological schools. Representatives from the church and, conceivably, society will need to assist the seminary in redefining the meaning of profession, the role of leadership, and the educational formats that will serve the goals that emerge from these conversations.

Carroll asks whether the professional model of ministry is worth saving, and John Westerhoff asserts that the professional model has outlived its usefulness—in terms of tendencies to power and control of specialized knowledge for the sake of its own guilds. If the specialization of the curriculum and the theory-practice dichotomy are not addressed, these statements will make no sense to church leaders increasingly committed to multiple staffs and complex organizational structures. The seminary will be less and less able to satisfy the church's perceived need for competent professionals, and training tasks will be taken over completely by larger churches and independent agencies. Any contribution the seminary may have made will be bypassed, and the churches' tendency to focus on the immediate, the pragmatic, and the quantifiable will further erode theological education for the whole people of God.

Increasingly, the separation of research and practice is being questioned as university-based and independent professional schools recognize that a significant distance exists between theoretical subjects and professional studies. The modern crisis in professionalism relates to practice grounded in pragmatism and expediency, lacking a foundation in broad knowledge, moral values, and ethics. Similarly, many academics presume that good theory need not be informed and/or reshaped by good practice. Further, in an increasingly technological society, the demand for specialized skills can overwhelm the need for professional character and commitment to values over against self-interest (see Schön (1987).

Citing the proceedings of a symposium on "the future of callings," Sharon Daloz Parks asserts that more are aware that something is amiss in the professions. "What is now reappearing is a reappreciation of the role of each profession in contributing to the quality, strength, and vitality of our common life" (Parks 2000, 175). Professional schools are giving renewed attention to how the professional confronts the problems and dilemmas of a changing world. Recognition of the need for mentors is shifting to a call for mentoring communities, where peers and specialists work together to address problems (ibid., 176–77). Those concerned about the future of theological education should see hope in this trend and may find helpful exemplars.

By the late twentieth century, pastors and thoughtful members of congregations began to question the preoccupation with success, efficiency, numbers, and performance in many churches.[24] If this pattern continues, the minister as professional specialist may assume a new role better suited to the biblically rooted identity of the congregation and its leadership and to its mission in culture. At the same time, the need to engage leaders and congregations about the fundamental character of the church as the people of God, and the nature of the church's mission in the world, may stimulate seminaries to envision the nature and role of theology and the organization of the theological curriculum in ways other than independent subject-matter disciplines alongside programs of ministry and leadership development. Finally, the ultimate priority of the church and seminary to stimulate the desire to know God may be rediscovered as the less desirable effects of institutionalism, rationalism, and professionalism are recognized and remedied. This consideration leads to the last of the four factors that have shaped higher education and, subsequently, theological education as we know it.

Factor 4: The Disposition of the Soul toward God
How the church and academy have understood and foster the desire to know God

(For background see also chapter 7, "*Theologia* and the Desire to Know God.")

---

[24]See Bandy (1998, 1999), Barna (1998), Bennison (1999), Callahan (2000), Cobb (1998), Cymbala and Dean (1997), Frank (2000), Halstead (1998), Kenneson and Street (1997), Peterson (1987), Webster (1992).

Edward Farley positions the meaning of *theologia* within three major historical periods: from the patristic era through most of the medieval period *theologia* was understood as the knowledge of God—that is, a divine illumination of the intellect. From the twelfth to seventeenth centuries, *theologia* became a cognitively oriented "state and disposition of the soul which has the character of knowledge." Finally, from the Enlightenment to the present, *theologia* was seen as "the practical know-how necessary to ministerial work." Theology in this period became "one technical and specialized scholarly undertaking among others; in other words, as systematic theology" (Farley 1983a, 35, 39). The meaning of *theologia* found in the first two periods has largely disappeared in the academy, and clearly Farley identifies the Enlightenment understanding as the source of most of the current problems in theological education. He argues that "in this period the two genres of theology continue but undergo such radical transformation that the original senses of theology as knowledge (wisdom) and as discipline [not in the sense of structured specialization] virtually disappear from theological schools" (ibid., 39). He continues, "With the Enlightenment and the modern university came the ideal of autonomous science, of scholarship, proceeding under no other canons than proper evidence" (ibid., 41). Then "with its pluralization into sciences, theology as a disposition of the soul toward God simply drops out of 'the study of theology.' Furthermore, there is no unitary science but an aggregate of disciplines whose unity is their pertinence to the tasks of ministry" (ibid., 43).

Farley favors a notion of *theologia* informed by the mysticism of the patristic era but shaped finally by the later medieval period through the Renaissance. The important distinction he makes between the patristic era and the later period is that, though the notion of divine illumination persisted, it was conceived in the later period as related to the schools and was regarded as a habit—a *habitus*. That is, it could be "promoted, deepened, and extended by human study and argument" (Farley 1983a, 36). Based on his interpretation of patterns in history, Farley concludes that *theologia* is best understood as the ecclesial counterpart of *paidea*.[25] The loss of this understanding in the current era has made theological education the "grasping of

---

[25]Farley defines *paidea* in relation to one aspect of the Greeks' view of the purpose of education: culturing a human being in virtue (Farley 1983a, 152–53).

the methods and contents of a plurality of regions of scholarship" (ibid., 153). Theological education, for Farley, should be concerned with the cultivation of theological judgment rather than presuming that theology (conceived as a system of rationally derived propositions) buttresses a functional understanding of ministry.[26] *Theologia* is best depicted as a mode of understanding—a process—rather than as a science; and like *paideia*, it is a preparation for life.[27] Properly understood *theologia* cannot be taught, but it can be the unifying principle for theological study and the orienting philosophy of the curriculum.[28]

In favoring the understanding of *theologia* that emerged in the twelfth to seventeenth centuries, Farley may not have taken enough account of the deep complexities in the understandings of theology and spirituality from the patristic era to the seventeenth century. The general consensus in the literature is that theology and spirituality, now seen as two distinct areas of knowledge and practice, were, for most of history, one unified essence. As institutionalism, academic rationalism, and professionalism proceeded, this essence fractured. Farley laments the loss of *theologia* and suggests that the specialization and fragmentation of theological education is due to a loss of unity in theology. However, this notion of the loss of unity cannot be fully apprehended without considering the significance of the one essence of theology *and* spirituality.

---

[26]The concern for intellectual process over theological propositions is also evident in Wood (1985b), who argues that critical inquiry is actually an act of obedience.

[27]Kelsey, reflecting on this, suggests that *theologia,* then, is not the "end point of the process but the process itself" (Kelsey 1993, 105).

[28]In Farley's judgment, Goclenius's *Lexicon Philosophicum* offers the most detailed treatment of the meaning of *habitus.* He summarizes Goclenius's analysis, picking up on the points that *habitus* is "a disposition or state of the human being, the most general category for affirming any human state .... Habits of the soul fall into either habits of will or of reason. It is in connection with the *habitus intellectus* that theology occurs .... Theology is a knowledge which occurs in the mode of certainty, and which is of a *composite* nature because it combines both a knowledge of conclusions (thus, *scientia*) and knowledge of principles (*neotikus*). The name for
this composite cognitive state or disposition is *sapientia* or wisdom." Farley concludes that "when seventeeth-century Reformed theologians argue, as they do, that *theologia* is in genre, wisdom, they are arguing for its composite character as a cognitive habit or state of the soul" (Farley 1983a, 47).

From the patristic era to the Middle Ages, the true unity of theology was found in its essence as affirmation of the Scripture and the creeds *and* as spirituality. Farley links *theologia* with a "cognitive disposition." Kelsey (1992) speaks of knowing God truly, and Dykstra (1991b) refers to theology in the context of the essential practices of the church. However, many efforts to describe a renewed theology are still embedded in the notion that theology, contemplation, and knowing are activities grounded in reason— and to a great extent dominated by reason. Suggesting that the meaning and purpose of theology can be recovered by a return to Western medieval understandings of theology tends to obscure the significant fact that theology for most of history was of one essence with the ineffable *mysteries* of spirituality, not reason. For many Western theologians and educators, the experience and knowledge of God rightly require the stabilizing force of reason. Spirituality without reason is out of control. However, reason too easily assumes the prominent, almost exclusive position of arbiter of the meaning of theology.

The Search for a Theology and Spirituality for Theological Education

Efforts to recover a theology for theological education must address the fundamental issue: humanity is not brought into right relationship with God and empowered for service through doctrine, or experience, alone. Clearly, then, if *theologia* is a missing element in theological education, it must be seen as a much broader realm than a cognitively oriented academic discipline of theology, however unified. The educative task is a holism of cognition, affect, and purposeful action. This is not a new idea. Only recently, in fact, was the notion of holistic learning almost completely banished from theological education. Charry argues that radical changes in how reason, knowledge, and truth were understood accompanied the Reformation.

> The new notions of reason, knowledge, and truth all eliminated affect. Being spiritually vulnerable to God's goodness and wondrous deeds no longer counted as truth or knowledge; nor was it rational because it attached the seeker to God. By the end of the seventeenth century the situation looks something like this: theology was no longer about the cure of souls but about ra-

tional assent to ideas; yet biblical scholasticism, developed to meet the epistemic crisis, proved inadequate to render theology a credible science. Theology was already moving toward the position it occupies today: emotionally inaccessible to believers and academically unacceptable to the wider academy. (Charry 2000, 82–83)

As unpopular as Charry's conclusions will be in some quarters, they are not easily dismissed. A consequence of the Reformation was to actually eliminate "attachment to God from the task of theology" and to give this task to preaching. The purpose of theology was not to cure souls "but to inform people of the coherence of the ideas to which believers assented.... The new reason, knowledge, and truth eliminated vulnerability and awe before the knowledge sought. Knowledge of God came under the control of human reason; the mind stood tall.... The new reason, truth, and knowledge required Prolegomena and system" (Charry 2000, 84).

It is now stating the obvious that the most tragic result of the loss of theology's primary purpose was to render it marginal to both the church and the academy. Rampant dysfunctionalities in both the institutionalized church and the academy were deepened when *living* theology was diminished as the central task of the believer. Living theology, of course, requires a lifelong commitment to interpretation of situations in the light of the gospel. In this regard, Farley is right in locating the task of interpretation in the church. In doing so, the question must be asked, "What would it mean to facilitate the interpretive life of the congregation and its members?" (Farley 2003, 11). Efforts to know God academically, to derive formulas and propositions that define God's essence and work, actually hinder the development of the people of God. One's understanding of God and one's life in relation to that understanding cannot be separated. The essential task of church leadership is to lead people to understand their identity and purpose as the people of God. If leaders are required who will facilitate the interpretive life of the congregation, theological education in its common institutional form will not do the job.

Nevertheless, many efforts to locate theological education in the church involve simply transplanting seminary or seminary-like courses. This replication of schooling in the church will not accomplish the task of developing the interpretive life of the congregation or assist the believer in the desire to know God. Farley's description of the development of the interpretive life is significant at this point. Our capacity for theological interpretation is developed along with participation in worship, remembering the Story of faith, and service. It is never simply casual religious opinion based on one's prejudices or experience. "Theological interpretation proceeds by way of self-conscious alertness, situational focus, and some degree of historical knowledge" (Farley 2003, 13). Unfortunately, this corrective could still leave us trapped in the notion that theological education is primarily a rational enterprise. "The problem with a purely intellectual search for God is that it necessarily regards what is sought as an object or a conclusion and an objective that can be reached. Equally, the determining factor of such a search is *me* and *my* understanding rather than the action of God" (Sheldrake 1998, 31).

An emerging conviction among Protestants is that any renewal in theological education and the church requires acceptance of the *unity* of theology and spirituality. Philip Sheldrake observes that acceptance of such a unity would lead those concerned about the development of the people of God to different, more expansive, ways of knowing and learning (Sheldrake 1998, 30).

> From the patristic period until the development of the 'new theology' scholasticism around the 12th century theology was a single enterprise. To say that theology was a unified enterprise does not simply mean that the later distinctions between *intellectual* disciplines were not present. The unity of theology implied that intellectual reflection, prayer and living were, ideally speaking, a seamless whole. Patristic theology involved the constant reading of the Scripture which was then shaped in the liturgy and in critical dialogue with Greek philosophical culture. This issued in reflection on such central themes as prayer, martyrdom, the state and stages of the Christian life and so on. (ibid., 36)

By the late Middle Ages, however, the spiritual life had moved to the margins of theology and culture. "By mid-seventeenth century, it became appropriate to distinguish the reasoning behind the doctrines from the effects of doctrine. Theology, concerned with the former, eventually became divided from the arts of Christian ministry. And so it is until this day"

(Charry 2000, 84). The theological curriculum isolates what was once a synthesis (exegesis and theology, theology and ministry) and separates doctrinal knowing from spiritual knowing (Sheldrake 1998, 37). Where every believer was once expected to belong consciously to the fellowship of the mystery, the arbiters of Christian knowledge are now those who have made their way through a course of studies in seminary.

If theology and spirituality were separated when the knowledge project became rationalized and the prerogative of institutions (schools), how can they be rejoined? The cultural situation is different, knowledge has expanded, and even if such an effort were desirable, it is impossible to return to the patristic and pre-Enlightenment eras. Sheldrake cites the positions of Sandra Schnieders and Bernard McGinn as complementary alternatives. "Schneiders believes that spirituality and theology are close partners that function in mutuality but respect each other's autonomy" (Sheldrake 1998, 84). In other words, spirituality is not a category *within* theology. "McGinn believes that spirituality is somehow primary in its partnership with theology" (ibid., 85). Both Schneiders and McGinn preserve the interdisciplinary or transdisciplinary nature of spirituality. It is not captured within theology as much as it is part of all theological discourse, and for McGinn, belief and practice are the "primary criteria of interpretation" (ibid.). Essentially, then, theology must recognize that it has a spiritual core. However, today theology and spirituality are separated, and education cannot proceed as if they were of one essence. Therefore, some form of dialogue between theology and spirituality is the only way forward. Retaining courses in theology and adding a course in spirituality is not sufficient. Retaining courses and adding a parallel system of group experiences without integration with other learning experiences is similarly inadequate. Because theology in the academy has been informed by the "familiar conversations with philosophy or other intellectual disciplines" (ibid., 86), Sheldrake warns that the rational discourse characteristic of academic theology will subsume spirituality into its own structures. A more humble theological discipline recognizes that spirituality serves to prevent a systematized or philosophical theology from imagining that it speaks the definitive word about God.

The major difficulty in embracing the possibility of an effective dialogue between theology and spirituality is that spirituality is seen as derived from experience. The experience of a genuine search for God has almost been lost in modern religious culture—a consequence of the separation of theology from spirituality in the seventeenth century. Therefore, when Sheldrake points out that "it is difficult to avoid the evidence of history that concrete spiritual traditions arise from Christian experiences or from the concrete realities of human existence rather than being derived from ideas and doctrines" (Sheldrake 1998, 86), many Protestants envision only contemporary "pop" spirituality, reflected in worship as entertainment and in self-serving ministry programs. But if "the Christian way began with *events* rather than with a shift of theory born of intellectual speculation," and if Jesus' followers experienced "their own lives and the nature of God's relationship with the world in a new way because of the impact upon them of the events of Jesus life," it follows that theological discourse can be "questioned and even deconstructed by the deeper insight that the reality of God is beyond the 'God' of rational argument" (ibid.). Sheldrake addresses inevitable concerns about the appeal to experience by defining experience in relation to the classic threefold formula of *sola fide, sola scriptura,* and *sola gratia.*

> The rational discourse of theology must be thought of as subordinate to three things: to the original act of faith of Jesus' companions, 'You are the Messiah, the Son of the living God' (*sola fide*); to the fact that this faith is brought about by the action of God, 'Flesh and blood has not revealed this to you but my Father in heaven' (*sola gratia*); and to the privileged expression of this faith in the pages of Scripture (*sola scriptura*). (ibid., 87)

Spirituality grounded in experiences of faith in relation to the event of the gospel, and buttressed by ongoing efforts to understand, is the best outworking of the human desire to know God. We can accept, with McGinn, that rational theology is in some way subordinate to spirituality, but we also need to accept that spirituality is undone without efforts of reasoned understanding. Finally, the fact that God will never be completely known perpetuates the mystery of the faith. In this respect, the temptation of rational theology toward closure is countered by the spiritual certainty that the journey of faith is always *toward* God. Spirituality, then, to a greater degree than academic theology, which tends to be dominated by Western reason, calls for the input and critique of the other. On the journey toward God, understanding and the enlightenment of faith are impoverished without the stories of God's acts among people found in Scripture, stories from the long history of the church, and the input and critique of men and women from other cultures and social situations. Insight from the human and natural sciences is needed at the intersection of theology and spirituality, because part of the journey toward God is understanding the nature and purpose of all God's creation. We then are obligated to confront issues of justice, power, self-interest, ethnocentrism, and institutional structures because injustice, the abuses of power, and oppression hinder the journey.

At this point we can return to Farley for help as we seek to determine how the relation of theology and spirituality is accomplished in theological education. Though McGinn and Farley would likely disagree on the place of spirituality and theology, and though Farley is not as explicitly concerned with the separation between theology and spirituality, they are moving in the same direction. "Theology in its primary meaning and as we are using it is a personal and existential wisdom or understanding. As such it is not tied to any specific course of studies such as clergy education. As such it sets its own requirements for studies, knowledge, and disciplines depending on the context in which it occurs" (Farley 1983a, 153). Once certain unproductive habits in forming the theological curriculum are abandoned, the study of theology is freed from the academy and its standard teaching practices. "The study of theology can and should occur in the churches, in the colleges, in universities, for ministers no longer attending schools, and in special locations in the culture" (Farley 2003, 25).

Allowing that clergy education is necessary, Farley maintains that theology cannot be "restricted to clergy education and its array of scholarly endeavors…. Because theology arises as an adjunct to the life of faith itself, *the inquiries and instructions of degree-granting schools are always derivative and secondary*" (Farley 2003, 36, emphasis added). He echoes Sheldrake's point by adding that various kinds of interpretive activity are needed because of the variety of faith-life situations among believers. The flawed assumption that academic theory (specialized, rationalized academic theology) can be applied "to practice, to culture, the self, the church, piety, and so forth" reveals a chief problem in theological education:

> It bypasses most of the structural elements in the situation of the believer and, therefore, suppresses most of the acts in which the believers interpret their own lives and situations…. Problematic

situations can range from global situations (the crisis in planetary ecology, the global phenomenon of political terrorism) to "metaphysical" situations (the course and destiny of human history) to very specific situations of the individual (the onset of an illness).... The Christian community typically has assumed that if the interpretation of the authoritative texts is done properly, all other interpretations will take care of themselves. It is just at this point that the believer (and the community of believers all) falls into uncritical and even idolatrous paradigms of the use of texts. Further, when the interpretation of situations is not itself subject to critical scrutiny, the believer reads the situation simply out of a kind of obliviousness, an inattention to most of its components. (ibid., 36–37)

But doesn't the array of practical subjects and their use of the social sciences indicate that the seminary is cognizant of the life situation of the believer? Not as long as theology and social sciences are severed *because of the nature of the theological curriculum and attitudes of some faculty who believe that God speaks only in the theological courses.* Productive insights are possible only as equitable conversation among the disciplines is encouraged. For example, following Alasdair MacIntyre's suggestion that moral philosophy presupposes a sociology, Richard Mouw proposes "that every theological system also has an associated sociology, such that we can fully understand the claims of a theological perspective only if we attempt to see what it would look like if those claims were fleshed out in the life of a community" (Mouw 2001, 73–74).

Though we should not deny a unique place for theology as the *critical knowledge of God* (see Dalferth 1996, 136–37), the undue separation of God's natural and special revelation ensures the withdrawal of theology into a narrowly specialized academic world. If theology is the critical knowledge of God in the midst of creation and human life, then the findings of both natural and special revelation are needed in the endeavor. Thoughtful interdisciplinary dialogue that reflects broadly on creation and on God's sixth-day creation is essential. Jeffrey Stout seems to recognize this as he affirms James Gustafson's argument that to ground theology in rationalistic, philosophical reasoning misses the point and removes theological discourse from its locus in "historically conditioned thought"—in other words, from the human condition (Stout 1988, 167). The point is not to abandon the contributions of the classical disciplines but rather *to avoid accepting these disciplines alone as those that define the parameters of the dialogue.*

Perspectives on the Nature of Theology and Spirituality

In the debates that swirl around the efficacy of theological education, there is a persistent concern as to whether the adoption of the research university model and the attendant separation of the disciplines obscured the original pietistic and formative intentions of theological education. In 1970, the ATS sponsored a task force on spiritual formation. Wayne Goodwin reports that in spite of difficulties of definition, members of the task force concluded that spiritual formation is dependent on the spiritual formation of faculty who model spirituality before their students. They also suggested that studies in spiritual formation be part of the academic curriculum (Goodwin 1989, 302–3). However, in many institutions there seems to be little impetus for adopting an emphasis that is difficult to quantify and almost impossible to program effectively. Faculty are not rewarded academically for modeling spirituality; in fact, if they spend too much time being spiritual mentors, they could suffer academically and their career progress might be jeopardized. Institutional and curricular forms do not easily accommodate the mysteries of the Christian faith.

Kelsey proposes that the task of the theological school is to "understand God truly"—noting that "Athens" and "Berlin" cannot be synthesized and that North American schools will have to negotiate between these emphases (1992, 227).[29] The academic study of disciplines is necessary, he argues, because God cannot be apprehended directly. However, he continues, academic study must be oriented in relation to the *practices* of congregations.

Cheryl Johns suggests a "Jerusalem" model as a solution to what she feels are the inadequacies of both "Athens" and "Berlin."

---

[29]"Athens" is identified by Kelsey as wisdom mediated by a scholar concerned about personal transformation. The one qualified to teach must possess learning and personal sensitivity. The context is communal. "Berlin" characterizes the "movement from data to theory to application of theory to practice" (Kelsey 1993, 22). The method is research. In Kelsey's judgment, the Berlin model is problematic in the effort to know God truly because it leads to professionalism. Can persons be competent and know God truly?

> Within the tradition of the Jerusalem Road as expressed in Scripture...there is an overarching theological purpose of *knowing* God truly. This knowledge, best expressed by the Hebrew word *yada*, is characterized as a dynamic versus static, experiential rather than contemplative, relational rather than individualistic, and transrational rather than merely cognitive. Therefore, knowledge of God is characterized by a relationship of encounter resulting in worship and obedience. This knowledge is available to anyone regardless of gender, race or social standing. (Johns 1997, 3)

The identification of theological education with cities as metaphors is intriguing, but one wonders if adding other cities to the mix would further shape the way we think about theological education. If theological education is about theology *and* education, surely more than three cities are required. Robert Pazmiño's linking of the history of educational philosophy with Jerusalem, Athens, Nazareth, Rome, and Prague is suggestive (Pazmiño 1997, 121). Though metaphors are never completely descriptive of reality, consider also the contribution to our thinking of the educators associated at points in history with Chicago, Capernaum, Paris, Hippo, Pietermaritzburg, Geneva, São Paulo, to name a few.

Robert Banks (1999) replaces Kelsey's city descriptors with the terms Classical and Vocational, adding a third, Confessional, and then proposes a Missional approach, which he describes as life-engaging service coupled with knowing and obedience. Theological education in both its dimensions—theology and education—is proving to be more complex than most realize!

To return to our theme: the desire to know God often generates multiple temptations. God can be known truly with the mind; the true presence of God can be acquired through contemplation and prayer; the perfect will of God can be known through biblical exegesis or spiritual feeling; and entry into the presence of the Divine is through acts of holiness and service. Is it inevitable that the desire to know God results in the separation of theology and spirituality, reason and piety, service and virtue? Can fallen humanity ever embrace a theological vision that is at once holistic, reasonable, and spiritual? Could the gospel, the ultimate act of God's love for humankind, provide the way for the "path of reason" and the "path of love" to be reconciled within a theological vision that is relevant for contemporary theological education?

Many of the values that shape higher education, including Christian higher education, are counter to the heritage of Christian belief. However, Christian educators continue to support institutional structures and professionalized forms of higher education that emerged from a dominant academic rationalism. Certainly, theological institutions will continue to uphold the importance of intellectual development; however, it is equally certain that theological education concerned only with the development of the mind or with the acquisition of information is less than Christian. To have clarified information and concepts as the highest goal of educational endeavor is not sufficient for what is required of us as Christians relating to the world (see Ward 1982). Theological education must be more than an encounter with ideas, or the passing of tests, or engagement in intellectual debates, no matter how mentally stimulating. "The best human knowing takes the form of discerning obedience" (Brueggemann 1982, 89) and Ward asserts that education grounded in obedient knowing *requires* responsible action.

> The biblical concern for obedience—acting on truth—should be the central purpose of education and life. It is not enough to argue that obedience requires knowing. The issue is that knowing, in Christianity, cannot be defined apart from doing. Both John and Paul are sensitive to the tendency to divide creed from deed, quite likely entering the early church from Greek philosophy and educational traditions (Rom. 6:4; 1 Cor. 3; Gal. 5:10–13; Eph. 2:10; 5:2; Phil. 3:12–16; Col. 2:6; 1 Thess. 2:1–12; 1 John 1:6–7; 2 John 6; 3 John 4). Their warnings are needed today as surely as in the first-century church. (Ward 1982, 292)

Charry weaves together from the history of Christian doctrine a defensible thesis that character formation, trust, love of God, and virtuous acts were once integral to theology and vital to knowing God. Her account seeks to recover the holism of Christian theology: the notion that integration of mind, emotions and behavior, within the context of a faithful community, is essential to the formation of Christian identity. "Communal practices such as participation in prayer, liturgy, sacraments, works of charity, and study all strengthen Christian identity. That is one reason why Christian communities have been fussy about ordering these communal tasks" (Charry 1997, 27). The habits of isolated linearity of the modern theologian are challenged in Charry's work. Rather than view knowledge about God as the precursor to loving God, Charry argues from the long history of the Christian church that communal practices reinforce knowledge and prepare the Christian for proper interpretation of knowledge. The idea that knowledge could be separated from practice would have mystified premodern theologians (Charry 1997, 28). Mark McIntosh concurs and follows McGinn and LeClercq in understanding mystical theology as making it possible for *all* Christians to partake of the divine nature (see 2 Peter 1:4). "If theology is able to do this, to show the spiritual seeker that the very heart of the Sought is precisely the source and goal of Christian theology, then it might suddenly find a great many people being interested, both in church and academy, in Christian theology" (McIntosh 1998, 40).

Since the late Middle Ages, it seems, Western Christians have been unable to hold intellect and piety in constructive tension.[30] Without intellectual rigor and the intent to inquire into God's revelation, spirituality tends to be shaped by personal experience, opinion, or the latest media personality. Without the desire to know God through the mysterious activity of the Spirit, intellectual inquiry and memorization of propositions tend to become meaningless activities of an empty soul.

The Great Divide

As one processes the trajectory of concerns in the literature related to theology and theological education, the suspicion emerges that the primary problem, after all, is not the specialization and fragmentation of theology into various disciplines. The greater problem for theological education, and consequently for the church, is that at some point, for reasons that seemed justified at the time, theology ceased to be described as of one essence with spirituality and became, in the West especially, a rational enterprise. In reality, the desire to hold together reason and piety, academy and church, virtue

---

[30] Note the tension in relation to understanding the meaning of ignorance. On the one side is the passion expressed in the North African proverb: "Ignorance is a disaster." On the other side is the monastic theme "Ignorance is the highest stage of spiritual formation."

and service, can be realized only if theology and spirituality are, in fact, of one essence.

A key impulse of the Enlightenment was the idea "that there is a *method* by which we can reach the truth.... Then method itself becomes differentiated into other methods—particular to disciplines—and disciplines become isolated from one another by the very methods designed to clarify them" (Louth 1983, 7). Several suggest that in the West, before the rise of the universities and Scholasticism, theology and spirituality were not programmatically distinguished and that a series of institutional developments contributed to the division (Lindbeck 1996, 293; see also Louth 1983; Charry 1997; Allen 1997; McIntosh 1998). For instance, by the sixteenth century, the notion that all clergy should be theologically educated was commonplace. Theological education for Protestants took place in universities. Catholics, under mandate from the Council of Trent, established seminaries. It would be another 250 years before the first Protestant seminaries (Andover and Princeton) were established. In the universities, clergy were to be intellectually prepared to interpret and defend the Word and to learn the skills they would need as leaders of the church. "Thus, the gap between theology and spirituality widened" (Lindbeck 1996, 294). This division "between thought about God and the movement of the heart towards God" is now so commonplace that it is taken as normative. Andrew Louth argues that the "specialization in theology, the remoteness of theologians...from the Church and the believing Christian, and indeed the remoteness of theologians from one another...are all part of a phenomenon we see much of elsewhere and have come to regard as inevitable." He asserts that this division is potentially damaging to theology, "for it threatens in a fundamental way the whole fabric of theology in both its spiritual and intellectual aspects" (Louth 1983, 3). McIntosh is concerned that if theology and spirituality remain separated, theology will actually begin to speak of a different God. "What kind of god does theology divorced from spirituality end up describing?" (McIntosh 1998, 15).

The Mystery of Faith and the Character of Theology
The past, present, and future met, wrote Augustine, in a stable in Bethlehem. The mystery that lies at the heart of the Christian faith is embodied in a miraculous birth and the death of God-become-human. Within this mystery is contained the necessity of a response of faith and a life lived in re-

sponsible service. If theology has nothing to do with this mystery, it is empty indeed. Any future for theological education that includes theology must also accept that intellectual justification for faith is in itself inadequate and counter to God's purposes for his church. "In order to reclaim the sapiential function of theology it will first be necessary to suggest how theological claims may be understood to refer to God. Once it is clear that we may speak about knowing God, it will be necessary to ask how we come to love God" (Charry 1997, 5).

The inevitable criticism that this perspective undercuts serious learning about theology ought to be rejected. Of course, much that has been gained over the centuries of the Christian church would be lost if learning were despised. Surely we have learned this lesson from history. The peril that confronts us today is that an impoverished theology will exacerbate the sense of loss of God's presence that already exists at the heart of Western culture and in the church. In this era, popular spirituality is not described in terms of reason and piety but in terms of how to have a meaningful experience of God and personal freedom within community. The quest is not to find some rational orderly, consistent, logical way to prove God but rather to find meaning in some experience of God and to determine if that meaning can be an adequate ground for life. Once again, in this generation, a view of spirituality that is grounded in experience is in tension with a view of spirituality grounded in reason. But the persisting polarities of reason and piety, experience and rationalism are not the defining issues in faith. The more critical issue is whether or not God is present. Clearly, a theology that is simply a quest for experiences that will prove God's presence is not sufficient. However, a theology that is merely a transmission of propositions is similarly insufficient. Only a theology that allows reason and piety, virtue and service to stand together will be convincing. Admittedly, when experience and the ineffable are encouraged, Christians may default to personal experience as the arbiter of faith. However, this only confirms the need for a theology that embodies within it the effective practices of the intellect *and* the mystery of piety. Reading Scripture without a corresponding desire to know the truth and to yield in obedience to the Logos will not foster spirituality. Similarly, to study the Scriptures as an exercise of the mind alone hinders the work of the Spirit in the life of the believer.

Thomas Oden delights in evidences that one postmodern inclination is to reach back across modernity to the premodern—to the patristics, and the medievalists—to recover a more holistic spirituality and hermeneutic (Oden 1995, 401). In the same vein, Charry asks, "What would be required for theology to reclaim its sapiential voice today? Given the postmodern criticism of Enlightenment rationality, perhaps some of the classical, especially patristic, interpretations of Christian doctrines may be more accessible now than at other times. This could spawn a renewed willingness to seek the wisdom of God in genuinely Christian categories" (Charry 1997, 238).

Christians still tend to be defined by institutional allegiances and commitments: champions of the intellect are generally found in schools, champions of piety in churches, champions of service in mission agencies. If the single essence of theology and spirituality is recovered in this era, it may be possible to attain a fresh union of reason and piety, virtue and service. If this occurs, the structures of theological education can be transformed, and the church can discover afresh its identity as the people of God and its true mission in the world.

CHAPTER 3

A Threat Matrix: Challenges Confronting the Seminary and the Church

Webster's Dictionary describes a matrix as an environment or source from which something else originates, develops, or takes form.

Arrangements of disciplines, assumptions about the nature of knowledge, and teaching methods, along with the social structures of academia, are today so familiar as to seem unalterable. The four interdependent factors explored in chapter 2 essentially created and continue to reinforce these structures, practices, and traditions. What follows is based on the conviction that a matrix composed of these four factors now threatens the future of theological education.

Implications from Four Interdependent Processes from the History of Higher Education

One of the more significant developments in North American higher education took place as the four factors identified in chapter 2 intersected with events in the seventeenth through nineteenth centuries. The English college philosophy imported in the seventeenth century encountered the German research university philosophy, imported in the nineteenth and early twentieth centuries. In the nineteenth century both philosophies suddenly had to cope with the Industrial Revolution and the rise of the professions. Much of what we love and hate in contemporary higher education stems from this period. The seminary, born in the nineteenth century out of ideological conflict with the university, retained university-style structures and curricular patterns. For this reason, the same confluence of influences has shaped what we know today as theological education.

The English College Ideal and German University Culture Miss the Mark in North America

A vestige of the English college is seen in the persisting ideal that character is formed primarily through exposure to the great ideas of Western civilization and interaction with scholars who present and embody them. The greatest scandal for many in the academy, however, is an impoverished mind, and the greatest priority, even over good character, is faculty with impeccable scholarly credentials. Research universities in North America were patterned after the German research university, most notably Humboldt University, and presumed that they were the universities of the future. That this model had been designed for a particular purpose in a very different situation seemed of little importance. In the Humboldt model, faculty were free to pursue research without hindrance and were expected to share the results of their inquiries with a small number of bright students. Further, the only degree program offered in the German research university was the PhD. It is not surprising that the model (which ultimately was found to be ineffective in Germany) has not been entirely effective in North American universities with large numbers of students, most of whom are not in advanced programs of study.

To complicate matters further, the Industrial Revolution provided nineteenth-century educational administrators with a way to manage large numbers of students. The assembly-line procedures of factories were adapted to the university to move students through various programs with minimum disruption and maximum efficiency. The persistence of the factory model of education is not without cause. As the professions took root in America, functional forms of education were valued. Because the professions emerged during one of the most pragmatic eras of North American history, the models of education in professional schools and professional departments of universities quickly developed a practical cast. The notion that the professional must be grounded in a broad knowledge base was lost as the demand for skilled professionals increased, even in churches.

Out of the intertwined processes of institutionalism, rationalism, professionalism, and the desire to know God, and mingled effects of the English college and German research university models, emerged the now-familiar structures and curricula of universities and Protestant theological education. By the end of the nineteenth century and into the twentieth, the forces of institutionalism, rationalism, and professionalism had become a mutually reinforcing matrix that, coupled with the rush to *Wissenschaft* and industrial models of organization, blunted spirituality in the academy and with it the desire to know God. Efforts to classify, organize, and systematize knowledge further defined institutional structures and reinforced a dominating rationalism that ultimately separated spirituality from the disciplines of knowledge and shifted it away from the center of discourse to the margins. Universities, colleges, and theological institutions evolved in similar ways because they borrowed structures and programs from one another. Even in divinity schools and seminaries, the separation of theology and spirituality has proceeded to a point where religious studies and biblical and theological instruction are often detached from the desire to know God. The demanding task of sustaining a healthy tension between reason and spirituality, along with the expectation of responsible obedience, tends to be neglected in favor of mastery of cognitive information, practice of basic research, or development of ministry skills.

Challenging the Institutionalized Silos of Theological Education

When Max Weber laid the groundwork for the bureaucratic model, it was an idea whose time had come. The bureaucratic model was an antidote to patronage and a class system in a society where pedigree had mattered more than ability (see Harris 2005). Over time, however, the positive benefits of bureaucracy led to unacceptable rigidity, control, and sameness. Further, in light of evidence that many seminary graduates struggle in their professional roles, that spirituality suffers in the often competitive and impersonal environment of academia, and that the survival of theological institutions is not guaranteed, more are willing to admit that the "grand project" of the theological academy is faltering.

Theological education is deeply institutionalized, and as literature and experience have amply demonstrated, there is nothing particularly theological or educational or even spiritual about it. A disconnected, overcrowded curriculum has not provided a convincing framework for development of the capacity of the capacity to reflect biblically and theologically on real problems; nor can it nurture spirituality effectively or refine ministry competency. Providing incentives for faculty to explore alternative approaches in teaching and learning is seldom a priority; assessment for learning and continuing improvement is seldom part of the academic culture; and education is identified with schooling rather than learning.

In one sense, the structuring of separate disciplines could be seen as a beneficial development that served to strengthen scholarship and understanding. But it is not necessary to use disciplines to structure departments and organize faculty. For example, why should a Ph.D. level of specialization in a discipline automatically translate into a corresponding department, a category in the theological curriculum, and a way of teaching? Imagine an alternative construction where faculty with hard-won specialized knowledge could bring their individual *and collective* insight to bear on persisting problems, seminal ideas, conflicting perspectives, and urgent tasks.

In reality, disciplinary boundaries make sense only to schools. None of the boundaries make sense when a student graduates and endeavors to minister in the world. Dan Aleshire has observed, "Disciplines are the inventions that make our lives in schools much better; they don't make the life of our graduates, at least in disciplinary units, better" (Aleshire 2000). Silos, or separated disciplines and departments, promote a form of introspection that does not serve the church well. Only the conversations within the boundaries of the discipline seem to matter (Chong 2003, 19). In extreme cases, conversation across the boundaries becomes impossible, like a visit to another country where the language of the other is incomprehensible.

> What the field areas have become, recent authors have pointed out, are loose political confederacies among scholars who share a training in the same professional academic disciplines…and share loyalties to the same professional academic guilds. The writing and discussion in this decade has raised forceful questions about whether these academic disciplines and guilds should continue to determine the structure of theological education. To permit this, say some authors, is to subvert the proper overarching goal of theological education, which is 'to do theology.' Instead, the character of the goal ought to define the structure of theological education and bend the disciplines to its purposes. That will mean a smudging of what now seem self-evident lines between disciplines, a demand for scholars capable of a good deal more 'interdisciplinary' scholarship, and perhaps the invention of some new 'disciplines.' (Kelsey and Wheeler 1994, 79)

The real challenge is to enable *holistic learning toward informed wisdom*. Such learning is accomplished only in conversation among knowledge areas and in the commitment to virtue and service. Theological education is utterly defeated in its task to assist the church's mission in the world if it is relegated only to schools consisting of narrowly circumscribed disciplines. Unfortunately, the power of schooling is such that the need for ordered knowledge and familiar institutional frameworks to hold and convey that knowledge have been seldom questioned.

Nevertheless, today corporations, including educational corporations, are implementing cross-functional, interdisciplinary, horizontal models in which communication pathways traverse the organization (see Harris et al. 2005). Should these trends take hold in theological education, new opportunities for growth and responsible service to the church and society may be possible.

Taking Education and the Quest for Truth Seriously

Bruce Wilshire notes the odd reality that "educators in universities seldom talk about education. Administrators talk about administrative problems, professors talk about problems in their special fields of study, and those who do talk about education, professors in education departments, are generally despised and shunned" (Wilshire 1990, 21).

Looking out his office window at his university, John Harris asked, "If a breakthrough in education were possible, what institution would be likely to accomplish it?" The implicit answer was 'Not schools.' Harris continued, "The schools haven't yet learned what kind of business they are in. The business of education is student learning but, astonishingly, many in the academy don't see the need to commit resources to this task. What would it look like if we actually shaped an institution around its primary function—learning?" In 1995, from their vantage point in other universities, Robert Barr and John Tagg say:

> We are beginning to recognize that our dominant paradigm mistakes a means for an end. It takes the means or method—called 'instruction' or 'teaching'—and makes it the college's end or purpose. To say that the purpose of colleges is to provide instruction is like saying that General Motors' business is to operate assembly lines or that the purpose of medical care is to fill hospital beds.

We now see that our mission is not instruction but rather that of producing learning with every student by whatever means works best. (Barr and Tagg 1995, 12)

If seminaries ever come to accept that the fostering of lifelong theological learning toward informed wisdom is central to theological education, then assessment for learning and the very nature of the quest for truth become significant issues. Aleshire has suggested that most ATS schools are limited in their capacity to assess

> the attainment of educational goals beyond the accumulation of certain kinds of knowledge, or the demonstration of certain kinds of critical thinking skills that can be traced through papers or other kinds of academic assignments.... It's much harder to know whether [a student] holds the information in a way that is going to be generative to the people of God, and can interact with human beings, on the one hand, feeling terribly responsible, but on the other hand, not being in control of anything, which is the character of much of congregational life. (Aleshire 2000)

Given the complexities in ministry, the *processes* of education are of paramount importance as learning and research tools for ministry development. Most fields of inquiry and professional development have a subcategory concerned about education; for example, engineering has a subcategory called engineering education—not to be confused with education *about* engineering. A major purpose of engineering education is research into issues that affect the practice of engineering. Systematic processes that evaluate the nature of research and education in engineering are considered essential. Typically, a field of study in the seminary sees its progress in terms of accumulation of information and theoretical (library) research into its particular content. Well conceived professional education (the seminary is still considered a professional school) demonstrates that ministerial education, at least, should conduct research into the appropriateness and efficacy of its theoretical constructs and education processes. Other fields of study—including theology and biblical studies—would benefit from research into how students and faculty engage the discipline and apply its principles and practices.

The Flawed Assumption of the Seminary as a Professional School

In spite of Edward Farley's concerns about the dominance of the clerical paradigm, seminaries are not even close to keeping up with current progress in professional education. At an ATS consultation in October 2003, issues related to what constitutes a good M.Div. program included the following:

1. The accrual of subject matter means there is more to teach, for older theories of the discipline are seldom left behind (as they are in medical schools, for example).

2. Though the M.Div. is considered a professional degree, it is pursued in the manner of a liberal arts degree, with an emphasis on academics.

3. Theory is assumed to eventuate in good practice without intelligent reflection on practice.

4. The educational process fails to take seriously experience-based learning.

In the period 2002–2005, M.Div. graduates rate areas of satisfaction in essentially the same ways. They report greatest satisfaction "with their *self-perceived abilities* to use and interpret Scripture, to think theologically, to preach well, to teach well, to conduct worship/liturgy, to lead others, and to relate social issues to faith. Students were less satisfied with their knowledge of the other religious traditions, ability to administer a parish, and knowledge of the church policy/canon law" (*Fact Book* 2002–2003, 21, emphasis added).[1] These observations reinforce the common presumption that the

---

[1] Student perspective in these areas remains constant through 2005. M.Div. students who graduated from ATS member schools in Spring 2005 (from the ATS Annual Report) rated their "level of satisfaction with progress in skills related to future work" on a scale of 1 (very dissatisfied) to 5 (very satisfied) as follows: ability to think theologically (4.4), ability to use and interpret Scripture (4.3), ability to relate social issues to faith (4.2), knowledge of my own religious tradition (4.2), ability to preach well (4.1), ability to teach well (4.1), knowledge of church doctrine and history (4.1), ability to lead others (4.1), ability to conduct worship/liturgy (4.1). They are less satisfied with ability to administer a parish (3.6), ability in pastoral counseling (3.8), knowledge of church policy/canon law (3.8), ability to give spiritual direction (3.9), knowledge of Christian philosophy and ethics (3.9). (From Annual Report 2005).

M.Div. programs in many seminaries give priority to theoretical studies and that quality assessment of student learning in relation to congregational and social realities is seldom done. Consequently, the curriculum and educational practices tend to remain fixed while the conditions in church and society change.

The Readiness for Ministry project in the 1970s demonstrated the resistance that exists to incorporating measures for the assessment of ministry competencies into accrediting standards (Cherry 1995, 136–37). At the same time, the effectiveness of the professional model in theological education was being questioned. Currently, ATS has secured professional assistance in the development of guidelines and helps for schools to assess M.Div. programs. What may follow from such assessment is curricular reformation that incorporates, as realistically as possible, the theological character of the church and its ministry, allows a broader range of educational formats, engages in *continuous* processes of assessment, and invites congregations into the process. In this respect, it has been observed that the Standards of the Association of Theological Schools in North America raise issues that *churches are typically more concerned about than schools*. Yet theological schools seldom have effective processes for involving churches as evaluators and contributors in their accreditation process. The complaint that churches are dysfunctional and tend to look for ministers who will help them be successful isn't a convincing enough argument to exclude them from the process. Theological schools have their own problems and are in many ways no less dysfunctional. Perhaps, over time, both the churches and the schools will benefit from working together to improve ministry education.

What would happen if the master of divinity, the flagship professional degree of most seminaries, lost its professional degree status? The ministry is one of the few, perhaps the only, professional fields that operates without requirements for continuous upgrading and external assessment. Lifelong learning and professional development are seldom high on the priority list of ministry professionals. This would be an unthinkable situation for other professions and one with serious consequences for professional credibility.

Currently, much of the concern related to the M.Div. degree is that the persisting incoherence of theory and practice is undermining ministry competence. David Kelsey and Barbara Wheeler observe, "The course of theological studies does not adequately integrate the disciplines of theological inquiry; it further fails to present theory in ways that make practice more effective; and the result of these two serious failures is a more comprehensive one: the basic purpose of theological education, to prepare people to fill competently the functions of ministry, is not often enough or fully enough achieved" (Kelsey and Wheeler 1994, 77).

However, they also note that the preoccupation with ministry problems can actually mask more fundamental difficulties. Once again they return to Farley's analysis that the most fundamental difficulty of the seminary is that the curricular pattern is incoherent, with no compelling rationale.

> The pattern is simply an aggregate of forms and ideas from the distant and recent past, fit into a structure, the four-fold pattern, whose principles of unity ceased to have power for us a long time ago. Even without a persuasive set of reasons for studying these things, to this end, in this order, rather than other things, to other ends, in some other order, however, the inherited pattern of studies is a heavy weight that holds in place many features of and ideas about theological education, whether or not we like them and want to keep them in the present form. The contradiction involved here—the practice of theological education is regulated by a pattern of studies for which we can produce no satisfactory intellectual explanation—is, Farley maintains, our fundamental problem, a problem so serious that it amounts to a crisis. (ibid., 77)

In spite of concerns about ministry development, Farley insists that the goal of theological education is not simply ministry competence and that functions or skills (the clerical paradigm) have come to define the curriculum. The solution, then, is to see theology as the goal of theological education. However, because theology itself is specialized to the point where it can no longer serve as a unifying center, even theology is not an adequate answer. Therefore, he asserts some reconceptualization of theology is necessary. However, even this proposal does not account for the lingering effects of the matrix of factors that have shaped contemporary theological education and contributed to its problems. The future of theological education may lie in a fresh look at the nature of institutions, the nature of knowledge and how it is communicated, the nature of professional development, and repentance for the loss of theological education's primary focus—to keep alive the desire for God. The next section presents a proposal from one of the more educationally conservative of America's university presidents. His proposal is intriguing as we move *toward* a renewed matrix for twenty-first-century theological education by exploring

The University of Utopia

Robert Hutchins, while president of the University of Chicago, offered a series of lectures in 1953 that laid out his vision for the University of Utopia. His lectures are all the more remarkable in that he personally did not support progressive education and was devoted to the task of making central and essential a liberal education informed by the intellectual heritage of the West.

Hutchins had a rather low view of the professions, particularly when their practitioners were not grounded in a broad intellectual tradition. He complained that professionals schooled merely in the techniques and subject matter of their own profession were unlikely to understand those from other professions or from other spheres of knowledge. "Society requires specialists; but even that specialism requires, if it is not to come to a dead end, that every specialty be able to throw light on every other. Every specialist must therefore be able to catch whatever light is being thrown from any quarter" (Hutchins 1953, 43). Of course, one could make the same argument for anyone who has spent a life time mastering any discipline without intentional effort to interact with other areas of knowledge.

In the University of Utopia, the worst outcomes of specialization are mitigated through a different form of organization. Traditional departments are abolished, to prevent faculty and students from speaking only to those who share their narrow specialization. "Therefore, the University of Utopia is arranged so as to force, in a polite way, the association of representatives of all fields of learning with one another. The University of Utopia is divided into institutions with faculties numbering about twenty-five and students about two hundred and fifty. Each faculty and each student group contain representatives of the major fields" (ibid., 44).

Noting the danger of producing professionals, even in theology, who have no sense of the intellectual content of the profession, Hutchins admits that it is difficult to master such content while engaged in the profession.

"The demands of a professional life are not favorable to study and reflection. On the other hand, universities are not well adapted to teaching the tricks of trades" (ibid., 39). The problem is compounded when professors must be involved in the profession if they are to teach it: if they are involved in the profession, they will seldom be good professors. Hutchins concludes, "The best division of responsibility between the university and the occupation would be to have the university deal with the intellectual content of the occupation, if there is any, and to have the occupation itself take charge of familiarizing its own neophytes with the technical operations they have to learn" (ibid., 40). To this end, Hutchins proposed that numerous organizations should surround the university to collect data, give technical training, and work on solutions to practical problems. The interchange between these organizations and the university should be deliberate and active (ibid., 64).

Traditional artifacts of American education are done away with in Hutchins's proposal. Students are accepted *only* if they demonstrate capacity for independent study and reflection. Criteria of time served, credit hours completed, and accreditation standards do not exist at the University of Utopia. Students seldom attend class for more than four hours a week, and even that attendance is not mandatory. Discussion among students and faculty is the chief mode of learning and inquiry. For Utopians, education is conversation with purpose. Hutchins observes that the customary structures of the university seldom provide natural channels for substantive conversation. If "education is a conversation aimed at truth" (ibid., 56) and not simply chatter, however, substantive conversation and some effort at relationship are required. Sitting, listening, and note-taking seldom encourage these capacities. University of Utopia professors are expected to be actively engaged in research and sharing that research with students for discussion and critique. The goal of the University, in short, is not agreement but communication in the service of truth.

For this quest, Hutchins posited the necessity of diversity as he understood it. Multicultural and gender diversity was not as great a concern in 1953 as bringing together faculty with different perspectives, backgrounds, interests, and temperaments for the purpose of promoting understanding (ibid., 68). The intended product of the University of Utopia is a person who achieves wisdom through the use of reason and experience—though Hutchins notes that education is *preparation* for one's later experience in a profession (ibid., 69). In other words, reflection on past or present experience is not a major part of learning at the University of Utopia.

Hutchins is irrevocably committed to education as the means to intellectual development of the populace. Societies, he maintains, require an organization "the purpose of which is to think most profoundly about the most important intellectual issues.... Extreme and premature specialization in the United States has carried the educational system into activities that have no connection with the intellectual development of the population" (ibid., 41).

Hutchins's vision reflects what could be assumed as the best of the German research model, with an English college model overlay. History demonstrates, however, that the presumption that the cultivation of reason and intellect alone leads to an enlightened citizenry and informed professional practice is flawed. The intellectual "grand project" of the academy has not led to utopia. However, Hutchins's proposal need not be dismissed entirely.

Toward a Renewed Matrix for 21st Century Theological Education[2]

One of the more interesting conversations we had during a meeting of the ATS Executive Board began with the question "What is a good theological school?" The question quickly became "What good is a theological school?" Then, more seriously, "What is theological education?"

Knowledge management is too complex, and the problems of society and church are too urgent, to permit the assumption that students can learn to think productively and develop informed wisdom and practice as they march in orderly columns through classes selected from a potpourri of departments, accumulating enough credit hours to a secure a degree. Can theological institutions advance serious scholarly and professional development by trying to accommodate every sort of student in an overcrowded curriculum littered with multiple, disconnected subject and professional areas? In this, Hutchins' concerns have merit. However, a reformed academy, a new Seminary of Utopia as *the* way forward, is an unlikely solution. Perhaps the day is dawning when the collaboration of several types of educa-

---

[2] See Chapters 4–7 for historical background.

tional ventures, formal and nonformal, church-based and public, academic and professional, is possible. Schools do have an unfortunate tendency to swallow anything that is not formally structured or credentialed; and many alternatives to schools do inevitably default to traditional school-like curriculum, structures, and credentialing. But, perhaps, an increased intercultural awareness, Internet access, and the unprecedented questioning of the hegemony and effectiveness of the schools by its own faculty and administrators, may yet lead to more productive relationships among several types of educational initiatives.

The task for twenty-first century theological education is not to do away with institutions but to create structures and processes that enable, rather than hinder, the achievement of desired outcomes. We cannot deny the need for reason, but human beings are more than reason, and that fact has educational implications. Leaders are needed, but how they are identified and developed requires input from multiple sources. These relationships will significantly affect educational process, assessment, and even accreditation procedures. To what extent can the forces of institutionalism, rationalism, professionalism, and the desire for God be used to redeem the service of theological education to the church?

The Seminary and Reconceived Institutional Identity

Institutions historically have been considered the stabilizers of society. In the past, employees believed that they would give all their working years to the employer institution and be taken care of in retirement. Charles Handy suggests that we are in a new era in which the bonds between individuals and institutions have been loosened. In Handy's analysis of the future of institutions, "our loyalty and responsibility are first to ourselves and our future, secondly to our current group or project, and only lastly, and minimally, to the organization. Without commitment to anyone or anything else, however, there is no sense of responsibility for others, and without responsibility there is no need for morality—anything goes, or at least anything that is legal, if it's what you want" (Handy 1998, 65–66).

Handy notes that the change in orientation toward institutions is largely a response to a world where little is stable and predictable and where survival depends on an individual's capacity to invent the future, creating new organizational forms or adapting old forms. However, what is the purpose that shapes our lives and the lives of others—and the ways in which we construe organizations? In the West, in order to protect individuals, corporate law views the organization as a person who can be held liable. However, in general, organizations tend to be responsible only to themselves and, recognized in the United States as persons under the law, can be construed as having constitutional protections. "Provided [investors, the workforce, customers, suppliers, and the surrounding community] all profit in some way from it, *the business can decide for itself what it stands for and what its goals are*" (Handy 1998, 68–69 emphasis added).

One could argue that in a similar way, the seminary is largely accountable only to itself—as long as it keeps its constituency, faculty, staff, students satisfied. It is when the satisfaction level begins to diminish that the seminary comes under increased scrutiny and critique. Even though seminary education has been the object of critique for decades, it is conceivable that renewed efforts to improve assessment, instruction, and faculty competence, increased diversity, and the emergence of other providers (i.e., church-based and other nonformal education initiatives) will significantly alter the landscape of theological education in the twenty-first century.

Winston Churchill once observed that we shape our cities and then they shape us. Institutional structures that resemble a series of loosely connected boxes of administrative functions and specialized disciplines have shaped the way we think about theological education and ministry for generations. The satisfaction level for this way of doing theological education has diminished significantly. Harris et al. (2005) observe that while universities recognize their problems and expend a great deal of energy in improving the organizational and educational processes, "they generally channel those efforts through the silos that define the system" (Harris et al. 2005, 6). They offer an organic analogy as a desirable future for higher education, drawing the following characteristics from the organic analogy:

1. In a healthy organism, cells operate in relation to the whole. Educational development and learning and application are fostered as faculty, administrators and staff, and students work together in teams on questions, issues, and tasks pertinent to the whole.

2. Healthy organisms are synergistic in nature. Educational institutions are synergistic when individuals work together in a climate of trust. Learning is seen as making connections. Analysis and synthesis are valued and encouraged (ibid., 17).

3. Purpose is the DNA of educational institutions. However, purpose statements are often vague, too broad to be of use, and too often imposed on the organization. "Where there is widely and deeply shared inter-subjective agreement [the DNA], there is little need for formal mission statements to discipline choices and set direction. Where inter-subjective agreement is absent, it is difficult to develop community through compelling mission statements or elaborate strategic plans" (ibid., 17).

4. Stem cells are vital to a healthy organism. "Viable institutions have 'stem cell' members who move easily from one role to another, connect past, present and future, and assemble new structures where old ones are crumbling. They embody the institution's ethos and are multitalented.... While most organizations have formal organizational charts, the actual work gets done through informal networks" (ibid., 18).

5. As the flow of nutrients among cells sustains life, so academic communities are "sustained by continuous, fluid interrelationships among faculty, students, staff, and administrators. Cells have walls, maintain their individual integrity, but those walls are permeable, open to the whole, conducive to the exchange of value" (ibid., 18)

Organizations that adapt and endure are more like organisms than rigid bureaucracies. Since education truly is about learning, educational organizations should be the most adaptable on the planet. Part of the reason why they are not is due to an ill-conceived rationalism

The Seminary and Reconceived Rationalism

The poverty of arid academic rationalism is well established. Seminaries bound by curricular fragmentation, simplistic efforts to integrate faith and learning, and a culture of academic rationalism will be unlikely to provide a framework within which discussion, discovery, and inquiry can proceed. The current overcrowded seminary curriculum is unable to shape more than a surface understanding of any discipline or to develop students' aptitude for scholarship.

Similarly, most courses that presume to offer ministry or leadership development are generally ill-timed and out of any context where the skills and professional behaviors can be learned effectively. There is no reason why scholar-practitioners in the seminary, professional development facilitators from whatever venue is appropriate, students, and church and community representatives, cannot interact concerning problems, issues, and significant questions that affect both knowledge and practice. If hope wins out over cynicism, the seminary may yet offer service to the church without being trapped by the fallacy that intellectual capacity comes from the cultivation of a mind devoid of human passion and blind to the great mystery of faith. Even the university, at times in history, endeavored to be a community of learner-disciples interacting in the quest for truth, with the goal of strengthening the mission of the church in the world.

Learning in community is predicated on the understanding that knowledge is not as much passed on as it is examined, studied, and continually revisited by teachers and students. Patricia Cross observes, "The current wave of interest in learning communities is not...just nostalgia for the human touch, or just research about the efficacy of small-group learning, but a fundamental revolution in epistemology" (Cross 1998, 7). It would miss the point to use phrases such as "learning community," "grounded in the church," and "service" without appreciating the need for a group of people, from diverse backgrounds and likely holding different perspectives, thinking and valuing in the same direction, open to questions that surface along the way, and committed to responsible service.

The Seminary and a Reconceived Professionalism

Thomas Edison left school in frustration and began inventing. The questions and problems he encountered while inventing drove him back to books and other sources of knowledge. Edison's experience is not uncommon. The point is that he demonstrated that the desire to learn is often (or perhaps only) stimulated when one encounters problems or anomalies.

The education of professionals for a complex age begs for different forms. Current forms are based on the historical presumption that men and women are being *prepared for* the ministry. If we assume that the best professional development occurs as men and women are involved with real situations, a more dynamic curriculum is possible. Today most professions make use of problem-based learning (PBL) and other curricular approaches that, when well designed, obligate learners to interact with real issues and deal with resource people from diverse disciplines as they seek information and strategies to address problems and questions. Where conventional assessment focuses on feats of memory, assessment related to experiences such as PBL obligates assessment for *learning and continued development*.

One seminary president envisions a day when lifelong learning is the expectation. He wants to see men and women involved in some form of professional and personal development from the day they graduate to the day they retire. These men and women will be involved in continuous assessment, and establishing and achieving goals for professional, personal and spiritual growth. Perhaps the seminary will do best to strengthen its capacity to nurture theological learning for informed wisdom and work in close conjunction with institutes and centers in the church and society that are better equipped for professional development. These centers will have different forms of education from seminaries, and if both educational venues are well designed, the interaction they foster will be lively and productive. Lifelong learning would be expected and rationalism would be less of a temptation in settings where reason informs responsible service and vice versa. With a new synergy of educational providers concerned about learning and development, the problem of the overcrowded curriculum could be alleviated as seminaries become one of several venues for theological education and leadership development.

But, perhaps, this vision is too idealistic. I should know better say my colleagues. Schools will never embrace such ideas. Perhaps a whole new thing *is* needed where the interplay of knowledge and service, and the obligation of lifelong learning for the sake of the church's mission in the world are possible. Consider a medical example that derives from problems similar to those that confront theological schools. Noted neurosurgeon Keith Black,[3] disturbed at the lack of progress in treating brain cancer, established an institute to bring together medical researchers and medical practitioners.

> During the years he worked on blood-brain barrier research, a parallel growth of medical knowledge had occurred in genetics, immunology, and molecular biology. Black grew frustrated that so little of that knowledge had been translated into effective new treatments for patients. The problem, as he saw it, was that the explosion of scientific knowledge had coincided with the implosion of academic medicine under the economic pressures of a

---

[3] See also http://www.thehistorymakers.com/biography/biography.asp?bioindex=781&category=medicalMakers Last accessed on October 2005.

costly health care system. The gap between clinical practice and laboratory science had become a chasm.... The result is a two track system in which medical research is conducted by Ph.D.'s and medical practice is conducted by physicians with little access to what is discovered by academics. (Schreiber 2004, 70)

Convinced that universities were not the answer, Black established a neurosurgical institute, where Ph.D.s and surgeons work together to find new treatments for otherwise untreatable brain cancers. Parallels with the problems of and possibilities for contemporary theological education are obvious.

As long as disciplinary silos dominate the theological curriculum, we are unable to address truly important matters, because there is almost no effective way to bring students and faculty from different disciplines together. Increasingly, in light of how difficult it is to change the theological curriculum, faculty, students, and other entrepreneurs are creating institutes, centers, and consultations as venues for interdisciplinary conversations, influence in church and society, and work on real tasks. Unfortunately, these institutes and initiatives are developing without much real awareness on the part of seminary leaders of the potential of such developments for the improvement of *learning*. Harris et al. (2005) have observed that faculty will collaborate across disciplines in communities of inquiry and special interests; but will seldom do so to promote learning among students.

However conceived, a different sort of intellectual and professional integration would be more constructive than what exists at present. Rather than attempting to integrate subjects or disciplines (which is not as achievable as we like to think), we may do best to integrate different sorts of learning contexts, where knowledge, significant questions, and important problems can be explored in many different ways.

If seminaries are unable to serve as intellectual centers interacting with professional development centers, perhaps Joseph Hough and John Cobb's alternative is the way forward. Hough and Cobb agree with Farley's basic analysis that the clerical paradigm is a problem and that theological education is for the entire church. But they do not agree that the problem is the professional paradigm *per se*. Stimulated by the pioneering work of James Hopewell, Hough and Cobb they suggest that "the current problem for the theological school is *not* that it is a 'professional' school, dominated by the 'clerical paradigm.' Rather it is that the church has become uncertain and confused as to what constitutes appropriate professionalism. There can be no clear unity to theological education until there is recovery of clarity about the nature of professional leadership within the church" (Hough and Cobb 1985, 5). For Hough and Cobb, the seminary *can* be a professional school, somehow holding together the theoretical and practical disciplines. They propose that the purpose of theological education is to prepare reflective practitioners. The task of theological education is a global task, where social issues are taken seriously by theological educators and every doctrine is linked to its practical result. Reflective practitioners operate out of the church's ecclesial memory, fashioning questions that stimulate reflection on how God worked in the past, how God is working in the present, and how God intends to work in the future. Thus trained, the practical theologian helps the congregation understand its identity and purpose in the world. Hough and Cobb believe that the structuring of the curriculum need not change substantially; however, the outcomes and the courses offered should be reoriented around a "congregational paradigm," a social agenda, and an intention to produce reflective practitioners.

It is likely that the theological curriculum will have to change significantly if academic and professional development is desired. But, however we conceive of the role of the seminary in relation to intellectual and professional development, one of our greatest needs is to inquire into how students are taught. The results of such inquiries can assist evaluation of curricular outcomes, identify factors involved when pastors are miseducated, reveal difficulties upon graduation, suggest better cultural and societal connections, and so on. The necessary question for theological educators is, what is involved in training others who will be able to train others also? Unfortunately, competencies and outcomes are ill-defined, and a culture of curriculum improvement is lacking. Because faculty own the curriculum only in their privatized areas, students tend to be more aware of the whole curriculum and its effects than are the faculty. We expect students to integrate knowledge from different disciplines when we as faculty may be unable or unwilling to do it! Further, curricular decisions seldom involve the church, and curriculum revision often occurs only when survival is at stake. The issue of curriculum development is becoming so acute that some are advocating that decisions about curriculum planning be removed from the exclusive ownership of faculty and that educational design professionals be engaged in the process.

In all of these matters, how does theological education foster a desire for God that eventuates in virtue and service? We could get so immersed in our dreams for alternative futures that we leave behind that which is most important.

The Seminary and the Desire for God: Theological Learning for Informed Wisdom

If it is true that the purpose of theological education is to serve the people of God, then the practices of the congregation are central to planning. These practices are fundamentally related to the nurture of the soul. However, because even the church seems to have lost its way in terms of what constitutes the desire for God, simply creating church-based models is not necessarily the answer to what troubles theological education. Arguments over professionalism, theory versus practice, loss of theology, and so on obscure a much greater problem: the separation of the "path of reason" from the "path of love"—in short, theological education exists to stimulate the desire for God.

No instructional approach, curriculum, or institutional context can bring reason and spirituality together or cultivate a sense of the divine mystery. This is a function of the intentional life of obedience of a community of faith and learning. The image of a relay race is proposed by L. Gregory Jones to illustrate why theological institutions and churches find it difficult to do foster these capacities. For most of the twentieth century, churches and schools functioned as participants in a race. The church held the promising leader (the baton) for a number of years, socializing and nurturing the beliefs and practices important to work with a denomination. After a time, the future minister was handed off to a school where the work of shaping leadership skills and theological formation was to take place. At graduation, the student was passed off to the congregation he or she was expected to serve. More recently, concern has been expressed that one or the other of the partners has not been running the race very well. The churches blame the schools for producing irrelevant leaders; the schools blame the churches for inadequate preparation of the future minister. Though many seminaries are engaged in serious self-examination, the evidence is now clear "that Christian practices and understanding within both congregations and the broader culture are diminishing" (Jones 2002, 187). Jones conjectures that the relay-race model itself is at the heart of the problem.

> What if the development of an ordained Christian leader is not a matter of following a predetermined, linear path toward a single, dominant endpoint? What if, instead, we conceive of this development as a pilgrimage that wends its way through a complex constellation of communities where practices, beliefs, and desires are formed and educated in a variety of ways? What if we think of the aim of this process not as graduation to pastoral responsibility but as membership in an ever-widening chorus that draws pastors, church members, seminary professors, and everyone else involved into the doxological praise of God? (ibid., 187–88)

Jones observes that the problem is not the idea of a race; after all, this was an image used by the apostle Paul. The problem is that much of theological education assumes that the development of leaders and scholars runs on a smooth, straight track. He proposes three intersecting communal settings as critical to the development of the minister: congregational life, formal education, and social settings that require engagement. Each of these settings contributes one or more elements: "catechesis, critical reflection, and faithful living in the world" (Jones 2002, 188). The congregation is a setting where desire is shaped by instruction, prayer, worship, and authentic social engagement. The awareness and practices of the believer will, in turn, be informed by habits of inquiry and self-reflection in the academy. Jones asserts that the crucial role of the academy is "in clarifying and testing the faith to ensure a more reflective, and hopefully less distorted, transmission of Christian life and thought from generation to generation" (ibid., 202). Finally, "faithful living in the world draws Christians into contexts in which the distorting and sinful desires, practices, and structures of our world ought to be challenged by the light of the gospel" (ibid.). The interplay of the three settings and *overlapping experiences* in each informs, shapes, and tests emergent beliefs and practices. For Jones, and many others, the institutional structures that support these experiences need not replicate familiar school and church structures.

The leader is a pilgrim, coming into these various settings and experiences at different stages of life and service. Failure to develop a pedagogy that embraces the pilgrim quality of education, along with an uncritical use of technology in education, will prevent seminaries from having any useful role in leading men and women to theological understanding, ministry competence, and the development of the life in Christ (see Jones 2002, 192). If congregations likewise fail to assist members to connect faith with service and worship with authentic life in the world, the effects on the mission and character of the church will be catastrophic.

Funding the Future of Theological Education

Theological education is not at its root a school; professional education need not be merely functional; academic learning need not be exclusively a rational enterprise. The face of higher education in the West is in a process of inevitable change. As educational leaders in other countries become aware that the forms they inherited from the West are no longer viable, even for the cultural West, they are becoming more intentional about seeking fresh and more effective ways to serve their churches and societies through education.

Angelo (1997) discerns seven shifts in higher education. Sufficient time has passed since he articulated these shifts to conclude that they are indeed being felt in the universities. The extent to which theological education has been affected by them, however, is still being determined. Angelo identifies these shifts as follows:

1. Practices that had been taken for granted are being questioned as processes of assessment become more common (e.g., the system of courses and credit hours).

2. Individual goals for teaching are giving way to shared goals, outcomes, and shared criteria for student learning.

3. Faculty are becoming more aware of research on teaching and learning.

4. A broader understanding of scholarship from simply research and writing to inclusion of integration, teaching, and application or service is emerging.

5. Greater attention is being given to the real costs of education and the evaluation of productivity.

6. Collaborative learning is more commonly accepted as essential for effective learning.

7. An additive, information-based notion of education as normative is being challenged.

The primary concern of this book is the nature and purpose of theological education. Today we tend to identify theological education with seminaries and in some cases with divinity schools. Concern about the effectiveness of institutionalized theological education is increasing. Change is an inexorable process, so even if we fail to act in relation to these concerns, theological education will change. However, focusing on one or two concerns at a time and polarizing ourselves in relation to those concerns is not helpful. As difficult as it is, the processes that have shaped higher education and theological education in particular must be seen as a whole—a matrix—that continues to affect how we view theological education. Remembering what a matrix is—an environment or source from which something else originates, develops, or takes form, a milieu that seems permanent but was itself the result of decisions made across centuries—may be more helpful as we search for "something else," alternative forms of theological education that will better serve the mission of the church in the twenty-first-century world. As in the past, our work of reformation will require the support of foundations and others willing to invest in the future rather than the past.

In the 1930s, the Rockefeller Foundation committed substantial funds to a survey of theological education that reoriented theological institutions in various ways, and mandated the creation of what became an accreditation agency. In our day, foundations are assuming greater importance as church and individual sources of funding are less available. However, foundations tend to look for focused and concrete solutions in order to bring stability to unsettled situations. In the case of theological education, it is too soon for solutions.

Robert Greenleaf has written of the importance of independent foundations and their potential to shape events for good or ill. Some foundations today are committing significant resources to experimentation in theological education. This commitment requires accountability to criteria that are not simply pragmatic, corporate, or personal—for the way forward is not clear. In recent decades, participants in numerous consultations (most funded by foundations) have talked and written about the problems confronting theological education, but these discussion have not yet produced consensus around clear action. Caution is necessary as a small number of foundations with substantial resources assume the task of guiding the future of theological education. What will result if one or two strong foundations assume an almost monopolistic position regarding the way forward in what should be a time of exploration of alternatives? Foundations could assist seminaries not to steer themselves into too narrow a vision of the future. Twenty-first-century foundations will best serve the future by contributing in the present to exploration and experimentation. The innate conservatism of foundation giving will not easily support disciplined inquiry into alternative futures for theological education. However, the cultural diversity of new leadership in the church worldwide demands such inquiry.

PART II

Historical Backgrounds

CHAPTER 4

The Development of Institutions of Theological Education

The existence of educational institutions from ancient times is well established (Barclay 1959; Crenshaw 1985; Ferguson 1987; Goldman 1975; Gutek 1972; Judge 1983a-b; Myers 1960; Ulich 1968; Wilson 1989; and others). Though patterns and structures of education have been widely diverse throughout history, formal schooling with a particular definition of structure and instructional process is today taken for granted in most societies. Universities and other formal expressions of education are so common that further description of them is unnecessary.

In reality, formal schooling and nonformal modes of education have coexisted for much of history. Prophet apprenticeships are described in the Old Testament. Socrates probed the minds of his followers through dialogue. Jesus, who probably went to school as a boy, later walked the countryside with his disciples, teaching them through formal discourse and informally through story, example, and experience. Martin Luther lived among the nonformal educational communities of the Brethren of the Common Life for the period of grammar school.

Until recently in the modern era, however, the terms *school* and *education* were used synonymously. As the limitations of schooling become more apparent and the effectiveness of nonformal learning more convincing, education is again less viewed simply in terms of its institutional expression. This chapter describes the historical relationship of formal and nonformal education and the gradual evolution of formal higher education, with particular attention to theological institutions.

The Monasteries and the Cathedral School

By the year A.D. 200, particularly in the West, loosely defined communities of believers began to assume organizational structures that would help them articulate and defend Christian doctrines. Monasticism was one of these structures. For Pachomius, Benedict and his twin sister Scholastica, Hilda, Augustine, Lioba, Basil, and others, a disciplined communal life, patterned after the communal life of the early church and expressed in service in the world, seemed the suitable context for the nurture of the spiritual life. The monastic life they helped to shape became a vital part of the church and a chief factor in the preservation of Western Christendom. By the eighth century, monasteries were the centers of Western culture and were occupied with the preservation of cultural documents and the development of monastic schools.

As a new Christendom emerged in a "world that saw the triumph of the barbarians, the decline of cities, and the consolidation of orthodoxy," new patterns of education were necessary. With the "end of the ancient schools and the birth of new types of education dominated by the Christian clergy," McGinn notes, Augustine's *On Christian Doctrine* became the "magna carta for medieval education" (McGinn 1994, 24). In this work, Augustine "encouraged the pursuit of grammar and the other liberal arts, but only in the higher goal of helping to understand the Bible." He wrote primarily for clerics but "did not exclude the educated laity from participating in this biblically-centered education" (ibid.). With the emergence of Christian advanced education, the time was ripe for the creation of a new system of schools, for which the monastic schools would provide the model. However, new schools did not mean new content and new methods. The Christian education coming to birth "was above all a biblical education that served to enculturate the clerical and monastic elite into their roles as leaders of Christendom" (ibid., 26). In general, the educational method was transmission, for the persons of the early medieval period lived in the "shadow of the [church] tradition," and the educational task was "to interpret, not to change and add" (Ulich 1971, 172).

In the early Middle Ages, the monastic schools provided instruction in reading, writing, arithmetic, and basic doctrine—subjects considered necessary for the service of the church (Ulich 1968, 52–55; Dawson 1991, 45–51). Instruction took two major forms: the *schola interior*, in the monasteries, for those training for religious orders, and the *schola exterior* for clerics (who today would be lay ministers and professional clergy). In the *schola interior*, the monks were guided by the abbot in study of patristic theology and the Bible. They copied manuscripts and wrote commentaries on biblical texts; but their style of exegesis, or "sacred learning," differed from that of later Scholasticism. The monastic commentaries tended to be less orderly, less "scientific," more allegorical and imaginative. The flights of allegory and the sometimes excessive literalism of monastic commentaries cause discomfort for modern exegetes, but clearly for the monastics the study of Scripture was at once an aesthetic, rational, and spiritual/mystical act (LeClercq 1982, 75).

The *schola exterior*, precursors of the Scholastic universities, were usually situated in cities, near cathedrals, and were intended to prepare clerics for pastoral activity. The Trivium and Quadrivium, or the seven liberal arts,[1] remained largely functional, focused on the skills needed for serving the church (e.g., arithmetic and astronomy were necessary to compute the date of Easter). Later, when the "new learning" penetrated the schools, the Trivium and the Quadrivium would be enlivened with new problems and new methods in a quest for forms of knowledge and integration unknown in the ancient world (Rashdall 1936a, 34).

Like the monasteries, cathedral schools dated from the fourth century. There are records of schools in the eighth century attached to the episcopal (i.e., the bishops') churches. Monastic schools were generally reluctant to take on the challenges of new methods in theology and philosophy; so, with expanding urbanization and the growing thirst for knowledge, students made their way past the cloisters to the cathedral schools, which had begun to expand their staff and curriculum. By the twelfth century, these schools were flourishing: the Lateran Council in 1179 "required every cathedral, or bishop's church, to maintain a school to educate priests, other clerics, and the poor" (Gutek 1972, 73).[2]

---

[1] The Trivium and the Quadrivium became the curriculum plan of the schools of the Middle Ages. The Trivium consisted of grammar, dialectic, and rhetoric, in that order. Successful experience with the subjects of the Trivium was necessary for mastery of the subjects of the Quadrivium: arithmetic, astronomy, geometry, and music. Boethius (c. 480–524) was considered the last of the Romans and the father of scholasticism. His translations and textbooks formed the basis for the extension of the Seven Liberal Arts (McGinn 1994, 25).

2 Gerald Gutek identifies several educational institutions (formal and nonformal) that developed during the Middle Ages.

The Scholastic Universities

Cathedral schools were prominent in the twelfth century, but, like the monasteries, they were soon insufficient for the demands of new learning. Through the Crusades, revival of commerce, urbanization, and contact with Arabic scholarship, the works of Aristotle, Ptolemy, Euclid, and the Greek physicians penetrated the twelfth-century world and changed the course of education. An influx of students led to the development of more formalized institutions—the universities. The most significant educational change at this time was the development and use of something approximating a scholarly method. In the early Middle Ages, doctrines and dogma had been precise and fixed, rigidly formulated and strongly tied to the tradition of the church. As social and political conditions allowed more time for the exercise and pursuit of knowledge, and as the fame of brilliant teachers spread, "scientific" inquiry into theology was espoused. The repetition of earlier commentaries was replaced by what was considered fresh thinking and dialectical technique.

At first, the word *university* referred to an entire group of teachers and students who resided together in a town. But a corporate structure would soon form in response to "town and gown" conflicts and a felt need to systematize learning.[3] In some of the early universities, teachers were expected to read and explain passages from required texts to their students. Often the only dialogue was between professors who would occasionally debate points of a text in front of the students. "In the schools of Italy…the guild was in the hands of the undergraduates…who hired teachers and set rules requiring the lecturers to finish the commentary on the prescribed texts before the end of a term of study" (Cantor 1969, 466). Some universities were formed by students to gain protection from the townspeople, who extracted exorbitant fees for books, food and lodging. Once "victorious over the townsmen, the students turned on their other enemies, the professors…. The professor

---

[3]"Already at the beginning of the twelfth century the fame of Abelard had made Paris one of the most popular centers of teaching in France, and by the middle of the century the multiplication of schools and the competition of rival teachers had made it the intellectual capital of Christendom…. The University of Bologna held a similar position in Italy…. As the [University of Paris] became the great international school of theology and philosophy for the whole of Western Christendom, so Bologna from the beginning was the great international centre of legal studies" (Dawson 1991, 184–86).

was put under bond to live up to a minute set of regulations which guaranteed his students the worth of the money paid by each" (Haskins 1957, 9).

In the thirteenth-century university environment, masters found themselves in strong competition. Popular teachers attracted students from all over Europe. Teachers who failed to interest and stimulate their students soon lost their followings and their careers. The enthusiasm for the dialectic method during this period should not obscure the fact that this was a serious, competitive, compulsive, often unhappy environment. Students lived mostly in poverty, made worse by the injustices committed by the townspeople. Their studies were long and hard. Students often vented their frustrations in gambling, drinking, and fighting.[4] If some of the most brilliant thinkers of the period were "disagreeable men and rather unstable personalities" (Cantor 1969, 467), it is not surprising.

The ideal of the medieval universities was to bring together student and master for the highest intellectual training, with practical application of knowledge for the improvement of society. Universities did not exist in the ancient world, yet today the influence of the medieval period is so great that it is felt they *must* exist.

> It is not necessary that the teachers should be united into a corporate body enjoying more or less privilege and autonomy. It is not necessary that the teachers of different subjects should teach in the same place and be united in a single institution.... It is not necessary that studies should be grouped into particular faculties, and students required to confine themselves more or less exclusively to one. It is not necessary that a definite line of study should be marked out by authority, that a definite period of years should be assigned to a student's course, or that at the end of that period he should be subjected to examination and receive, with

---

[4] Charles Haskins includes material related to student affairs in his history. "There are for one thing, the records of the courts of law...like the case of the Bolognese student who was attacked with a cutlass in a classroom, to the great damage and loss of those assembled to hear the lecture of a noble and egregious doctor of laws...like the enactment of New College against throwing stones in chapel, or the graded penalties at Leipzig for him who picks up a missile to throw at a professor, him who throws and misses, and him who accomplishes his fell purpose to the master's hurt" (Haskins 1957, 61).

more or less formality and ceremony, a title of honour. All this we owe to the Middle Ages. (Powicke and Emdem 1936a, 459)

Patterns of Education during the Renaissance and Reformation Eras

As the relationship between secular and ecclesiastical powers became more fluid in the fourteenth century, the secular and Christian humanist educators[5] of the Renaissance were able to act more freely than their medieval counterparts. They could criticize the structures of learning in the schools and create their own patterns of education. The importance of education during the Renaissance is reflected in Paul Grendler's assessment that the schooling initiatives of the Renaissance united a potentially chaotic Italy and stimulated a similar cultural accord in much of Europe.

> The extraordinary political, social, economic, and even linguistic diversity—divisiveness would be the better term—threatened to pull the peninsula apart at any moment. But schooling united Italians and played a major role in creating the Renaissance. Humanistic pedagogues developed a new educational path very different from education in the rest of Europe in the early fifteenth century…. The humanistic curriculum unified the Renaissance, making it a cohesive cultural and historical epoch of great achievement. When humanistic education crossed the Alps, it created a similar cultural accord that endured beyond the shattering of religious unity. (Grendler 1989, 410)

Petrarch in Italy and the representatives of German mysticism (such as Meister Eckhart and Johannes Tauler) were successful in criticizing the rational objectivity and narrow speculativeness that had come to character-

---

[5] A. G. Dickens suggests that at the time of the Reformation the term *humanist* did not refer to the self-made "Renaissance man," the rugged individualist, or the person who has discarded God in favor of scientific progress. "Around 1500 a humanist was a teacher or student of the ancient classics" (Dickens 1994, 87). Dickens describes this humanist as a "poor scholar, still a Christian believer, somewhat on the periphery of university life" (ibid., 88), barely noticeable in the company of the much more luminous theologians and scholastic philosophers.

ize the Scholastic universities of the late Middle Ages. Numerous private discussion groups, where clerics and teachers met to discuss classical authors as well as scientific topics, evolved into learned societies and academies that spread throughout Europe (Rüegg 1992, 448–56).[6] Much of Renaissance education, though secular, was concerned with classical morality. "Humanistic and vernacular schools taught morality through classical examples. They did not stress Christian religious doctrine and practices until the advent of the Catholic Reformation. The church played no institutional role in Renaissance education until the late Renaissance" (Grendler 1989, 409–10).

In the sixteenth century, Schools of Christian Doctrine were begun by Castellino da Castello to provide religious instruction for the poor. Once these schools were endorsed by the Council of Trent and promoted by local bishops, large numbers of children were enrolled in them. Grendler notes that

> In Milan in 1564 about 200 adults taught more than 2,000 students in 28 Catechism schools. Bolognese schools enrolled close to 4,900 children in 1568. In 1577, the next year for which figures are available, average Sunday and holiday enrollment ranged from 3,000 to 4,000.... Milan had about 120 catechism schools in 1591. Approximately 7,000 Milanese boys and 5,750 girls attended Schools of Christian Doctrine in 1599, when the city had about 200,000 people overall. At that time about 7,700 adults (3,730 men and 3,970 women) participated in the confraternity, a figure that may have included casual and inactive members. (Grendler 1989, 337)

The purpose of these schools, as for much of Renaissance education, was to inculcate religious knowledge in the laity and encourage moral behavior. Catechetical instruction was not concerned with inquiry or the deepening of knowledge. Students were not encouraged to question their faith;

---

[6]The invention of the printing press in the fifteenth century stimulated the desire for literacy and spread the ideas of those who sought reform in the church. When the church ordered the burning of all heretical works in 1502, this served only to fuel the literary renaissance that had been under way for a generation.

those who sought "to learn more than what is suitable" or asked "about difficult and hidden things" were silenced by the teachers (ibid., 350).

The Brethren and Sisters of the Common Life established schools throughout Europe in an effort to teach practical Christianity. The movement stimulated widespread monastic reform, touched the masses, and brought new vitality to learning (Hyma 1950, 11–12; Ulich 1968, 89–90). But, the various houses of the Brethren and Sisters of the Common Life disbanded in 1517, having failed as a movement to affect significantly the religious life of nations caught in the controversies and battles of the Reformation era (Dickens 1964, 20). Political, religious, and economic conflict took precedence over the simple life of piety and service.

About fifty years prior to the posting of Luther's theses,[7] numerous universities had been established in Europe, and, as in the case of Cambridge, colleges were added to existing universities. These academies became places where new ideas were developed and discussed. The agitations of the Renaissance humanists and Reformers ultimately weakened the Scholasticism of the later Middle Ages, and the medieval universities buttressed by it declined.[8]

However, the universities of the fifteenth and sixteenth centuries failed to live up to their promise as centers of reform (Oberman 1981; Dickens 1966). The dream of humanist curricular reforms seemed unattainable. A conservative, politically careful climate overtook the universities (Dickens 1966, 49–50). At the University of Tübingen, Philipp Melanchthon eventually resigned because he felt he was "being forced to behave more as schoolmaster than as professor" (Oberman 1981, 58). By the eighteenth

---

[7]The common consensus is that the posting of the theses occurred on October 31, 1517.

[8]Manchester notes that attendance at Oxford was about 1,000 students by the fifteenth century and that academic freedom had vanished with the expulsion of John Wycliffe from Oxford in 1381 (Manchester 1992, 104). Hastings Rashdall cites figures placing 10,000 students at Bologna in the twelfth century and 30,000 students at Paris and Oxford in the thirteenth century. He estimates that there were 3,500–7,000 at Paris and hardly more than 1,000 at Oxford by 1438 (Rashdall 1936a, 325–26, 330–33). Wycliffe is reputed to have said that there were once 60,000 students at Oxford, a number that had fallen to about 3,000 by his own time. These figures are no doubt inflated, given the common practices of estimation and exaggeration; but granting that there were several thousand students in the twelfth and thirteenth centuries, the numbers had indeed greatly diminished by the fourteenth and fifteenth centuries.

century, the university had degenerated into a system deemed ridiculous by populace and rulers alike. In German-speaking Europe, for example, genuine intellectuals considered universities to be "sites of rote disputation inhabited largely by pedants" (Fallon 1980, 3). Even efforts by some such as G. W. Leibniz to found an academy of science as an alternative to the university could not be sustained. The king of Prussia was so disgusted with the universities that he appointed his court jester president of one of them! "The state of the university through the eighteenth century in Germany was seen as medieval, frozen in time, bound by a trade school mentality and preoccupied with transmitting to students (by reading aloud from texts) knowledge perceived locked in closed systems" (Fallon 1980, 4).

The Idea for a New University in Berlin

Germany in the eighteenth century was largely an intellectual wasteland. After the defeat of the Prussian army by Napolean in 1806, the universities at Jena and Halle were closed, prompting Johann Gottlieb Fichte and Friedrich Schleiermacher, and later Friedrich Wilhelm Humboldt, to propose that a new university be established in Berlin. By 1809, the idea of a new university was forming; at the same time Humboldt was active in the reform of elementary education employing the methods of Johann Heinrich Pestalozzi in teacher education. Humboldt's commitment to the educational ideals and methods of Pestalozzi is not insignificant, for it shaped his conviction that the university exists to enlighten and humanize the state. He was unshakable in his conviction that the best scholars committed to research and inquiry can cause knowledge to flower in the human spirit, which will, in turn, transform character. Persons of transformed character will then benefit and lead the state.

Humboldt ultimately became the spokesman and predominant architect for the new university. His chief founding principle was to find the best minds available and to give them full freedom to pursue research wherever it led. The ideal of the German model for higher education was that knowledge (*Wissenschaft*) is always to be treated as a problem yet to be solved, and thus research is a persisting habit of the scholar. The boldness of this enterprise is reflected in Fallon's observation: "Perhaps the most remarkable fact about the widely admired German University of the nineteenth century is that it had no clear precedent. The university idea was struck, virtually *de novo*, by scholars and aristocrats of the enlightenment from only a few fleeting practical examples and with only a passing glance at history. It was an idea deriving force as much from reaction to intellectual chaos as from consolidation of intellectual growth" (Fallon 1980, 3).

In the nineteenth century, the German university model was spoken of with a reverence appropriate to deities. Freedom to do research and to discuss it freely was a breath of fresh air for students from the New World who studied in Germany. They took the German methods back to America and influenced the founding of similar universities there. Abraham Flexner described Charles Eliot's pace setting reforms for the medical school at Harvard (Flexner 1910, 12). Undoubtedly, these reforms can be attributed to his experiences in Germany shortly before he became president of Harvard.

The three functional principles that shaped the German university, and that remain more or less prominent in universities today, are the unity of research and teaching, academic freedom, and the centrality of the arts and sciences. Formerly, the arts and sciences had been considered the foundation for all later study in specializations such as law, theology, or medicine. The arts and science faculty were considered lower, while the professional or specialized faculties were considered higher and more important than the lower faculty. In restoring the prominence of the arts and sciences, Humboldt turned this pattern on its head (Fallon 1980, 28–31). Schleiermacher maintained the pattern by insisting that clergy were to be educated first in the broadest possible knowledge base and then allowed to pursue a narrower specialization. In other words, the essential foundation for professional development was a broad base of knowledge coupled with habits of inquiry and continuing research.

However, subtle factors embedded in the decisions and structures of the German university were ultimately of greater importance when the model was transferred to North America. Daniel Fallon (1980), who wrote his history not to applaud the success of the German university but to suggest reasons for the decline of its influence, noted that after some eighty years of the highest intellectual activity, and a devastating world war, the German university seemed locked forever in the nineteenth century and irrelevant to the modern age. Significantly, the only degree offered at the University of Berlin in its formative years was the doctorate. Even though Schleiermacher maintained that the terminal degree in theology should be the Lizentiat and the doctorate "reserved only for truly remarkable universal contributions" (Fallon 1980, 38), the clear intent of the founders of the University of Berlin was to assemble an intelligentsia focused on the highest of higher learning. Evidently, enthusiastic supporters of the German pattern for North American universities failed to see that the founding premise of the University of Berlin in particular was that elite scholars and a small group of elite students would come together for doctoral-level education.

Related to this premise was Humboldt's belief that strength of intellect is the most important factor in selecting faculty. If students are influenced by the best minds and exposed to the highest of academic research, he believed, character development will follow. However, many of the intellectuals Humboldt invited to become faculty were actually unruly, jealous, arrogant, narrow-minded, and self-serving. His dream of an intellectual elite that would enlighten and humanize the state foundered on the realization that a well-stocked and well-trained mind is no guarantee of virtue, wisdom, or a capacity to reach beyond oneself into service.

Further, given Humboldt's commitment to intellectual strength as primary, he paid almost no attention to *learning*. We struggle today, in universities and seminaries, with this legacy. For the most part, curriculum is structured in disciplinary silos—departments peopled by faculty, each totally unrelated to other silos that also shape and affect students.

Much of the concern about the future of American higher education stems from the effort to take the essentially elite model of the German university and use it as the template for a university that would be very different in its culture and clientele. It should not be surprising if similar concerns are expressed about the future of divinity schools, seminaries, Bible colleges, Christian universities (and, now, some church-based theological initiatives), since to a large extent they copied the university model.

Digging a little deeper, one soon discovers that understanding and analysis of the problem is not a simple matter. Higher education in North America, though shaped by the German university, was also influenced by the English model of the academy and Pietism and was formed in the unique culture and professional expectations of the nineteenth century.

Educational Institutions in North America

The founding of universities and theological institutions in North America in the nineteenth century proceeded rapidly. Faculty went to Germany to study, and many returned full of enthusiasm for the German methods (Farley 1983a, 10; Brubacher and Rudy 1968, 178). They copied the German curriculum structure (though placing biblical studies as the first of the disciplines to be studied in a fourfold scheme), established research libraries, university presses, and learned societies, instituted the radical new seminar approach, and assigned research papers. But perhaps because the church was caught up in the spirit of a burgeoning, progressive nation, many seemed to miss Schleiermacher's intent that development of professional clergy include early exposure to the broad base of knowledge found in the liberal arts. Nineteenth-century Americans seemed to be more impressed with German practices and methods. In the North American context, practices came to be defined as functions or skills, and the practical departments identified more easily with their social science counterparts. Theologians identified more closely with their academic guilds than with the church or practical departments. In time, theology became the realm of schools and ministry the realm of the church. It can be argued that the early rationale for the fourfold model (which included the desire to turn people to God) has been modified by a theory-to-practice linearity, resulting in a fragmented curriculum where faculty are specialists in their field and involved in presenting a series of often disconnected courses.

As institutions were formed in North America, the German research university, though powerful, was not the first or only influence. While the lingering effects of copying the elite German university cannot be denied, it would be a mistake to assert that early university presidents in America intended to clone the German research university. Clearly, the English college ideal, Pietism, and factors within the emerging American culture were all influential as well. The German system, with its emphasis on research and professional training, concentrated on the advancement of the discipline while deemphasizing (though not excluding) the development of character. English educators, while not denying the importance of research, retained the ideal that a university education should first shape the character of the student. A desire that piety and learning should be united was characteristic of English schools. Typically this led (as was Humboldt's desire) to an emphasis on the liberal arts, with the expectation that the society would be improved through education.

Fleeing the oppression of government and church in England, many Puritans emigrated to America. Here they felt they could fulfill their dream for a perfect society founded on their religious and educational ideals. They founded Harvard College (1636) and Yale (1701), patterning their curricula after that of Cambridge University but conscious that they had an opportunity through the schools to shape new leaders for their new society.[9] For almost a century they continued to follow English patterns of education, incorporating aspects of the Scholastic curriculum and method with piety. Doctrinal purity was the primary concern in the academic program of the colleges. Mary Latimer Gambrell notes that Yale was founded largely out of a fear that Harvard had strayed from the fundamentals—even though Harvard's liberalism, at least though the eighteenth century, was considered mild in character. The Westminster Confession and the Articles of the Church of England were still required, and the overseers of the university remained conservative until the end of the century. When Harvard became Unitarian in 1805, "Yale was experiencing a series of revivals destined to hold it faithful to tradition for another generation" (Gambrell 1937, 58). Tests of doctrinal orthodoxy for students and prospective Yale faculty remained stringent until the 1820s. Louise Stevenson (1986) traces the development of Yale from its roots in an evangelical tradition, through intentional efforts to provide students with an intellectual basis for the Christian faith, to the ultimate adoption of the curricular model and character of the research university. Educational forms incorporating the transplanted and revisioned German emphasis on professional ministerial education would not appear until the nineteenth century, resulting in the now familiar fourfold design of the theological curriculum.

Eric Springsted observes, "Virtually all of the universities founded in the American colonies, with the exception of the University of Pennsylvania, were avowedly Christian.... By 1861, 162 permanent colleges...had been established (only 29 of them before 1830). Of these schools, the Pres-

---

[9]Samuel Willard, vice president of Harvard from 1701 to 1707, in a tract entitled *Brief Directions to a Young Scholar: Designing the Ministry for the Study of Divinity*, outlined a system of education that differed little from that offered at Cambridge in the sixteenth century. Analytical and doctrinal methods were recommended for study of the Scriptures; students were to read widely (the content carefully selected), and descriptions of heresies, ancient and modern, were to be provided to prepare the student for "controversy" (Gambrell 1937, 23). At both Yale and Harvard, this ministerial education was the only course of studies available for all students, regardless of their chosen profession. By the end of the eighteenth century, however, different programs were available for those entering the ministry and those preparing for other professions (ibid., 75).

byterians could claim forty-nine, the Methodists thirty-four, the Baptists twenty-five, and the Congregationalists twenty-one" (Springsted 1988, 5–6). He suggests three reasons for the founding of these Christian colleges in the mid to late 1800s: first, America had just experienced the Second Great Awakening and some of these denominations wanted to increase their influence on the frontier; second, colleges were needed to train clergy; and third, church leaders desired to civilize and bring intellectual culture to the frontier. "This emphasis on learning is important because, contrary to what fundamentalists think, it shows that few people who sought to establish piety on the frontier saw knowledge as any threat to Christianity" (Springsted 1988, 6).

Changes in American culture following the American Revolution led ultimately to the secularization of the colleges, which, in turn, stimulated the development of denominational colleges[10] and the creation of the seminary. As the social changes that followed the American Revolution stimulated changes in congregations' expectations concerning ministers, corresponding alterations in theological education would be seen by some as a challenge to the traditional scholastic curriculum. Through the eighteenth and into the nineteenth centuries, churches would be challenged by changes in culture, clergy and laity would reexamine their respective roles, and ministerial education would change.[11] As in previous centuries, members of the Christian community had yet another opportunity to reconsider the nature of ministry and leadership and the purpose of theological education. Theological education for the remainder of the nineteenth century and into the twentieth would be affected by their decisions.

The functional needs of churches, the state of ministerial education, and dissatisfaction with diminishing theological orthodoxy prompted the formation of the theological seminary in the second decade of the nineteenth century. The limitations of these early efforts are attested to by Leonard Woods, writing from the standpoint of a former ministerial student at

---

[10]By the Civil War, 180 denominational colleges had been formed, which Wayne Goodwin assesses as "out-of-control" development. The motivation for the founding of these schools was the renewed religious energy of the Great Awakenings and dissatisfaction with science and secularism (Goodwin 1989, 206).

[11] See Bradley (1996) for detail on the influence of the Puritan tradition, the tension between piety and learning, and implications for practical theology.

Harvard. He provides a vivid description of these factors in his history of the development of Andover Seminary. The state of ministerial education, in his judgment, was defective—much more so at Harvard than at Yale. "During the four years of my education at the [Harvard] university there were not, so far as I recollect, more than three or four resident students in divinity" (Woods 1885, 17).

The Revolutionary War had broken the pattern of sending students to Europe, and the new frontier needed ministers. Andover Seminary became a prototype for future development of graduate theological schools. To enter Andover, a student had to be a college graduate or pass an examination in Latin, Greek, and the sciences. Andover offered a three-year course of studies, completion of which was not required of students. The first year included study in Greek and Hebrew, biblical exegesis, and the history of Scripture. The study of Christian doctrine occupied the second year, and the third year included studies in preaching, ecclesiastical history, and pastoral duties (Gambrell 1937, 146). Timothy Dwight, then president of Yale, gave the founding address and spoke of the advantages of a school where students had the time and resources for study that ministerial apprenticeship could not provide.[12] The seminary was not, in his view, an alternative to existing colleges. It was intended to replace the "parsonage seminary" and the conventional practice of private tutoring.[13] If this view reflects a negative judgment on the simplicity of the tutors, then Roland Bainton portrays these parsonage seminaries, popularly called "schools of the prophets," and their plain-speaking pastor-tutors in a more favorable light. In the eighteenth century it was common for a ministerial candidate to spend some time in further study at Yale or as an apprentice to a resident pastor. This pastor was in many cases a graduate of Yale and considered part of the teaching staff.[14] These pastor-tutors, however, "were not selected by the College nor by the churches, but were chosen by the students who often

---

[12]Timothy Dwight was an American Congregationalist minister and educator, grandson of Jonathan Edwards. In 1795 he became president of Yale College, where he established professional schools of medicine and theology and attempted to modernize the curriculum.

[13]It was common at schools such as Harvard and Yale for students after graduation to continue to study divinity privately with the college president (Ringenberg 1990, 379).

[14]Bainton identifies Jonathan Edwards as one of these pastor-tutors. In most cases, the wives were as influential as their husbands (1957, 53–54).

reined up at a parsonage door, unannounced, with a request for admission. When a tutor considered his candidate qualified he was recommended to a church. Following a call he was rigorously examined by neighboring churches, and if deemed qualified was ordained" (Bainton 1957, 49).

Woods, a graduate of Harvard College, provides a balance between Dwight's concern and Bainton's approbation. In his much earlier description of the apprenticing of ministerial candidates, Woods observed:

> The time which the candidates for the ministry devoted to professional study was generally very short, frequently no more than a few months. Even when they extended their studies to a year or more…[they] gained but a very inadequate knowledge of the different branches of theological learning…. Some studied alone, reading such books as they could procure, and writing a few sermons. But in most cases they pursued their studies under the direction of some distinguished divine. Besides enjoying his assistance, they had the advantage of a little company of students who pursued their studies together, and frequently engaged in profitable discussions of important subjects. True, the clergyman who became their teacher had for the most part a very small collection of books, and was himself so occupied with his ministerial duties, that but little time and attention could be given to his pupils, and it was moreover very rarely the case, that parish ministers with such an education as they themselves enjoyed, were qualified to carry students through the various departments of a theological course. There were, however, some real advantages in the method of study which was then pursued. Young men had opportunities to acquire a direct and practical acquaintance with the duties and trials of a minister, and with the affairs of a church and parish. (Woods 1885, 18–19)

The success of Andover Theological Seminary stimulated the founding of other divinity schools: Harvard Divinity School (Congregational/Unitarian, 1811), Princeton Seminary (Presbyterian, 1812), Auburn

(Presbyterian, 1818), Yale Divinity School (Congregational, 1822),[15] Protestant Episcopal (1823), Union of Virginia (Presbyterian, 1824), Lancaster (German Reformed, 1825), Newton (Baptist, 1825), and Union of New York (Congregationalist/Presbyterian, 1836). Over fifty seminaries had been established by thirteen denominations by 1840. By 1860, this number had increased to sixty. Between 1860 and 1890 twenty-five seminaries were founded, primarily in the Midwest and mostly by German and Scandinavian immigrant groups (see Ringenberg 1990, 379). The seminary had become a permanent fixture in American religious life.

Reasons given for the founding of Princeton Seminary were the rapid growth of the Baptists and Methodists, the spread of religious infidelity, the need to address shifting cultural values, and the dramatic increase of vacant pulpits among Presbyterian churches. While Mark Noll suggests that the intent of the seminary was to ensure a pious clergy and to advance piety in the people (Noll 1979, 80–89), George Marsden cautions against drawing lines between groups that stressed reason and intellect in education and ministry and those that stressed piety and experience.

> The Calvinists tended to stress intellect, the importance of right doctrine, the cognitive aspects of faith. and higher education. On the other hand, more pietistically and emotionally oriented groups, such as the Methodists, tended to shun intellectual rigor and to stress the practical and experiential aspects of faith. Yet many groups in America stressed both the intellectual and the experiential-practical aspects. Many Congregationalists and Presbyterians, especially those of the revivalist branches known in the nineteenth century as "New School," combined educational and doctrinal emphases with intense emotion.... Even "Old School" Presbyterians, including those at Princeton Seminary renowned for their doctrinal conservatism and severe intellectual demands, had a place for sentiment and some pietist leanings. The Baptists, who were less centralized and standardized, had some similar

---

[15] See Bainton (1957) and Sloan (1971) on the establishment of the American colleges.

pro-revivalist intellectual leadership along with some distinctly non-intellectualistic elements. (Marsden 1980, 44–45)

Princeton had no articulated curriculum during its early years.[16] Soon, however, a three-year program was established (as it had been at Andover) and became the prototype for the schools that followed. Students spent considerable time in churches, and faculty spent considerable time in research and writing. The integration of piety and learning was an important value; students were encouraged spiritually and received frequent exhortations from pious men. From the end of the nineteenth century into the early twentieth, prayer meetings, chapels, revivals, spiritual retreats, and exhortations to the godly life were common in university divinity schools. Most faculty believed that scholarship was no threat to piety (Cherry 1995, 34–35). However, Conrad Cherry also observes that most divinity schools were unable to maintain a balance between piety and intellect.[17]

In 1909, the students petitioned the board of directors to reduce the stress on exegesis and biblical languages, citing certain courses in Old and New Testament in the petition. They agitated for more practical courses, such as those being offered at Union Seminary (New York)—among them sociology.[18] Their petition was denied. However, with the appointment of a new president in 1913, the curriculum was revised, much to the dismay of those who disparaged the practical inclusions (Meeks 1990, 28–30). Unfortunately, the students' need for practical help and the faculty's desire to uphold traditional academic standards caused a polarization between the practical and academic rather than stimulating creative conversation about ways to provide both. It appears that though the 1913 revision alleviated an

---

[16]See G. S. Smith (1996) for further detail on the purposes, curriculum, and contribution of Princeton, the development and influence of Methodist schools, and the differences in perspective between the Methodists and the Presbyterians at the time. See also D. B. Calhoun (1994–1996).

[17] The surveys of the 1930s and 1950s concluded that the multiplication of departments and the demands of scholarship, fieldwork, and family responsibilities were contributing factors. "In the 1970s and 1980s, the student bodies of most of the divinity schools became so diverse that there was no apparent shared religious experience that could issue in common religious devotion" (Cherry 1995, 37–38).

[18]Auguste Compte (1798–1857) is said to invented the term *sociology*. At this time it was a new science which promised some understanding of social patterns.

immediate problem, it failed to address seriously the purpose of the seminary and the nature of the curriculum.

As the nineteenth century progressed, theological education was both shaped and fundamentally altered by the complex interplay of modernism, revivalism, critical methods of study, liberalism, neo-orthodoxy, the theory of evolution, and social and political forces. A dramatic increase in involvement in organized religion and an educational revolution are considered two hallmarks of this century.[19] The response to the educational revolution within the Protestant community was mixed. Baptists and Methodists, though different in their organization, were similar in that their clergy had little formal education. "Unlike the Congregational, Presbyterian, and Episcopalian ministers, who typically were of genteel origin and were highly trained and well educated, the Baptist and Methodist clergy were of the people. They had little education, received little if any pay, spoke in the vernacular, and preached from the heart" (Finke and Stark 1992, 76). Methodists, slow to establish schools, ridiculed the schools of the East for manufacturing ministers who did not understand the needs of the West. A prominent Methodist preacher, Peter Cartwright, argued that training while in ministry would be more effective than the education offered by all the colleges and Bible institutes (Mead 1956, 240; Hatch 1989, 8–9). "As was true of most Methodist leaders of the time, including Bishop Asbury, Cartwright was opposed not to higher education but, rather, to the use of theological schools to design 'man-made ministers'" (Finke and Stark 1992, 76). At the 1844 Methodist General Conference, Cartwright estimated that "fewer than 50 (of approximately 4,282 travelling ministers)" had much beyond an English grade-school education. But he boasted that these clergy "'preached the Gospel with more success and had more seals to their ministry than all the sapient, downy D.D.'s in modern times'" (in Finke and Stark 1992, 7).

Suspicions regarding the corrupting effects of development of the intellect, though they slowed the development of graduate theological education in these groups, would not prevent it. In spite of the objections to an educated clergy, the development of seminaries continued. Between 1831

---

[19]See Finke and Stark (1992) and Wind and Lewis (1994, 24–28, 216–53) for a discussion of congregational development from the Colonial era through the nineteenth century.

and 1859, student enrollment at Congregational seminaries increased from 234 to 275, at Presbyterian seminaries from 257 to 632, at Episcopalian seminaries from 47 to 130, and at Baptist seminaries from 107 to 210. The first Methodist seminary, founded in 1847, had 51 students by 1859 (ibid., 77).[20] Roger Finke and Rodney Stark note that the number of Methodist schools now increased rapidly. By 1880 there were 11 theological seminaries, 44 colleges and universities, and 130 women's seminaries and schools (ibid., 154). Finke and Stark conjecture that the growth of Methodist seminaries was caused partly by a national expansion of higher education but also, more significantly, by the desire of "the larger, more affluent Methodist congregations" to have "educated clergy on a social par with Congregationalists, Episcopalians, and Presbyterians" and the desire of clergy for the "social status and increased pay that a well-educated clergy could obtain" (ibid., 155).

Both the university and the seminary in North America were bound by history to the Colonial college model, and both struggled to establish their identity in relation to it. Though most early seminaries were founded to preserve the Christian educational ideals that many universities were rejecting, they inevitably patterned their curriculum and administrative structures on those of the universities. Consequently, the development of the modern university and the concerns expressed about its future offer important insights for those concerned about the future of the seminary.

The Development of Universities and University Divinity Schools in North America

Prior to 1870, religion was a pervasive influence in American colleges. They were founded and supported by churches, most of their professors and presidents were clergy, and society assumed that the colleges would care for the religious welfare of its citizens. During the eighteenth and most of the nineteenth centuries in the United States, undergraduate colleges upheld the British tradition of character formation in the context of a broad liberal education. In 1814, Timothy Dwight observed that Yale and Harvard were still more like collegiate institutes than universities (Brubacher and Rudy 1968, 177).

---

[20] See Richey (1996) for further information on Methodist education.

As professional specialization evolved within the universities, they followed a course characterized by a layering of the German research method over the Colonial college tradition. Unfortunately, in the context of burgeoning technical interests, ideological conflicts, pluralism, cultural change, and the new positivist spirit in post–Civil War America, the Colonial college ideal (with its religious orientation) and the notion of advancement of knowledge through research could not coexist (Brubacher and Rudy 1968, 199; Marsden 1991, 88). By the end of the nineteenth century, the emerging research universities had relegated religion to the periphery, in the belief that amateur clergy-professors could not provide the kind of scholarship that was needed (Marsden 1994, 89; Cherry 1995, 32).

In the Stoors Lectures delivered at Yale in 1935, Robert Hutchins (then president of the University of Chicago) more than suggested that because theology was irrelevant to this "faithless generation" it could no longer be the unifying principle of the university—any university. Theology as a "science" based on revealed truth was no longer adequate for the rational and scientific tasks of higher learning. He argued that the metaphysics of Plato and Aristotle should replace theology as the unifying principle for the universities and would help higher education achieve its major goal, the development of wisdom. That there was still some recognition of the place of theology in the university was evident in the national storm of protest that followed his lectures. William Adams Brown, former acting provost at Yale, countered with a series of lectures at Chicago entitled The Case for Theology in the University. Arguing that Hutchins had confused all theology with dogmatic theology, Brown insisted that Christian theology, in its broad sense, could provide a philosophy that could give meaning to life and consistency to education and serve as a unifying force in the fragmented curriculum of the universities—a point Hutchins later conceded (Longfield 1992, 159–60; Cherry 1995, 276–78). For Brown, the survival of Western civilization was at stake in this debate. America, established on faith in God and a sense of the dignity of humankind, could dismiss neither without opening the door to totalitarianism. "Theology, understood not as a matter of doctrine but as 'the philosophy of the Christian religion,' which insisted on a moral, meaningful universe and the essential importance of personality, could not only provide the means to a unified university but also support the future of democracy" (Longfield 1992, 163).

Marsden notes, however, that secularization of the academy was not necessarily the product of a reaction against Christianity. Many of those who advanced processes of secularization and specialization in the universities were themselves committed to Christianity. Daryl Hart's account "Faith and Learning in the Age of the University: The Academic Ministry of Daniel Coit Gilman" (1992, 107–45) provides an example of how the university leaders of this time dealt with religion in relation to the new scientific quest. Arguing that the "intellectual gospel" in America never approached the secular agnosticism represented in Britain by T. H. Huxley, Hart writes: "Instead, academic reformers such as Gilman, Eliot, and Cornell's Andrew Dickson White believed that their institutions, while advancing knowledge, would also bolster an enlightened and non-sectarian Christian faith. Rather than inciting hostilities between scientists and theologians, America's leading universities would reassure believers that science encouraged religion, a message that Protestant leaders themselves embraced and promoted" (Hart 1992, 110; see also Hart 1999).

Though the universities had broken their ecclesiastical ties, and though religion tended to be seen as moral truth where the sciences and the professions determined the curriculum, there was still in the nineteenth century the desire that the university support a Christian worldview and encourage moral growth (Marsden 1992, 27; Hart 1992, 200–202). Many of the supporters and founders of the modern university believed that the divinity school was a natural part of the university—one of several specializations important to the changing American culture. For example, Harper's[21] vision for a divinity school as an integral part of the modern university led to the transfer of the Baptist Union Theological Seminary to Chicago in 1890, "thus making the Divinity School the first professional program at the University of Chicago" (Cherry 1995, 5). It was Harper's intent that the divinity school "serve the University internally by bringing religion into connection with the various branches of learning, and it was to aid the society at large by dispatching a legion of well-educated ministers to Christianize and civilize the globe" (ibid., 4). However, as higher education in North America developed in the context of a burgeoning, industrialized society, it was perhaps inevitable that the concept of specialized systems that

---

[21]William Rainey Harper, founding president of the University of Chicago (1892).

worked so well for factories would become part of the language of the culture and would be adapted to the curriculum of schools.

Hart observes that by the middle of the twentieth century the university was showing signs of ill health. Publications appearing from the 1930s into the 1960s suggested that "a recovery of Christian thought and ideals was crucial to the recovery of the university" (Hart 1999, 115). With theology once again poised to reenter the university, W.A. Visser't Hooft, then the secretary of the World Student Christian Federation, attempted to rouse the church to a better understanding of its mission in the world. "Part of that mission was to form a Christian intelligentsia that would present the Christian message to the 'secular world' and translate that message into a plan of 'concrete action'" (ibid., 115–16). However, Visser't Hoof't, Robert Hutchins, Arnold Nash, Walter Moberly, and Henry P. Van Dusen were among those who brought to public notice the purposelessness of the university and its inability to provide the environment for pursuit of truth in order to bring meaning to the knowledge contained within the disciplines of the university. Hart traces the problem through historical circumstances dating back to the Reformation and Enlightenment and postulates that, over time, the university had so emphasized bringing the applied sciences to society, that it lost the common framework provided by philosophy and the humanities. However, even these disciplines seemed unable to overcome the malaise created by the narrowness of scientific specialization. Visser't Hooft stressed that the church could not abandon the university for in it was found the best hope for integrating truth. Van Dusen argued that the way out of cultural decline was for the universities to reclaim Judeo-Christian values and Christian theology. Others such as Hutchins would argue that the way forward for the university was to seek *intellectual* coherence and that theology was not necessarily the remedy for the current malaise. Those who did see a place for theology, encouraged Christian scholars to move away from the margins and to reform the university from within. A return to the faith that had founded the universities was considered the university's best hope (see ibid., 116–123).

Between 1870 and 1920, the traditional divisions of the university—law, the arts, medicine, and theology—evolved into the natural sciences, the social sciences, and the humanities. Among those concerned that a narrowed specialization of the university curriculum would impoverish the humanities, Allen Bloom asserts that neither the natural sciences nor the social sciences can answer the fundamental questions of human life. Predictably, he offers the humanities as that set of disciplines which, out of their rich storehouse of human knowledge, can provide answers to the question of how people should live (Bloom 1987, 336–82). Jaroslav Pelikan (1992), in his turn, asserts that a storm is breaking upon the university again, necessitating a critical reexamination of the idea of the university. The university has not discharged its intellectual and moral responsibility if it is not able to respond to the wholeness of the human condition.

Cherry expresses pessimism that the various subspecialties of the university could be unified at all, much less by a divinity school. "Certainly the divinity school, as it has been surpassed in power and influence by other university programs on most campuses, has enjoyed no opportunity to serve as a unifying force within the multiversity" (Cherry 1995, 287). He concludes that not only did powerful cultural forces sweep away the dream of a Protestant America unified by the work of the university divinity schools, but in embracing the forms of the modern university and its specialized curriculum, the divinity schools were unable to be a unifying presence in the culture. By establishing ministerial education in the university, the founders "inadvertently cut ministers off from the life of the churches. And as they took up the role of 'prophetic criticism' of church and society behind the safe walls of the university, the schools further alienated themselves from the churches they sought to serve. The founding vision of the divinity schools overestimated the compatibility of university and church, specialized learning and ministerial task, theoretical sophistication and practical application" (ibid., 297).

In their efforts to imitate the practical training designed for the prestigious professions, the founders of divinity schools perpetuated an approach to professional training that fails to support the presumption of the compatibility and inherent coherence of theory and practice. Between 1910 and 1926, the curriculum of Yale Divinity School was oriented to distinct, functional tracks with little effort to create an educational whole. In the 1930s, Dean Luther Weigle insisted that Yale's system of vocational tracking allowed the student to focus on current ministerial problems, provided the opportunity to specialize in a particular ministry, and encouraged students to integrate their own learning. This system of vocational tracking based on the hope that students could integrate learning with practice was adopted at the divinity schools of Union, Boston, Drew, Vanderbilt, Emory, Duke, and

Southern Methodist University. An alliance with Andover Seminary permitted Harvard Divinity School to expand into the practical disciplines between 1908 and 1926. Fieldwork was required at all the schools, but increasingly they struggled with how to integrate fieldwork with academic study (ibid., 140). Through the 1930s, many had to admit that professional education and graduate theological study had not been integrated effectively. Though William Adams Brown of Union maintained his conviction that every course should include practical application, he admitted that students were not integrating the different functions of the curriculum into a practical theory and that the practical courses were too quickly outdated. He recommended that ministerial education should lead students to develop a theological perspective on the ministry rather than assuming the individual integration of separate functions.

Dean Robert Cushman of Duke Divinity School insisted in 1961 that "the principal aim of theological education—'perhaps of all education properly conceived—*is not function but an integral being who can function appropriately*'" (Cherry 1995, 141). Several believed that this would be achieved through a curriculum that emphasized the classical disciplines rather than training in technique. However, it soon became apparent that the effort to provide a unifying perspective from the classical disciplines was not uniting the theoretical and practical dimensions of the divinity school curriculum. It was also evident that the practical courses and fieldwork were not preparing students for ministry. "By the middle of the 1960s, some divinity school educators were persuaded that the AATS-sponsored study of professional education for the ministry may have sharply stated a disquieting truth: *"Ministry today is generally discontinuous with the preparation provided for it"* (ibid., 146).

In the 1960s, it could no longer be assumed that ministerial education took place in the context of a predominantly Christian culture, that Protestant churches would remain static while their future leaders were being trained, that students would enter divinity school after years of socialization in the church, or that students would be biblically literate. In America, traditional institutional structures were challenged as men and women were caught up in the spirit of revolt that characterized the 1960s. The fourfold structure of the curriculum was not replaced, but underlying presumptions of authority were challenged, and the educational expectations of students changed. Since that time, theological education has had to define itself in relation to increasing diversity and pluralism.

As efforts to use theological perspectives from the classical disciplines to under gird and inform ministry foundered, divinity school leaders proposed a more rigorous system of supervised ministry that would synthesize theory and practice. Pastoral psychology and clinical pastoral education represented efforts to contextualize the curriculum of the divinity school. However, by the 1980s it was evident that the effort to synthesize theory and practice through a contextual model of professional ministerial education was not achieving the hoped-for result. Similarly, even though departments of religious studies were accepted in the twentieth-century universities, they seemed more suited to the preparation of professional scholars than to preparing persons for professional leadership in the church or church-related agencies (Hart 1992, 216; Cherry 1995, 120).

Through the last third of the twentieth century, it became apparent that the project of the divinity school and professional ministerial education had stalled. At the same time, critiques of seminary education had escalated significantly. At this point, revisiting the findings of surveys of theological education in the early to mid-twentieth century may be instructive. They reveal a trajectory of problems that contributed to the malaise at the end of the century and that seem to have persisted to the present. The relevance of the surveys' findings to the present condition of theological schools will be obvious.

Surveys of Theological Education, 1924–1956

A series of complex influences[22] with origins in the German university and English college, and in the unique conditions and controversies of the North American scene, had produced a structure for theological education characterized by a fourfold curriculum and a primary outcome expressed in

---

[22]See the historical surveys of Miller and Lynn (1988), Brubacher and Rudy (1968), and Miller (1991) for more thorough treatments of the complex forces affecting the development of American theological education from the seventeenth through early twentieth centuries. Mark Noll, George Rawlyk, and David Bebbington have written on the context of evangelicalism during this period; see Noll, Bebbington, and Rawlyk (1994) and Rawlyk and Noll (1993).

mission statements as "preparation of persons for ministry."[23] The fourfold pattern generally included biblical studies, theological/philosophical studies, historical studies, and practical studies. Charles Wood notes, "The persistence of this pattern ever since, despite the many ways in which both theological studies and church leadership have changed over the years, is attributable in part to the power of a common perception that its divisions still represent what the church's leaders need" (Wood 1985b, 3).

In some schools, the curriculum had a primary orientation to piety in learning; in others, the key orientation was to the development of the mind. Beginning in 1924, these developments were evaluated by a series of studies, which in their turn influenced the form of theological education in both the United States and Canada. In 1924, Robert Kelly[24] surveyed 161 theological schools in North America. The study was driven by the widespread belief that "the machinery and the methods used in educating Protestant ministers were inadequate" and that ministerial leadership was in serious decline (Kelly 1924, vii). The resulting report—the first major analysis of American theological education—was oriented to issues of ministerial leadership. The report, *Theological Education in America*, painted a far less than positive picture of the schools as "centers of intellectual and ethical power" (in Kelsey 1993, 56) and warned that churches would seek their ministers from Bible colleges and religious training schools (a practice that continues to the present). "There are evidences that goodness rather than intelligence is often held up as an end of theological training. With rare exceptions the seminaries are not conspicuous as centers of scholarly pursuits" (Kelly 1924, 235). While the

---

[23]Mark May et al. affirm the persistence of the general categories of the fourfold curriculum. "For more than a century after the founding of the first seminary for the training of minis
ters in America, the situation varied little among the existing institutions. In each there was a required curriculum embracing the four divisions of theological study as then understood: (1) exegetical theology; (2) historical theology; (3) systematic theology; (4) practical theology" (May et al. 1934, 34).

[24]Robert Kelly, formerly president of Earlham College, was the first president of the Association of American Colleges founded in 1915 to support the smaller denominational and non-demoninational colleges in their mission to counter the lack of unity in undergraduate education around Christian principles (see Hart 1992a, 205–206).

report allowed that some ministers were leaving seminary and going into the churches with transforming power "because they have received a new vision and have been free to pursue it," the majority formed in these institutions, it said, simply maintained the denominational status quo. "The didactic if not dogmatic methods of teaching, which are very prevalent, tend to emphasize in the student's mind the authority of men. Prophetic preachers may be spoiled through theology if that theology is after the tradition of the elders and not after Christ" (ibid., 236). Kelly's methodology was seriously questioned by angry seminary administrators, who felt the study was flawed and would drive away needed support for the schools.[25] As a result, a new survey was commissioned.

The Rockefeller Institute of Social and Religious Research agreed to fund the new survey, on the condition that an overseeing organization be formed as a basis for peer review and external assessment (see Miller 1989, 192). In time, this association would accredit member schools, and presidents would be obligated to give attention to educational administration—a task that became more complex with the professionalization of the curriculum. The president, who once served as an academic voice for the faculty and as the moral compass for the student body, became an administrator. With the proliferation of levels of administration, theological schools were on the way to becoming corporate enterprises.[26] This seemingly subtle shift in orientation had a profound impact on theological education. Pragmatic pressures related to institutional success and survival more easily overwhelmed issues related to learning, spirituality, and mission driven by theological meaning. Institutions concerned about accreditation could find it easiest to report on procedures and statistics as marks of institutional suc-

---

[25] The criticisms of Kelly's report focused on what was judged to be inadequate observational methodology and interpretations, conclusions unsupported by data, the inadequacies of reporting, and so on. To support their claims critics pointed to comments scattered throughout the report itself referring to the incompleteness of the data (Miller 1991, 26; Goodwin 1989, 36).

[26] Jeanne Meister (1998) notes that the emergence of universities as corporations is related to the belief that knowledge must be managed. Much of the innovation occurring in higher education is in the corporate university, encouraging multiagency partnerships and use of technology. It is inevitable that this trend will affect the evolution of the seminary as an institution. Bill Readings argues that the contemporary university is not as much linked to the destiny of the nation-state as it is becoming a transnational bureaucratic corporation (Readings 1996, 3).

cess. The 1996 ATS Standards have been significantly revised to encourage schools to be concerned with learning, spirituality, and mission. This is a needed corrective to earlier tendencies to quantify theological education, but it remains to be seen how the schools will respond to the changes in emphasis.

Agreeing to Rockefeller's stipulations, Mark May with William Adams Brown selected sixty-six seminaries considered to be representative of all seminaries in the United States and Canada. The four-volume report, published in 1934, recommended that the task of the seminary be to train ministers for the professional ministry and that the curriculum should relate to this task (see May et al. 1934). The curriculum of medical and legal professional education was given as an example of the type of rigor needed in the theological schools. The case-study approach in law schools and the clinical experiences of the medical student were described as ways to solve the persistent problem of the separation of theory and practice.

The observation that schools of medicine and law were associated with universities, and that improvement in educational standards seemed to be linked to their association with professional accrediting societies, led to proposals that seminaries form similar alliances. May et al., recommended the formation of an association of theological schools that would have authority to establish and maintain the standards of ministerial education. In 1934, the Conference of Theological Schools became the first accrediting association. In 1936, the American Association of Theological Schools in the United States and Canada was formed; in time it became the Association of Theological Schools. Cherry notes that from the beginning "the movement for the creation of standards for ministerial education was dominated by the ideals of university graduate education" (Cherry 1995, 135). This link with the university, as well as a clarification that these early linkages were not with the *research* university, is confirmed in May's report:

> A survey of the history of ministerial education shows that the first theological seminaries were, as a matter of fact, not seminaries at all, but institutions of higher learning, predominately theological in character—the educational heritage of the first American colonists from the mother country. Harvard College, the first American institution of higher education, was founded in 1636 by the Massachusetts Bay Colony, largely for the purpose

of providing a suitable ministry.... Similarly, the main purpose for the founding of Yale College (1701) was training for the Christian ministry. (May et al. 1934, 21–22)

In *The Purpose of the Church and Its Ministry* (hereafter *The Purpose*), a 1956 report from another survey of theological education, H. Richard Niebuhr added an important element to the critiques of theological education. He suggested that the confusion and uncertainty he perceived in theological schools was due to a lack of theological clarity about the church.

Without a definition of Church it is impossible to define adequately the work of the ministry for which the school is to prepare its students. It seems impossible also to organize a genuine Course of study including the Biblical disciplines, church history, theology, the theory and practice of worship, preaching, and education on other grounds than those of habit and expediency unless there is clarity about the place of these studies and acts in the life of the Church. (Niebuhr 1956, 18)

Even though he defined the proper context of theological education as the church, Niebuhr stressed that the purpose of theological education is not simply to train ministers to sustain the programs and structures of a particular church or denomination. He observed, "There is an internal contradiction in a theology and a Christian educational system that regard the work of the Church as the final activity to be considered." This tendency leads to the confusion of "its work with that of its Lord and equates devotion to [the Church] with loyalty to the kingdom of God" (ibid., 41).

Niebuhr was convinced that confusion of the proximate and ultimate goals of theological education would create a context that exalted the church (as institution) and would emphasize not the reconciliation of persons to God but the conversion of persons to the institutions of Christianity. "When [this confusion] prevails...[theological] education necessarily becomes indoctrination in Christian principles rather than inquiry based on faith in God; or it is turned into training in methods for increasing the Church rather than for guiding men to love of God and neighbor." A similar confusion ensues when the Bible becomes so central in theological education that it "takes the place of the God who speaks, and love of the book replaces devotion to the One who makes himself known with its aid" (ibid., 43). The end of his argument was that the work of the theological curriculum is theoretical and informs practice. However, he did allow that reflection without action is bad theory. Observing that preachers, Christian educators, and church administrators cannot learn theory without involvement in the relevant activity, Niebuhr concluded, "The point is not that we learn by doing. Sometimes we learn nothing by doing except the bare deed.... The point is rather that we do not learn the meaning of deeds *without* doing" (ibid., 128–29). In spite of Niebuhr's stress on the formation of the intellect, his views on theological education were clearly holistic. Theological education requires what David Kelsey and others would later identify as the "practices" of the church. Worship, hearing the Word, and service are essential correctives to an education oriented to ministerial functions or parochialism. In this way Niebuhr developed his logic for the relationship of the school to the church (ibid., 130).

Niebuhr's assessment of North American schools was that in educating persons who will lead the church, they

> tend in consequence to neglect the first function of a theological school—the exercise of intellectual love of God and neighbor.... Their concentration on the task of educating ministers gives them their unique character, it determines the content of their courses of study and influences decisively their choices of students, teachers and administrators. It also involves them in great difficulties, since the contemporary church is confused about the nature of the ministry. Neither ministers nor the school that nurture them are guided today by a clear-cut, generally accepted conception of the office of the ministry. (ibid., 49–50)

It is not immediately clear how Niebuhr's concern for the neglect of the "first function" of theological schools is related to his sense of the church's confusion about the nature of the office of the ministry. Nor is it clear how he would accommodate the necessity for leaders to develop skills and capacities that are predominantly organizational and sociological in nature. He did argue that persons once knew relatively clearly what was expected of ministers, even though the specific nature of their function differed in different periods of church history. He referred to earlier studies by Mark May et al.(1934) and Hugh Hartshorne and Milton Froyd (1945) to show that considerable confusion had developed among churches, denominations, seminaries, and laypeople about the function of the minister (Niebuhr 1956, 49–53).

In this regard, the chapters of H. Richard Niebuhr and Daniel Williams' *The Ministry in Historical Perspectives* (1956; hereafter *The Ministry*) are held together by a common, and, one suspects, intentional effort to trace what the servant/priest/minister did in each major period of history. Each chapter treats the religious and cultural climate of the time, but basically to show the context in which certain functions of the ministry became important. Taken alone, *The Ministry* contains little that would lead one to think in more than functional terms about the nature of theological education that shapes the minister. But in *The Purpose*, Niebuhr (and presumably his colleagues) revealed his concern that ministers were being prepared for "the varieties of ministerial work without reference to a common function to be carried out by all ministers" (Niebuhr 1956, 53). He noted that when this common function is not understood, ministers are subject to the pressures from churches and denominations, and have no clear sense of vocation, which contributes to the laziness and frustration cited as reasons for failure in ministry (Niebuhr1956, 54).

In *Purpose*, Niebuhr revisited church history to show that even though the minister in each age was responsible for certain tasks, there was a relatively clear sense of the ultimate purposes that defined the ministry (Niebuhr 1956, 58–79). He identified what he considered to be the emerging conception of the ministry with the term *pastoral director*, a term that did not refer simply to one who directs the tasks of the church. He understood the temptations inherent in the word *director* and addressed them by describing the minister as one in community who does not function as a business manager or exercise the type of authority characteristic of hierarchically ordered societies (ibid., 90). Niebuhr never denied that the minister's business is to preside over or perform specific church functions; however, he maintained that the first and most important function is the edification of the church. The minister is concerned to "bring into being a people of God who as a Church will serve the purpose of the Church in the local community and the world" (ibid., 82). Noting that the work of the church is to increase the love of God and neighbor, he added, "It is significant that when ministers reflect on their theological education they are likely to regret more than any other deficiency in it the failure of the school to prepare them for the administration of such a church" (ibid., 83–84).

Niebuhr, like those before him, was not kind to the theological schools of his time. In spite of new disciplines, new challenges, and new ideas, the schools continued to be bound by traditional concepts of the institution and the curriculum. He complained that the curriculum was a collection of studies rather than a course of studies. When attempts were made to integrate the curriculum, they involved comprehensive examinations, theses, or integrative courses, which did little to address fundamental curricular problems. Bible, church history, theology, and preaching continued to be taught as separate subjects, and without a controlling or unifying idea for theological education, churches and ministers continued to be confused about the true nature of their work. The constant rivalry between different theologies and philosophies and between academic and practical disciplines exacerbated the problem and made it difficult for the schools to address deeper issues. All they could do was tinker with what Niebuhr called the academic machine. In spite of his concerns, Niebuhr was hopeful that faculty and students who were concerned with the ultimate purposes of theological education would one day change the institutions (Niebuhr 1956, 99–102). We're still trying.

The Niebuhr, Gustafson, and Williams study (1957) was, like previous studies, concerned with the profession of ministry and education appropriate to that ministry. However, a revisiting of their language concerning the profession, and the type of education that fosters it, is suggestive of their understanding of the term *profession* as applied to ministry, and of their views concerning the nature and purpose of contemporary theological education.

In *The Advancement of Theological Education* (1957; hereafter *The Advancement*), H. Richard Niebuhr, Daniel Williams, and James Gustafson made several recommendations about the shape of the theological curriculum that reflected their larger vision for theological education: it enables students to "enter into dialogue with contemporary thought and culture" and is not preoccupied simply with preparing students to perform ministerial tasks. "It is necessary to underline just what is at stake here. It is not enough to say that philosophy, psychology, and sociology are necessary to the understanding of certain aspects of the minister's task…. These and other disciplines are essential to the full understanding of the Christian faith itself "(Niebuhr, Williams, and Gustafson 1957, 87). After considering the role of these disciplines, the authors suggested that in three years students will only have begun mastery of one discipline "and some slight acquaintance with a few others." Only three things can be required of theological students: first, that they develop "a general acquaintance with the main areas of human thought"; second, that they "discover that angle of approach to Christian truth which is vital [for them]"; and, third, that they "begin to formulate [their] conception of the normative elements in Christian faith so that [they have] a principle of judgment which [they] bring to thought and action." Niebuhr, Williams, and Gustafson stressed that theological students should be able to sustain a dialogue between the "normative character of the Christian faith" and "inquiries into human life." Students "should have sufficient mastery of some particular discipline in science or the humanities" to allow interaction between the Christian faith and the chosen discipline (ibid., 88).

Glenn Miller assesses all three surveys and notes that all began with the assumption that the theological curriculum was flawed in that content was isolated from its application. Though they criticized the diminishment of theological inquiry, they did affirm that the schools were functioning well as centers for professional education. Consequently, in his judgment, the three reports did much to popularize the professional model in theological education (Miller 1991, 26). The unfortunate result of this popularization remains an inexplicable separation between professional education and mature theological inquiry. However, the concerns for the nature and purpose of theological education articulated by Niebuhr, Gustafson, and Williams put their conclusions in a different class from those of Kelly and Brown and May. Niebuhr, Gustafson, and Williams do not define professional education for ministry in exclusively functional or technical terms.

The Final Surveys of the Twentieth Century

Three less highly profiled studies concluded the era of surveys of theological education. Sponsored by the Lilly Endowment, Bridston and Culver (1965) proposed to determine the essential educational requirements for ministry and to study the relationship of pre-seminary and graduate education. In general, their findings reflected the earlier studies without significant differences in recommendations. They proposed that "secular cultivation, professional competence, and vocational integration" characterize the training of the minister, and encouraged a more seamless integration of undergraduate and graduate studies (Bridston and Culver 1965, viii). The ministerial student was described as almost wholly socialized by their upbringing in religious families, the church, and church-related colleges—to the extent that theological education was simply training members of a ghetto for the ghetto (ibid., 15). In asserting that "the most urgent dilemma facing theological education today is the need for finding a criterion through which, in the face of proliferating course offerings, decisions can be reached on what should be, what might be, and what need not be taught to ministerial students to prepare them for effective service (ibid., x), they anticipated today's concern about the crowded curriculum of theological schools. Observing that some schools were experimenting with curriculum revision, they recommended that the seminaries share their new thinking and experiments with one another. One of their more controversial recommendations derived from their criticism that the liberal arts tended to be the exclusive pre-seminary program for prospective ministry students. They suggested that a more pluralistic approach to undergraduate education should not be discouraged (ibid., 151). In general, their report recommended greater communication among the schools, greater consideration to the integration of undergraduate and graduate education for the minister, and greater awareness on the part of college and university presidents as to the extent to which their colleges provide pre-seminary training (ibid., 150–154). Noting that a relatively small percentage of seminarians (33%) actually anticipated parish ministry as their vocation, Bridston and Culver reiterated H. Richard Niebuhr's earlier concern that there was as yet no clear cut idea of the purpose of the theological school (ibid., 154–155).

The Feilding Study in 1966 reported on developments in theological education such as continuing education, the doctor of ministry degree, more rigorous supervision of fieldwork, emphasis on professionalism, increasing demands from the churches, and improvements in mass communication. However, the study also revealed that little had changed from earlier studies. Theological education was still criticized as irrelevant, bound by tradition, hindered by denominationalism, and threatened by change. Charles Feilding's words in the introduction to his report are prophetic: "The study was undertaken during a period of unusual ferment in theological education which is likely to continue for a long time to come. It is no longer left to radical critics to announce that theological schools are in crisis, it has become a commonplace in the schools themselves" (Feilding 1966, 1). He stressed that the pace of social change required more open-minded ministers with a greater tolerance for ambiguity. His words seem to echo the concerns of churches today.

> The outlines of such an education can be seen not only in the best schools but perhaps more clearly in the working ministries of men and women who have succeeded in breaking through the adamantine barriers of moribund ecclesiastical institutions to establish renewed parishes and experiment with new ministries. The much maligned parish clergy here and there are beginning their own revolution and challenging the seminaries to send them better trained associates and leaders. Even more maligned church bureaucracies have demonstrated to schools in some instances that they can place valuable research facilities and leadership at the disposal of the educational system. (ibid., 2)

The study reported growing frustration with the university model, lack of clear purpose, theory and practice discontinuity, and a curriculum in disarray. It reflected the criticism of clergy who wondered "why their theological education did not prepare them for their work; I have heard from many of them including old students whose judgment I know well enough to trust. There are also the frustrated church leaders who cannot understand why theological schools are not grappling with the needs which seem so evident to them" (ibid., 3).

In light of these concerns, Feilding offered four goals for professional theological education: knowledge acquisition, development of professional competence, development of personal maturity, and spiritual formation. He suggested that institutions adapt their curriculum to the characteristics of students who attend; he encouraged lifelong learning goals and experiences that would equip students for life and relationships; he recommended that spouses be included in the educational process and that professors have ministry experience; and he challenged schools and churches to be more aware of issues in the world.

> How can pastoral imagery and a pre-scientific world-view be of help to the millions in teeming cities alternately threatened with

nuclear war and promised life of unlimited leisure in an automated world? Do not the writers of our own times interpret them better for us and do they not equip us better, and without illusion, to meet the possibility that life at bottom is absurd? The churches can no longer take for granted a respectful hearing for anything whatever in their traditions. Theological education isolated from those who ask such questions is useless. (ibid., 4)

The third of the surveys was sponsored by the Henry Luce Foundation and directed by Claude Welch. At the time of this study (1969–1971), the academy was under attack and facing financial crisis. However, following a 1963 Supreme Court ruling that "legitimated the formal study of religion for all United States public education," religion had "emerged vigorously in the colleges and universities as a field of studies distinct from theological training in a seminary or divinity school" (Welch 1971, vii). Observing that both public and private education were in foment, Welch's rationale for his study "arose from the judgment that the clue to the future of these changes lay in graduate education: in the training of scholars who are to be the teachers and researchers in the field" (ibid., viii). The primary focus of the study was doctoral programs in religion at sixty-nine institutions of higher education in the United States and Canada, which included fifty universities and nineteen independent theological schools (ibid., ix).

Welch's nineteen conclusions and recommendations are worth noting in light of current concerns about theological education.

1. Graduate religious education is experiencing a crisis of identity that requires a redefinition of the core material of the curriculum. Welch suggested that religious studies needed to broaden beyond the professional studies of the bachelor's or master's of divinity to include different religious traditions and to explore different methodologies: linguistic, anthropological, sociological, historical, phenomenological, and so on.

2. Greater integration is needed between graduate and undergraduate studies of religion.

3. Studies in Eastern religious traditions, Islam, African religions, and the religious experience of blacks in North America must be included.

4. Graduate study in religion needs to be strengthened by inclusion of the social sciences, including sociology, psychology, and anthropology.

5. Development of teaching competence should be included in the graduate program.

6. Dissertation research requires a more thorough understanding of existing research in the field, greater cooperation in research efforts, and better direction.

7. Master's level programs require greater definition of purpose.

8. Experimentation is needed regarding the role of religious studies in interdisciplinary programs.

9. Greater exchange of students between doctoral programs should be encouraged.

10. Inclusion of women and minorities should be encouraged.

11. Overall planning is needed, given the fact that institutions have proceeded with graduate studies in religion without consultation or review and that needless duplication of resources has resulted.

12. Doctoral programs in religion need to be an integral part of the university and freer from professional school interests.

13. Financial support for students needs to be increased and the number of students at the doctoral level reduced.

14. Given the extensive involvement of public institutions in the academic study of religion, greater attention of academic associations is required apart from church-related schools or professional interests.

15. Ways must be found to represent the study of religion in the civic community.

16. Coordination among the several regional accrediting bodies and the American Association of Theological Schools is needed for the certification of doctoral programs.

17. The different schools need to be encouraged to allocate fields of specialization and to be accountable to one another for work in their particular specializations.

18. More rigorous standards of admission should be developed and intensive training of faculty undertaken.

19. The number of existing doctoral programs in religion should be reduced and new programs begun in specific situations. (Welch 1971, 3–9)

Daryl Hart judges that Welch's report served to widen the gulf between theological education at seminaries and religious studies in the university, probably because of his emphasis on the university's ability to prepare academic scholars and his consequent de-emphasis of church-related and professional schools. Consequently, schools that were not connected to well-respected universities offering traditional theological subjects and whose purpose was the preparation of ministers were considered inferior (Hart 1992a, 214–15). Wayne Goodwin observes that Welch was heavily criticized for using poor research techniques, for favoring prestigious schools, and for allowing personal bias to affect his results. His study was the last of the surveys of theological education and was seldom referred to after 1972 (Goodwin 1989, 239, 277–90). Even if these criticisms are legitimate, Welch's recommendations for greater accountability and coordination, better admissions criteria, less duplication among programs, inclusion of a broader knowledge base, development of research competency, development of teachers, and engagement with the public sector are surprisingly similar to current concerns and recommendations.

Chapter 5

The Shaping of Academic Theology

The organization of learning around rationalistic philosophies and cognitively oriented modes of curriculum structure and presentation has a long history. Augustine (or perhaps Boethius) was the first to distinguish two parts in the curriculum of the medieval universities: the Trivium and the Quadrivium. As noted earlier, the Trivium preceded the Quadrivium and was the necessary preparation for it. It consisted of three parts: grammar—students were to learn how language functioned; dialectic—students were taught how to define terms, make accurate statements, and construct an argument; rhetoric—students practiced the art of elegant, persuasive expression. The Quadrivium followed this training in the art of thinking and communication and consisted of subjects: mathematics, literature, and so on.

The issue here is not that such a structure—involving courses that stimulate thinking and awareness of subject matter—is inappropriate and should be dismantled; many would agree that higher education today would profit from more careful attention to the skills reflected in the Trivium. The issue is that logic, reason, and mastery of intellectual skills and subject matter *in the service of developing the mind* are perceived by too many as the primary, if not the only, legitimate rationale for education.

In the High Middle Ages it seemed that only a new breed of scholar, the Scholastics, could satisfy the desire for knowledge stimulated by the revival of commerce, urbanization, and the discovery during the Crusades of the works of Aristotle, Ptolemy, Euclid, and the Greek physicians. "The twelfth-century masters were avid for new forms of knowledge and were not afraid to break with tradition in exploring them" (McGinn 1994, 369). Through the influence of these scholars, the method of rational inquiry into theology spread and changed the course of education. For three hundred years the new learning flourished in loosely structured communities, the *universitas*. The Scholastic scholars around whom the students gathered were not as interested in defending the faith as they were in rediscovering it and harmonizing it with the ideas of the newly discovered pagan philosophies. They searched the non-Christian philosophies to find ways the ancient ideas could help Christians better understand what they believed. "The Scholastics...were not radical liberals, seeking to establish a new, rational form of the Christian faith. Rather they used both ancient philosophies and traditional doctrines in new, refreshing, vital ways to make Christianity meaningful to a new age" (Roberts 1981, 114).

At the best of times, masters and students in medieval universities came together out of a desire to explore the new knowledge uncovered during the Crusades, particularly the writings of Aristotle. Gradually, as the material was set in order, categories of knowledge were developed and divisions or faculties were created. These faculties and their teachers became confined to buildings, timetables, courses, and degree specialties. A major critique of Scholasticism is that it ultimately separated knowledge and practice, spirituality and reason.

Scholastic Theology and the Universities

In time, the disciplines of arts, law, medicine, and theology were consolidated into faculties, and the now familiar institutional forms emerged.[1] In medieval universities, each of the disciplines was considered to have an essentially religious character. Theology was envisioned as the discipline that integrated the learning from all the other areas of knowledge into one whole. Secure in this ideal, some of the most brilliant doctors of the church endeavored to harmonize faith and reason. John of Salisbury, a courtesan and twelfth-century educator, is representative of this effort. He expressed concern that the liberal arts curriculum had become vastly overspecialized and argued for an integrative education that would take wisdom and virtue seriously. In his view, the liberal arts should be in conversation with theology, and moral and intellectual learning should be integrated (Colish 1998, 177).

When the medieval scholars became absorbed with the works of Aristotle, it appeared that academic theology had triumphed over monastic

---

[1] See Rüegg (1992, 26–30), for a discussion of why other faculties were not included and why these four remained the traditional faculties of the university. Probable reasons include the nature of the distinction between the liberal and mechanical sciences, a common way of thinking in these disciplines, and the presence of controlling guilds.

theology. Reason was once again the defining characteristic of humankind. Reason, not the love described by the mystics, qualified the relationship between persons and God. By the late Middle Ages, fundamental disconnects had occurred among theology, prayer, rational reflection, and monastic meditation. The tendency to treat themes in individual treatises gave way to the creation of syllabi organizing in coherent form all that students needed to know. "The goal of pedagogy was now to train professional, full time scholars with a substantive and methodological grasp of entire fields of knowledge, enabling them to push back frontiers and to define their own positions against rival views" (ibid., 265)

Many of the Scholastic theologians, Thomas Aquinas in particular, taught that divine illumination of the intellect is essential for control of the will and emotions, which in turn ensure spiritual wisdom. Aquinas believed that the intellect is derived from the soul and is therefore unaffected by the Fall and capable of achieving true wisdom. However, the idea of a superintending role of the intellect, though present in Aquinas's thinking, is not a fair depiction of Aquinas's whole thought on education and the role of the teacher.

In 1256, Aquinas delivered his inaugural address as a master at the University of Paris. Having chosen to speak about the calling of Christian teachers, he described them as those who enlighten others about the highest wisdom, the sacred doctrine that comes from God and is contained in Scripture. Aquinas argued that everyone has some awareness of God, that some can apprehend higher things through human reason, but that the highest wisdom transcends human reason and is contained in the Sacred Scripture. It is this highest wisdom that Christian teachers pass on to their students. Therefore, the highest of moral character, the capacity for sound judgment, and humility become essential characteristics of human teachers (see Jenkins 1997, 213)

For some, a notion of *theologia* rooted in the philosophy of Aquinas and other later medieval philosophers is preferable to the fragmented and specialized ways of doing theology characteristic of contemporary theological education. The *theologia* that would under gird the new curriculum is understood as the contemplation of God, a disposition of the soul that is grounded in a strengthening intellect. For others, this understanding of *theologia* tends toward elitism and exaltation of the rational, thus capturing neither the essence of theology nor providing an adequate basis for spiritual inquiry. Though these scholars and academicians are equally concerned about the specialization and fragmentation of the theological curriculum, the understanding of *theologia* as a "cognitive disposition" is not sufficient.

Hans Küng's analysis of Aquinas's struggle to understand the new Aristotelian sciences in relation to the existing Augustinian theology and philosophy is helpful at this point. Küng begins with two assertions: (1) "The spiritual basis for [Aquinas's] existence was not the study of Aristotle but the *discipleship of Christ*. This made Thomas capable of steeping himself in the philosophical thought of antiquity precisely for the sake of Christian faith" (Küng 1994, 104). (2) Aquinas believed that the task of theology, even a theology grounded in the intellect, is to let God speak (ibid., 108). These assertions anticipate Küng's conclusion that although Aquinas proposed a radically new method for theology, he did not actually create a new paradigm to do away with the Augustinian notion of the integral relationship of faith and reason.

The discovery of the whole of Aristotle's writings and the scientific methods he proposed fascinated Aquinas and led him to turn his mind to implications for theological method. The need "to prove the justification of faith alongside reason (*rationem fidei*)" as opposed to justifying reason alongside faith was a completely new challenge for Aquinas, one that "forced him to think though the relationship between faith and reason in a new, fundamental way" (ibid., 109). When the young professor Aquinas needed to expound the theological textbook of the Middle Ages, he was confronted with "the gigantic task of combining the new knowledge from ancient philosophy with scripture and traditional theology" (ibid., 106).[2] However, Aquinas undertook this task not out of some fascination with knowledge for knowledge's sake but "for the sake of people in the present,

---

[2] Küng summarizes this textbook as encompassing the "doctrine of God, the doctrine of creation, christology and the doctrine of redemption, the doctrine of the sacraments and eschatology" and makes the point that this structure and sequence have been "maintained in theological curricula down to the present day" (Küng 1994, 106).

with a theological and pastoral intent.... So Aquinas did not intend a revival of Aristotle but his transformation" (ibid., 106–7).[3]

Aquinas's procedure was to keep separate his analysis of Aristotle's philosophical and scientific reasoning and his commentaries on Augustinian theology. His conclusions that one could no longer simply rely on reference to the Bible and church tradition to answer questions of faith and that much greater use of reason and conceptual analysis was required would lead ultimately to his condemnation and excommunication in 1277. Arguing that the Creator endowed human beings with the capacity for reason, Aquinas created a rational basis for theology. The former union of theology and spirituality was challenged as Aquinas proposed two distinct modes of knowledge: what humans can know from their own reason and experience and what can be known only through revelation. Aquinas proposed that some insights can be known apart from divine revelation, because God has created human beings with the capacity to know. Faith is necessary to accept the "higher truths of revelation" (Küng 1994, 110). However, in our quest to understand *theologia* as the under girding principle of theological education, it is important to realize that though Aquinas distinguished between philosophy and theology as two different ways of knowing about God, he did not propose a *separation* of philosophy and theology. They both speak of one God, he said. Reason and faith are therefore compatible and should support one another (see ibid., 108–12). The "cognitive disposition" of Aquinas must be understood, therefore, in light of this integration of reason and faith, just as his theological method must be understood in light of his spiritual, pastoral concern and his academic argument.

One cannot presume certain understandings of *theologia* predicated on medieval thought without at least considering the implications of Küng's observations that Aquinas did not actually separate his theories from Augustinian theology, that the source for much of the rational theory of knowledge that characterizes Catholic (and Protestant) education today was the worldview of Greek antiquity, and that Aquinas was an apologist for the

---

[3]Küng notes that Aquinas's reliance on Augustine identified him not with monastic theology but with university theology—his writings were intended primarily for students and colleagues. However, Küng persists in characterizing Aquinas as having maintained the tension between writing out of pastoral concern and for university colleagues, between seeking a new rational method and commitment to letting God speak (ibid., 107–8).

church. Aquinas retained the Augustinian notions of the supernatural and the mysteries of salvation, accepting Augustine's patristic positions on matters such as the doctrine of the Trinity, redemption, and original sin while using Aristotelian categories to propose conceptions of grace. Aquinas' theological method was bound to Augustine while at the same time based on views of physics, chemistry, and biology derived from Greek antiquity that would later collapse with the discoveries of Copernicus. Aquinas served the church by constructing a theology focused on the papacy. He proposed "a *magisterial* teaching office for theologians" that was "to rest on the academic competence of the Magister" (ibid., 121). In light of these observations, one is justified in questioning the use of Thomistic philosophy as the ground for a rationally oriented, cognitively disposed, contemplative *theologia* as the way forward in theological education.

Aquinas developed theological categories that made systematic study of theology possible. The student could now go beyond the older authorities, utilizing the method of rational inquiry into matters of faith as a way to spiritual wisdom. The effects of Aquinas's philosophy (known variously as Thomism, neo-Thomism, neo-scholasticism, and perennialism) linger, along with questions as to the appropriateness of Scholastic forms of knowing for contemporary theological education. Fortunately or unfortunately, Aquinas was captivated by Aristotle's notion of forms or categories and proposed that the wisdom of God could be identified only if the appropriate categories or systems were in place. This led to Küng's judgment that "Thomas' theology—unlike the more contemplative monastic theology of the church fathers and still that of Augustine—is quite essentially a *rational university theology*, composed by professors in the *schola*, the school, and intended primarily not for the people and pastoral care, but for students and colleagues in theology" (ibid., 107).

Yet to depict Aquinas as a thoroughgoing rationalist and then to use this judgment to create cognitivist models of education is called into question by an incident during a morning mass that occurred within a few months of his death. "When [Aquinas] met his God in a consummating vision, all of the volumes on his shelf turned to straw. He had delighted in pure reason and had loved to pore over Aristotle and the Bible. For twenty-five years he had studied, taught, preached, and argued, but in a mystical moment all of that fell away" (Carmody and Carmody 1996, 22; see also Jenkins 1997). Küng acknowledges the significance of the incident but is more cautious about its motivation. "Even now people puzzle over this self-assessment and over what had happened at that service." Did Aquinas have a stroke or some other health crisis? Did this man, who was described by his contemporaries as praying constantly, have a truly ecstatic experience—a "visionary experience of heavenly glory or insight into the transitoriness of his two-storey theological system? All straw?" (Küng 1994, 124-25). Whether or not the incident can be described as a vision from God, it demonstrates that in the pre-Enlightenment, pre-scientific medieval world, the cultures of mysticism and Scholasticism were not easily separated. Rationalistic models of education and a cognitively disposed *theologia* cannot be presumed from the medieval period if we do not understand that theology and spirituality were integrally linked.

Though Dan Treier generally agrees that the problem in theological education is not a loss of the unity of theology but a loss of the unity of theology and spirituality, he stresses that the fissure between the monastics and the Scholastics was real: spirituality and reason were *not* exquisitely balanced in the pre-Enlightenment era. In effect, the method of the Scholastics and monastic spirituality ultimately separated, as that which was prized in the cloister could not be sustained in the university. Unfortunately, the fissure opened out into a chasm between reason and piety in the Enlightenment. Treier warns against the temptation to claim that the pre-Enlightenment scholars and monastics had it right and that we simply need to recover a lost synthesis. The more appropriate perspective is that the pre-Enlightenment ideal *respected the possibility* of a unity between the path of reason and the path of love and that the present effort is to recover that possibility without necessarily rejecting altogether the gains of the Enlightenment era.[4]

Evidence of the fissure can be found in the fact that though the ideal of many in the medieval universities was to bring together student and master for the highest of intellectual training, where society would be improved by the practical application of knowledge, the university system, at least after its golden age, seemed to develop the intellect at the expense of creativity and imagination. "For the fairly competent student the main defects of a medieval education may be summed up by saying that it was at once too

---

[4]From a personal conversation, Wheaton College, Wheaton, Ill.

dogmatic and too disputatious" (Rashdall 1936b, 453). It seems that theological study and piety were seldom integrated at the level of instruction and that student life was typically lacking in moral and spiritual quality. The educational method "ignored the imagination and the senses and produced men of capacious memory and mental subtlety who were nevertheless often vicious and uncouth" (Lawson 1967, 50).

On the other hand, the broader university life of the Middle Ages was not divorced from spirituality. Communal religious life was encouraged in university settings, and monastic orders created houses to protect monks in the university from the abuses of townspeople. No doubt some of these settings were characterized by authentic piety and spirituality. William Courtenay cites evidence that study of the Bible was central in universities and that theological students were required to have attended lectures on the Bible for several years before they attained the bachelor of theology (Courtenay 1987, 111). Though some of these practices were likely as perfunctory and secular as similar exercises that can be found in modern divinity schools and seminaries, a warm, genuine piety was probably present.

A case can be made that the project of the Scholastic theologians was not to separate theology, spirituality, reason, emotion, and volition. To stereotype Scholasticism as the polar opposite of spirituality is unfair. The quest was not to *create* a rational understanding of knowledge or a rational theological method; rather, the quest was to make sense of the "new" sciences and perspectives from the writings of Aristotle in relation to the former knowledge. Even Aquinas was not disposed to abandon Augustine and the patristic conceptions of Christian thought. That project would be the task of a later age. However, even with these tendencies toward what today would be described as a more holistic understanding of knowledge, Scholasticism became narrow and excessively disputatious, its method captured in forms that persist to the present. The legacy of the medieval universities is clearly evident in the forms and practices of the modern university. In spite of developments in the Renaissance and Reformation eras, North American universities continue to retain the shape of the medieval university while being influenced by the English college emphasis on the shaping of the mind for character formation and by the German universities' emphasis on research and professionalism.

One does wonder whether the educational movements and reforms of the Renaissance and Reformation would have been necessary, or would have been as radical in their scope, if the Scholastic universities had been able to forge a more coherent and widespread synthesis of spirituality and reason in their instructional practices and curriculum.

The New Universities of the Renaissance and Reformation

The Renaissance humanists sought out the *paideia* and *humanitas* of the ancient world, attempting to recover it and embrace it without "scholastic and ecclesiastical overlays" (Manchester 1992, 104). Men and women responded to what they perceived as the fresh teachings, ideals, and attitudes of the Renaissance scholars. Universities, rejuvenated by the new *humanitas*, were once again crowded; books circulated, and the old learning was replaced by the new humanism. The humanists attacked the popes, the monks, and the Scholastics. According to A. G. Dickens, humanism can be credited with "altering the mental map of Europe" in the fifteenth and sixteenth centuries (Dickens 1994, 89), especially after the invention of the printing press made it possible for the social and religious opinions of the humanists to filter down to the masses. The humanists were described as energetic analysts of their own and preceding cultures. Through the sixteenth century, they dominated the schools and fostered among their students a desire to document all evidence and to study materials and issues in relation to their historical and cultural settings, free from specious Scholastic interpretation, allegory, and clerical inventions. It was inevitable that these methods, refined on the ancient classic texts, would come to be applied to the Scriptures (ibid., 90).

The Scholastic tradition did not interest a population that had declared its independence from the authorities of society and church. "Behind Renaissance education lay the optimistic presupposition that the world was susceptible to understanding and control. Through education the mind can be trained to understand, the will can be persuaded to choose good. With a few notable exceptions, [the humanists] believed that through learning people could improve themselves and their world" (Grendler 1989, 410; see Oberman 1981, 267).

It is precisely at this point that the different emphases of the Reformation become interesting. Luther and the Reformers who shared his passion were concerned, among other things, about the renewal of lay piety. "Those reformers who considered the educational aspirations of the Renaissance as both a signal and a basis for a renewal of the church concentrated their attack on the *enforced ignorance* of the common folk and transformed the preaching of the gospel into a pedagogical mission" (Oberman 1981, 188). In general, the Reformers adapted the fourfold structure of the universities (arts, law, medicine, and theology) for the training of the clergy. The emphases of the Reformation required new content and outcomes for theological education, and most of the Reformation leaders were active in developing academies or programs of study for the new ministers, with more emphasis on preaching and the study of Scripture than on patristic and medieval theology. Luther expected ministers to be university trained and "able to exegete scripture, defend the gospel's true message, and assess the quality of dogmatic positions" (Goodchild 1992, 1,211).

Thus challenged by the Renaissance humanists and the Reformers, the church could no longer dominate its clerics or the universities. Theology ceased to be the integrating discipline in the university. In the universities' newly envisioned curriculum, arts, law, medicine, and theology became separate disciplines.[5] Once the Renaissance humanists separated the four faculties of the university from one another, theology never recovered its position as the foundational discipline that gave meaning to the others. The universities of the fifteenth and sixteenth centuries, for the most part, fell back into the pedantry of the late Scholastic period.

Using the University of Tübingen as a case study, Heiko Oberman describes the consequences for universities that were unable to recognize the implications of the simultaneous development of a popular lay piety and the emergence of an urban populace that was increasingly culturally and intellectually alert. In the sixteenth-century world, "the universities received a public image still popular today. They were caricatured as arrogant, irrelevant, anti-social and reactionary.... Thus, when the master craftsmen gained control of city hall, they too took measure of the academic masters' gowns and, not surprisingly, discovered them to be mere cosmetic coverings for minds distended by arrogance" (Oberman 1981, 266).

Through the seventeenth century, there was no shortage of criticism of the university and many suggestions for reform. For example, it was said

---

[5]Colin Brown identifies this separation as the beginning of modern secularism and as the first opportunity for the disciplines to each have their proper function (Brown 1990, 139). Other contemporary critiques would suggest that this laid the groundwork for the ensuing specialization and fragmentation of the disciplines.

that universities should prepare people for the service of the Commonwealth, that theological studies should be curtailed or abolished altogether, that students had become negligent and profane. Several complained that universities contributed more to the corruption of students than to their piety (Greaves 1969, 42–45). Debates between the religious Puritans and more experimentalist reformers about how to remedy these problems continued through the seventeenth century. In keeping with the growing experimentalism of the time, some reformers recommended eliminating many of the traditional subjects and increasing emphasis on the study of mathematics, the natural sciences, and some foreign languages. They attributed the problems in the universities to excessive reliance on theory and disputation, foreign and/or dead languages, and the antiquities.

Schleiermacher and the Founding of the University of Berlin

In 1809, at a time when the university was widely perceived as a failed enterprise, the University of Berlin was founded as a place where professors and students were free to seek truth. Impartial investigation, research, and teaching were considered the most important functions of a university, and faculty were expected to maintain the delicate balance between their roles as teacher and researcher. The fruit of research was to enrich teaching, and teaching was to give purpose to research. This balance was necessary to engender within students the "spirit of search and research," ensuring that their specialized studies would not be limited "to the narrowly technical or the dogmatically prescribed" (Stroup 1984, 157). Accordingly, the founders of the University of Berlin resisted the favored practice of dividing the university into specialized departments; instead they sought to develop an educational climate that represented the totality of knowledge. The university was to be a place where young minds were awakened to the interconnectedness of knowledge, which in turn would make specialized study possible (ibid., 156–57; Sykes 1982, 104). The founders also felt that seekers of knowledge should not be constrained by looking first for its usefulness, for once usefulness is determined, the quest for knowledge ceases. Friedrich Schleiermacher affirmed philosophy as the highest science that connects and unifies all knowledge. These ideals are significant in light of how German university methods influenced North American universities and, subsequently, theological schools.

Faced with the impending removal of the theological department from the university because it did not fit the new scientific paradigm, Schleiermacher undertook the task of recasting theology as a theological science. His 1830 *Brief Outline on the Study of Theology* (hereafter the *Outline*; see Schleiermacher 1966) set out his rationale for the place of theology in the university. However, his concern for the revitalization of theology in the university paralleled his concerns to revitalize religion for the ordinary person who had become weary of religion, and to restore religion to the intellectual life of the time. In order to touch the lives of people in his culture, he recast religion as intuition and feeling. He defined religion as a holy experience, that which happens when souls are touched by the infinite in the deepest part of their being (Küng 1994, 167).

Schleiermacher wished above all else to be a "convincing Christian." He was active as a theologian with an impressive interdisciplinary education and as a lecturer, administrator, and political activist. He was pastor to a congregation and a public preacher. For him, religion was a matter of life and heart that must be expressed in a totality of being, not just in thinking. This passion is in the background of Schleiermacher's efforts to redefine theology for the German university and qualifies Edward Farley's criticism of Schleiermacher's legacy as the "clerical paradigm." Farley claims the shift that resulted from Schleiermacher's articulations was from "study which deepens the heartfelt knowledge of divine things to scholarly knowledge of relatively discrete theological sciences" (Farley 1983a, 10). To blame this shift entirely on Schleiermacher, however, is to miss the lingering effects of his pietistic upbringing on his conceptualization of the model for the German university,[6] and the effects of the American context on the subsequent development of the university and seminary in the United States in particular.

In the *Outline* Schleiermacher defined theology as a "positive science" whose methods of study and organization are rational and orderly. With the use of these methods, a "particular kind of knowledge" is assembled which can be verified in experience (Schleiermacher 1966, 14). His safeguard against the problem this presented was to ground the formation of judgments on the basis of one's experience in the ecclesial, corporate nature of Christianity. The church is therefore the proper context for theology, and the purpose of theological study is to develop leadership for the church (ibid., 16, 20). For Schleiermacher, theologian and church leader should unite in one person. Without this integration the theologian "would merely be engaged in working over various theological subjects in the spirit of whatever particular science is proper to them. Likewise the clergyman's activity would lack both the skill and the foresight of good leadership, degenerating into a mere muddle of attempted influence" (ibid., 22). Only when pastor and theologian are united in one person can the true purpose of theology, as the "reflection upon God's presence with his people," be realized (ibid., 117). Similarly, integration of all the theological disciplines is necessary if the task of theology is to be achieved. The church will be

---

[6]Schleiermacher was influenced in his early years by the Pietism of the Moravian Brethren. In later years he would reject Pietism, but its effects lingered as he synthesized later influences into his theological perspectives. His early pietistic influences battled with his acceptance of Enlightenment rationalism as propounded at the University of Halle. While a student at Halle, Schleiermacher absorbed the writings of Plato and a new writer, Immanuel Kant. "For him, too, pure reason has no competence outside the horizon of human experience" (Küng 1994, 159; see also DeVries 2001, 329–49). Schleiermacher had abandoned the pietism of his youth and yet could not embrace Enlightenment rationalism wholeheartedly. He continued to believe that there is a "last mystery" not accessible to reason (Küng 1994, 159). At twenty-eight years of age he took a post as a hospital chaplain in Berlin. The six years of this ministry proved a formative experience. His experiences with pietism and rationalism were reexamined through his chaplaincy and by his passion to be the people's pastor and shaped his later conceptions of theology and the theological task. Undoubtably, he was aware of the educational philosophy of Comenius (seventeenth bishop of the Moravian Brethren and one of history's most notable educators) and his efforts to create a "great didactic," a compilation of all knowledge that would allow men and women to engage in productive discourse. Schleiermacher likely read, or was familiar with, Comenius's *The Great Didactic*.

edified by its leadership only to the degree that all the theological disciplines are interrelated.

Schleiermacher succeeded in retaining theology as a field of study within the university. Was the cost of his success too high? Abraham Kuyper (c. 1837–1920) differed from Schleiermacher in asserting that though theology is tied naturally to the church, the church's needs can never dictate the nature of theology. The church can advocate for the inclusion of those studies necessary to maintain its life, "provided she does not presume to determine in what way her requirement shall be met" (Kuyper 1954, 617). This insistence reflected Kuyper's view that any division of theology, any outside attempt to determine how it should be taught or applied, potentially destroys its essential organic nature. Kuyper also maintained that a proper link between theology and spiritual reality is necessary. Without this link, rationalism attacks theology at its heart, or theology disappears in sentiment or mysticism. "For this reason the theologians of the best period of the Reformation ever insisted strenuously and convincingly upon the linking together of the theology to the Word, to the Church, and to personal enlightenment; for in these three factors together is found the guidance of the Holy Spirit, without which no theology can flourish" (ibid., 625).

As pastor, teacher, and theologian, Schleiermacher reacted against what he saw as intolerant orthodoxy in the religious institutions of his day. He argued that in humanity there is an inner God-consciousness operative at the deepest level of human emotion, that religion is rooted in deep emotions such as those aroused by poetry or song, and that the purpose of preaching and the task of theology is to stimulate this God-consciousness (Cross 1911, 106–9; Weborg 1978, 45). He stressed the nature of religious life as a *community* life, the truth of the faith as unknowable apart from the community, and the work of the Holy Spirit mediated within the community (G. Cross 1911, 332; Weborg 1978, 45–46). Reinhold Niebuhr underscored the importance of this concept when he described Schleiermacher's view of theology as the "disciplined and critical thinking of those men to whom has fallen the responsibility for guiding and vocalizing the common life shared by believers.... If the thinking of such men is shorn of its relationship to that common life and its needs, the content of their thinking can no longer be called theology, and its elements fall to the lot of the other sciences" (Niebuhr 1962, 23).

The tensions reflected in the positions of Kuyper and Schleiermacher persist in present theological education and are implicit in any discussion of the role of theological education in relation to the church and of the role of theology in relation to the academy. The role of theology in the academy would retain some of the influences of its Continental and British parentage, but would be shaped in unique ways as higher education took root in North America.

Theology and Education in Colonial America

Max Weber, considered the father of modern democracy, theorized that organizations can be united by a charismatic leader, common beliefs, *and* hierarchical relationships in which each part can perform a task without needing to be aware of the whole and without recourse to purposes. "It was a theory perfectly suited to the industrial age, an age that sought identical results in operations performed time after time, no matter who performed them" (Vest 2000, 64). Nicholas Wolterstorff delineates two major factors that Weber felt were the essence of modernization: (1) Differentiated spheres of activity free art, economics, law, ethics, science, and so on from the external control of the church and state. *Wissenschaft,* or 'scientific' research, is among these liberated spheres of activity.[7] (2) Once the spheres are liberated, Weber said, the activity within each sphere is autonomous, each possessing its own inner logic. Rationalization is the essential dynamic of sphere activity, "oriented as that thought is toward prediction, grounded as it is in sensory experience, and intertwined as it is with technology.... Characteristic of the modern academy in general has been a regnant understanding of the structure or, if you will, 'the logic' of well-formed *Wissenschaft*" (Wolterstorff 2002, 6; see also Wolterstorff 2004, 172–87).

Wolterstorff adds that the fundamental characteristic of well-formed *Wissenschaft* is that learning is generically human. That is, it has to be without bias or subjectivity; it is objective. The curriculum that resulted from

---

[7]David Kelsey avers that to translate *Wissenschaft* as "science" is misleading because the word in English generally connotes the physical sciences. He suggests that *Wissenschaft* is better understood as disciplined critical inquiry. The paideia model used critical inquiry but acknowledged certain sources as unquestioned authorities. However, critical inquiry (*Wissenschaft*) in the research university "requires that no alleged authoritative source of truth, either sacred or secular, be exempt from rigorous testing of its veracity" (Kelsey 1992, 84).

this view was a hierarchy of disciplines—the sciences at the top, humanities at the bottom, the social sciences someplace in the middle, and theology changing places depending on by whether the shapers of a curriculum considered it a rational enterprise. Therefore it was critical for the university to propose that Christianity is rationally grounded. As Christianity moved to the margins of academic rationality in ensuing years, theology came to have little or no place in the academy. But Wolterstorff believes that the self-understanding of the modern university as a well-formed *Wissenschaft* has been shattered in recent years. Scientific progress does not proceed by a systematic application of the scientific method—it is more intuitive than that. As the "regnant self-understanding" crumbled, so too did the structure of disciplines. The humanities, for example, are no longer inferior to the sciences, and learning is not as objective as first believed. As a new self-understanding for the academy is coming to birth, scholarship grounded in religion will, affirms Wolterstorff, have a place (Wolterstorff 2002, 6–8; see Marsden 1997).

Mark Schwehn, in his turn, identifies Weber's address at Munich University in 1918 as a key influence in the shaping of a rationalistic view of knowledge in the German universities and hence in the universities of North America. Weber defined the academic vocation as a rational, detached enterprise where scholars attempted to advance knowledge by research and study in their specialized disciplines. The cost of maintaining this rigorous specialization is that inquiry into the wholeness of things and the meaning of human life cannot and should not be carried out by the academy (Schwehn 1993, 10). Weber argued that coherence in the specialized disciplines is possible, because the separate and specialized vocations (that presumably derive from these specialized disciplines) would be orchestrated according to God's purpose. Human beings could therefore find meaning in their individual vocation, trusting God to know the total framework and to order the world accordingly. Schwehn cites this argument to support the notion that Weber's understanding of the purpose of specializations is no longer viable for the academy—if it ever was. There is no longer the sense of a larger whole orchestrated by God. More significant, in the absence of any larger framework, *the making of knowledge itself becomes the chief end of the academy*. Schwehn suggests that because the making of knowledge is ultimately unsatisfying as an academic vocation, the modern university seeks meaning in community service or in a revisitation of the ideal of character formation (ibid., 13–16).

In a later work, Schwen argues that the historical synthesis of religion and higher education can be regained and offers a proposal to counter what Weber had so effectively undermined—the true purpose of academic inquiry. Where Weber posited that *making* knowledge is the purpose of the academy and that knowledge is based on an instrumental rationality whose end is mastery of the world, Schwen proposes that the purpose of the academy become inquiry into truth. Instead of Weberian mastery of the world through rationality, academics ought to "seek understanding of the world through communal inquiry" stimulated by the "affections of awe, wonder, and gratitude that together constitute piety." Schwehn then offered that the "the means-end rationality that defined the academic mind for Weber" be replaced or absorbed "into a far more capacious epistemology that views qualities of character, mind, and spirit as integrally related to one another" (Schwehn 2002, 55).

Schwehn may have overstated the reversion in the German universities to a purely objective, highly specialized form of education (which replaced an earlier emphasis on character formation). The emerging concept of professional education in the German universities was probably a complex mixture of earlier ideals regarding holistic education and the emerging emphases on specialized research. However, his observation that a purely objective research model grounded in specialized disciplines could not be sustained in the North America universities, shaped as they were by the English college traditions of liberal learning and character formation, by the influence of seventeenth-century religious movements, and by the German professional model, is no doubt accurate.

Before German university enthusiasts brought the research model to America (where Schleiermacher's original vision for the university was significantly altered by factors within the new cultural context), the English college ideal would be the first to shape the emerging culture of the American university. Puritans in England, dissatisfied with the quality of preaching and the spiritual vitality of ministers, agitated for the removal of clergy they considered unfit for the pulpit (Gambrell 1937, 11–12).[8] Through the early 1600s, they petitioned the Crown for reform in ministerial education, despite the fact that in 1603 nearly half the clergy held university degrees and the monarchy had passed legislation for reforming ministerial education. The real issue of concern was the growing number of lay clergy. Influential Puritans considered a university-trained clergy a necessity and appealed to English law, which prohibited anyone from occupying the pulpit who was not properly ordained (which included university credentials).[9]

However, in 1650 advocates for the uneducated lay clergy disputed the view that a university education is a qualification for the ministry and argued that there is no distinction between ordained and lay clergy, that all who are so gifted have the right to preach publicly. Some, believing that education in theology causes the minister to glory in academic achievements, suggested that the study of theology be abolished from the universities (Greaves 1969, 18). The controversy raged through the 1650s, with both supporters and opponents of lay clergy found among the heads of colleges as well as among the clergy. In an analysis of the gradual disengagement of the colleges from their sponsoring churches, James Burtchaell argues that pietism was a causative factor in the growing separation of religion and learning.

---

[8]Puritan ideals concerning the ministry and ministerial preparation were laid out in two books. Richard Baxter, in *The Reformed Pastor* (1655), developed the ideal of the Puritan ministry. In his advice to clergy he stressed a balance between spirituality and rigorous academic training. Jonathan Edwards, in *The Preacher* (1705–1709), outlined the course of studies he considered necessary for ministerial preparation.

[9]Though it is apparent that the tradition of a university education for ordination persisted in New England, an individual could be ordained only if called by a local congregation. "The people in the local community conferred the office upon the individual, and, once ordained, the minister became a central figure in that community. He was the glue that held the community together" (Wind and Lewis 1994, 228). By the early eighteenth century, ministers had adopted an identity as one separate from the community. (The fact that they were better educated than most was seen by some as the major contributing factor in this distancing and fueled arguments against an educated clergy.) Ministerial associations were formed, which increased the ministers' sense of themselves as a special clerical class. However, congregations still wielded authority over the clergy, who, began to see themselves as an *embattled* special class (ibid., 228). The struggle for control tended to alienate clergy and congregation, effectively eroding the seventeenth-century relation of the minister to the community.

Religion's move to the academic periphery was not so much the work of godless intellectuals as of pious educators who, since the onset of pietism, had seen religion as embodied so uniquely in the personal profession of faith that it cannot be seen to have a stake in social learning. The radical disjunction between divine knowledge and human knowledge had been central to classical Reformation thinking, and its unintended outcome was to sequester religious piety from secular learning. The older pre-Reformation view, that faith was goaded by revelation to seek further understanding, and that learning itself could be an act of piety…succumbed to the view that worship and moral behavior were to be the defining acts of a Christian academic fellowship. Later, worship and moral behavior were easily set aside because no one could imagine they had anything to do with learning. (Burtchaell 1998, 842)

The Puritans rejected Scholastic theology, but they did not feel it necessary to reject the entire Scholastic curriculum. They continued to require scholastic disputations for all undergraduates and retained the Scholastics' juxtaposition of spirituality and reason. However, the "Puritan instructors at Cambridge were really interested less in making their students scholastic disputants than preachers. Sermons were the subject of emphasis, with the primary authority being the Bible rather than Aristotle and his fellow ancients. Presumably the entire range of subjects in the curriculum was examined with a view to the application of that knowledge to ministerial duties" (Greaves 1969, 11). The Puritans shared with the Reformers a belief that the chief function of the clergy is to expound the Scriptures. Through preaching. the soul is stimulated to commune with God; edification will be achieved through attention to good preaching. Only a spiritual person who has experienced rigorous academic training can offer this kind of preaching.

The Puritans believed that after the New Testament age the Spirit had ceased to impart knowledge by extraordinary means. Therefore, a university-trained mind is essential to discern the knowledge revealed by the Spirit and to communicate this knowledge clearly to others. However, Greaves notes that the more conservative Puritan epistemology "was not truly rational, neither was it truly intuitive (ibid., 115). If something was beyond the power of reason to understand, the Puritans relied on authority to resolve the difficulty. Reason and Spirit were not to be disjoined; though knowledge gained through the Spirit was compared to reading a book by sunlight, and knowledge gained from reason to reading the same book by candlelight (ibid., 115). Other Puritan reformers urged their readers to subordinate reason to faith to such an extent that dependency on reason ceased. They believed that the Spirit can give wisdom by extraordinary or mystical means. They criticized the emphasis on reason and the educational system that trained for it. Knowledge available from personal spiritual experience is superior to reason, they argued, and this knowledge is available to the educated and uneducated alike (ibid., 116–25). However, it was the more conservative Puritan idea of the university that prevailed through the nineteenth century and, in a sense, prepared the way for acceptance of the German scientific and professional approach to theological study in North American schools.

As the Puritans and other groups emigrated to North America, they inspired a culture whose everyday language and affairs were rich with biblical allusions understood by all. In a sense, the Bible became the common language for all the immigrant groups as they looked for principles that would bind them together into a new nation. Because of this religious culture, the core values of virtually all the institutions established in America in the seventeenth and eighteenth centuries were patently religious. Debates concerning reason and faith, theology and science, though present in the seventeenth century, would not seriously distress the schools and denominations of North America until the nineteenth century.

The Great Awakenings of the 1730s and 1740s, which followed on the heels of Newtonian empiricism, created tensions and fostered new initiatives in clergy education. The revivals "forced the clergy to acknowledge that their power and prestige did not come from ordination or membership in a ministerial association; rather it came from their ability to work with their people as pastors" (Wind and Lewis 1994, 229). Clergy who were not seen to have a "converted heart" (as opposed to merely a clever mind) were deserted by their congregation. But it is also clear that clergy who sensed that their congregation was not responsive to the themes of the revivals would desert it and become itinerant preachers. Prompted by the spirit of the revivals, some rejected appeals for a university-educated clergy and established schools for the training of revivalist preachers. In response, laws were passed declaring that only those educated at Harvard, Yale, or another approved institution could receive financial benefits (Gambrell 1937, 33). Overall, the universities were challenged by the religious enthusiasm of the revivals, encroaching liberalism, and the criticism of those such as George Whitefield, who believed the university could no longer produce ministers of vital spiritual character and preaching. Denying Whitefield's charges, leaders of the schools warned students against the excesses of the revivals.

Then, in response to the Unitarian takeover of Harvard in 1805, Andover Theological Seminary was formed in 1808 as "the first American Congregationalist institution whose sole purpose would be training for the ministry" (Gambrell 1937, 37).[10] Here ministers would not be "contaminated" by the swirling doctrinal controversies of the time and the impoverishment of theology in the universities. In 1811, Harvard established a program of advanced studies in theology,[11] but this was not sufficient to turn back the tide of protest that had led to the founding of Andover (Goodwin 1989, 204–5).

While some such as Jonathan Edwards—a significant voice during the revivals and representative of the educational ideals of Puritanism—stressed the value of learning doctrine, history, languages, the sciences, and philosophy, leaders in the growing Baptist and Methodist groups added their voices to those warning against the dangers of an educated clergy. The value of learning prevailed. Of eight hundred ministers ordained between 1740 and 1810 in New England, fewer than twenty were not at least college educated—even though some felt that the quality of ministerial education had declined since the seventeenth century (Gambrell 1937, 52).

Following the revivals of the early eighteenth century, the American Revolution created a nation—and a populace that considered itself capable of independent thought and action. Enthusiasm for political independence and growing religious fervor, expressed through burgeoning religious movements and revivals, were equally characteristic of the early decades of

---

[10] The University of Berlin was founded a year later. It would be some years before the influence of the German research university model, over against or alongside the English college ideal and Pietism, would be felt in North America.

[11] Harvard had established a chair of divinity in 1721 to accommodate the need for advanced study in theology and to provide a framework for the mentoring of students by an experienced pastor (Goodwin 1989, 202). This two-year program marked the consolidation of a separate department for theological study.

the new republic. The traditions of Western society were challenged by the populist spirit, which in turn affected the church. With increasing involvement of "common people" in political and religious matters, a delicate tension developed in relation to ecclesiastical authority. It was not usual to give laypeople institutional ecclesiastical authority. Yet laypeople and unlearned populist preachers were free to express their opinions about church matters, and many exerted considerable influence in ecclesiastical matters. After the Revolution, an untutored religious leadership became normative. Though Nathan Hatch acknowledges the almost paradoxical situation of a populist spirit amid the authoritarian church hierarchies of the Methodists and others, he asserts that the church operated within its authoritarian structures in such a way as to allow an "illiterate laity to experience some degree of freedom of religious expression" (Hatch 1989, 9–11). Likely the populist spirit made any repression of the illiterate clergy ill advised. The hierarchy seemed to be able to control the structures of their denominations and their churches, but they could not control surges of religious fervor or the free-ranging popular preachers who found pulpits and a crowd wherever they chose to stand. In this climate, people were less inclined to defer to an educated elite composed of clergy and learned theologians. Tradition was less of a controlling factor in religious experience. Further, the religious experiences of the people were less subject to the "scrutiny of orthodox doctrine and the frowns of respectable clergyman" (Hatch 1989, 10).

Clearly, the American Revolution stimulated a new vision with regard to the nature of ministerial leadership and church authority, as well as concerns about the effectiveness of academic theology. The style of the German research university was poised to almost overwhelm the influence of the English college tradition, while concerns about the erosion of theology in the university stimulated the development of the seminaries. The university divinity school, and a new era in academic theology, would come into prominence in the midst of these changes.

The Compartmentalization of Academic Theology

Noah Porter, president of Yale University from 1871 to 1886, defended the idea that the college should have a distinctly Christian character in order to counter atheistic tendencies in science, literature, and culture. In college, students should learn habits of character and culture that would remain with them throughout life, he said, and the capacity to think was to be preferred over the acquisition of special knowledge (professional) knowledge. Porter assumed that students would come to Yale with a faith learned in home and church. At the college, they would test their faith against contemporary thought in a safe environment. The result would be a faith with an intellectual basis less vulnerable to atheistic tendencies.[12] His comments were consistent with the English college traditions and hinted at the tension that would soon alter the place of theology in the university curriculum and the shape of theological education. Porter and his colleagues were determined to create a college that would serve society by nurturing in its students the full-orbed life of the scholar, with religious faith and values at its heart. This goal was not always popular: some felt that Yale should give less attention to the cultivation of a Christian gentility and more time to preparation for careers (Marsden 1994, 126; Stevenson 1986, 50–57, 64–65). George Marsden judges that in defending these ideals Porter failed to "address the issue of the relationship of Christianity to the emerging universities" (Marsden 1994, 128). In time, the colleges would become universities, and in the universities science was the new orthodoxy. The opposition and the ultimate loss of the religious ideal should not obscure the fact that Yale, from the 1840s to the mid-1880s, managed to fuse "religious faith with scholarly vocation, teaching and writing with social action, individual with social improvement, elite education for the few with democratic society for all" (Stevenson 1986, 138).

In the first half of the nineteenth century, most colleges were tied to denominations and offered religious and moral instruction. Students were housed in dormitories, where they would not be tempted by city life, "and faculty were as much concerned with their moral development as they were with their intellectual formation" (McClellan 1999, 29). Moral philosophy, taught most often by the president, was the capstone course in these colleges, and required of graduating seniors. This course sought to bring Christian ethics to bear on a variety of personal and social issues. Edward McClellan notes that "the antebellum era was remarkable for the extent to which a uniform approach to morality prevailed up and down the largely Protestant

---

[12]Porter traced the history of ideas from Immanuel Kant, Alexander Hamilton, Johann Gottlieb Fichte, and Friedrich Schleiermacher in *The Human Intellect* (1868), in an attempt to show that German thought was not a threat to Christian belief (Stevenson 1986, 69).

educational ladder" (ibid., 30). In the late nineteenth century "science began to raise new questions about conventional beliefs, but in the antebellum years, the college experience only reinforced the basic values that children had first learned at their mother's knees" (ibid., 29–30). Students who sought other intellectual traditions often had to go outside the prescribed curriculum; some even created student-run libraries to stock Enlightenment texts.

However, the effort to maintain a clerically controlled classical education mixed with some modern courses and crowned by a course in moral philosophy taught by the president had collapsed by the end of the nineteenth century (Marsden 1994, 89).[13] The increase of discrete disciplines, the fragmentation of the curriculum, the splintering of the moral philosophy course into its subdivisions of ethics, psychology, sociology, and political science meant that there was no one capstone course that would focus issues of moral decision for students. Change was apparent as early as the 1870s, when the expansion of knowledge and a growing demand for professional training began to shatter the tightly prescribed curriculum that had characterized higher education in the antebellum era. The ancient dream of a broadly educated people who could integrate the spheres of learning and develop a comprehensive view of the world quickly disappeared as a new generation of educators emphasized the production of new knowledge and preparation of students for specific careers. As research and specialization became the dominating ideals of the universities, educators found it increasingly difficult to integrate intellectual and moral concerns, and character

---

[13]Marsden notes that Scottish Common Sense Realism dominated American colleges in the nineteenth century. This philosophy held that "God's truth was a single unified order and that all persons of common sense were capable of knowing that truth" (Marsden 1980, 14). Marsden suggests that the Princeton view of truth, for example, "was based on the assumption that truth is known by apprehending directly what is 'out there' in the external world, not a function of human mental activity. The mind discovers objective truth, which is much the same for all people all ages" (ibid., 114). However, the Common Sense view of knowledge finally collapsed in the face of the commonsense observations that "if truth is so objective and common sense so reliable, how does one account for the wide prevalence of error?…How is it that there are so many rational and upright people of good will who refuse to see the truth which consists of objective facts that are as plain as day?" As confidence in objective knowledge was shaken, cultural and religious diversity gradually began to erode the "Anglo-Saxon Protestant religious and moral consensus" (ibid.).

education moved to the margins of higher education in all but the most religious of the colleges (McClellan 1999, 63).

English college traditions and ideals had dominated early Colonial American education. However, by the end of the nineteenth century, the German research university method of teaching and research in the service of professional development had come to define the major American universities. Theology and ministerial education were deemphasized as the administrators of the new universities came to believe that the purpose of higher education is to prepare persons for public life (Kuklick 1985, 197). The leaders of the new research universities were convinced that religion cannot provide the structures of knowledge needed for a technological and pluralistic culture. Both George Marsden and Daryl Hart note that Daniel Gilman, the founding president of Johns Hopkins, was a "serious liberal Christian" who had studied theology in the 1860s and received a license to preach from the Congregationalist Church. After his retirement, he served as vice president of the American Bible Society and is said to have appreciated its broad ecumenism and its contribution to the elevation of human society (Marsden 1991, 91; Hart 1992b, 108). The seeming contradiction between the new administrators' efforts to dismiss theology and clerical emphases from the universities and their religious affirmations may be better understood in light of Hart's observations that Gilman had early rejected the "technicalities of theology" with its impracticalities and abstractions, in favor of a religion that could address everyday concerns, and that presidents such as Gilman, and Charles W. Eliot at Harvard, could view scientific inquiry as "so morally demanding that it became religiously fulfilling" (Hart 1992b, 109).

Since theology was no longer viewed as an organizing principle for the curriculum, they could assign the work of religion to what they felt were its appropriate agencies—divinity schools—while planning for the universities to play out their own envisioned roles in society. Protestant leaders were able to accept this compartmentalization because most university presidents and many faculty affirmed that university study can encourage virtue and that the goals of scientific inquiry and religion go hand in hand. Through the universities, professional ministers would have access to advanced learning and the latest in professional development. "And by finding a home in the intellectual centers of the nation, the divinity schools could absorb the exciting climate of diverse outlooks and still bring the unifying perspective of religion to the diversified city of the university" (Cherry 1995, 295). This vision of professionalism would founder, however, in the academic climate of the university.

CHAPTER 6

The Emergence of Professionalism in Theological Education

In lectures presented about the year 1800, Johann Gottlieb Fichte outlined his ideal for the university. Departing from the ideals of Immanuel Kant, Friedrich Wilhelm Humboldt, and Friedrich Schleiermacher, he intended to eliminate all professional courses from the curriculum. Such courses were more appropriately assigned to "special institutes separate from the university and under the direction of experienced professional men and officers of the state" (Lilge 1948, 49). Though his views were unpopular and ultimately ignored, Fichte may have been prophetic in his concern that "university study would be so crowded by practical requirements and technical courses that the general theoretical disciplines would suffer progressive amputation and students' imaginations would be crushed by factual information. As educational developments since have shown, his fear was not unjustified" (ibid., 49).

The notion of the profession has its origin in medieval orders, where it meant "to be professed in vows," set apart as special agents of the faith (Westerhoff 1982, 158; Miller 1991, 22; Clarke 2001, 73–79). "By the Middle Ages the 'professions' had come to connote offices defined by the act of professing authoritative knowledge and belief" (Cherry 1995, 129). In time, the professional became one who graduated from a university and was deemed able to put theory into practice. Through the Middle Ages, the professional was a cleric as well as a doctor or was a lawyer with theological knowledge foundational to professional practice. As separate professions of divinity, law, and medicine emerged, the definition of professional shifted from one who was grounded in a confession of faith to one who possessed specialized knowledge. From the twelfth to sixteenth centuries, the professions of law and medicine were grounded in either or both of the disciplines of theology and the arts (Miller 1991, 22).

Significantly, in the medieval universities, the ideal of rational inquiry into truth as the way to informed wisdom that grounds action could not be sustained (or fulfilled). Debates between mystical and Scholastic theology were subsumed by the need for answers to specific questions occasioned by controversy, and by a need of clear guidelines for pastoral administration. Scholastic theology was shaped ultimately by the practical (functional) interests of the church, and for large numbers of students the university became the door to a church vocation (LeClercq 1982, 224; Rashdall 1936b, 442–45).[1]

The polarity of theology as philosophical study versus theology as preparation for the clergy through the study of canon law was clearly evident at the Universities of Paris and Bologna from the twelfth through fourteenth centuries. The University of Bologna was the center for the study of canon law, which was essential for ecclesiastical administration. The University of Paris "possessed a unique prestige as the center of Christian philosophy and theological studies" (Dawson 1991, 189). Through the *quaestio* and public disputation, the University of Paris transformed the intellectual atmosphere of Western Christendom, at least during the golden age of Scholasticism. However, it was the University of Bologna, where clerics (studying canon law in preparation for a professional career in the church) and civilians (who studied canon law but were involved in government and science)[2] studied together, that established the pattern for professional education. In spite of John of Salisbury's[3] warning against the "Philistine view of education as a utilitarian preparation for a successful professional career" (ibid., 184), the universities did produce a group of

---

[1] Initially, theological study and a university degree were not required for entrance into the priesthood or other professions, but it could help if one had only limited ability. By the fifteenth century, "the academic degree was recognized as evidence of scholarly qualification to such an extent that it became important in the competition for appointment to ecclesiastical and secular posts" (Rüegg 1992, 22).

[2] Copernicus, a student of canon law at Bologna, worked out the calculations that became the foundation for modern astronomy.

[3] John of Salisbury was an English scholar who, after studies at the University of Paris and Chartres, became bishop of Chartres in 1176. Christopher Dawson considers him the most complete embodiment of medieval humanism, asserting that he was one of the first to recognize the value of the Aristotelian revival for transforming older scholastic disputations (questions and answers on prescribed topics approved by the church) into "a theory of science and a science of thought" (Dawson 1991, 184).

professionals who became key figures in government and church administration. Over time, the study of theology conformed to the needs of ecclesiastical administration, which contributed ultimately to the partition of the curriculum into separate disciplines, with theology no longer the common course of studies for all students.[4]

During the fifteenth and sixteenth centuries, successive wars created chaos and engendered a sense of foreboding throughout much of Europe. Unprecedented numbers of pilgrims visited shrines and read devotional literature. However, this resurgence of popular piety was often characterized by shallowness, fear, and superstition. Thousands were killed in witch hunts; thousands more flocked to shrines to touch or look at holy relics to ensure their salvation. Due to this increase in religious activity, more clergy were required who could officiate at mass. "Crash courses" inaugurated many uneducated and morally unstable men into the priesthood. Provoked by abuses perpetrated by the church and its clergy, most of the Reformers sought ways to upgrade the education of Protestant clergy. The professional development of these clergy was not yet, however, an accepted program of the university.

Tom Bloomer, the provost of the University of the Nations, once took me into the cathedral in Lausanne, Switzerland, where I stood on the very stones where Calvin's Reformed seminary *really* began. Outside, he pointed to a site, just yards from the cathedral, where archaeologists were unearthing the remains of what appears to have been an early cathedral school. Then across the street he showed me a house where committed Reformers and university faculty took it upon themselves to call out and give noncredentialed instruction to committed men who could never attend a university but who would become preachers of the Reformation. When these men were handed their diploma, their teachers said, "We are giving you your death warrant." Perhaps because of the urgent reality of their education, some believe that these nonformal educational experiences of apprenticeship to determined and godly teachers were more effective than the academic programs of theological study.

---

[4]During this period, virtually all professionals (diplomats, physicians, secretaries, architects, and so on) received ecclesiastical training.

The dominant model for professional education through the seventeenth and eighteenth centuries was apprenticeship. This mode ultimately proved unworkable, as the complexity and knowledge base of the professions increased and as the number of willing masters decreased. The professional had enough to do without taking on an apprentice. Also, the strength of the apprentice relationship was also its weakness: ministers in training were influenced by the idiosyncrasies of their mentor. In time, training was taken over by full-time teachers in professional schools, which had the effect of removing the student from the field. Since professional schools tend to be expensive, the shift from apprenticeship to formal schooling with an internship also limited access to professional fields.

Emergence of the German Research Model for Professional Preparation

In nineteenth-century Germany, Schleiermacher's vision to integrate practical theology with theology as a whole was never realized. Practical theology fragmented into a number of disparate areas, each concerned with a particular function (e.g., preaching, pastoral care). After Schleiermacher, asserts Edward Farley, practical theology became increasingly the training of persons for the *functions* of ministry. "Thus a single area of theological studies that mediated biblical and historical materials and the issue of the community of faith's self-perpetuation, world-oriented mission, and institutional tasks never developed. In other words, practical theology never has existed, and does not now exist as a discipline" (Farley 1983b, 32; see also Farley 2003).

The German research university was envisioned as a way to prepare professional leaders for the church, and an effort was made to tie that education to the larger tasks of theology. Though Farley and others characterize even the shaping of these larger theological tasks as a movement away from the earlier theological synthesis and *habitus*, Schleiermacher's vision for theological education was not what it ultimately became in the schools of North America. He could not have anticipated the pragmatism of North American churches and their desire for leaders who can *do things*. John Stroup observes that even in the University of Berlin by the 1840s, a decade after Schleiermacher's *Outline*, theological study had withdrawn from the ideals of the scientific quest and became more like an institute for training pastors (Stroup 1984, 160). Is the apparent difficulty of retaining an integrated, unified vision of theological education because it cannot happen, because we expect too much of formal schooling, or because we have wrongly envisioned the nature and purpose of theological education?

While Farley affirms a deep understanding of theological unity in Schleiermacher's writings (Farley 1983a, 93–94), he also critiques him for paving the way for the more functional clerical paradigm that, to Farley's mind, troubles contemporary theological education. Perhaps this was the fault not as much of Schleiermacher's vision as of the pragmatism of nineteenth- and early-twentieth-century North American churches and theological schools. To evaluate Schleiermacher's impact on North American theological education curriculum, it is important to understand as much as is possible the differences between North American expectations and his view of the relationship of theological education and church leadership. It would seem that Schleiermacher's idea would be more profitably examined not primarily as the thing that caused our current difficulties but as something that was intended to fulfill a particular theological vision for his own day. Even though some theological educators would quarrel with his theological views and reject aspects of his rationale for the theological curriculum, an examination of his educational design, and of the way he envisioned the interrelationship of the parts, is instructive.

A subtle shift occurred in the curricular model between the time of the Renaissance and Reformation and the work of Schleiermacher in establishing theology as a professional, scientific discipline at the University of Berlin. Although Schleiermacher didn't invent the divisions of the theological curriculum, he is often considered the founder of what has become its fourfold model. His need to justify the continuance of the department of theology at the University of Berlin led him to define theological education in a particular way, which resulted in a change in the orientation of the curricular model. Charles Wood notes that Schleiermacher has been criticized for making theology dependent on philosophy and that "his placing of both exegetical and doctrinal theology within historical theology amounted to a surrender of any stable norms for the faith." Wood believes that though this criticism is not entirely valid, it did result in a reiteration of the fourfold model, with biblical studies first in line as a safeguard against these "Schleiermacherian tendencies." The linearity developed as follows:

- biblical studies, which deals with the normative beginnings of Christianity

- historical studies, which deals with less normative though significant developments

- theological studies (particularly systematic theology), which provides a "rational account of the faith for the present moment"

- practical studies, which "ostensibly draws principles from the theoretical studies to guide ministry" (Wood 1985b, 15–16)

Schleiermacher actually proposed a threefold model with several subsections[5]: philosophical theology, which was to clarify the distinctive nature of Christianity over against other kinds of human experience; historical theology, the core of the curriculum, which "was a reflection upon God's presence with his people" (1966, 117); and practical theology, which gives order to whatever action is required in the church. Exegetical theology was a subdivision of historical theology, a study of the primitive documents of the church, including the Scriptures. This effort to accomplish a unified theological system was necessary for two reasons: (1) Schleiermacher had to justify theology as an appropriate department of study within the University of Berlin. In other words, he justified theology as a scientific discipline (orderly and cohesive) with a professional outcome (the training of church leaders). As a scientific discipline, it would also fit the character of study at the university, where the search for new knowledge and new ways of integrating that knowledge was permitted. (2) Only a unified system could produce the proper kind of church leader. "The tasks of practical theology…will be most accurately stated by the person who has most thoroughly and completely developed his philosophical theology. The most appropriate method will occur to the person whose historical basis for living in the

---

[5] Walter Wyman traces the logic of the threefold organization to the introduction of Schleiermacher's *Entwurf eines Systems der Sittenlehre* (roughly translated "Design for a Systematic Teaching of Ethics"). Following the dialectic of Being as material and Being as spiritual, Schleiermacher extrapolated two principal sciences, reason and nature, and two forms of knowing, speculative and empirical. Combining these, he created four sciences: physics, natural science, ethics, and historical science. Wyman provides this background to show that for Schleiermacher historical theology was related to historical science—that is, the empirical knowledge of a specific belief system, the Christian faith. Philosophical theology was a critical discipline connecting the "empirical data of history with the speculative knowledge of the essence of reason developed in the famous 'propositions borrowed from ethics.' And practical theology was a technical discipline, providing the 'rules of art' for church service and church government" (Wyman 1991, 105–6).

present is the deepest and most diversified" (ibid., 114). Without this careful integration, "the Church lives in confusion over its own origin and history, its own present condition, and the function of its total mission within God's purpose for the world" (ibid., 124).[6]

Abraham Kuyper criticized what he saw as Schleiermacher's arbitrary divisions and the linking of those divisions with the church. For Kuyper, the natural divisions of theology were studies centering on (1) the Holy Scriptures, (2) church history, (3) Christian doctrine, and (4) homiletics. Other divisions were unsatisfactory because they proceeded from the subject—the human mind—not from theology itself. "But by itself the assumption that there are four organic groups in the body of Divinity...is not enough. To be scientifically established, these four groups must of necessity proceed from a common principium of division" (Kuyper 1954, 628–29), which for Kuyper was the Scripture. Then the logical order of studies was bibliological, ecclesiological, dogmatological, and diaconiological, "just by *these* names and in *this* order" (ibid., 631). Kuyper, like Schleiermacher, ended his course of studies with disciplines that made the necessary bridge to the church. However, Kuyper insisted that only the term *diakonia* is compatible with the previous three divisions of study. *Practical* was not acceptable because it simply reflected technical products of the human mind, which were not related to supernatural elements.

David Kelsey describes the impact of Schleiermacher's proposal as a change in the *movement* of theological education and says that the underlying rationale for the curriculum structure changed, even though the organizational structure of theological education remained relatively unchanged (Kelsey 1992, 243–44). He argued that in early theological education (at

---

[6]Though the current fourfold configuration of the theological curriculum, and the blame for its subsequent problems, is commonly attributed to Schleiermacher (see Rowen, reflecting Farley, 1996, 98; Farley 1983a), the model has a much earlier precedent. Olav Guttorm Myklebust, in detailing the contribution of Gisbertus Voetius (1589–1676) to the formulation of a theology of missiology, notes that his model for theological studies consisted of four main sub
jects: dogmatic theology, practical theology, exegetical theology, and *theologia elentica*, which was understood by the Dutch as the "confrontation of the Christian gospel with non-Christian systems of life and thought" (Myklebust 1955, 40–41). This particular fourfold structure preceded Schleiermacher's by almost two hundred years.

least in the early medieval period and the Reformation) the movement or organizing principle of the curriculum was one's personal Christian formation in relation to Scripture. (This orientation is apparent in the early Middle Ages and the Reformation, but even then it was mixed with the practical concerns of preparing clergy for church functions.) Kelsey continues that in the seventeenth century, the organizing principle was the application of doctrines (derived from Scripture) to church leadership. He concludes that the subtle difference that resulted from Schleiermacher's work was to recast the movement of the curriculum (i.e., from early conceptions of Source to personal Christian formation, or from Source to doctrine to application of the doctrine) as a process of forming theories about Christian phenomena through research—not necessarily beginning with the Source. Resulting theories could then be applied to problems confronted in the tasks of church leadership. This conclusion is consistent with Schleiermacher's descriptions of the purpose of theology within the university. "Thereafter doing theology, which had been seen as 'sapiential,' the cultivation and exercise of the wisdom that is inherent in faith, came to be seen as a type of theorizing which could subsequently be applied to solve problems in Christian life and thought" (ibid., 244).

However, since theology and educational ideals in the medieval period and the Reformation cannot be described as *sapientia* to the exclusion of *scientia*, it is doubtful that Schleiermacher's vision caused the movement Kelsey describes. Moreover, Wyman suggests that any investigation of the nature of the study of theology is inadequate if it does not consider the implications of the shift in historical consciousness from the pre-critical, pre-Enlightenment era to the modern world through the Enlightenment. The assumptions under girding the fourfold structure during the time of the Reformers were necessarily different from the assumptions under girding the fourfold structure of the modern era (Wyman 1991, 91–92). Further, it is apparent that even the composition of the fourfold model differs from one era to another. The implication is that in comparing curricula one may need to consider more than a shift in orientation. However, irrespective of opinions concerning the movement of curricula and regardless of any difficulties with Schleiermacher's theological views, it would seem that North American theological educators generally accepted his organizing principle for the study of theology (i.e., the practice of church leadership) and retained a basic structure that would be familiar to Schleiermacher, but proceeded to envision the purpose and relationship of curriculum divisions in ways it is doubtful he ever intended.

Schleiermacher sought to retain a place for theology in the university. In his *Outline* he described theological education as a search for the totality of knowledge and the process as a balance between research and teaching. He insisted that theological skills and data divorced from the guidance of the church ceased to be theological. These convictions make it seem unlikely that he would have supported the type of theological education that is often attributed to him. Though he supported earlier conceptions of structured curriculum with his own threefold model, it is doubtful that he would have supported a curriculum design with fragmented, isolated specializations ultimately focusing on pastoral skills, in which the functions of ministry and the specializations of the curriculum override concerns for theological integration, in which schools and the church are often isolated from one another and even deeply suspicious of one another, and in which research and teaching can be separate functions.

Likely Schleiermacher did contribute to the linearity (theory to practice) of curriculum structure, because he did not seem to recognize that practice can also influence theory. Don Browning has observed, with others, that though Schleiermacher considered practical theology the crown of theology, he still assumed a movement from philosophical theology to historical theology to practical theology. Browning cites Schleiermacher's assertion in the *Outline* that the elements of theology belong together *because* they are necessary for practice. Although it appears that Schleiermacher viewed all theology as a practical task, he never allowed that congregational practice could (or should) inform philosophical and historical theology (Browning 1991, 301). For Schleiermacher, practical theology derives from "thought done elsewhere" (Burkhart 1983, 52–53), or he insisted that the *only* thing that distinguishes theology from the secular studies is theology's orientation to church leadership.

Schleiermacher's insistence has led to the concern that if theology is only as valid as the use to which it is put, it becomes susceptible to all manner of external pressure (e.g., church expectations). However, Schleiermacher himself desired that the nature of church leadership be determined by theological inquiry (Wood 1985b, 13). Further, the assumption of theory-to-practice linearity in Schleiermacher could simply be the result of confusing practice as clerical function (contemporary) and practice as piety

(Schleiermacher). It is unlikely that Schleiermacher would be concerned about reflective practice—that is more common in contemporary education. He was, however, concerned that the practice of Christian piety shape the professional activities of the minister. This nuance in his thinking was lost or deemphasized over time. In effect, the growing dominance of a three- or fourfold pattern for the curriculum led to the inference, by virtue of the positioning of the disciplines, of a theory-to-practice linearity.

In Germany, membership in a profession was tied to higher education. "The most important professions in the German states in 1860 were the traditional callings of clergyman, physician, graduate in law, and academic professor. All clergymen and professors as well as a large proportion of the legal graduates practiced their professions as officials of the church or state. Partly for this reason, private professional organizations were weak or nonexistent" (McClelland 1983, 307). The German research universities became the chief places for scientific inquiry into knowledge and the development of the professional.[7] The architects of the curriculum stressed the importance of unfettered scientific research and mandated that students should have free choice of courses, without attendance requirements or examinations, considered "schoolboy practices" of lower schools. In the desire to shape mature scholars and professionals, educational methods such as the seminar, the laboratory, and the scholarly lecture were developed (Brubacher and Rudy 1968, 175).

In time, specialized professional schools were established which both expanded and diversified German higher education. However, in the German universities a distinction was maintained between the concepts "professional" and "practical." Practical studies were rejected as the universities "accepted instead a mission of providing almost exclusively 'theoretical' training" (McClelland 1983, 312). Fritz Ringer notes that the traditional emphasis on research and teaching of German universities was rooted in a fear that the state would insist on practical learning, thus reducing them to training schools for high officials (Ringer 1979, 412). Consequently, applied research (without an integral link to "pure scholarship") came to be disparaged.

---

[7]Johann Gottlieb Fichte, Friedrich von Schelling, Friedrich Schleiermacher, and Friedrich Humboldt, founders of the University of Berlin, were among the first to articulate the necessity of teaching *and* research in the curriculum of the German university.

Many North Americans who had studied in German universities returned, determined to reform higher education in America.[8] They were convinced that the German research university offered a suitable curricular framework for the kind of professional education needed in post–Civil War America.[9] Piety and emphasis on expertise in the classics as major purposes of higher education were challenged by these graduates and by a broad demand for university training that would allow America to compete in the modern world. The implicit assumption that the purpose of Protestant higher education was to "shape the whole society according to Protestant standards" (Marsden 1992, 25) gave way before a vision of scientific progress and increasing cultural pluralism. Although Christianity in and of itself was not rejected, theology (the doctrinal formulations) and clerical authority were (ibid., 10–15).

In the theocentric culture of eighteenth-century New England, the ministry had been a public office. The "sacred office defined and sustained the community as a public" (Scott 1978, 148). However, Donald Scott notes that by the mid-nineteenth century, the church and the minister were positioned differently in society. The church, understood especially in terms of denominational affiliation, was sought out by new members of a town, but the church was less a public center than a private, devotional center. One's personal relationship with God was not correlated with one's views on social issues. Similarly, by the 1850s the clergy were no longer central to the life of the public society. By virtue of this movement from the center to the boundaries of society, the clergy became a profession "organized and defined by a set of institutions which were outside lay or public control" (Scott 1978, 155). Scott (1978), Burton Bledstein (1976), and Daniel Calhoun (1965) all refer to an emerging culture of professionalism that affected the self-perception of the professional class, including the clergy. While not at the center of public life, clergy were recognized as occupying a particular

---

[8]Germany was one of the few places to go for graduate study. "Between 1815 and the outbreak of the First World War, more than ten thousand American students passed through the halls of German universities" (Brubacher and Rudy 1968, 176).

[9]Though the precise impact of the German universities on American higher education is difficult to determine, most of these graduates brought back the methodology but failed to reproduce the "philosophical context" of the German universities (Brubacher and Rudy 1968, 178; Marsden 1994, 104; Cherry 1995, 32–33).

position in society. In short, as society recognized the need for various sorts of professionals, it included the clergy among them; "its character as a profession enhanced the clergy's collective legitimacy as the overall guardian and definer of God's word and presence in society. Under the culture of professionalism, monopoly over the appropriate lore and authority to control and dispense it properly belonged to the collective body of certified practitioners, those who had gone through the rituals and training" (Scott 1978, 155).

Scott asserts that while the move to professionalism did not eliminate the church or clergy from nineteenth-century societal affairs, it did reposition clergy and church authority in society (ibid.). Furthermore, the shift to a professional orientation redefined the character of the church, reinforcing the need for professional leadership, and this, in turn, affected the purpose and curriculum of theological education. These observations are intriguing in relation to contemporary critiques of seminary education and ministerial competency. Accreditation, ordination provisions, and the professional conferences that faculty, ministers, and other church leaders attend may assume certain responsibilities for continuing professional development and evaluation, but faculty, pastors, and other church leaders are typically not obligated to undertake systematic and ongoing evaluation and upgrading. The ministry (and by implication theological education) is one of the few (if not the only) professions without consistent requirements for continuing education and assessment of continued suitability for the profession. Though hundreds of church schools were founded in the late nineteenth century in response to increased numbers of churches, the demand of the frontier for ministers, and an influx of people seeking higher education, the impression is that the professional education of clergy began to diverge from patterns of professional education in other fields. However, a noteworthy attempt by Abraham Flexner to take principles and practices from a particular professional field to inform all of professional education—ultimately including theological education—continues to be important in the literature on professional education.

The Flexner Report

By the second half of the nineteenth century, the professions were well established in America, and the new middle class was demanding education primarily as a means to professional advancement (see Light 1983, 351–52).

All manner of schools (vocational schools, trade schools, universities) were established to meet the need. Abraham Flexner's report on the state of American medical education was the chief contributing factor to sweeping changes, not only in American medical education but in the nature of much of professional education. His report changed the process from learning a profession by acquiring information to learning a profession in an educational environment that couples theory with clinical experience. In time, most professional schools, and later many theological schools, developed a format in which the theory of the profession was coupled with a certain period of experience in the field. The assumption was that the experience would provide clues for areas where further research was needed.

Flexner's campaign was really against proprietary schools that doctors ran for profit. As he recounts the story of the establishment of medical schools, his disdain is evident. "But with the foundation early in the nineteenth century at Baltimore of a proprietary school, the so-called medical department of the so-called University of Maryland, a harmful precedent was established" (Flexner 1910, 5). Noting the vast number of schools that sprang up between 1810 and 1876, "whenever the roster of untitled practitioners rose above a half a dozen" (ibid., 6), he is clear that the primary motive was profit.

> A hall could be cheaply rented and rude benches were inexpensive. Janitor service was unknown and is even now relatively rare. Occasional dissections in time supplied a skeleton—in whole or in part—and a box of odd bones. Other equipment there was practically none. The teaching was, except for a little anatomy, wholly didactic. The schools were essentially private ventures, money-making in spirit and object.... Income was simply divided among the lecturers, who reaped a rich harvest, besides, through the consultations which the loyalty of their former students threw into their hands. (ibid., 7)

Flexner cites the inconsistencies of the apprenticeship system of the seventeenth and eighteenth centuries as a motivating factor for the development of university-based medical education (ibid., 3). The apprentice's experience was only as good as the quality and integrity of the master.[10] The ready availability of profit spawned a vast number of medical schools, many of which had severed connections with research universities.

In light of contemporary concerns about the relevance of theological education, Flexner's comment that the *practice* of medicine had outstripped medical *education* is telling. While the knowledge of techniques and resources grew in the field, professional schools "continued along the old channel, their ancient methods aggravated by rapid growth in the number of students and by the lowering in the general level of their education and intelligence.... No consistent effort was made to adapt medical training to changed circumstances. Many of the schools had no clinical facilities whatsoever" (ibid., 9). Glenn Miller notes that Flexner, a graduate of John Hopkins University, "did not believe that professional education was the best way to train leaders" (Miller 1991, 24). However, it is apparent that Flexner was not philosophically opposed to professional education or clinical practice. More likely, with the founders of the German research university, he was against purely utilitarian education and against practice disconnected from theory. Clearly, his antipathy to the professional schools, as they severed their attachment to universities such as Pennsylvania, Yale, and Harvard, was largely because of their exploitative practices (Flexner 1910, 8).

Flexner was determined to locate (or relocate) medical education in the universities or in specialized research facilities supported by foundations, and to change the nature of medical education (Miller 1991, 32). He accomplished his goal. His report on the state of medical education stimulated the creation of standards, which caused most of the schools-for-profit to go out of business. Flexner observed in triumph, "Practically without exception, the independent schools are scanning the horizon in search of an unoccupied University harbour. It has, in fact, become virtually impossible for a medical school to comply even in a perfunctory manner with statutory, not to say scientific, requirements and show a profit" (Flexner 1910, 11).

---

[10]This criticism persists in relation to contemporary practices of on-the-job training (OJT).

The Growth of Professionalism in Theological Education

As the industrial economy developed through the nineteenth century and as cities grew, the segmentation of American society was reflected in the churches. In some instances, churches became private organizations servicing the devotional needs of congregational members who influenced society primarily through volunteer associations related to but independent of the churches. This development contributed to the debate concerning the nature of ministry, as clergy tended to isolate their preaching and ministerial tasks from social responsibility (Wind and Lewis 1994, 237). A concomitant development was the professionalization of the clergy.

Denominations established colleges and seminaries in response to the perceived need for professional education. By the latter part of the nineteenth century, the newly formed seminaries were faced with the dilemma of how to establish a system characterized by the now familiar academic administration, required courses, credit hours, and hierarchy of degrees. The degree structure remained chaotic until the American Association of Theological Schools mandated in the 1930s that the bachelor of divinity be the first theological degree. The master of divinity degree was established in the 1960s as the professional degree of choice for clergy. Theological study became increasingly specialized, and new disciplines such as religious education and sociology of religion were added to the curriculum.

Following the turbulence of the 1960s, enrollment in theological schools declined, and many clergy left the ministry for other vocations. A new doctor of ministry degree was proposed (following the earlier advice of H. Richard Niebuhr) and approved by ATS in 1970. The unique in-ministry structure of the doctor of ministry program was designed to enhance ministry proficiency—and to temper the threat posed by declining enrollments. The doctor of ministry experiment proved successful, and enrollment increased in North American seminaries from 201 in 1969 to 6,430 by 1986 (Goodwin 1989, 297). However, the project was not without its detractors. Some questioned the motives of clergy in pursuing doctoral status. Others criticized the program's lack of rigor as a doctoral degree. In some seminaries, experiences in the degree program seemed helpful to ministers in providing a forum for discussion of problems in ministry, opportunities for networking, stimulation of study, and improved competency in ministry. However, the shape of professional clergy education is still not clear.

Kelsey, commenting on the importance of the various surveys of theological education in the early twentieth century, contrasts the understanding of the term *professional* of the Kelly and Brown and May surveys with Schleiermacher's concern for the development of the ministerial professional at the University of Berlin. Robert Kelly and Mark May and William Adams Brown suggested that because of limited educational methodologies and standards, the ministry profession was losing ground to the other professions in terms of esteem and competence. However, Kelsey expressed surprise that neither survey provided any sustained theological reflection on the meaning of ministerial competency. Both surveys suggested the inclusion of more skill-oriented education as well as knowledge (*Wissenschaft*). The surveys presumed that the purpose of theological schools was to educate ministers for the churches. Given this, Kelsey concludes, "if we want to know what the relevant competencies are for the ministry, we must ask the churches what they expect in their ministers" (Kelsey 1993, 57).

Where Schleiermacher defined the ministerial profession in relation to society as a whole, Kelsey argues that the case is different in North America and suggests that churches therefore should specify the "practices for which religious leadership needs to have competencies" (ibid.). The practices he describes are those that are essential to the life and ministry of the people of God. But, according to Kelsey, it was implicit in Kelly's survey and explicit in May and Brown's survey that competencies for ministry are defined functionally rather than theologically. Kelsey's overall assessment of the influence of the surveys is that though they used the language of the German research university founders, they actually encouraged a functionalist modification that fragmented the relationship between critical inquiry and professional development.[11] The irony of this is that

> although it celebrates the sense of 'rationality' associated with the Enlightenment and institutionalized by the research university, such theological schooling would not in fact cultivate that rationality in its students! Moreover, the functions for which students are to be prepared are largely socially defined and are divorced from critical inquiry that might help to check ideological captivi-

---

[11] See Kelsey (1993, 54–64) for more specific references to these surveys.

ty of accepted ministerial functions. Under the impact of this modification of the 'Berlin' model, theological schooling tends to undergo a movement from pure academic research to applied academic research (both done at the hands of academic theologians) to popularization of the applied research (by theological school teachers) to repetitions of the popularizations by practitioners (the students). (ibid., 64)

Though Kelsey is correct that the May and Brown survey encouraged professionalism, their definition of professional education does not necessarily support a functionalist notion of it. They do describe all "true professional education" as functional but make a clear distinction between "the type of education that aims to furnish a man with the type of training required of all ministers, and that which trains for a specialized ministry." For May and Brown, the vocational school offered specialized education, while the professional school was to give the minister a foundation in principles and to develop the capacity to think about real problems; the assumption was that the minister would then acquire specific competencies on the job (May et al. 1934, 57). May and Brown actually raise objections to a functionalist curriculum even as they observe that many of the seminaries they surveyed believed in it.

Some of the more obvious objections are, first, that the function of the ministry is rapidly changing, and that one cannot build a curriculum for tomorrow on a list of the duties and activities of ministers today; secondly, and more potent, is the objection that most intelligent preachers will acquire these practical skills much more efficiently and quickly on the job than in the seminary. Therefore, the seminary should not devote too much time to them, unless it wishes to go in for clinical work. (ibid.)

Kelsey's observation about the separation of theological reflection from ministerial education is correct in that with the rise of concern for the training of ministerial competency theological studies devolved into a separate department. Even though doctrine was emphasized, it tended to be parochial and denominational (see May et al. 1934, 23). It can be said that partly as a result of these surveys, the curriculum was broadened to include courses from the professional disciplines, and curriculum requirements were extended to ensure that students would be exposed to what they needed to function in ministry. Unfortunately, the most apparent result in North American theological education has been to overload the curriculum, restrict theological reflection, frustrate spiritual formation, and therefore work against the ideals of a professional education.

Challenges to Professionalism

A third survey (1956–1957) by H. Richard Niebuhr, James Gustafson, and Daniel Day Williams is considered the pivotal study of theological education.[12] In addition to statistical data, it provided a richer, more deliberately theological language for interpretation of the purposes of theological education, especially in relation to a theology of the church and the role of the minister in contemporary society. The committee visited more than ninety seminaries, interviewed most of the deans and scores of individual faculty members, met with over forty faculty groups, examined the documents of schools they were unable to visit, and received detailed information on all schools except one. Thirty-six schools were sent a questionnaire requesting data for the period 1934–1954. For additional perspective, the team interviewed denominational leaders, pastors, students, and, for the first time, a limited number of laypeople (Niebuhr 1956, xi). "It is commonly agreed that three points made in the study were important to the future development of theological education.... (1) The mission and purpose of the church could be summarized as "the increase among men of the love of God and neighbor," (2) the emergent new concern of the minister was as a "pastoral director" and (3) theological schools should be the intellectual center for the church" (Goodwin 1989, 44–45). The authors of the study were concerned that the curriculum of the relatively new seminaries of the 1950s was subject to the empiricism of the churches and anti-intellectualism. However, they also observed that churches, regardless of denomination, were seeking to develop a Christian theology (Niebuhr, Williams, and Gustafson 1957, 4–5).

---

[12]This study resulted in a series of bulletins and three books: *The Purpose of the Church and Its Ministry* (1956), by Niebuhr; *The Ministry in Historical Perspectives* (1956), edited by Niebuhr and Williams; *The Advancement of Theological Education* (1957), by Niebuhr, Williams, and Gustafson.

The dilemma implicit in these observations continues to trouble twenty-first-century seminaries. How do seminaries respond to the demand for competent practitioners *and* help churches understand the need for a theology that defines congregational life, organization, and ministry?

In *The Advancement*, the authors noted increased rigor in the standards of theological education (in admission policies, facilities, preparation of faculty); however, they were concerned that the effective teaching of theology was being undermined by increased student load and administrative duties; curricular tensions; the demands of denominations, churches, and other agencies; and the financial difficulties that often require faculty to "supplement income by activities outside the schools" (ibid., 20). This concern for teaching effectiveness was connected to the authors' observations that since 1934 there had been a resurgence of interest in the traditional disciplines. This was fostered by a "concern for 'professional' understanding of principles versus the interest in purely vocational skills" (ibid., 21), along with a desire to correlate the traditional disciplines with one another and to relate theological understanding to issues of contemporary culture. Niebuhr, Williams, and Gustafson did not disparage the addition of nontheological subjects, believing they reflected in part a desire for continuous dialogue with contemporary thought, expressed in how theology was interpreted and applied. The authors suggested they had found a new trend in the schools toward communication among the disciplines.

> Co-operation among biblical scholars and theologians, among psychologists and theologians, between church historians and sociologists and between all these and the teachers who are dealing with Christian education, preaching, and other pastoral responsibilities is now a requirement for an adequate theological program. The discovery in our world and in the Church that it is too easy and too dangerous to split apart realms of life which ought to be held together has become potent in redefining the collective responsibility of the theological faculty. If we are right, if a movement toward internal communication and redefinition is taking place within the schools, it becomes pertinent to ask how it can be furthered. (ibid., 68)

However, they expressed concern that opportunities for independent and advanced study were being reduced because of the addition of new courses in worship, administration, pastoral care, and Christian education and the attendant fieldwork requirements. Intellectual rigor, perception of ultimate issues, and application of Christian faith to contemporary problems are diminished, they said, when a curriculum consists primarily of required courses, many of which are introductory in nature (ibid., 20–22).

Niebuhr, Williams, and Gustafson were unrelenting in their lament that the schools tended to be spiritually and intellectually ingrown, that their faculty were not interacting significantly with faculty in the university even when they were part of a divinity school on the same campus, that students tended to develop an intellectual grasp of ideas with little understanding of their meaning—especially in relation to a Christian enterprise that demands more than simple, predictable application (ibid., 69–70). They cited several interconnected problems in relation to the curriculum: uncertainty about the purpose of theological education, overloading the curriculum especially in relation to professional courses, requiring the same, rigid course of studies for all students, extending requirements without extending the time required for the degree, and a piecemeal, fragmented curriculum consisting of a number of specialized courses with little demonstrable unity or internal consistency (ibid., 80–82). "Unity then, in theological education, means more than logical unity, though that is a value to be prized. It is a matter of the interconnection of all topics in the curriculum and their being bound up with life experience in such a way that the student discovers exciting new possibilities through that central reality in his faith which gives meaning to the whole" (ibid., 83).

The three surveys of theological education in the twentieth century—Kelly, May-Brown, Niebuhr-Gustafson-Williams—paved the way for a more professional understanding of theological education. The Conference of Theological Schools, angered by the harsh criticism of the Kelly report, commissioned a new study, which John D. Rockefeller's Institute of Social and Religious Research agreed to sponsor only if seminaries made a commitment to use the results (Miller 1989, 190). The May et al. report that resulted encouraged seminaries to create curricula based on the real work of the minister, and their recommendations formed the initial standards of the Association of Theological Schools. The Niebuhr-Gustafson-Williams report in the 1950s "showed that the schools had made real progress. Despite problems, they were functioning centers for professional education" (Miller 1991, 26). The Association's Readiness for Ministry project, begun in 1973 and completed in 1976, pursued two goals: determine the skills needed by ministers and establish a system of evaluation.[13] Evaluation keyed to needed skills would help seminaries know if their graduates were ready for ministry. Miller notes that the report stimulated discontent regarding whether ministry could be described in the terms stated by the project. Does professional education produce leaders? Evidence from the churches suggested that professional education was often not attained. Examination of the seminary program suggested that each discipline considered itself a discipline in its own right, with its own associations and theory base—not a discipline that contributed to some idea of the profession of church leader (ibid., 27). Criteria for the ministry were not informed sufficiently by theological principles and an understanding of what God expected of his people.

Expansion of University-Based Professional Education

Tension between the liberal arts tradition and professional education is a recurring theme in the universities of Germany, Britain, and ultimately North America, and forms a backdrop to the development of professional programs in theological schools. With the influx of laity into universities and the provision of endowments for colleges, the need for the income derived from professional faculties diminished, particularly in England. A new tradition developed which viewed the study of the liberal arts as an end in itself rather than as a grounding for the professions. Once cultivation and discipline of the intellect became the goal of the universities, it was inevitable that models of apprenticeship and systems of private academies and societies would emerge outside the universities to satisfy demands for professional education (Cornell 1982, 31; Engel 1983, 293–94).

Later, especially in England, nineteenth-century reform movements called for a revival of professional education within the university—and this, of course, threatened the now independent professional schools. By the late nineteenth century, universities were developing degree programs in areas such as dental surgery, engineering, and architecture, organized along

---

[13] Go to the Association of Theological School's resource page for the current Profiles of Ministry resources. http://216.151.81.21/resources/student_information.asp

the lines of professional schools (Cornell 1982, 29; Engel 1983, 298). The universities attempted at least to sustain a curriculum in which professional education was identified with "ordered bodies of knowledge" (Engel 1983, 302). The curriculum structure that developed over time for training of the professional had three parts: theoretical knowledge, applied knowledge, and clinical experience. It included foundational courses, methods courses, and structured practice. The intent was for professionalism to be "based on (1) technical skill, (2) theoretical knowledge on which the skill is premised, and (3) acceptance by a community of other professionals" (Doll 1993, 44).

Evidently, as the universities embraced the professions, both were changed (see Light 1983, 345). Certainly the pragmatism of post–Civil War culture, coupled with rapidly increasing demand for practitioners (in both society and the church), contributed to the tension that university professional schools experienced between the need to train competent practitioners and the ideal of educating persons in the core knowledge grounding the profession. It was Schleiermacher's intention that students be exposed to the totality of knowledge before they entered professional development. While this ideal proved unattainable, many in the German universities defined the education of the professional in relation to scholarship and rejected any suggestion that professional studies were synonymous with practical or vocational studies. However, the climate of North America in the eighteenth and nineteenth centuries seemed to favor an understanding of professional education that emphasized the practical and downplayed scholarship (which, in turn, affected the understanding of professional education in seminaries and Christian colleges). In the absence of a coherent vision for the role of theology and the humanities, and reflecting pressure to move students through their specialized studies, disjointed courses in theology and the liberal arts seem merely tacked on to the curriculum of professional specialization. The presumption that research universities could support and enhance the professions through an interconnected network of specialized disciplines foundered. What was envisioned as a unified approach to learning became fragmented departments. The idea of theories informing practices could not be sustained. Faculty members in the various departments identified with their professional associations. In time, the wholesale disjunction within both theoretical and practical disciplines further limited any efforts to fashion curricular models of integration (see Marsden 1992, 32–35; Bloom 1987, 356–359).

The Morrill Act of 1862, in response to pressure for more practical and scientific courses, endowed land to universities with professional schools and inaugurated an era in which education was to be available to all. Then, when Harvard introduced its elective curriculum in 1869, the monopoly of the classical curriculum in American higher education was effectively ended.[14] Johns Hopkins University, founded in 1876, is reputed to be the first American research university established on the model of the German research university.[15] Like the German universities it emulated, it was to be nonsectarian and unfettered in its search for truth.[16] "With its exclusion of 'ecclesiasticism or partisanship,' Johns Hopkins heralded in yet another way the coming of a new kind of American university" (Brubacher and Rudy 1968, 180). It became the first university in America to have graduate, professional education as its defining purpose.

It would be surprising if Johns Hopkins, though modeled on certain German precedents, did not reflect distinctive emphases in nineteenth-century American culture.[17] For example, President Daniel Gilman's effort to retain the religious and moral character of Johns Hopkins, along with the freedom of the scientific and professional enterprise, illustrates the forces at work in American higher education. George Marsden avers that Gilman's effort was actually a concession to the Baltimore constituency that wanted

---

[14] Margaret Louise Cornell notes, "The creation of the state universities and the land-grant colleges along with the adoption of the German research model and the introduction of broad-range professional education all contributed to the various facets of the modern American university. By the end of the century, four purposes had emerged—teaching, pure and applied research, professional training, and community service—which together characterized the modern American university" (Cornell 1982, 41–42).

[15] Daryl Hart argues that the influence of the German university on Johns Hopkins University was not as great as historians have assumed. For the most part, he suggests, the university drew from American standards and "bore the imprint of Yale's Sheffield Scientific School" (Hart 1992b, 114).

[16] There was much criticism at the time that Thomas Henry Huxley was invited to present the opening address and that the opening ceremonies did not include prayer. However, the
university had been opened officially some months before, and President Daniel Gilman had been inaugurated with prayer and many references to the religious character of the institution (Brubacher and Rudy 1968, 180; Marsden 1994, 152).

[17] See Hart (1992, 114–15) for a more thorough discussion of this mixture of influences.

to retain an undergraduate college. Gilman distinguished between the college, where it was appropriate to provide for students' moral and spiritual welfare, and the university, where knowledge could be pursued without sectarian interference. This distinction between graduate and undergraduate education was accepted by the Christian community almost without objection. In reality, the new spirit of specialization in the context of scientific inquiry further compartmentalized religion. The developers of the universities believed that though science and religion could be in harmony, the university was the place for scientific enterprise. Therefore, as the denominations concentrated on the religious life of the colleges, professional and technical schools multiplied with little regard for religious issues (Marsden 1994, 153–54).

With the founding of Johns Hopkins and provisions made for Land Grant universities, the American university was pressed into national and community service. Ideals of service to the nation and enrichment of human life replaced former religious allegiances. As in German research universities, the basis for a professional education was the advancement of knowledge and application of the "fruits of research to problems of daily living" (Brubacher and Rudy 1968, 181). In his inaugural address at Johns Hopkins, President Gilman presented his vision for the social responsibility of the university. He "expressed the hope that university reform would make 'for less misery among the poor, less ignorance in schools, less bigotry in the temple, less suffering in the hospital, less fraud in business, less folly in politics'" (in ibid.).

Clearly, many founders of the early research universities were enthusiastic in their conviction that the church and the university could be allies. Because the universities were at the leading edge of professional education, it was believed that through their divinity schools they could supply a superior education for ministers and thus elevate the profession of the ministry. Many churches, realizing the important cultural influence of the universities, welcomed the alliance as a way to extend their own influence and that of the divinity school in shaping "the values, ideals and aspirations of the American people" (Cherry 1995, 24–25).

However, this vision for the professional education of the clergy actually created several areas of tension for the divinity schools. They found it difficult to sustain effective relationships between scholarship and piety, professional specialization and the multifaceted religious needs of churches, theological learning and the diversity of the university. Administrators of divinity schools soon realized that they "would have to deal with a gulf separating two communities of responsibility, the university and the church, quite as much as they would have to face a division separating theory and practice" (ibid., 156).

As an example, William Rainey Harper, founding president of the University of Chicago, offered his vision for the university, which included "the ceaseless investigation into every realm of knowledge…an active ambition to put knowledge to use for human service…a greater accessibility involving the maintenance of more ways of entrance to the university than had been true in the past and many more direct channels of communication with the outside world" (in Brubacher and Rudy 1968, 187). Harper attempted to hold scientific philosophy and religious thought in tension, but in time at many schools the divinity curriculum was dropped or assigned to a position disconnected from university affairs. Faculty selection shifted from clergy to university-trained professionals. Christianity was downgraded "to a moral and natural religion which had to become ethical, rational, and tolerant to fit into the university scheme" (Goodwin 1989, 212–13). Boyer noted that academics in Europe and in America "were moving inevitably from faith in authority to reliance on scientific rationality. And to men like Daniel Coit Gilman, this view of scholarship called for a new kind of university, one based on the conviction that knowledge was most attainable through research and experimentation" (Boyer 1990b, 9).

The Seminary and Professional Education

By the mid-1800s, hundreds of church schools had been founded in response to several factors: growth of the professions and the need for professional training, increased involvement in organized religion, an influx of new immigrants, increased numbers of churches, the demands of the frontier for ministers, and increased numbers of persons seeking higher education. At the same time, the perceived inadequacy of theological study and ministerial education in the universities, along with the fact that the Revolutionary War had broken the pattern of sending students to Europe, stimulated the establishment of seminaries. Andover Seminary and Princeton were the prototypes for the future development of graduate theological schools.

Timothy Dwight and Lyman Beecher, among others, railed against the illiterate and unlearned preachers invading the parishes of the land, especially in New England. In their minds, the fate of Christianity was dependent on an educated clergy. "If ministers appeared contemptible, ignorant, and vulgar, religion itself would sink to a sordid level and be regarded, not by superior minds only, but ultimately by the people at large, as a system of groveling doctrines, and debasing precepts…. In this vein, Dwight was delighted that Andover had established one of its five professorships in 'the eloquence of the Desk'" (Hatch 1989, 19). Beecher was convinced that preachers who despised learning and who were therefore theologically ignorant were actually hindering the work of the gospel in the lives of America's citizens, exposing people to error. Arguing that the ignorant were never chosen to fulfill God's cause, he used the example of Christ's teaching of his disciples for three years to lend support to his objections (ibid., 18). Unfortunately, he seemed to miss the fact that Jesus chose not to found a school (even though schools existed in the ancient world) or to establish a structured curriculum leading to a degree. Further, even after their three years of education at Jesus' side, Peter and John were still identified as ignorant and untrained, but nonetheless feared and honored and able to turn their world upside down (Acts 4).

Was the formation of the seminary a reasonable answer to the loss of a spiritual center for the university and the need for a different context for ministry education? The matrix of influences that affected the universities was apparently not well understood by those who established seminaries to accomplish what they felt the universities were unwilling or unable to undertake. Confusion and tension arising from a failure to terms with this matrix of influences contribute to much of the difficulty in theological education identified in contemporary literature. Seminary founders, for the most part, adopted the forms and structures of the university, maintained a view of knowledge as organized in specialized and fragmented disciplines, attempted to develop professional education with a rationalized curriculum, *and* hoped to foster the students' character and spiritual development.

CHAPTER 7

Theologia and the Desire to Know God

Since both Eastern and Western churches trace their theological heritage to the early church, the search for a *theologia* that holds reason and spirituality in dynamic tension must begin in the patristic era, explore the early medieval period, and then consider the implications of the Great Schism between the Eastern and Western churches in the eleventh century. "In 1054, a schism had officially separated the church of Rome from that of Constantinople, but, thanks to the interaction that continued to take place among some monks, there was a unity on the level of spirituality that was stronger than the division introduced on the level of religious politics" (LeClercq 1985, 129). Jean LeClercq's observation is important because it suggests that something important endured in the interplay between Eastern and Western mysticism. If a return to *theologia* is considered a way forward for theological education, some understanding of the use of this term *in relation to other terms* is necessary. A summary of the concepts of mystics who influenced the West is included in this chapter, because the ways their theories were interpreted and applied shaped monasticism and ultimately the academy.

Clearly, it is too simplistic to suggest that the schism caused a dominating and problematic Western rationalism along with the separation of theology and spirituality. But was something important lost in relation to theology, reason, and spirituality in the schism between Eastern and Western mysticism, just at the time when Scholasticism, along with an ascendant rationalism, was prevailing over monastic education? Only qualified patristic and medieval scholars could hope to do justice to the complexities of understanding and definition in these eras; however, even a cursory survey may be instructive.

The Meaning of Theology in the Early Church

A major task of theology in the early church was to "articulate the Church's experience of God's presence in its life" (Greer 1986, 2). Theology, constrained by its inability to describe the glory of God, nonetheless sought to give shape to Christian experience. Rowan Greer cites Irenaeus as his source for what experience meant in the early church: it was understood as the apostolic witness to the incarnate Christ. In other words, the term incorporated the experience available through the apostolic gift to the church and the Rule of Faith (creedal affirmations) and safeguarded by the bishops (see Greer 1986, 4; Bouyer 1990, 183). Given that the incarnation, Scripture, and the creeds were considered the basis for the church's experience, theology was concerned with the exegesis of Scripture and extrapolation of meaning from the creeds. "Theology, then, is largely the attempt to put into words this past and common experience of the Church" (Greer 1986, 5). However, since the early church theologians conceived of their task as a continuing effort to know the unknowable God, theology was not a strictly cognitive enterprise (ibid., 11–15).

Augustine distinguished between *scientia* (knowledge perceived from the external world through the senses) and *sapientia* (knowledge, or wisdom, concerned with eternal reality). Augustine understood knowledge (*scientia*) and wisdom (*sapientia*) as "separate instruments for learning God." Concluding that both *scientia* and *sapientia* are necessary for the theological task, Ellen Charry observes, "Modern academic theology has largely limited itself to *scientia*. While it is essential for pointing seekers in the right direction, in Augustine's view *scientia* alone is unable to heal us. The goal of *scientia* is to move the seeker to *sapientia*, wisdom" (Charry 1997, 133). Though Augustine "selected the mind as the seat of human dignity and personhood" (ibid., 137), he did not separate mind and affect. The function of the mind is to direct the affect. The mind, however, is not to be trained for knowledge's sake. It is trained to enable the whole person to enjoy God.

In the patristic era, it was assumed that God cannot be known simply through reason and academic study. The mystery of spiritual understanding is necessary, an understanding developed not simply by study but by experience with the Holy. The possibility of knowing the mystery of holiness is grounded in the seeming paradox that God is utterly inaccessible yet can be known through disciplined spirituality. The Christian who would know the

Unknowable should read the Bible, engage in the silence of prayer and contemplation, and participate in the traditions of the church. The fundamental rationale for *lectio divina* (reading the Bible) was that for the person engaged in everyday life in the world, reading the Bible is essential. *Lectio divina* presumes a prayerful reading of Scripture. The text is first read, usually aloud, the reader inviting the Lord to reveal something; the reader then prays the words of the text back to God. Scripture nourishes the mind, but it is never to be used as an object of knowledge for knowledge's sake. The reading is to be done in the attitude of prayer that continually invites God to reveal the meaning of the Scripture, to lead one to have the mind of Christ. Through waiting on God in the silence of prayer, the second discipline, God's presence may be known to the soul.

Louis Bouyer argues that the mystics understood contemplation to be a gift of God. God is unknowable except through revelation; therefore contemplation cannot be a purely rational undertaking (Bouyer 1990, 194–95). For this reason, the boundaries between the theological disciplines remained diffuse and imprecise. In relation to the third spiritual discipline, Andrew Louth suggests that "participation in the tradition of the Church implies participation in a life of love, of loving devotion to God and loving care of our neighbor. Participation in the tradition…implies a growing attentiveness to Our Lord, and a growing likeness to him…. The idea that theology must work within the alleged heritage of the Enlightenment now looks much less compelling" (Louth 1983, 65).

In the patristic era, experiencing God was greater and more mysterious than simple reliance on intellectual knowledge, emotion, or the senses. God is revealed to human beings who are capable of transcending reason, emotion, and the senses in "a 'contemplation greater than knowledge' to which the Fathers referred as the 'eyes of faith,' 'the Spirit,' or, eventually, 'deification'" (Meyendorf 1979, 13). In the patristic era and through much of the medieval period, there was thus no conflict between theology and mysticism. Mystical knowledge accepted the inadequacy of the intellect and language to find and express truth. Love, not reason, was considered the primary means whereby access to the Holy is possible: love that apprehends the "continuous communion with the Spirit who dwells in the whole Church" (Meyendorf 1979, 14; see also Wilken 1996, 24748).

The theologians of the early church attempted to integrate the meaning of Scripture (incorporating added understanding from the creeds) with the liturgical experience of the church. In this way they sought to order the church's experience and to link its past with the present (Greer 1986, 8–9). Significantly, the theological efforts of the patristic fathers were not scientific or systematic. The creation of categories of dogmatic theology and mystical theology, each with its own separate knowledge base, would occur later in the academic context of the medieval universities. Louth asserts that the coinherence of mystical and dogmatic theology "scarcely survived beyond St. Anselm in the eleventh century, [and] in the twelfth century…we see a wedge being driven between heart and head" (Louth 1981, 180).

Ongoing contributions of historians and theologians allow better understanding of the complex patterns in theology and spirituality from the patristic era through the Middle Ages. Though their efforts cannot be reviewed exhaustively in this book, their findings are suggestive of what may have been lost in the changing perspectives on theology and theological method through this period. The purpose of the following sections is not to propose a reunification of the Eastern and Western Church, though that is being attempted in some quarters. The purpose is to explore the coherence of theology and spirituality, and from this understanding to ponder the implications of a more holistic understanding of reason and spirituality for the future of theological education in the West and in countries to which the West has exported theological understanding, forms of higher education, and church practices.

Evagrius's Influence on the Meaning of *Theologia*

After Constantine recognized Christianity in the fourth century, the monastic experience to varying degrees consisted of efforts toward moral virtue, spiritual contemplation, asceticism, and service. Some in the monastic movement warned against the solitary life and established communities; others practiced a solitary life of holiness; others objected to strict asceticism, believing it could become an end in itself. The dynamic tensions of monasticism were between the individual and the communal life and between contemplation and action (Greer 1986, 172). In time, the communal ideal won out over solitude, and "the dialectic between contemplation and action [was] worked out in the hospitality of the monastery" (ibid., 169).[1] Origen, along with the Cappadocians, believed that hospitality, caring for orphans, establishing schools, and so on engender the life of virtue. The life of virtue enables the intellect, which stimulates contemplation, which is then expressed in virtue (ibid., 179). Origen conceived of a vital interaction among service, virtue, intellect, and contemplation. In the fourth century, Evagrius Ponticus,[2] whose spiritual doctrines were used by Eastern Christianity for centuries, disrupted this interaction by giving contemplation the highest place (ibid., 181; Meyendorf 1979, 67).[3] The order of contemplation in relation to the practices of virtue in Evagrius is important. One practices virtue to gain capacity for contemplation of the inner essence of created things. From this the believer achieves the state of contemplation of the Logos from which created things derive their meaning. Arduous practices of "pure" prayer were, for Evagrius, prerequisite to "certain forms of theological knowledge—direct contemplative knowledge of the Logos" (Coakley 2002, 88). In spite of a ban of his teaching in the sixth century because of his association with Origen, Evagrius was among the most significant of the monastic writers and theologians. The logic of his incorporation of the practices of the virtues with practices of prayer leading to contemplation, which then leads one to an ever greater understanding of and conformity to God, continues to compel those attracted to his writings.

---

[1] Bernard McGinn suggests that Christian thinkers, beginning with Clement of Alexandria, "adapted and transformed the ancient Greek paradigm of the distinction between the *theoria* and praxis" (1991, 256). In shifting the meaning of *theoria* from discursive reasoning to suprarational insight, these Christian thinkers insisted that contemplation and action were inseparable.

[2] McGinn identifies Evagrius as one of the great Greek Christian mystics at the end of the fourth century, one who exerted considerable influence on Western Christian mysticism (ibid., 144). Diogenes Allen notes that "Evagrius was a friend and pupil of the Cappadocian fathers, who were the principal theologians of the Nicene Creed and orthodox trinitarian faith" (Allen 1997, 65).

[3] In Origen's system, "monastic asceticism and spirituality find a justification, but contradict the basic presuppositions of Biblical Christianity. As a result, Origen and his disciple Evagrius were condemned in 400 by Theophilus of Alexandria and in 553 at Constantinople" (Meyendorf 1979, 25; see also Louth 1981, 100). Origen's system, however (presumably through the work of Evagrius), continued
to influence the theology and spirituality of post-Chalcedonian Eastern Christianity (Meyendorf 1979, 25).

Evagrius, while a devoted follower of Origen's teachings, modified the nature of Origen's linkages among contemplation, action, and virtue. His theories were carried from Eastern to Western mysticism by John Cassian (see Louth 1981, 179–80), who took up Evagrius's belief in contemplation and prayer as the means for overcoming the vices that kept men and women from God. Thus service as a companion of contemplation, intellect, and virtue was deemphasized in Western mystical theology. Personal acts of spiritual discipline in order to overcome sin, and the assumption of reason as the root of contemplation, reoriented Western monastic theology and paved the way for Scholastic theology—which in turn paved the way for academic theology. "According to Evagrius, Jesus Christ was not the Logos taking flesh, but only an 'intellect' who had not committed the original sin and, thus, was not involved in the catastrophe of materialization. He assumed a body in order to show the way toward a restoration of man's original union with God" (Meyendorf 1979, 26; see also Vest 2000, 68–69).

Evagrius believed that the enemy of the soul is to be found in thought, "for which the monks used the word *logismos*" (Tugwell 1985, 25). *Logismoi*, or wrong thoughts, were considered the work of demons, whose intent is to trap the soul and prevent the knowledge of God that comes through prayer. Prayer was understood as the way to reach true participation in God (ibid., 28); therefore pure or genuine prayer was seen as the goal of the human life, achieved only as one progresses successfully through several stages. Progress through the stages would cleanse the mind of the *logismoi*, preparing the soul for harmony with God, i.e., perfect contemplation. Evagrius believed that it is not possible to achieve the knowledge of God unless one has entered the state of contemplation. However, lest one get caught up in the "luminosity of the mind," prayer is necessary (Meyendorf 1979, 67; Tugwell 1985, 28, 30).

Evagrius's theories, carried to the West through the interpretations of Cassian, shaped monastic education by consolidating the view that contemplation and prayer are the essential acts of the life of faith. The monastic schools embraced the ideal that education should encourage a life of spirituality and contemplation. This ideal was to be realized in sacrament and liturgy, meditation and contemplation, prayer, and clearly in the insistence that the Scriptures be read and studied, primarily by the clergy but also by the laity. Gregory the Great, bishop of Rome from 590 to 604, insisted that only through the study of Scripture is contemplation possible, and that the deeper meanings of Scripture are revealed in mystical fashion to the one who studies God's Word. He was concerned that clergy learn the sacred text, but through preaching and teaching he also sought to make the Scriptures known to congregations (McGinn 1994, 41). Methods such as meditation and active reading, where the lips move to produce a muscular memory, were common. In these ways, a Scripture passage became part of the soul and was "tasted" as the reader probed its meaning. The reading and study of Scripture were considered an act of prayer and worship. Throughout the monastic era, monks treasured the sacred writings—patristic literature and the Scriptures—as literature, and because they satisfied their desire for God.

Evagrius's theories seem unnecessarily convoluted and tedious, and his distinctions are controversial, at least for many Western Protestants, who dismiss them as beyond the bounds of biblical acceptability. Sifting through Evagrius's terms to determine their meaning is an inexact exercise, but attempting to understand what Evagrius meant, in relation to what Cassian and medieval theologians and academicians actually heard, may help us as we seek a way forward in theological education.

To guide those who would seek the highest state of contemplation, Evagrius divided spiritual knowledge into two categories: the practical and the theoretical. Though he claimed that practical knowledge is possible without the theoretical, he argued that "the theoretical or contemplative cannot be gained without the practical. The practical consisted in the renunciation of vice and the acquisition of virtue, and so is to be understood as the ethical stage of the Christian life. The theoretical knowledge turns out to be largely an understanding of Scripture" (Greer 1986, 180; see also Gawronski 1995, 49; Happold 1970, 36, 68–74).

In Evagrius's system, as the soul learns to contemplate reality, it becomes aware of its capacity as a mind, which leads to *theologia*, a third stage or category. This third stage is the inexhaustible realm of the unknowable; for *theologia* was defined as the contemplation of God—of the Trinity. Essential knowledge will be found in this stage of knowledge, where the knower and the known are one. The mind *is* what it contemplates in *theologia*, the contemplation of the Trinity. This unity is possible because the mind has been stripped and made naked in the two previous stages (Louth 1981, 103, 108–9). However, "there is indeed *progress* in *theologia*, there is always more to know of the infinity of God, there is an unlimited ignorance: but it is an ignorance that is continually yielding to knowledge" (ibid., 109). Prayer, the state of being in prayer, is found in *theologia*. Prayer in this state depends on *apatheia*, a state of the soul in which the irrational is under control. To attempt prayer without this control was for Evagrius a dangerous undertaking. Prayer as "mere thoughts" (the antithesis of *theologia*) distracts the soul from God. Pure prayer, the contemplation of the Holy Trinity, is beyond mere thoughts (ibid., 110)—in short, it is wisdom.

Theologia, then, involves a seemingly paradoxical identification of pure prayer, passionlessness, and perfect harmony of the soul with God with the pure activity of the intellect. *Theologia* is the state of being wise; the wise person is a *theologos*, a theologian, one who can speak about God, one who knows God (ibid., 111). The theologian is one who prays in truth; the one who prays in truth is a theologian. Gregory adds that the theologian is, of necessity, a "person of high sanctity." Later, when appeals to reason allowed the knowledge of God to be separated from the experience of God, the theologian could be an immoral person and still be a theologian. Gregory Nazianzen complained "about those who seem to be skilled in talking about God but who practice none of the virtues and pursue no form of asceticism" (in Ramsey 1985, 19).

Clearly, most of the mystics allowed for reason and the exercise of the intellect; however, their intellectualism must be understood in relation to medieval mysticism and not equated with Enlightenment rationalism. Mystics sought for the unity of such capacities as contemplation, reason, virtue, and service in their search for the union of the soul with God. For a post-Aristotelian, post-Enlightenment Western mind, the notion that these capacities make up one essential mystery that can be understood only as the soul finds its way to God is almost impossible to grasp. It is the same difficulty that a Westerner has with the Hebraic notion that knowledge and action are of one essence—inseparable. We are more comfortable with the Hellenistic view that knowledge can exist as a thing in itself, apart from virtue and action. Compare Evagrius' notion that service, contemplation, and virtue are inseparable with Sir Isaac Newman's idea that pursuit of knowledge in the university is a good in itself, regardless of any application to service. Ultimately, in the West, practice has tended to be synonymous with activity and little else; prayer became an exercise too easily isolated from virtue, obedience, and service; *theologia* came to be defined as essentially rational contemplation.

It seems that postmedieval usages of terms such as *reason, contemplation, virtue, practice,* and *service* developed in a different direction from their usages in the patristic and medieval periods. Perhaps the primary reason for this difference is that the mystics were not unsettled by holding together qualities that the modern mind wants to separate. For the early church fathers and mothers, and for the medieval mystics, theology and spirituality were of one essence. Disciplines such as contemplation, prayer, service, resistance to evil, and reason were integrally linked.

Certainly, twenty-first-century theological educators are not obligated to recover the past as the formative principle for the future, though some consider the patterns established in the late medieval through Enlightenment period valid for the present (see Muller 1991). However, there seems to be a broad consensus that unnecessary problems for the current theological curriculum were created through the period of the Enlightenment. Perhaps a way out is a return to pre-Enlightenment notions of *theologia* as the unifying principle in the theological curriculum, but contemplation, the method of *theologia*, cannot be understood simply as a less specialized and less fragmented form of theological cognition. In essence, theology in the patristic and early medieval periods was oriented to knowing God in Christ, in the Scripture, and in tradition and was viewed as one whole rather than diffused through several disciplines.

Many recommendations for future development in theological education presume that the way forward is to return to some cognitive disposition without the overlays of the professionalized, specialized fourfold model. If we are looking to the theologians and mystics of the early church for help, they will tell us that our *theologia*, along with its cognitive disposition, must also incorporate virtue, service, and some notion of a mysterious, mystical union with God.

The Development of *Theologia* and Spirituality in Western Mystical Theology

Cassian was dependent on Evagrius for his ascetic theory and introduced the concept of the *logismoi* to the West. He divided his ascetic theory into two parts: the practical was the activity of moral discipline, while the theoretical was the contemplation of the divine and the understanding of the deep meaning of Scripture. Cassian taught that there are two parts to theoretical knowledge: historical interpretation and spiritual understanding

(McGinn 1991, 219–21). For Cassian, proper understanding of the Scripture is contingent on moral effort and does not depend on study alone. He defines *theoria* as the contemplation of God, and contemplation as the "progressive conformation of the soul to God" (ibid., 225).

Throughout Bernard McGinn's magisterial study *The Presence of God: A History of Western Christian Mysticism*, he describes Christian mysticism as a way of life. Everything that prepares the individual for the encounter with the divine presence, and everything that flows from that encounter, is mystical. However, Western medieval mysticism was not properly understood as an exclusive encounter of the *individual* with the divine. McGinn frequently envisions mysticism in communal terms. In his discussion of the roots of Christian mysticism in Judaism, Greek religious philosophy, and early Christianity, he argues that the experiences and language of mysticism were made possible through the assimilation of the Scriptures *by the worshiping community* (ibid., 3). At least through the twelfth century, the Christian community believed that consciousness of the divine presence was gained through *corporate* involvement in reading, meditating upon, preaching, and teaching the Scriptures, and through the observance of the sacraments, which stimulate contemplation and mystical union with the divine. McGinn identifies three essential themes in communal monastic mysticism: (1) Solitude depends on one's separation from the world and is the best context for true contemplative prayer. (2) Reading and meditation involved reading done aloud, with pauses for reflection and absorption of the meaning. This "prayerful, slow, and audible reading of scripture and of other classic sacred texts" (McGinn 1994, 132) was not merely a private effort; it was also to be done as part of the communal prayer of the entire church. "*Lectio divina* was created within the community of the monastery and the wider community of the church and is only understandable within that context, however much the ideal was or was not realized in real life" (ibid., 133). "*Meditatio*...was originally used to indicate the repeating of a scriptural text in order to commit it to memory." Later, meditation came to be defined as a "physical exercise of repetition aimed at an internal effect, the personal appropriation of the word of God" (ibid., 135). By the eleventh century, the meaning of meditation shifted somewhat to include written meditations. (3) Meditation naturally served as the stimulus to the third theme: contemplative prayer. In McGinn's judgment, the distinctive characteristics of early Christian mysticism were its ecclesial setting and the medieval mystics' belief that God is never sought for individual benefit but for the edification of the church (ibid., 184, 418).

The significance of the monastics' desire to orient theology and education around the search for God is better understood in LeClercq's and McGinn's elaborations of terms used by the mystics to describe aspects of spirituality. The word *theoria*, for example, appears frequently in medieval literature and is "often accompanied by adjectives which prove that it is understood as a participation, an anticipation of celestial contemplation" (LeClercq 1982, 100). A phrase such as *theorica studia*, LeClercq argues, in light of its usage in the medieval context, should be translated not as "theoretical studies" but, rather, as "love of prayer." McGinn cites a complex mix of terms from the vocabulary of the monastics for the rich meaning of contemplative prayer: *theoria, speculatio,* and even *theologia* (McGinn 1994, 139). Notably, *theologia* was used by the monastics in relation to the habits of the soul, the nurture of which was the vocation of the whole people of God. It was not used to denote religious experience or techniques for practical Christian living (LeClercq 1982, 192). Significantly, especially in light of current efforts to use *theologia* as the unifying principle for theological education, the term was defined by the purpose of monastic life—the search for God. McGinn notes: "The relation between love and knowledge in the path to consciousness of the immediate presence of God is one of the essential themes of western Christian mysticism. Gregory the Great played a crucial role in the development of this theme...because of his practical teaching on the necessity for both knowing and loving in the growth of contemplation" (McGinn 1994, 58). Pope Gregory used the term "internal understanding" (or "saving knowledge") to refer to his theory of practical knowing, which "involves the whole process of turning away from exterior sensible perception to the interior knowledge that culminates in the vision of God" (ibid.). Gregory spoke of love as that which draws the mind away from the world and lifts it to God. Because God is love, taught the medieval Christian mystics, love is the power that unites persons to God. "Intellect by itself, especially since the fall, represents a block to reaching God; but the *cooperation* between intellect and love is still *necessary* for attaining the goal [of unity with God]" (ibid., 201).

The monks feared that processes of disputation conducted outside an environment supportive of spirituality, sincerity, and humility would lead to arrogance and detached curiosity. "To offset these undesirable effects, the mind must be brought back to a single occupation and preoccupation. A single quest and a single search must be substituted for all these questions. To seek God, not to discuss Him, to avoid the inner turmoil of overly subtle investigations and disputes" was the ideal of the monastic theological method (LeClercq 1982, 205). Monastic theology allowed that there can be objective knowledge of God but emphasized that this is simply a preparation for personal knowledge of the Holy. The ultimate purpose of the knowledge of God is to unite one to God. This knowledge can utilize intelligence and the dialectical method, but "it infinitely surpasses them" (ibid., 216).

LeClercq and McGinn stress that the monastics and Scholastics shared a concern for knowledge and contemplation of God, but the orientation of their theology and method differed. Monasticism was built on foundations of prayer and humility and was dependent, to a great degree, on religious experience and mysticism. The monks sought to order their lives and contemplation by the mysteries of God. LeClercq describes monastic theology as a "theology of admiration and therefore greater than a theology of speculation. Admiration, speculation: both words describe an act of looking. But the gaze of admiration adds something to the gaze of speculation. It does not necessarily see any farther, but the little it does perceive is enough to fill the whole soul of the contemplative with joy and thanksgiving" (ibid., 226). Scholasticism, on the other hand, was more impersonal and objective. The Scholastics attempted to remove subjective elements so that the faith could be revealed without human interference (ibid.).

However, both LeClercq and McGinn are careful to stress that the difference in perspective was a matter of emphasis rather than a divergence (ibid., 212–217; McGinn 1994, 367–374). Like the monastics, many of the Scholastics insisted that the goal of learning was an increase of love for God. Like the Scholastics, many monks believed that a foundation in the seven liberal arts was necessary for the study of the Bible, because this would produce a skilled reader and would lead to greater biblical understanding

(McGinn 1994, 368).[4] However, the monks would not speak of study as *scientia*, "convinced as they were that it was essentially *sapientia*, the wisdom sent down by God for our salvation." On their part, the Scholastic masters "took up issues that had not concerned the monks, especially with regard to the scientific status and organization of the effort to understand Christian teaching" (ibid., 368).

To presume, then, that mystical theology and Scholastic theology were distinct and separate categories, even in the Middle Ages, is to miss the point that patristic and medieval scholars cannot be easily understood on this side of the Enlightenment. Many of the Scholastics were mystics and vice versa (LeClercq 1982; Greer 1986; McGinn 1991 and 1994). "If the general aim of the scholastic method concentrated on establishing a new ordering of theological tasks to better achieve the *intellectus fidei*, the famous *credo ut intelligam* (I believe in order to understand) that Augustine had striven for, the monks continued to insist that all theological effort was essentially directed to increasing our love for God—*credo ut experiar* (I believe in order to experience)" (McGinn 1994, 154). This dynamic tension reflects the two dominant streams of medieval mysticism: the path of reason and the path of love. Exercises of contemplation, meditation, prayer, reading of Scripture and acts of charity were commonly found on both paths.

When Edward Farley, David Kelsey, and others argue for a new understanding of theology embodied in terms such as *theologia*, *habitus*, *wisdom*, or "to love God truly," they clearly identify with the "path of reason." The "path of love" was not and is not commonly found in academic institutions.

---

[4]In the twelfth century a Carthusian monk, Guigo, imaged the stages of spirituality as the rungs of a ladder: reading, meditation, and contemplation. Reading (*lectio*) and meditation (*meditatio*) were activities common to all people and fundamental to the activity of prayer, which led one to contemplation. In early expositions of the spiritual exercises, a quest for meaning was seen as the important underpinning for meditation. In time, reading was downgraded, and the quest for meaning in meditation dominated the spiritual exercises. By the fifteenth century, some manuscripts omitted the practice of reading altogether (Tugwell 1985, 106). "Reading eventually resurfaced, but only in the very debased form of 'spiritual reading,' as an exercise in its own right, consisting in the reading of 'spiritual books,' designed on the whole to tell people how to be pious, rather than to enlighten their minds with truth" (ibid., 107). Reading and meditation fell into disfavor as emphasis on intellectual reasoning increased. As a corrective perhaps, in the sixteenth century St. Ignatius, among others, stressed that meditation must be properly grounded in the biblical narrative and not replace Christian activity but be energized by it (ibid., 107, 110).

Yet this lesser known contemplative tradition, when held in tension with the "path of reason," forbids the isolation of theological education from the *ecclesia*, the whole people of God, and prevents it from becoming the peculiar province of a professional class of clergy or academics. Heiko Oberman calls for a blend of the two paths that would lead people away from an exclusive, elitist intellectualizing of God's revelation. He is concerned about the use of methods that make Scripture an object of analysis without the method of meditation that makes the student a loving listener. Similarly, didactic preaching needs the corollary of the shared journey to inner faith. Without mystical faith, as he understands it, "the Church that is called 'the salt of the earth' does not and cannot exist" (Oberman 1994, 90).

The quest of the mystics was to understand the extent to which God can or cannot be revealed to humanity. In this quest, the interplay of reason and mystical spirituality was accepted for much of the medieval period. There was constant interplay in the currents of thought articulated by the Western Christian mystics and Scholastic theologians such as Aquinas. Through the medieval period, there was no time when monastic mystical theology[5] disappeared and Scholastic theology triumphed. Even though scholastic reasoning came to dominate the academic culture, there was still a dynamic interplay between different perspectives on how men and women can come to know God, the Unknowable. No one approach can be said to be *the theologia*, or even the wisdom, of the medieval period. Mysticism

---

[5] Heiko Oberman distinguishes between mysticism (and by implication medieval mystical theology) and seventeenth- and eighteenth-century mystical theology. "'Mysticism' means the experience of faith tending toward union with God"; mystical theology analyzes mysticism with a view to providing rules to guide others in their efforts to follow the practices and experiences of the mystics (Oberman 1994, 78). Oberman's perspective is that mystical theology obscured the true quality and character of mysticism. He maintains that in their preoccupation with definitions, rules, and analysis of experience, seventeenth- and eighteenth-century theologians hindered access to the experience of mysticism. Clearly, Oberman's conviction is that mystical

theology has colored current understandings of mystical experience. "Protestant reference books and manuals of the late seventeenth and eighteenth century rarely lead to genuine mysticism. Fearful concern for orthodoxy and denominational boundaries harrowed and dried out the field of experienced mysticism. As a result, our understanding of mysticism has also been prejudiced. There is little in Protestant orthodoxy that would be useful in exploring mysticism, because it sees mysticism as a phenomenon of a Catholicism far from Scripture, a Catholicism which, along with its sacramental and Marian mysticism, was refuted and superseded by the Reformation" (ibid., 80).

could properly be understood as a dialectic between intellect and spirit, intuition and reason, rationalism and experience. It embodied humanity's search for union with God in love, and God's search for humanity.

In light of the thickly textured descriptions of the quest for the Holy throughout the medieval period, LeClercq's enthusiasm for the monastic understanding of the relationship of learning and piety is compelling. However, it is difficult to embrace the monastic ideal as the model for theological education today. Monastic education tended to move along narrow channels, bounded sometimes by an excessive literalism, sometimes by undisciplined mysticism, and always by church dogma.[6] What Robert Ulich sees as the monks' "uncritical acceptance" of the Greek and Roman classics (Ulich 1968, 65) suggests that their educational method and view of Christian experience could not allow the kind of interplay of arguments and ideas needed to extend the boundaries of Christian knowledge and possibly promote a richer understanding of the life of faith. This work was to be attempted by the Scholastics. The resurgence of ancient ideas and methods, reforms in the church, the stimulation of urban life by the economic prosperity of the eleventh and twelfth centuries, and the challenge to piety that these movements represented could not be contained by the monasteries. They declined but did not disappear, and the major centers of learning became the universities.

Yet though the ideal of patristic theology and medieval mysticism—to link the church's experience to the life of obedience in the Spirit—often faltered in excesses of allegorical and spiritual imagination and asceticism, Scholastic efforts to systematize theology were also problematic. In succeeding centuries, these efforts led ultimately to a dependence on reason that tended to downplay or sever the connection between *scientia* and *sapientia*. However, notable examples following the medieval period suggest a natural

---

[6]In a collection of materials related to the history of education, Robert Ulich includes a portion of a document by a priest, Hrabanus Maurus (c. 776–856), entitled *Education of the Clergy* (in Ulich 1971, 174–90). Maurus, referring to the seven liberal arts, defined the dialectical method as the science that can lead to knowledge and as the skill that shows "what is valid in argument and what is not." However, it is apparent that for Maurus the conclusions of thinking were predetermined and had to be consistent with church dogma (ibid., 177).

tendency to maintain a productive tension between the path of reason and the path of love.

The Brethren and Sisters of the Common Life

By the fourteenth century, the laity had slipped out from under clerical control. The church attempted to curb preaching and translation of the Bible, but laypeople began to establish associations and institutions for spiritual activity. One of the best known of these associations was the Brethren and Sisters of the Common Life. Geert De Groote, around 1374, abandoned a promising clerical career, gave his house to poor religious women, and sought a life of spirituality. He resolved that he would become a deacon and, without joining any established religious order, preach his message throughout the diocese of Utrecht in the Netherlands. By the time of Groote's death of the plague in 1384, a group of disciples living in the vicarage of Florens Radewijns, a priest in Deventer, founded the Brethren of the Common Life. "A parallel development was that of the Sisters of the Common Life, a community that emerged from the group of devout women who had lived in Groote's house since 1374 under statutes written by Groote in 1379" (Gründler 1987, 176–77; see also Van Engen 1988, 12–13).

Groote's vision emerged at a time of great religious, social, and political upheaval. The church was corrupt, torn apart by intrigue, greed, and claims to leadership by competing popes (see Enns 2000a). The aim of the Brethren and Sisters of the Common Life was not to develop a new body of writings or a new devotion (in this sense the term *devotio moderna* or "modern devotion" is misleading). John Van Engen asserts that the *devotio moderna* was Catholic and late medieval in its origin, linked to the Renaissance and Reformation only by virtue of the fact that many of the themes of the *devotio moderna* were reminiscent of the renewal themes of those periods (Van Engen 1988, 10; see also Enns 2000a, 13–14). Otto Gründler adds:

> During the early part of the twentieth century, the *devotio moderna* has frequently been described in various studies as a radical break with medieval monasticism and as a forerunner of the Protestant Reformation. It has been credited with initiating widespread innovative changes in public education and with having influenced nearly every humanist of the fifteenth and six-

teenth centuries. Evidence of the "modernity" of the movement has been found in its lay character, nonconformity, modern individualism, rejection of externals in religious practice, alienation from the church, and in its rejection of binding vows.

> That the above claims do not apply to the monastic branch of the *devotio moderna*, that is, the Windesheim Congregation, is obvious. But neither do those claims, on the whole, apply to the Brethren and Sisters of the Common Life, as recent scholarship has shown. On the contrary, the institutions and literature of the *devotio moderna* represent a revival of traditional monastic spirit rather than a radical innovation. (Gründler 1987, 179)

The Brethren and Sisters sought to recover the teachings of the Scripture and devotional life as described and practiced by the desert mystics and medieval masters (Van Engen 1988, 40). Though they incorporated the concept of "spiritual ascents" common in medieval mysticism as a way to nurture purity of heart and moral perfection, Groote stressed that those who ascended must also descend in service to others (Van Engen 1988, 57–58). Groote understood the dangers of a devotion that was not grounded in the teachings of the Scriptures, and throughout his life he insisted that devotion and experience be tested against the teachings and "images" of Scripture. He allowed meditation and the practice of forming mental images to stimulate religious devotion; however, the images and sensations aroused in meditation must be purified by the Scripture (Van Engen 1988, 43–44). Because of their belief that much of the teaching of the Scripture should be in the vernacular, the Brethren had a powerful influence on the laity.

Any learning that would distract from the desire to love and serve God was rejected by Groote. Though part of his strategy to reform the church was to provide education that included the study of pagan and Christian literature, and though the traditional subjects of logic, mathematics, philosophy, grammar, and rhetoric were to be part of the curriculum, the prior orientation of study was to be conformity to Christ and "attending to the words of the Gospel" (Dickens 1964, 20; Gründler 1987, 184). All education had to have a practical end. It had to be evident in life. Scholastic theology and philosophical discourse were considered ineffectual for true understanding and irrelevant for the spiritual life.

Progress in moral virtue, increasing in personal holiness was the central point...of the *devotio moderna*; all else was secondary. Not that reading, copying, or whatever else one did was not important; but it needed to serve one goal: advancement in sanctity. And in this context, it needs to be emphasized also that the endpoint of their religious lives was neither *ascesis* (although poverty, fasting, chastity were emphasized), nor mystical union or extraordinary experiences. (Enns 2000a, 16)

Marlene Enns concludes that the consensus of the literature is that Groote did not despise learning and that the *devotio moderna* was not anti-intellectual. His correspondence to a friend at the University of Paris suggests that after his conversion he did not reject but was disappointed with Scholastic learning and preaching (ibid., 51).

Despite persistent opposition from the clergy, the Brethren and Sisters of the Common Life were within a decade an established presence in the Netherlands and Germany. By 1390, the houses had so increased in number that local magistrates were forced to rule on the legality of their gatherings (Van Engen 1988, 12). They lived communally, without establishing a formal order, and aimed to practice a life of simplicity and holiness patterned after New Testament teachings, the writings of the desert mystics, and teachers of the early church (ibid., 47). Church leaders looked on their common way of life with suspicion until they saw that the Brethren and Sisters were self-supporting (not beggars) and that many continued to be active members of their parish churches. Ultimately, they were recognized as legitimate gatherings of ordinary men and women simply seeking a more authentic expression of spirituality. The church even allowed the use of the vernacular in their meditations and reading of Scripture, having become convinced that their practices were indeed private and for the purpose of personal edification (ibid., 15–16).

Though the movement is generally described as a lay movement, Oberman, citing medieval documents, suggests that the notion of the common life was just as applicable to priests. Gründler notes, "In contrast to the Sisters, who were laywomen, the Brethren of the Common Life were by no means a lay community. The majority of its members were priests or candidates for the priesthood (clerics). The few lay brothers, the *familiares*, usually carried out the menial tasks of cooking, cleaning, and tailoring"

(Gründler 1987, 177). The distinction between lay and clergy orders was not intentional; it existed primarily because the "monastic landscape had appeared so bleak at that moment as to make a merger with existing orders seem ill-advised" (Oberman 1981, 55). However, anticipating that their life and discipline would resemble those of a monastic order and would therefore provoke accusations that they were violating the "Fourth Lateran Council's prohibition of new orders in 1215...Groote, shortly before his death, had urged his followers to found a monastery" (Gründler 1987, 178). By 1460, eighty monasteries belonged to the Brethren.

Following the teaching and example of Groote, the Brethren and Sisters of the Common Life established schools throughout Europe in an effort to teach practical Christianity.[7] Though their schools were not numerous, Oberman observes, "the Brethren were unusually active in furthering education. Their concern ran more in the direction of *sapientia* than *scientia*, but...they did pursue an ultimate synthesis of wisdom and knowledge" (Oberman 1981, 47).

The various houses of the Brethren and Sisters of the Common Life disbanded in 1517. Historian A. G. Dickens concludes that the *devotio moderna* ultimately failed as a movement, unable to affect significantly the emerging religious life of a region caught in the controversies and battles of the Reformation era (Dickens 1964, 20). As true as this may be, the assessment is certainly only partial. The movement encouraged hundreds of men and women to progress in morality and devotion. In an era of indifference and corruption, these men and women found the courage to put their faith into action and to live out their piety in everyday life (Enns 2000a, 20–21).

As one movement wanes, another comes to birth. This pattern is repeated throughout the history of Christian devotion. After the Brethren and Sisters of the Common Life diminished in influence, in the fifteenth century Jean Gerson would stimulate the resurgence of a piety and mystic-

---

[7]Though he left the monastic life in 1379 and preached against its besetting sins—immorality, simony, and indolence—Groote continued to commend it as a lifestyle. He valued the desire to separate oneself from the world and to live a life of holiness and contemplation, but he felt that people should practice this life not in a monastery but in the world. Likewise, though he criticized the church, Groote did not want to withdraw from the church. He tried on several occasions to silence those who taught contrary to the established teaching of the church (Hyma 1950, 34–37). For a description of the practices of the communities of Brethren and Sisters of the Common Life, see Hyma 1950, 109–15, 140–44.

ism that relied less on "intellectual vision" and stressed once again the "path of love" (Oberman 1994, 84).[8] This mystical tradition had elements in common with many previous movements: it appealed to laity who desired a mystical union with God but were unable to give up their livelihood to pursue it. "This form of piety led to the reading of Holy Scripture and to common prayer after work or during breaks at work. Mysticism was in this way 'democratized,' made accessible to all believers" (ibid., 85). The movement fashioned yet another non-Scholastic alternative to the *via rationis* (the path of reason). "Modern scholarship has not yet accorded this alternative mysticism the attention it deserves. When we think in a general way about medieval mysticism, we usually associate it with a spiritual movement that had turned away from the world, that was far from all social and political crises of the time. No matter how often this is repeated, it is still wrong" (ibid., 85–86).

Seventeenth-Century Pietism

Ernest Stoeffler suggests that the influence of seventeenth-century Pietism in orienting theological education to the "practical concerns of the churches" has become more apparent in recent decades (Stoeffler 1983, ix). Philip Jakob Spener[9] developed a proposal, outlined in *Pia Desideria*, that reflects his intent to reform theological education, restore an emphasis on the heart as well as the head, and situate faith in life. He insisted that since suitable ministers were necessary for the reform of the church, it was essential that they be trained in the schools and universities of the period. The role of professors was to suppress un-Christian behaviors and attitudes so that the "schools would, as they ought, really be recognized from the outward life of the students to be nurseries of the church for all estates and as workshops of the Holy Spirit rather than as places of worldliness" (Spener 1964, 103).[10] Spener described theology as a practical discipline, consisting

---

[8]Gerson is identified by Oberman as a church father of the fifteenth century (Oberman 1994, 84).

[9]Often referred to as the "Father of Pietism." He influenced August Herman Francke, a leader of German Pietism.

[10]Dutch Pietists were also influential in shaping higher education in the American colonies. Gisbertus Voetius (1589–1676), a professor at the University of Utrecht, wrote a guidebook for students which was used at Harvard to reinforce "true godliness and right learning" (Tanis 1976, 34).

of more than knowledge and the accumulation of information. "Accordingly thought should be given to ways of instituting all kinds of exercises through which students may become accustomed to and experienced in those things which belong to practice and to their edification" (ibid., 112).

Unfortunately, initial enthusiasm for Spener's proposals waned when clergy realized the importance he gave to the role of the laity.[11] As the resistance of clergy and professors of theology increased, Spener returned to *collegia pietatis* or small groups of true Christians. Predictably, these groups tended to become little churches within the church, their members criticizing the organized church and its clergy. Spener was an important voice for the Pietist movement. His emphases on personal and spiritual formation and on what today would be termed lifelong learning added to the rich mixture of influences that shaped America's Colonial colleges.

Spener's themes were also significant at the University of Halle, under August Francke's leadership. Francke insisted that theology can be understood only in the "convergence of Scripture and life.... Pietistic theological education, therefore, both informs and forms persons; it instructs and inspires; and it provides a definitional body of knowledge while it disposes people in life toward the world" (in Anderson 1997, 4; see also Weborg 1986, 184). Following the ideals of Comenius and other Pietists, he made prayer, meditation, and the battle against temptation crucial elements in theological education. "There can be no growth in grace apart from these activities, and that growth is the true aim of theological education rather than a merely intellectual grasp of dogmas and related interests" (ibid., 54). Even though Francke's vision for theological education could not be fully realized, his influence was such that hundreds of pastors went from the University of Halle committed to improving the world. Further, the goals of theological education infused other departments of the university, such that

---

[11]C. John Weborg lists Spener's six proposals, which reflect his integration of the laity in the ministry: (1) Increase the use of the Word beyond what was typically prescribed and encourage its study and application through the conventicles. (2) Again through the agency of the conventicles, encourage the development of lay ministry consistent with the doctrine of the priesthood of all believers. (3) Both knowledge and practice confirm one's profession. (4) Even religious controversies must be dealt with in a manner consistent with the practice of Christianity. (5) Seminaries should be considered "workshops of the Holy Spirit." Both spiritual formation and intellectual development are to be encouraged. (6) Seminaries should provide practical experience in ministry (Weborg 1986, 206–7).

thousands of others in all locations and professions were taught in an educational system that sought to combine competence and scientific modernity with growth in grace, which inculcated at every opportunity the God-given duty to be of use to the neighbor, to be God's instruments in improving the Church and the world. Converted men and women were called to convert all human institutions, bending them toward the better times which Spener had prophesied. The school as an ecclesiola received in Halle an elaborateness of expression that may never have been equaled since. (ibid., 57)

The Pietist influence encouraged the ideals that faculty teach by example, that they give attention to the lives of their students, that Scripture cannot be understood until it is worked out in life, that education defines a body of knowledge *and* disposes a person to God.

However, Pietism in North America suffered from internal shifts in the meaning of piety. Initially, subjective individual experience was a corrective to arid Scholasticism and was kept in the context of Scripture, group accountability, and commitment to service. In later years, emotional experience became the mark of piety and led the movement toward anti-intellectualism. (Erb 1983, 25).

In North America, education of clergy in the colleges was shaped by Puritans, Methodists, Baptists, Presbyterians, Anglicans, and other immigrant groups. Most of these groups were nurtured in a Pietism that was grounded in the historic church, characterized by a practical theology critical of Enlightenment rationalism, committed to the doctrine of the priesthood of all believers, and unwavering in its intent to transform culture through a renewed church. One of its means for renewing the church was conventicles, or small groups of believers. In these small groups the Scriptures were accessible to every person, and believers were encouraged to admonish and encourage one another based on the Word (Weborg 1986, 205). "By means of group Bible study, free prayer and testimony, Pietism sought to raise the consciousness of Christians that they were priests of God and to exercise their spiritual priesthood in prayer and service to neighbor" (ibid., 183).

In the seventeenth century, the Puritans established an American colony, founded schools and churches, and for the most part exemplified the effort to maintain the tension between the path of reason and the path of love. As it was for the monastics, the heart of Puritan devotion was prayer and meditation (Hinson 1986, 170). "Although Puritans would not have distinguished as precisely as the monks did between levels of prayer (*cogitatio*, *meditatio*, and *contemplatio* of Hugo of St. Victor), they did differentiate meditation or contemplation from ordinary prayer, which is perhaps best characterized as 'mental' prayer'" (ibid., 173). Richard Baxter taught that contemplation and prayer require a spirit empty of all worldly concerns in order to apprehend the presence of God. In this act of contemplation, however, consideration or rational control was needed, because the Puritans "feared the emotions and the imagination" (ibid.). Rational control coupled with such an empty spirit would prevent the soul from harmful excess.

Schleiermacher and Pietistic Influence in the German University

This debate between theology as intellectual apprehension and theology as reflection on human experience was refocused by Friedrich Schleiermacher in the nineteenth century. Though he came to doubt many of the orthodox Christian doctrines, he retained his belief in religious affections or devotional feelings. At the University of Halle he was influenced by Kantian skepticism and Enlightenment philosophy, and while pastoring a Reformed Church in Berlin he was caught up in Romanticism, a movement seeking to counter the rationalism of the Enlightenment. The Romantic emphasis on poetry, the feelings, imagination, and intuition appealed to Schleiermacher. In 1806, after a short professorate at the University of Halle, he returned to Berlin to pastor Trinity Church; he later participated in the founding of the University of Berlin.

It helps to understand Schleiermacher's decisions and actions to realize that the age in which he lived was characterized by religious indifference. The French Revolution had disestablished the church and elevated reason in its place. Voltaire, among others, was active in criticizing the church. German philosophers questioned the role of theology in the university. In response, Schleiermacher proposed that theology become a "positive science" oriented to the church's professional leadership. The effects of this emphasis have been discussed in previous chapters. However, Schleiermacher also sought to provide a new role for theology by grounding it in human experience. In his mind, a theology grounded in human experience would demonstrate that religion is essential to true humanity. He described God in such a way that he was not elevated above humanity but became part of humankind. The source of theology then became "*human* reflection on human experience of God" rather than "timeless, authoritative propositions" (Grenz and Olson 1992, 44).

Clearly this position and the professionalizing of theology create serious problems for those who believe that the Word of God is a source greater than human experience and that theology is about God, not about church leadership. However, if we reject Schleiermacher altogether, an important insight could be lost. Schleiermacher's attempt to make experience and feeling the foundation for theology is clearly problematic. However, the word *feeling* as used by Schleiermacher should not be understood as simple sensation but as a "deep sense or awareness" or piety. This implies that feeling can incorporate a significant cognitive element that is deeper than that experienced in a merely rational approach to theology. Because this form of cognition is difficult to understand, Schleiermacher's perspective on the role of feelings in theological understanding is often bypassed. Perhaps this feeling that incorporates cognition is like the inner experience of looking intently at a magnificent painting or listening to a complex symphony. The power, beauty, and complexity of such a creations is overwhelming. One's feelings in such a case require cognitive involvement but in a way that cannot be easily defined. For Schleiermacher, then, the task of Christian theology was not simply a descent into capricious feeling but necessitated far deeper levels of the intellect to be operative than is customary in theological learning. Without affirming his dismissal of an authoritative Word, we may acknowledge that Schleiermacher's understanding of the place of feelings or experience in theology is significant in relation to contemporary concerns about the division of theology and spirituality that seems to have been fostered when reason was in its ascendancy.[12]

---

[12]Mark McIntosh confirms that the mystical writers warned against a preoccupation with religious feelings or experience. He also notes that a purely rational effort to know God is point
less. Theology is not simply the study of God; it requires involvement with God (McIntosh 1998, 23–26).

Toward a Holistic Understanding of Reason and Spirituality

Regaining the unity of theology and spirituality is a much-desired goal, yet such an integration is almost incomprehensible on this side of the Enlightenment. Western Christians generally are uncomfortable with the esoteric, affective nature of Eastern spirituality, while Eastern Christians do not understand a Western theology that is defined almost exclusively in cognitive terms. It is difficult for those enculturated in the West or in the East to apprehend what theology and theological education in their respective countries may have lost in the separation of Eastern and Western spirituality.

For the West, attempting to use spirituality *as a corrective to* academic theology in theological education is not a helpful solution. It would seem that a more holistic understanding of reason and spirituality would provide a better framework for theological education and the practices of the church.

Significantly, movements that sought to stimulate spiritual renewal in medieval and Reformation Europe coexisted with the growth of the universities. For example, Scholasticism and Christian mysticism, *scientia* and *sapientia*, intersected and interacted with one another as they each sought the proper relationship between scholarship and piety, prayer and study, doctrine and service, personal holiness and justice. It would seem that the Reformers, for the most part, understood the inevitability of a tension between intellect and piety. John Calvin, for example, can be understood only if doctrine and piety, academic and pastoral theology, are held together. Interestingly, Calvin's *Institutes* are sometimes referred to as preferred devotional reading. "For Calvin," says Ellen Charry, "the purpose of treating articles of religion is to enhance godliness.... The modern academy eliminated spiritual and moral formation from scholarly inquiry, rendering the modern disciplines of marginal use to the church. Calvin would stand down from this decision" (Charry 1997, 199). Charry also observes, "Calvin's *Institutes* contains no prolegomenal statement but instead plunges directly into the core concern: how does God make himself known to us, and what is to be the tangible fruit of that knowledge?" (ibid., 203). Calvin and other Reformers understood that sinners—and society—will not be transformed by a purely rational explication of the faith.

Throughout the pre-Enlightenment era, neither emphasis would ever completely displace the other, and this interplay between the path of reason and the path of love continues to the present. The most significant insights from the pre-Enlightenment eras involve expressions of *theologia* and the desire to know God in ways that were unquestionably multifaceted. Reason and spirituality were not in opposition; apprehension of what can be known and contemplation of what cannot be known were equally valid; virtue and action were in most cases conjoined; and it was demonstrated that the individual life and communal life could, at the best of times, exist in healthful tension.

Contemporary theological education presumes that through the accretions of the theological curriculum God can be known. If, however, God can be known only in part, and if the way of the Spirit is critical to knowing, reason is neither the sufficient nor the ultimate measure of our knowing. If *theologia* is the unifying principle, the pre-Enlightenment theologians teach clearly that theological education must allow room for a God-filled silence. Paul's notion of a greater mystery in the Christian faith (see 1 Cor. 2: 6–12; Eph. 1:7–10; Col. 2:2–3) would seem a corrective to the excesses that tend to occur in both mysticism and rationalism. In this the duty of theological education is clear: to uphold a reasonable apprehension of the faith but never to presume that God can be known thereby. As the people of God, our acknowledgment of a greater mystery leads us in humility to worship and prayer eventuating in service. Those who claim to be teachers must never be guilty of influencing leaders for the church who will allow that which cannot be known to be obscured by reason, or by piety.

Part III

Implications for 21ˢᵗ Century International Theological Education

CHAPTER 8

Recovering a Focus on the Church

In the simplest terms: God is the solution to the problems of the world, not the church. The church, although orientated to, and governed by, the solution, still remains part of the problem.... Since the primary aspect of the church is penetrated by the activity of God it must be understood as a theological mystery and, as such, is essentially indefinable. – Nicholas Healy

Healy's words mark the tension that confronts the contemporary church. As a sociological organizational entity, the church bears the inevitable flaws of all organizations—thus Healy's first observation. However, as a theological entity, the church is the mystery of God and bears the mystery of God to the world. A thoughtful pastor once wrote, "I realize now that for all my ideas and skills eagerly put in practice, the truth is, I had no theology of the congregation. I had various notions of what to preach. These I advocated fervently. I was sure of the biblical mandate to help the helpless. These I pushed into action. But I had no sure ground for understanding the congregation itself as *ecclesia*, that is, people of God called together and gifted for ministry in a particular place" (Frank 2000, 12).

If the Scripture is to be taken seriously, the church is God's chosen means for making known the mystery and the wisdom of God (see Eph. 3:9–10) and the agency for reconciling the world to God (see 2 Cor. 5:18). One could argue that the institutional church, which should be a reflection of the church as God sees it, is the *foundational* community; that is, principles of life and faith learned in the church inform and transform all other human communities and functions in society. To the extent that this community is dysfunctional, other human relationships and communities in society are impoverished—including the families that are embraced by the church.

It follows, then, that organizations such as theological institutions serve the mission of the church in the world. In themselves, they bear no special mandate from God as the church does. When the church gave away two of its central functions, education and mission, to schools, mission agencies, and other serving organizations, three interdependent functions of the church that have defined the community of faith from the Old Testament time to the present—the worship of God, obedience to God's Word (a function of learning), and justice to one's neighbor (the heart of mission)—were pulled apart. The loss of the synergy of these practices has contributed to many of the concerns expressed about the loss of the church's relevance and vitality. George Barna, a sincere Christian, tried for years to find the formula for a successful congregation. By 1998 he was no longer hopeful about the future of the organized church in North America. "Let's cut to the chase. After nearly two decades of studying Christian churches in America, I'm convinced that the typical church as we know it today has a rapidly expiring shelf life" (Barna 1998, 1). He has repeated his disillusionment more recently about trying to foster pastoral leadership that would serve the church (Barna 2002).

Barna's view may have idiosyncratic elements, but I can sympathize with his judgment. For several years I worked among congregations and theological schools in Canada. After one particularly difficult church board meeting, I wrote the following:

If Churches Were Parks

If we tore down our church buildings and replaced them with parks, would the buildings be missed? If churches were parks, there would be trees and grass and places for pleasant walks, neighborhood families enjoying the changing seasons, and our "old ones" sitting on benches telling children stories of their lives and faith.

In the fall, as the leaves changed from green to yellow, orange and red, we could invite our friends and neighbors to corn roasts and BBQs; invite them to laugh with us, talk with us, and enjoy the beauty of God's creation—in the park. We could leave the children something wonderful in a world gone mad.

In the winter we could roll in the snow with the neighborhood children, throw snowballs, create snow sculptures, and grow to know each other again as we walked under trees heavy with hoarfrost. At Christmas, we could string colored lights, decorate a Christmas tree, savor the story of the nativity and sing carols under quiet stars.

If churches were parks, we would have to forsake our games of power and our dreams of empire for pleasant walks, snow forts, corn roasts, Christmas trees, carol sings, Easter pageants, and heart-to-heart talks with those who need to know why we still believe in God. If our churches were parks, all people could gather there; they could come whenever they wished, for there would be no locked doors or security windows on our parks—no stained-glass windows to hide behind. Members of the church eating lunch in the park could strike up a conversation with a businessperson, university student, or shopper resting before heading home, admire the multicolor of a group of teenagers and ask them if they are afraid of the world we have created for them, or angry because of the future we may have taken away from them.

Of course, we would find pain in our parks. Lonely people, unhappy children, sullen youth. We might confront those trying to buy drugs in our parks. We might fear those who would hurt us and steal from us. If our churches were parks we would have to confront the world outside our buildings. We would have to be those who make peace and speak of redemption and hope rather than those who hide behind fortress walls and wish the world away.

At the start of the world, God put the man and the woman in a park. God chose to walk and talk with the man and the woman in a park. When we were cast out of the park, we began to build towers, empires, cities, and temples. We had to acquire and possess—not only the present but the past and the future. We found ways to control our world and other persons. It's hard to do this in a park.

Admittedly, this short essay grew out of youthful disappointment that the church was not living up to *my* personal ideals. As I have grown older, I am both less naive about the nature of institutions and more hopeful because of a larger view of the church. The reality is that the institutional church is an organizational mess; because humans are involved, it always will be a mess.

Interestingly, after Barna's series of indictments he observed that "the stumbling block for the Church is not its theology but its failure to apply what it believes in compelling ways.... Christians have been their own worst enemies when it comes to showing the world what authentic, biblical Christianity looks like" (Barna 1998, 5).

Perhaps without realizing it at the time, Barna intermingled aspects of the church that must be understood as two distinct realities: its institutional and theological character.[1] Since ecclesial or institutional perfection is impossible in light of a fallen creation, we will become discouraged if all we see is the organized expression of the people of God. While we accept the sometimes dismal realities of the institutionalized church, we must look deeper to its fundamentally spiritual character and purpose.[2] Missing this, we will always struggle with pessimism about the role of the church in the world. Only a theology of the cross in light of the eschaton gives us the freedom—and the faith—to assert that if the institutional church as we know it crumbled into ruin, the church as the people of God would persist.

Ted Ward's image of organizations as leaky boats is apt. As leaders we will spend all our years of service in institutions, bailing. However, even as we recognize that organizational entropy is inevitable, we are obligated to give constant attention to what God demands of the church, to teach and lead faithfully, and to speak prophetically when necessary. These are the tasks of theological education as well. "A Christian community has no

---

[1] The effort to understand the church as both a theological and an institutional entity is spawning a growth industry in publications. Among the books are Webster 1992, Bandy 1998, Frank 2000, Ortiz 1996, Kenneson and Street 1997, Cymbala and Dean 1997, Peterson 1987, Nouwen 1989, Guinness 1993, Posterski and Barker 1993, Posterski and Nelson 1997, Van Der Ven 1996, Clowney 1995, Barna 1998, Giles 1995, T. Hawkins 1997, Küng 1967. These range from a charismatic, emotive response, to a deeply felt organizational-leadership response, to a theological-historical response. We may not have found the way forward in this matter, but concern for the church and its true nature and function is growing.

[2] The emergent church movement illustrates the pattern common throughout history of efforts to restore a productive tension when rationalism or institutionalism threatens to overwhelm the "path of love" or spirituality and mystery. When any such movement appears, controversy also emerges. See www.emergent village.com Last accessed in October 2005.

choice as to whether theological education, for all its members, will be an element of its educational work; it only has a choice as to the kind of theological education it will be" (Wood 1996, 307–8).

Many who have struggled with the dysfunctionality of churches and seminaries tend to believe that the only way forward is to bypass existing institutions and start afresh. This chapter reflects two premises: the inevitable *institutional* dysfunctionality of churches and schools must be accepted, and understanding of the *theological* character of the church as the people of God is fundamental to what theological education becomes in the twenty-first century. Dallas Willard reminds us, "We have this treasure in earthen vessels. And the earthen vessel is never right.... No man [sic] can see the church; only God sees the church. The church lives before God; it is greater than any of its manifestations" (Willard 2000b). Theological education, then, becomes viable only as it develops in relation to the church as institution *and* as the invisible reality seen only by God.

Until recently, concerns related to churches and schools were cataloged in mutually exclusive domains: school problems and church problems. Increasingly, theological educators and church leaders attribute the disconnect between theory and practice and lack of relevant leadership development, at least in part, to an ineffective partnership between the church and theological schools. Envisioning the problem in this way, however, tends to generate three common, potentially unproductive responses:

1. Churches, particularly multicampus churches, bypass theological institutions and create their own seminaries, or conduct conferences to teach what they perceive the seminaries have taught inadequately.

2. Theological schools seek to connect with the church by teaching existing courses at a church site or by placing more of their students in churches as interns.

3. Individuals and groups form institutes or training centers to train leaders and develop resources for the church.

The potential benefits of such initiatives are obvious, but more important are the potential difficulties. In the first instance, church-housed seminaries and conferences can be controlled by a single focus or dominating agenda. Further, the church-housed seminary may have little to no contact with broader communities of the church and scholarship.[3] On the other hand, when courses are simply transferred from the school to the church, or when a school sends interns to a church, the church provides the space, but the school and its particular agenda can control all matters related to the educational process. In this case, the seminary tends to be out of touch with the realities of the church and its ministry. Since theological schools were established as centers for leadership development for the church, this disconnect defeats the purpose of the school and further weakens the church.[4] Finally, when agencies see their role as developing leaders and resources for the church, the dominating emphasis can be program as ministry, or leadership as effective management, without a corresponding effort to understand the church as God sees it.

Wallace Alston argues that the reformation of the church will require and include the recovery of the church as a theological community and the ministry of the church as a theological vocation (Alston 2000a, 19). He maintains that the recovery of a theological community (as opposed to a market-driven, program-oriented, worship-as-entertainment center) will lead to a corresponding resurgence of theologians who write in the service of the church. The two sections that follow attempt to treat the church as both a theological community and a sociological or organizational entity and argue that a productive tension between the two must be sustained.

The Church as a Theological Community

Numerous theological texts have been written on the nature of the church. Here we shall consider simply the more obvious attributes of the church

---

[3]For this reason, some are making a distinction between church-based and church-housed theological education. Church-based theological education, as it matures, is increasingly aware of the implications of the *ecclesia* as base, recognizes the need for greater diversity of perspective, and is more intentional about the design of the education process. See Reed 1992 and 2001.

[4]Dan Aleshire, executive director of the Association of Theological Schools, has reminded us that the ancient tradition of theological education was church- or cathedral-based. However, it doesn't necessarily follow that church-based theological education is better. The issue is not church-based theological education, or nonformal education, or a richer pedagogy *as corrective*. The issue is a reformation in understanding of the character expected of the church, the people of God as clearly identified in Scripture. It is understanding and living out this character that determines the nature of theological education.

that can be derived from a reading of the letters to the churches in the New Testament. What would result if we took seriously even these most obvious characteristics of the church?

- The church is the community of the redeemed.

- The church is gathered by God for God's purposes.

- The church exists as an agent of reconciliation.

- Christ is the head of the church.

- The congregation called together by God for God's purposes is under the leadership of Christ and empowered by the Spirit.

- The church is a community of people on mission and as such must fulfill God's purposes.

- The church is a community where the Holy Spirit is active.

- The Spirit of God empowers, gifts, sustains, and sets apart the church for the accomplishment of God's purposes.

- Authority resides in God and God's revelation.

- Congregations have particular responsibility over matters of decision making and discernment of error.

- The church is a community where church discipline is practiced—where members help each other follow the path of obedience.

We are not expected to recreate the forms of the New Testament church, but a consideration of what God expected of the early church is instructive. One day I determined to read all the letters to the church in the New Testament and write down every phrase, every word, every statement that was addressed to the congregations who received these letters. What were the congregations being admonished to do? To be? To know? It was readily apparent from the long list that resulted that very little explicit direction was given to the churches with regard to organization and structure. However, there was substantial, sober, explicit direction given as to the character of the church—the people of God. Significantly, the New Testament letters are not intended primarily for individuals. Even those addressed to an individual were to be read over the shoulder, as it were, by the congregation. The admonitions, the encouragement, the instructions to the church, then, are minimally structural and addressed to the congregation *as a whole*.

What difference would it make if all the people of the church were *expected* to demonstrate to the world a particular sort of character? A theme that appears frequently in Willard's writings on spirituality is that the American church has made the serious error of presuming that discipleship, or the expectation of obedient followership, can be separated from belief in Christ as Savior. Belief in the right things without attention to character is incomplete. "The natural bridge from faith to obedience or abundance is precisely discipleship to Jesus Christ" (Willard 2000b). Nicholas Healy asserts that the church is constituted by the activity of the Holy Spirit but also "*by the activity of its members as they live out their lives of discipleship*.... The identity of the concrete church is not simply given; it is constructed and ever reconstructed by the grace-enabled activities of its members as they embody the church's practices, beliefs and valuations" (Healy 2000, 5, emphasis added).

Regarding a theological expression that can inform what we do as the church, Kevin Giles argues that the "best solution to the quest for the fundamental church concept, under which all other titles and descriptions of the church can be subsumed, is 'the Christian community'" (Giles 1995, 15). This conclusion is reflected in many contemporary writings that attempt to call the church back to its fundamental identity. Yet Scripture provides numerous descriptions of the church; perhaps the real picture of the church is a shimmering kaleidoscope. However, it is valid to see the church as a community characterized by the many other attributes given in the New Testament. Whether or not Giles's conclusion is completely agreeable, in an age when churches are adopting the term *community* in their name or when church advertising appeals to those searching for a warm community, his warning about the ways community is practiced and defined is important.

Though the word *communio* (or *koinonia*) can be translated "fellowship," Giles says, our customary usage of *fellowship* is inadequate for what the word means in the original. Community or fellowship is not expressed by just getting along or by feeling good in a certain place. Community emerges as people participate together in suffering, in giving, in the gospel, in the body and blood of Christ. "The word is thus used of the relationships that constitute the Christian community, the church—but, we add, never of the social reality thereby created" (ibid., 16). In other words, *communio* or *koinonia* is never applied to a concrete group of people or an institution. The term speaks of the relationship Christians have with Christ and, then, with each other. Willard's observation is pertinent:

> We are not here to create a community. God is creating a community, and we are a part of that. But we're here to redeem community by living in the kingdom of God. We are here to create something with God, if you wish, but not by ourselves. When we set out to produce community, I believe that we are stepping into an area where God will not bless. It may be that we'll do good things—God knows we need community. But it is one of the great temptations historically to suppose that human beings are capable of creating community. (Willard 2000b, 1)

Giles reminds us that "God's work in history, as it is presented in the biblical drama, involves the gathering together of a people who are united to him and to each other" (Giles 1995, 18). *In other words, community is first and foremost defined by what God expects.* The church God envisions is a unity (John 14; Rom. 12:4; 1 Cor. 12:12; Eph. 4:12)—a people that worships and serves God. However, as Gordon Fee has observed, Paul's concern with the body metaphor "is not that the body is one *even though* it has many members, thus arguing for their need for unity despite their diversity. Rather, his concern is expressed in v. 14, that *even though the body is one*, it does not consist of one member but of many, thus arguing for their need for diversity, since they are in fact one body" (Fee 1987, 601). In other words, unity *requires* diversity!

This diverse community *must* be defined by obedience, service, community, and the desire to glorify God. In this respect, it is significant that the people of God existed long before there was the Bible as we have it today. A danger for evangelicals in particular is to assume that God is interested only in the preservation of the Bible (a distortion made worse when its interpretation is assumed to belong to a privileged group) and that cognitive mastery of that Scripture is sufficient; this diminishes the imperative of growing as a people toward Christlikeness. Furthermore, the very purpose of the congregation is weakened when prohibitions and practices are imposed on the church with the use of isolated passages, divorced from context and experience. In this respect, we can miss the New Testament emphasis on the authority that is *given to congregations*, which implies the need for greater attention to congregational development (not church growth in the numeric sense). Don Carson notes that New Testament congregations are involved in decision making alongside the apostles and elders (Acts 15:22). Congregations hold decision-making responsibility over a wide range of issues affecting internal order (1 Corinthians 11:20-26; 2 Cor. 8-9). Congregations have authority and responsibility to protect themselves from false teachers (Galatians; 2 Cor. 10-13; 2 John). When discipline is needed, the appeal is to the entire congregation to act (1 Cor. 5; Gal. 6:1). Congregational members are responsible participants in the selection of leaders and delegates (Acts 6:3; 15:22; 1 Cor. 16:3; see Carson 1984, 228-30). The need for more than transmissive teaching and preaching in the congregation and for leaders who lead from the midst of the congregation becomes apparent if these significant areas of congregational authority are taken seriously as areas of development. To use this authority wisely necessitates that *congregations* be growing to maturity in Christ.

At this point, a consideration of the sociological or organizational nature of the church is necessary. The congregation of God's people is expected to live as God demands. It is a community under one head, Jesus Christ, and empowered by one Spirit. What are the significant implications for organization, leadership, relationship, and style of ministry for a church that understands its identity as a people gathered for God's purposes, whose head is Jesus Christ, and whose purpose is fulfilled only through the gifting, guidance, and empowerment of the Holy Spirit? What types of organizational structures and patterns of relationship will make possible the development of the spiritual character clearly described in Scripture? If Christ is the head of the church, what is the role of leaders in the congregation? What is the nature of authority, power, responsibility, and accountability? In what ways would worship, education, and mission be affected if a congregation made these connections and took the implications seriously?

The Church as a Sociological Community

To a great extent, the search for a theological understanding of the church grows out of a concern that emphasis on organizational and social dimensions of the church has diminished the emphasis on spirituality and accountability to God. However, it must not be forgotten that the organizational and social concern emphases were themselves a corrective for a church considered bound by theological rigidity and irrelevant to human concerns. A healthy interplay is needed between the theological and sociological dimensions of the church, such that organization, leadership, human interaction, intercultural interaction, care, advocacy, and so on are stimulated by the rich literature of the social sciences *and* assessed theologically. Because the church is also a human construction, we have to deal with structures and procedures for the organized church—what they are and how to evaluate them. Organizational structures profoundly affect the behavior and attitudes of persons in the congregation. Organizational patterns and practices communicate. They speak to the world of our sincerity, of the quality of our relationships. They reveal our understanding of the nature of power and authority. Insights from the social sciences informed by theological principle, and vice versa, can help us understand these dynamics.[5]

The church has both a sociological and a theological character. As an institution it is informed by institutional principles and procedures and organizational and relational dynamics. At the same time, organizational practices (e.g., styles of ministry, leadership, organizational structures, planning processes) should be consistent with the character God expects. The theological character of the church provides criteria for how we interpret, apply, and evaluate organizational principles, procedures, and relationships. Without attention to the fundamentally theological issues of identity and character, the role of the church in culture is confused, often indistinguishable from most other organizations. Sadly, for many in North American society, and for many in congregations, the church does not have the kind of persona that even nonbelievers instinctively feel it should have. Without a lively integration of its theological and sociological character, the church becomes incomprehensible, not only to the world but also to Christians.

Part of this chapter was written at a resort center in Nova Scotia. As we looked out at the Atlantic Ocean one day, the owner said, "If you want to see church on Sunday around here, go to the local Wal-Mart!" How do we answer the owner's implicit criticism? If we are unable to disentangle the

---

[5]In this respect, see literature that attempts to recast organizational practices in light of the nature and mission of the church as God sees it. Representative examples are Rendle and Mann (2003) and Hudson (2004). See also www.alban.org. Last accessed in October 2005.

institutional forms of the church that we have created from the church as God sees it, we have no answer. Clearly, the answer is not to be found in Wal-Mart–style communities with better programs, user-friendly services, and efficient organization. In a culture searching for community, the institutionalized expression of the church alone is not an option.

In my judgment, the organizational pattern we have established for congregational communities is upside down. We often begin our planning with discussion about what programs or ministries we need to establish, believing that effective programming characterizes a successful church. If the ongoing challenge for the church in the world, renewed in each generation, is to learn its identity as a people gathered by God and to live out that identity in the world, then the organizational pattern must be turned on its head. Think first of the church as the people of God, rather than as an organization defined by programs. Then envision those experiences that are necessary for the maturing and spiritual development of the entire congregation: worship, learning, authentic service, prayer, relationship, and so on—defined as the congregation seeks to ascertain their meaning and the nature of their practice from Scripture and the history of Christian communities. As the life of the community of faith emerges and as people come to know one another, specific needs, concerns, ministry options, and ways to communicate the gospel within society will become apparent. *Only then should programs and specialized activities be developed.* Some of the programs and ministries that emerge will be age related, many will be time specific; most should grow out of the gifts of the Holy Spirit given through individuals to the community of faith. In a success-oriented culture, beginning with matters related to the formation of the congregation's spiritual character may seem a waste of time. However, without such consideration, the church is simply one more helping agency in society, and God's presence in the body is optional, or worse, unnecessary!

Before we can think productively about theological education and leadership development for the church, the dual character of the church must be apprehended; and the institutionalized church must be demythologized. Its organization is essentially a human creation—no matter how hard we try to justify it theologically. Yet the existing institutional structures of the church have become so deeply entrenched that they have taken on a pseudotheological verity. The problem, of course, is that we don't know what would emerge from a robust interaction of the theological and sociological character of the church. The familiar is comfortable, and because it is comfortable, we are shaped by it. When we have an investment in the institution and a stake in its continuance, it is hard to let it go or to allow it to change. We may become loyal to the institution to the degree that our service is to preserve the institution, and we are soon unable to critique its nature and function on the basis of biblical and theological principle.

Theological Education and Leadership Development

A commonly suggested antidote to the perceived problems of today's church is to develop leaders who know how to manage an organization and who communicate in an appealing fashion from the pulpit. As necessary as it is to have someone in a congregation who can assist with organizational matters, the more urgent need is for leaders who are able to assist congregations to understand and live out their identity as the people of God in the world.

Today seminaries are under pressure from denominational leaders and congregations to train better leaders. However, the nature and role of leadership is distorted when churches seek to be successful or efficient rather than being the people of God. Churches seeking strong leaders who can create successful churches should always be unhappy with the products of seminaries. Churches who are simply seeking pastors who can function well (in preaching, teaching, relationships, office management) should likewise be unhappy with the product of seminaries. The seminary, with a functioning community of scholars, should provide assistance to the church as it seeks to embrace more biblically consistent understandings of leadership. Where this is lacking, the answer is not to create church-based seminaries *for the purpose of* creating strong leaders for successful churches. Nor is the answer for seminaries to enhance and enlarge functional aspects of the curriculum in order to develop the pastoral skills that many churches want. If the church has departed from the most basic descriptions of its character and purpose in Scripture, leaders will be in the undesirable position of "trying to make an organization work that has departed from its function" (Willard 2000b).

Churches and schools that fashion leadership-development experiences based on understandings of the nature and purpose of the church other than what Scripture itself identifies are not serving well the people of God. They are actually setting church leaders up for failure. Without question, leaders are needed who both understand the spiritual realities of the people of God and have some sense of the needs of an organization. However, we make the mistake of equating organizational charisma with spiritual leadership. Eugene Peterson is one of many who sharply criticize churches and denominations who don't understand the difference between these tasks.

> The pastors of America have metamorphosed into a company of shopkeepers, and the shops they keep are churches, They are preoccupied with shopkeepers' concerns—how to keep the customers happy, how to lure customers away from competitors down the street, how to package the goods so that the customers will lay out more money.
>
> Some of them are very good shopkeepers…. Yet it is still shop keeping; religious shop keeping to be sure, but shop keeping all the same. (Peterson 1987, 1)

Toward a More Appropriate Approach to Leadership Development

In the late twentieth century, theological institutions began to align themselves with large, corporate-style, multicampus churches who offered training programs that were once part of the theological curriculum. Isn't this a good thing? It seems that the seminary is finally becoming aware that these churches offer a more relevant way of training men and women for ministry. However, these large churches represent a very small proportion of churches in North America, and their corporate philosophy is only one perspective on the nature of the church and its ministry. Men and women trained in these venues may be no more able to serve the church's mission in the world than those trained in existing programs criticized for being out of touch.

Certainly, theological institutions and large churches want to bring the best resources to bear on leadership development for the church. But many theological educators and church leaders alike are also concerned about consequences for the church. Churches, especially those struggling for survival or wanting the world to see them as important, tend to respond first to factors related to the marketplace, human need, or even the agenda of powerful individuals. They see what is and respond with program and ministry, before they have also considered the theologically driven what-ought-to-be questions. For instance, ministry as meeting needs can easily devolve to sustaining dependency and can even become a subtle form of control over the other. Is there a theologically driven what-ought-to-be response that should inform our understanding of ministry? My commitment to the priesthood of all believers, and to the imperative of development implicit in the creation, leads me to view ministry as development of the other. In other words, simply meeting needs may never help the needy become ministers themselves, or more fully human.

Flawed views of the church and ministry inevitably lead to flawed leadership-development strategies. Graduates of seminaries inevitably find themselves deficient and seek out assistance from what they perceive as successful enterprises. Consequently, the twenty-first-century church is in danger of being buried alive by an avalanche of ideas intended to stimulate leadership skills and programs. Church leaders flock by the hundreds and thousands to the latest conference on how to have a successful church—and too often come away unable to effect significant change or renewal in theirs. The barrage of survival concerns, the television images of the successful pastor, the messages of innumerable how-to conferences, and the dizzying swirl of expectations from their congregation often leaves church leaders in doubt about their role and vocation. Concern for institutional survival compels church leaders to seek advice from those they consider successful or effective. However, images of leadership and organization borrowed from presumed successful churches or from the world of business are nearly always inadequate and incomplete. If chosen or adapted without good judgment, borrowed images will fail, and without appropriate guidance, church leaders will be compelled by this failure to seek another image, and another. They will remain caught in the maze of literature and conferences, searching for the best image for themselves and their church.

The rhetoric of church-growth strategists, organizational planners, trainers, and promoters is empty when it is grounded in motives oriented to success and effectiveness.[6] These motives tend to create a perspective in which church growth is seen as the result of strategic planning, leadership training, management, and marketing. Church growth becomes an entrepreneurial effort driven by a strong leader rather than a work of the Spirit of God. Efficiency, effectiveness, and success are powerful gods in the contemporary church, but they are false gods—often unrecognized as such in contemporary church life. One who knows something about marketing strategies, who understands the kind of music and style of speaker that attract a crowd, who knows how to manage the platform, who is able to plan programs that meet the sociological needs of a community would be able to build a large church without much difficulty. However, one wouldn't have to be a Christian to do it!

The problem that afflicts the Christian community in many regions of the world is not the existence of large churches *per se*; the problem emerges when size becomes a *human* quest and obsession rather than accepted as something God will grant if God chooses (note the emphasis in Acts 2:37–47 and 5:12–14). It may be a fine point; after all, it seems that God added to the number of this first church because its people did something. But look carefully at what they did. Walter Liefeld, distinguished professor emeritus of Trinity Evangelical Divinity School, in a sermon entitled "The Church That Nobody Dared to Join," noted that Acts 5:1–14 presents a picture of congregational development unfamiliar to most North Americans. Ananias and Sapphira lied to the Holy Spirit and were struck dead for their deception, causing great fear in the church and among all those who heard about the event. After their deaths (not exactly a church marketing strategy) and the performance of many signs and wonders by the apostles, *no one dared to join them, but many believed in the Lord and were added to their number.*

Willard is concerned that congregational commitment in North America is considered voluntary—exclusively a matter of personal choice;

---

[6]One should never assume that all efforts by superchurches of America are without merit. Many leaders are concerned about underlying spiritual values. However, a tendency to export the latest "flavor of the month" is becoming particularly problematic: in other countries, pastors desperate to learn how they too can have large, successful churches flock to conferences that are often planned and presented with little or no understanding of local struggles and local culture, and even less awareness of how culture makes a difference in practice and in the definition of problems.

this leads pastors to feel it is their responsibility to entice people to come to their churches. Suggesting that the user-friendly church may be nothing more than a reflection of a personal need to get people into church, he expresses doubt that "Jesus could have carried on his ministry if he had to...try to get people to come and hear him" (Willard 2000b).

One consequence of this trend is efforts to enhance the profession of the ministry. Unfortunately, the nature and formats of professional education are not well understood by theological educators. For instance, the M.Div. is considered a professional degree by North American accrediting agencies; but as already observed, in seminaries it is treated as if it were in the same educational category as a liberal arts degree. Since the 1960s, professional initiatives in theological education have helped the church, but in today's high-pressure climate, professionalism is increasingly a problem.

Effects of the Professional Model of Ministry on the Church

As North American churches increased in complexity through the nineteenth and twentieth centuries, the notion of professional leadership, borrowed from the German university model and modified substantially in postrevolutionary America, was embraced by the churches. Churches, in effect, evolved into corporations managed by CEOs with special skills. The role of the minister as pastor and preacher did not disappear, but the relation between the minister and the community seemed to become that of a specialist serving a particular sector of society.

In seminaries, the dominance of professional and corporate images of leaders led to a curriculum focused on preparation: the schools existed to *prepare* leaders for ministry in the church and the world. Often the implicit assumptions were that the schools are best equipped to prepare leaders, that churches have little to no role to play in the affirmation of suitability and giftedness, and that leadership is a matter of developing skills and acquiring information.[7] The experience of the candidate became unimportant, for his or her preparation would begin and end with the school. Over time, as lea-

---

[7] Charles Van Engen avers that "only students called by God, empowered by the Spirit, and acknowledged by the church for ministry in the world are indispensable. Administrative infrastructures, permanent buildings, well-stocked libraries, published books, resident faculty, and classroom instruction are all luxuries" (1994, 15).

dership has become more functional and churches more corporate, the capacity of churches and schools to contribute meaningfully to the continued development of leaders has declined.

Through the early decades of the twentieth century, theological education was tailored (consciously or unconsciously) to produce clergy and, ultimately, other professional staff for church. In the 1970s, the call to "liberate the laity" was heard for a brief time, and the theme of the priesthood of all believers resurfaced in the literature. However, the corporate structures of the church were now so deeply ingrained, and the relationships of clergy and laity in relation to those structures so defined, that only as questions began to be raised in the 1990s about the liberation of structures would the nature of leadership assumed by clergy be seen by some not as a biblical imperative but a corporate invention. With the increasing professionalization of the church, leadership became a theory to be applied or a set of skills to be learned and practiced. Numerous books promise that effective leadership results from applying a number of "keys" or "habits" to circumstances.

It has been observed that a word translatable as "leadership" does not appear in the Greek New Testament. This omission may not be significant, except to underscore that the Scripture's emphasis is clearly on leaders and not on some abstracted theory of leadership. The more important lessons to be gained from the leaders described in Scripture are found in how they came to understand God's purposes for his people and how they responded—*with considerable variation in style*—to that understanding.

Willard suggests that the church is in trouble in North America, not because of leaders but because of an idolatry of leadership—which leads to inevitable "evasion of responsibility by the followers" (Willard 2000b) Carson notes that even the Pastoral Epistles' lists of qualities applied to leaders are really qualities that are expected of the whole people of God. Only two qualities might possibly be singled out as particular to a leader: that a person should be "an apt teacher" and "must not be a recent convert" (1 Tim. 3:2, 6). All other qualities in the lists are elsewhere mandated of the entire people of God (Carson 1984).

The work of the pastor-teacher is to equip or make fit God's people for acts of service (Eph. 4:12). Paul describes a threefold pattern for the development of leaders in his instruction to Timothy: a leader teaches another, who in turn teaches others, so that they can teach others (2 Tim. 2:2). The understanding that people are to be developed so that they will in turn be able to develop others challenges assumptions that pastors are being trained to lead their flock. The shepherd image is an appropriate and biblical image; however, important questions have to be asked: When do sheep become shepherds? What is the role of the shepherd in creating a climate wherein the sheep can become shepherds? If valid, these questions imply that theological education must be for the whole people of God.

Theological education can no longer be restricted to the training of a ministerial elite. However, if we accept the premises that leaders are necessary and that the Spirit of God gives diverse gifts to the church, theological education that fosters the development of leaders *and* serves the whole people of God will likely require different, though integrated, educational strategies, different curricular forms, and different educational venues.

Emerging Initiatives in Theological Education Related to the Church

Concern is building over the perceived ineffectiveness and mounting costs of school-based theological education and its distance from the church. In response to such concern, concrete initiatives and ideas that allow more productive connections between the church and the theological school are emerging.

Church-Based Theological Education

Reasoning that theological schools are not only dubious centers for ministry development but that they take students/leaders out of the very contexts where their skills and awareness need to be enriched, the growing church-based theological education movement sees its mission as developing leaders in context. The more mature expressions of church-based theological education contribute what Ted Ward describes as a dominating ecclesiology within the scholastic approaches to theology. That is, reflection on the theological meaning of the church as God sees it in relation to its institutional expression grounds theological education (as opposed to teaching men and women who can then build a successful institution called a church). Where theology in the seminary tends to begin with abstractions, Ward suggests that many church-based leaders are growing in their capacity to foster theological reflection in relation to the practices of the church and the question of how God wants his people to respond. Theological education is not "content packed in boxes and delivered to students," but learning of knowledge in relation to issues of importance for the church and service.[8] As church-based efforts continue to mature and as their leaders discover criteria and principles that will guide their practice, they could effectively replace existing seminary models.

The most obvious vulnerability of church-based efforts is the tendency to bypass the seminary as one place for equipping leaders for today's church. As supporters of church-based efforts disparage the seminary, they flirt with the danger of losing the depth and missing the vital questions that a true community of scholars brings to the development of the whole people of God. When churches relegated their responsibilities for education and pastoral and missionary development to schools, the habits, attitudes, and skills required to be a center for theological education were diminished or lost. Now, as churches complain about inadequacy in the seminary's product and react by bypassing the schools, they make almost no corresponding effort to create new settings and new roles for a community of scholars. *A community of scholars in some form* is desperately needed by churches that tend to base decisions about leadership, organization, and ministry on other than biblically informed principles and sound scholarship. However, the community of scholars must not be disconnected from the church and its mission in the world.

In-Ministry Models of Theological Education

The in-ministry approach is related to the church-based approach but doesn't necessarily require a shift from the seminary to the church. Robert Banks (1999) suggests that theological education is directed to three audiences: the laity, the clergy (or those who lead), and the scholar. The resulting model of theological education is oriented to the whole people of God—not just to the training of a ministerial elite; it involves learning in ministry, may entail "coming apart" for a time, and requires a closer relationship between the church and seminary. Banks places the Bible at the center of the curriculum, with other disciplines added as derivative. Study is integrative and collaborative. Faculty and students are together involved in ministry. The movement of the curriculum is toward personal formation, theological reflection, and ministry.

---

[8]Ted Ward, personal conversation.

Multiple Sectors for Theological Education

Ted Ward suggests that theological education may split into two sectors: the more academic and longer programs for churches that believe they need leaders with advanced master's degrees and doctorates, and more functional shorter programs that will serve the majority of churches. If there is a defensible difference between the kinds of educational experiences offered for those who are now or will be congregational leaders and for those who have gifts of scholarship, the formats of theological education may well be reshaped into three distinct but mutually permeable categories:

- *church-based theological education*—holistic educationally, concerned with the development of leaders in context, intentional in the inclusion of professional ministers and laity in learning experiences

- *apprenticeship of the scholar*—men and women with significant gifts in scholarship (to be distinguished from formidable feats of memory), affirmed by the church and connected with the church and society, are brought into relationship with mature scholars in various disciplines who are likewise connected with the church and society

- *professional development of the leader*—utilizing his or her context, as well as experiences away from it, to shape capacities and enable reflection on authentic practice

A variation on this suggested model is that theological education could come to consist of three *movements*: (1) Responsible education initiatives in the local congregation would stimulate adults to reflect on the life of faith in relation to real-world issues. (2) When questions emerge that require specialized input, one or more scholars are invited into the process—not to give the right answer but to introduce knowledge, ideas, and new questions into the process. (3) If men and women with particular abilities and interests in scholarship emerge through this process, the church would support their apprenticeship to a community of scholars. The role of existing seminaries could be to serve the church in developing those who have the gifts of scholarship.

Niche Seminaries

As institutions realize that their survival is threatened by their attempts to maintain a large number of programs and that passing burgeoning financial deficits on to students is seriously depleting enrollment and creating ministry-threatening financial indebtedness for graduates, "niche seminaries" could emerge, each embodying a particular specialty. Whether this will exacerbate an already fragmented educational effort remains to be seen. Theological education could decentralize into mobile centers around the world, connected by face-to-face consultations and through technologically mediated networks. Temporary intentional communities could then be created, where configurations of scholars, laity, students, and church leaders would come together in retreat-style settings for one or two weeks to engage one or more particular problems or issues.

Communities of Discernment

The notion of the seminary as a community of discernment recalls a former emphasis on the seminary as the intellectual center of the church. This notion has a long history and is not without merit; however, when it is assumed that all the information a person will need must be acquired through a degree program, the role of the intellectual center devolves to the number and types of courses offered. Consequently, the number of courses has proliferated to the point where the curriculum is not sustainable as a framework for the development of leaders. Intellectual development understood as merely the acquisition of information is not adequate. Ross Bender envisions the intellectual task more holistically: "The fundamental task of our seminaries...is the task of discerning the Word and the will of God for our day. I would go further and affirm that the task of spiritual discernment is the fundamental task of the church and that the seminary, being a seminary of the church, shares in this task" (Bender 1997, 179–80). He proposes that discernment is "carried out within a cognitive frame of reference which involves first, the perception that God is acting in human history; second, a lively sense of being caught up in God's purposive activity; and third, an awareness of the eschatological character of our existence." Bender qualifies "cognitive frame of reference" by describing the task as involving intellectual reflection and a "total response to the God of faith, obedience and love" (ibid., 187).[9] Bender's continuum of discernment includes two types of activity: critical reflection and purposeful activity that "issues out of the response of obedience to God" (ibid., 193). However, in his efforts to describe a unique role for the seminary, he seems to stumble over a distinction between the seminary as a community of reflection and the church as a community of action.

Communities of Faith

The specialization of theology into cognitive categories and the distancing of theological education from the church has desperately weakened the Christian community. Nicholas Wolterstorff, discussing the distancing of university theology from the church, argues for a refashioning of theology in relation to the gospel and the life of faith: "If ecclesiastical and theological interest in doctrine is not directed toward this faith but rather to doctrinal development in and of itself, then it misses life and with it its own real task" (Wolterstorff 1996, 131). The task of the church is to awaken a sensibility of God's presence. "And one of the most important theoretical tasks of theology today is to provide the conceptual clarification necessary for this task, that is, to develop, probe, and critically investigate what *God is present* means" (ibid., 132–33). Theology, then, must not be understood simply as a social science. "And neither can it be a guiding science for some religious system or for the church if it is not first something different and much more basic, namely, *critical knowledge of God*" (ibid., 133).

Wolterstorff defines theology as "sustained reflection about God" (ibid., 36). When does the community feel a need for this kind of reflection, and who leads the community in it—the theologians? With the fragmentation of theology and its persisting specialization, sustained reflection is virtually impossible. To be fair, the educational structures don't exist that would bring theologians, students, and church members into a sustained dialogue characterized by mutual respect—a dialogue that would allow critical questions to be asked and examined. Even if the educational structures did exist, Wolterstorff observes "that the root of the alienation of uni-

---

[9]In 1983, John Fletcher reported on a survey of 136 seminary administrators. Of the goals cited for theological education, the most often cited was "To be a center for theological and ethical reflection to the churches, denominations, and the communities in which seminaries are located" (Fletcher 1983, 102).

versity theology from the church lies in the modern church wanting the wrong things of its theologians, and that the theologians of the modern academy are often nothing short of heroic in refusing to give the church what it wants—forcing it to ask the questions it *should* ask rather than those it prefers to ask, forcing it to accept the answers it *should* accept, rather than those it would like to accept" (ibid., 37). This claim of heroism presumes (1) that modern theologians are in fact aware of the complexity of the issues confronting the church and the theological challenges these present, and (2) that churches are actually asking questions of theologians. Stanley Hauerwas takes a more blunt approach in his criticism. "Modernity marks the time when theologians began to believe that their task is to explain the truth of what Christians believe in a manner that assumes the explanation is truer than the belief itself. Such theology is no longer the servant of the church but tries to be its master" (Hauerwas 1999, 15). One conclusion from the debate is that theological education is valid only if the community is broadened to include the church. In such a community of faith, theologians and church leaders become partners in the task of theology.

A Congregational Paradigm: A Dilemma for Theological Education

The term *paradigm* is so overused, or ill used, that one can hardly manage the effort to describe yet another proposal for a new paradigm. Perhaps the proposals are better understood as efforts to bring together elements that have for too long been separated, with the primary culprit being the fragmented and specialized nature of the theological curriculum. James Hopewell (1984) and Joseph Hough and Barbara Wheeler (1988) have proposed that a congregational paradigm replace the current paradigm of theological education. Their proposal allows for a community of scholars but shifts the focus of educational efforts from the cognitive and character development of the student to the cognitive and character development *of the church*. The congregation thus is conceived as the organizing principle for the curriculum.[10] But if the church is viewed as an institution that needs to be managed, without careful thought to the implications of scriptural characterizations of the church, congregational and leadership development emphases in theological schools, conferences, and seminars will stress skills, programs, tactics, and corporate growth almost to the exclusion of spiritual reflection, discernment, and perception. As a result, the relationship of theological education and the church will falter.

In the literature, the notion of a congregational paradigm seems to have lost momentum. However, efforts to ground theological education in the church persist. Each attempt demonstrates how difficult it is to distinguish between the institutional form of the church and the *ecclesia* or people of God. Developing leaders in church-based approaches defaults most often to training in skills, or, in an attempt not to be trapped in a solely functional curriculum, church-based efforts will attempt to rival the scholarship of the academy. Church-based efforts to replicate the academy in a new setting do not reflect a new paradigm. Similarly, if seminaries and church-based efforts focus on the institutional needs of the church, the people of God will neglect their missiological, prophetic, and pastoral responsibilities in culture.

The dilemma that confronts efforts to ground theological education in the church is the inevitable disappointment leaders face in serving the church. Numerous former staff members in churches can be found among the ranks of seminary faculty, employed by helping agencies in society, or bereft of faith. In many cases, these men and women have left the church because of disappointment and a sense of failure. If a proposal for a congregational paradigm for theological education is met with cynicism, most of us are not surprised. The ideal of a church and school partnership is well founded; the reality is much harder to realize.

---

[10]To test his vision, James Hopewell initiated a program at Candler Seminary that brought together a pastor, a professor, twelve laypeople, and twelve senior students to work on a problem of congregational significance for a term. However, Hopewell wasn't necessarily seeking alliances between seminaries and congregations. "If church and school adopt the same norms and perspectives, each institution loses its prophetic and constructive power" (Hopewell 1984, 64). Theological institutions need the freedom to help congregations evaluate and reflect theo
logically on their mission and practices, just as churches need the freedom to interact with schools about tendencies that are incompatible with kingdom values.

The next generation of efforts to foster a congregational paradigm to replace or at least to supplement theological institutions may find theological education for the whole people of God a more productive ideal. In equipping church members who enable the church to live out its Christian identity, theological education becomes more inclusive. But those who shape theological education for the whole people of God will find that more than conventional school-style approaches are needed. Joseph Hough and John Cobb point the way to understanding the primary role of leaders as helping congregations understand and learn how to live out their identity as the people of God. They believe the problem with theological education is not that it has been oriented around a clerical paradigm but that the church has fundamentally misunderstood the nature of church leadership (Hough and Cobb 1985, 5). Eugene Peterson describes the role of leaders as keeping the community attentive to God. He continues, "Three pastoral acts are so basic, so critical that they determine the shape of everything else. The acts are praying, reading Scripture, and giving spiritual direction." Peterson then describes these acts as acts of attention. "Prayer is an act in which I bring myself to attention before God; reading Scripture is an act of attending to God in his speech and action; spiritual direction is an act of giving attention to what God is doing in the person who happens to be before me at any given moment" (Peterson 1987, 2).

As efforts to foster a congregational paradigm proceed, it is likely that at least three modes of theological education will be needed: a professional school, a setting where scholars are apprenticed to a community of scholars, and a more fluid series of learning experiences for the whole people of God (including those recognized by the congregation as leaders). Each of these modes will accept as prior its responsibility to understand and serve the church's mandate to be the people of God in the world. Each mode will be learning-focused and characterized by a relational pedagogy. Those involved in the development of each mode will interact and plan together.

Even though most in seminaries have little to no understanding of developments in professional education, it is likely that they will continue to be construed as professional schools for some years to come. However, the purpose of the school is not to train skillful managers but "practical theologians" who can critically reflect on the church's life and practice (Hough and Cobb 1985, 18, 91–92); and who can assist congregations to understand their identity and service as the people of God. However, the church also requires leaders with administrative ability, and at this point the interaction of the three modes becomes especially necessary. Pastors often find themselves consumed with administrative detail, often to the detriment of the acts of attention Peterson describes. In order to share this responsibility, business men and women are often placed on church boards, with the assumption that they are most able to govern an institution. The fact that business people are on church boards is not the problem. The problem emerges when these men and women are not enabled to think and act *both* organizationally and theologically in relation to their mission as leaders in a congregation. If time and opportunity are not given to explore this dimension, business professionals are generally such busy people that they will automatically default to the skills, conceptions, and habits of mind and behavior they know best—organizational behaviors. These behaviors and ideas will be laid over the church, and in time the church will be no different in its ethos from any other institution in society. Only when leaders are present who can help members understand their identity as the people of God will the implications of this identity for organization and ministry be considered.

It follows, then, that some of the more important tasks of theological education are for scholars, congregational leaders, and the laity to engage the multiple dimensions of the church's mission in society; to understand the nature and identity of the people of God; to address particular institutional realities (power, authority, organizational dynamics, decision making, and so on) from biblical principle and in relation to Scripture's clear accounts of what God expects of the character and behavior of his people.

Daniel Schipani uses the term "ecclesial paradigm" to describe a model of theological education that is "focused on the church's identity, nature and purpose, namely its very life and its ministry." Theological education then "will take place within contexts of authentic evangelical piety and spirituality, genuine Christian ethics and moral behavior, and an epistemology…governed by the very Spirit of God" (Schipani 1997, 22–24). Such education serves and supports outcomes within the church's community "*to enable persons for worship, to equip them for community, and to empower them for mission*" (ibid., 26). The theological curriculum is shaped around the text of the Bible, the life and story of the ecclesial community past and present, and cultural and intercultural circumstances. Learning processes are "communal, dialogical, collaborative, and discipleship/ministry-oriented" (ibid., 30). Schipani's conception is not what some would describe as a church-based model. The ecclesial paradigm is worked out in relation to both graduate (i.e., academic) and professional schools, as distinguished from the ministerial paradigm in which the seminary is exclusively a professional school.

Schipani suggests that in the ecclesial paradigm the educational process is related to the purpose of the church, its focus is on the formation and transformation of congregations, and its outcome is to support and renew worship, community, and mission (ibid., 35). Summarizing Schipani, Marlene Enns identifies the characteristics of theological education operating within an ecclesial paradigm—some of which are similar to those suggested by Hopewell, Hough and Wheeler above. First, the nature, identity, and purpose of the church constitute the starting point. Second, theological education is concerned with the formation and transformation of the church. "The primary focus is not on the development of the students (potential and present leaders of the church), but on the development of the church" (Enns 2000b, 4). Third, theological education is an extension of the church's teaching ministry. Fourth, ecclesial theological education is an alternative to both the academic and clerical approaches to ministry development. Most notably, the ecclesial paradigm posits that the Christian community is fundamentally responsible for the educational task, not individual theologians. Theologians are not removed from the process, but they work in dialogue with the ecclesial community, as part of it.

Based on these characteristics, Enns discusses the need for a conversation between the Bible, the ecclesial community, and real-life situations. The conversation is not simply a cognitive exercise but one that draws on the mystical heritage of Christian faith (ibid., 9). The Anabaptist tradition within which Schipani and Enns speak stresses obedience and the revealing power of the Holy Spirit as keys to knowing that eventuate in wisdom and justice. It follows, then, that the practices of the church are organically linked to education. "Theological education is 'in the business' of helping the church to be more faithful as a People of God, more spiritual as a Body of Christ, and more incarnational as the Spirit's Temple" (ibid., 19).

The move to a congregational or ecclesial paradigm, related to the schools, is threatened by the fact that theological schools are receiving less ecclesiastical and denominational support and are increasingly driven for funding to sources outside the church. Many incoming students are less involved with churches, and some are seeking a theological education for reasons other than a career in the church. Further, the perceived need for credentialing, and the assumption that credentialing is accomplished in relation to formal, classroom-based models and through forms of testing common in the academy, makes it unlikely that theological schools will embrace the ecclesial paradigm. The academic model is not terribly effective at measuring that which matters in the life of faith, ministry, and leadership.

However, the notion of the theological school as the only, or even primary, source of trained leaders is no longer sustainable. Increasingly, small groups of faculty and church leaders, independent associations or foundations, and students themselves are experimenting with a variety of initiatives in theological education. Though it is relatively simple to fashion alternative curricula and learning experiences, the momentum of such initiatives often falters when confronted with the perceived need for academic rigor and credentialing. Thomas Thangaraj has been bold enough to try to demystify the notion of academic rigor: "Almost all the recent writers in theological education plead for an increase in academic rigor.... Though there is a widespread agreement that there should be more academic rigor, what we really mean by 'academic' is still unclear" (Thangaraj 1992, 13). If academic rigor is understood in terms of conceptual understanding, examined knowledge, vital questions, holistic development, reflection on practice, mutual learning, and so on, new initiatives will be well served. If academic rigor is simply understood as the transmission of the content of particular subjects by qualified scholars who are hard on their students, emerging initiatives will indeed falter.

Credentialing and accreditation are assumed necessary to guarantee a certain level of academic and professional performance and to simplify the movement of students from one school to another. However, it is not necessary that accreditation be based on one particular set of standards, nor is it necessary that accreditation be the exclusive province of the academy. In higher education generally, challenges to current models of accreditation and credentialing are gaining momentum.[11] In theological education, evidence of less than adequate competency and increased urgency about learning will lead increasingly to experimentation in the standards and agencies of accreditation. As church-based movements and other initiatives mature, they will develop their own forms of accreditation.[12] These experiments will succeed in some areas; however, temptations to power and prestige are also part of the dynamic of institutions. Whether in North America or on another continent, the persisting need for recognition, status, and social power is part of the pressure on institutions to maintain familiar systems.[13] If this pressure is recognized for what it is, leaders may realize the importance of affirming values that are more appropriate for institutions concerned about development, lifelong learning, and service and examine accreditation and credentialing procedures in relation to these values. Admittedly, these values are beginning to be reflected in the accreditation standards that relate to North American theological education, but it appears increasingly that theological institutions are slow to recognize their importance.

It has been noted that the revised Association of Theological Schools standards reflect areas that were once the prerogative of the church. It appears that the seminaries have determined that the churches aren't accomplishing the tasks detailed in the 1996 standards and that if these various gifts and graces are to be available for ministry, it will have to be because they developed, for the most part, in ATS theological schools. We have yet

---

[11]Concerned about flawed assumptions in university credentialing procedures, Charles Hayes writes, "While proof of qualification is clearly necessary in the professions, the current system allows credentials to represent a transfer of power rather than demonstrated competence. The process often leads to pointless restrictions that prevent many talented people from realizing their full potential. You can have a good education without having credentials just as you can have credentials without a good education" (Hayes 1995, 18).

[12]Some decades ago, Ward and others proposed a framework and criteria for a church-based accrediting body that would provide school input that is currently unavailable through the academy-based accreditation associations. See also Sweeney and Fortosis (1994).

[13]Paul Stevens and Brian Stelk offer a hard-hitting critique of the Western degree as the ultimate credential in many countries. "While Western political, economic, and military imperialism is not acceptable in the Two-Thirds World, cultural and educational imperialism is both acceptable and, by and large, welcomed. It holds the promise of success" (Stevens and Stelk 1993, 33).

to see if the seminaries can accomplish the tasks any more effectively. The 1996 standards raise accrediting issues that theological education has never before faced. And because the association, the member schools, approved the standards, no ATS member seminary in North America is free to say that the standards are not its responsibility.

For several years I was involved in a consultation on the aims and purposes of theological education under the leadership of Richard Mouw, president of Fuller Theological Seminary. About twenty faculty from different evangelical seminaries in America and representing a variety of disciplines met twice a year for several years. George Barna was invited to one of our meetings. We found him an engaging person, and our interaction with him was useful. During his presentation, Barna used two different sets of overhead transparencies. One set summarized his findings from interviews with pastors. The other set presented information he had gathered from congregations. He dealt with each set separately. The findings from interviews of American clergy could be summarized thus: Clergy feel confident in their understanding of the Bible, their knowledge of theology, and their capacity to teach and preach. They feel less confident about their ability to manage a changing organization and to work effectively with people. As Barna presented the other set of transparencies he said, in effect, "Members of congregations are not growing in their understanding of Scripture or in their spiritual lives, and they are confused about the nature of *their* ministry." I'm sure I wasn't the only person thinking, *What's wrong with this picture?* The chasm between what church leaders feel are their primary capacities and abilities and what members of congregations affirm is not happening in their lives is a critical issue for the future of theological education.

Recovering the Focus on the Church

God's primary interest is the church, defined as the people of God. It is doubtful that God mandated Christian schools, mission organizations, nonformal organizations, or even institutional expressions of the church. These are human creations and should always be seen as supportive to the mission of the people of God in the world. Therefore, their organizational structures can never be cast in concrete. God desires the strengthening of the *ecclesia*, but there is no particular reason to take theological schools, or theological education as we know it, as a given.

The burden of this chapter is that an understanding of the dual character of the church is essential in any effort to move forward in theological education. As long as we are on this earth, the dysfunctional nature of institutions will disappoint and frustrate all our efforts. However, we must accept that we will spend all our lives bailing in these leaky boats and move on. There are a few important premises and observations as we move on:

- The church is the community in which attitudes and behaviors critical to societal life and organizational development are nurtured.

- Theological education is conceived as professional schools, settings where scholars are apprenticed, and for the whole people of God.

- The appropriate development model for leaders reflects 2 Timothy 2:2 (developing leaders who in turn will be able to develop others).

- A shift is occurring: where institutional-instructional modes had been primary, there is movement toward lifelong learning communities in multiple modes.

- A trend is developing toward international partnerships among institutions and nonformal leadership-development initiatives.

- Theological education is slowly confronting its responsibilities to be church-focused and responsive to social issues.

At a consultation with theological faculty and administrators from various schools and countries in Central and Eastern Europe, a theologian affirmed the importance of a suitable framework that "really works for the church." For him, the least suitable framework is the institutional framework, for it is utterly inadequate to do justice to the role of the church. A trinitarian framework, as suggested in this chapter, is more suitable because it positions the role of the church in relation to kingdom principles and values. In his judgment, we must begin with the premise that God is restoring creation and that the church has a role to play in this task. "Real transformation comes from transformed people, not from well-organized churches." The church is a way of life, and in order to restore the meaning of the church as both a theological and a sociological entity, we will need to transform systems. This was his particular concern for postcommunist countries, but it should be a concern for the rest of us as well. When we view the church as the people of God, we acknowledge that Christians are in the world, and one of the tasks of church leaders is to help the people of God make better connections with the world. The Eastern European theologian suggested that if we "train Christians to serve society, they will be better prepared to serve the church. Get Christians into the world, not into the church!" This statement will be upsetting to some, but think about it. If a recovery of focus on the church only deepens our commitment to the institution, we will consistently employ or recruit people to serve church purposes. But if the church is seen as a people gathered by God to accomplish God's purposes, Christians are set free to serve the mission of the church in the world. As we serve the mission of the church in the world, I suspect that the mission and purpose of theological education as a center for learning will become much clearer.

CHAPTER 9

Toward a Learning Century for Theological Education

What if learning were the purpose of education?—Richard Boyatzis, Scott Cowen, and David Kolb

Buckminster Fuller used to say that you should never try to change the course of a great ship by applying force to the bow. You shouldn't even try by applying force to the rudder. Rather you should apply force to the trim-tab. A trim-tab is a little rudder attached to the end of the rudder. A very small force will turn it left, thus moving the big rudder to the right, and the huge ship to the left. The shift to the Learning Paradigm is the trim-tab of the great ship of higher education. It is a shift that changes everything. —Robert Barr and John Tagg

Over time, American higher education has adapted and reinvented itself repeatedly in response to social, economic, and political changes. And it will again. Today, as at the end of the nineteenth century and again after World War II, new ways of envisioning and organizing academic life are emerging. This time, however, the attention centers less on building new institutional structures, redefining the curriculum, or expanding access and more on the very heart of education: the improvement of teaching and learning (see Angelo 1997). Literature on educational renewal suggests that the prevailing instructional paradigm is giving way gradually to a learning paradigm. The role of the teacher is being recast from that of an expert who distributes a store of knowledge to one who shapes tasks that compel a search for knowledge, develops capacities such as judgment and evaluation, and encourages skills of lifelong learning. A mere presentation of information does not equal learning and is insufficient for today's learners who need to grasp the meaning and application of knowledge. The use of disciplines as the sole organizing principle for the curriculum is being questioned, and assessment of learning is slowly replacing conventional and sometimes unjust methods of testing. Similarly, the tendency to equate particular methods with good teaching is giving way to efforts to foster a learning culture. This chapter is built on the real possibility that a shift from an instructional paradigm to a learning paradigm may be the next sea change in the historical development of theological education.

Will the twenty-first century be the Learning Century in theological education? If so, a number of factors, taken together, could create a new matrix for theological education. This chapter presents a set of factors different but not totally separate from those that have shaped what we know today as higher education. Learning is predicated on more than rationalism; theory and practice are better understood as *praxis* and go beyond professionalism; the learning community operates in organizational frameworks but is more than institutionalism; and lifelong learning is a cluster of sustainable habits that support one's desire to know God truly.

Factor 1: Learning—A Holistic Process of Development

Does an emphasis on learning (or learning in community) undermine the importance of the teacher? In fact, the role of the teacher becomes even more critical. If a faculty member is merely a deliverer of content, he or she is easily displaced where information is readily accessible through technology and print resources.[1] In an era where the flood of information threatens to overwhelm us all, teachers have particular responsibility to discern when a careful structure of ideas and argument is needed to guide a community of learners responsibly through a body of knowledge or a problem. As an experienced learner, the teacher models the art of questioning and interactive dialogue, articulates values and behaviors that sustain the learning community, and guides students in the use of group resources. Teachers help students gain practice in identifying and defining problems, making judgments about their importance, and conveying their judgments with clarity. Teach-

---

[1] I accept that when I am facilitating a seminar that the participants are surfing the web (and their email) using the wireless internet connection that we have created for them. Frequently they find resources at various reputable sites that supplement or provide different perspectives on the issue under consideration. Part of the work of the seminar, then, is to assist in the judgment of the repository of knowledge now available on the web.

ers help students present arguments and ideas with a sense of style, helping them to communicate with grace, confidence, and humility. Teachers encourage tolerance of the complex and ambiguous, the validity of seemingly contradictory positions on the same issue, and humility before the reality that we cannot know most things with certainty. Teachers rebuke ethnocentrisms and champion diversity. Teachers discourage the tendency to reduce the world and ideas to simple categories; they challenge simplistic responses and seek to awaken a critical and discerning outlook. Teachers introduce students to the aesthetic dimensions of knowing, stimulating a sense of wonder. Teachers encourage personal reflection and reflection on the example of others, contemporary and historical, who demonstrate what is most valued.

The art of teaching entails several difficult and demanding skill sets that are understood best in relation to the teacher's responsibility as a facilitator of learning. The nature of learning suggests that the role of the teacher will not be fulfilled through cognitive processing alone. "It is interesting that in North American society we so much admire people who put information together in new ways and come up with new conclusions. Yet, in college we reward people who simply gather and remember information—who conform in their thinking" (Stronks 1991, 98). Some may find Stronks's comment overly cynical; for others, it is a valid critique of educational institutions that have forgotten that education is about learning.

Learning as a Multidimensional Process

In one of the early surveys of theological education, H. Richard Niebuhr et al., suggested that much of the problem in seminaries was to be found in what he termed the "didactic stance." Disturbingly familiar complaints are reflected in the survey's findings: the lecture dominates students' experience, teachers feel pressured to cover content, assignments are mechanical, tests are based on excessive memorization, and there is so much reading that thought and reflection on the reading is impossible. Niebuhr was concerned that theological students have the sorts of experiences that would develop their intellectual capacity (Niebuhr, Williams, and Gustafson 1957, 134–35).

Thirty years later, David Kolb (1984) suggested that learning consists of two major processes: (1) the various ways learners receive information and store it and (2) the various ways adult learners process knowledge and make it available for use. These two processes are embodied in four quadrants framed by two sets of polar opposites: Concrete Experience and Abstract Conceptualization, Reflective Observation and Active Experimentation. Kolb asserted that *the effort to integrate the opposite modalities of learning* leads to more mature capacities in complex reasoning. Intentionally created learning experiences that foster students' skills in integrating and reconciling these opposites are, in Kolb's judgment, essential to the development of understanding. It is not without reason that many of the theorists in cognitive development build on Jean Piaget's account of the rhythm of intellectual development: assimilation, disequilibration, accommodation, all leading to a new equilibration. Appreciation of the importance of this process in the formation of complex reasoning led John Dewey and others to insist on the use of real problems in learning[2] and to ground the processes of learning in the authentic experience of human beings.[3] Far from being "just the sharing of experiences," this approach to learning requires teachers who have well-developed questioning technique,[4] proficiency in guiding dialogue, capacity to discern the relationship of present experience to previous knowledge, the ability to fashion a conceptual framework to guide thought, and the wisdom needed to help learners examine their values and presuppositions.

Once theological educators overcome the debilitating stereotypes of "education is just about methods" and that experience and problem-based learning are simply the "sharing of ignorance," the real work in theological *education* (or theological learning) can begin.

---

[2]John Dewey, who was badly misrepresented by his some of his followers, stressed that the use of experience in education must be directed by wise and broadly knowledgeable teachers who make responsible choices about the nature of the experiences and problems that will be used in the learning situation. Dewey's writings are readily available but Ryan (1998) offers a summary description of his work and theories.

[3]Dewey's notion of the mind as a verb rather than a noun is apt.

[4]The importance of the question in shaping thoughts, attitudes, and behavior is often unrecognized by teachers who are preoccupied with their content and delivery. Yoram Harpaz and Adam Lefstein noted that predictable, thoughtless questions create an "answering pedagogy"; skillful questioning motivates investigation. Poor questioning is a device for control or to fill time; good questions stimulate learners to find connections and to probe their assumptions. A teacher skilled in questioning technique will nurture communities of discourse. Good questions "reveal involvement in and deep understanding of the subject" (Harpaz and Lepstein 2000, 54). Skillful questioning is hard work!

Developing a Wider View of Cognition

Meeting with Czech leaders involved in nonformal education, I noticed that the translator was having difficulty conveying the term "learning experiences" when I used it. He said that there is only one word in Czech that describes the educational task—the word English speakers would translate as "to teach" or "to educate." For a Czech, "to teach" is synonymous with what typically happens in formal schooling.

I have learned since that this difficulty is found in other languages as well. And even though English has a range of words to denote the educational task, the concept of *learning* in North American higher education is equally difficult to convey. Richard Boyatzis, Scott Cowen, and David Kolb stress that "learning is a broad concept encompassing many ways of knowing. In the new learning paradigm, intelligence as the single, universal measure of the capacity to learn is replaced by recognition of diversity in ways of knowing" (Boyatzis et al. 1995, 231).

In the 1950s, Benjamin Bloom proposed three domains of learning: cognitive, affective, and psychomotor (or skill, or volition, or purposeful action).[5] He suggested that teachers can affect only these three domains, that the domains overlap, and that learning is never be confined to just one of the domains. Since then, attempts have been made to reinforce the inseparability of the dimensions of human learning.[6] In this regard, Elliot Eisner asks, "What would a wider view of cognition look like? What would it suggest for the curriculum of the school and for educational evaluation?"

---

[5] See B. Bloom (1956), Krathwohl, Bloom, and Masia (1964), and Anderson, Krathwohl, and Samuel (2000) for more information. The description of the taxonomy is readily available in educational literature. Unfortunately, as the practice of giving grades based on tests entered American education (the first use of grading in higher education in America appears to have been at Yale in 1783) and as the measurable objectives movement spread through formal education in the 1970s, the cognitive domain was excised from its context in the three domains and given prominence. Though Bloom intended the taxonomy of levels of learning in the cognitive domain to help teachers design questions, learning tasks, tests, and other elements of the learning process that would foster complex reasoning capabilities; inevitably that which was easiest to measure became the focus of testing and assignments.

[6] Robert Marzano (2001) notes that after almost half a century, nothing has developed to replace Bloom's Taxonomy of Educational Objectives. In his book he offers a new taxonomy for a new century. Similarly, Lorin Anderson, David Krathwohl, and Benjamin Samuel (2000) recast the taxonomy to reflect what they believe are contemporary realities in learning.

(Eisner 1994, 22). Many of the instructional practices of conventional theological education are predicated on the assumption that learning is purely a mental activity. Reason is exalted, affect is suspect, and skills and application belong to something less than real school. Student Services takes care of the person, chapel takes care of the spirit, the counseling department weeds out the misfits, and the classroom takes care of the mind. There is relatively little in conventional classrooms that is compatible with the life most students experience.

In life and work, humans are constantly seeking ways to convey meaning, information, ideas, values, practices, and so on. In life, we generally accept that multiple forms of what Eisner calls representation are necessary.[7] One reason communication of ideas and sharing of experiences require multiple representations is that no one form of communication will represent the whole. "*Every* form of representation neglects some aspect of the world" (ibid., 41). Similarly, conventional forms of instruction are inadequate in their ultimate effectiveness because they are too limited in scope. "The kinds of nets we know how to weave determine the kinds of nets we cast. These nets, in turn, determine the kinds of fish we catch." Then the capacities or habits we have developed related to a particular form of representation influence "the extent to which what we know conceptually can be represented publicly" (ibid.).

Seminary faculty, in the main, want their students to develop the capacity to think, to deal with concepts, to communicate ideas and beliefs to others. Most seminary faculty are concerned that students demonstrate a vibrant spirituality, a humane regard of others, and godly leadership. However, to manage the academic structures we have created, we have presumed these capacities to be separable and assigned them to different departments for treatment and/or development. In the academy the capacities are also ranked, consciously or unconsciously, in order of importance or status. The rituals of the academy demonstrate this ranking and reinforce it. Further, even though most seminary faculty would admit that life and ministry are

---

[7]Forms of representation are the devices humans use to make public conceptions that are privately held. They are the vehicles through which concepts that are visual, auditory, kinesthetic, olfactory, gustatory, and tactile are given public status. This public status may take the form of words, pictures, music, mathematics, dance, and the like (Eisner 1994, 39).

not predictable or easily managed by rules and formulas, school culture and expectations generally support the quest for certainty.

Unfortunately, these assumptions and practices do not transfer well to life and ministry.

> There is no question that complex tasks—by definition—require different sorts of skills, skills that often relate to different forms of representation and that require different kinds of problem solving abilities. When such tasks are made available—and this is a curriculum development problem as well as a pedagogical problem—opportunities for students to achieve competence and recognition are increased, *provided* the school values such accomplishment.... The devaluation of some forms of cognition is especially acute at the university level. (Eisner 1994, 80)

In the 1960s, curriculum reform presumed that each discipline had a unique conceptual structure. In order to understand the discipline, one had to understand the structure. Since the structures were unique, it followed that each discipline was cataloged and presented independently. Since then, concern about integration of students' study and life has emerged, along with the notion that knowledge and practice would be enriched, and transferability of principles and practices strengthened, if students could see relationships among the disciplines. What followed was the realization that greater variety in ways of presenting and processing subject matter and concepts was needed to foster understanding and responsible action. "We cannot continue to offer programs in schools in which high levels of student performance predict nothing but performance on school-situated tasks. If a school performance is only useful for predicting success at more schooling, the practical meaning of what students learn in school for their life outside school will be small or nonexistent" (ibid., 84). Clearly, recovering the single essence of knowledge and responsible service, or knowledge and obedience, is part of a recovery of learning as the centerpiece of education.

Learning as Service

Someone once said that we define ourselves not by how much we know but by our commitments. *Service learning* is a contemporary term for this ancient concept. If the Hebraic notion of knowledge as embodying action is accepted, the notion of knowledge as power or control is indefensible and any faith in pure rationalism must be challenged. Responsible action or service is central to understanding. Timothy Stanton, Dwight Giles, and Nadinna Cruz explain that renewed interest in service learning was stimulated by activist efforts of educators who "in different settings and in varied roles...found themselves groping for programmatic and pedagogical means for connecting community service with academic learning, linking social action with critical reflection" (Stanton, Giles, and Cruz 1999, 53; see also Boyer 1990b). Service learning at its best strengthens social responsibility, promotes greater sophistication in the understanding of complex problems, and sensitizes people to the effects of institutional behavior and structure on human life and activity. "The needs of the community, rather than of the academy, determine the nature of the service provided" (Stanton, Giles, and Cruz 1999, 3). Service learning enables reciprocity, empowering those who are served to shape the nature of the service and to participate in it.

Most in theological education recognize that the disposition to serve is not an automatic result of ministry education. Even though the language of "preparation of men and women for the service of the church" has long been printed in seminary catalogs, service learning is not a well-developed concept in theological education. To ask, then, if service learning can be added to an already crowded theological curriculum is to miss the point. Service learning is an attitude, a spiritual commitment, not a course. Like spirituality, the values and practices of service must be part of the culture of the entire school. Citing outcomes of the Search Institute's studies of service learning in relation to congregations, Peter Scales and Donna Koppleman identify five conditions that are likely to sustain the effects of service learning: the environments in which service learning takes place are supportive, faculty care for students, students are integrated into the whole organization that is the context for their service, service is a normal part of the curriculum, and the values of service are reflected throughout the entire culture of the theological school (Scales and Koppleman 1997, 133).

Should service become the organizing principle for the organization or remain simply a line in the school catalog? If theological educators took hold of the contemporary idea of service learning and imbued it with values central to Christianity—worship of God, obedience to God's Word, and justice to neighbor, lived out in communities of faith and learning—the entire culture of their school would be affected. Service, rather than specialized and fragmented disciplines, would guide curriculum development; learning experiences would include inquiry, problem solving, and integration of knowledge and action.

Most seminary faculty want their subject matter to be relevant, and many do what they can to help students apply knowledge to life and ministry. However, the structures and reward systems of higher education, focused as they are on research and presentation rather than on learning and service, tend to reinforce unhelpful assumptions about the nature of knowledge, who owns it, how it is communicated and structured, and what is assessed. Further, in many cases, the curriculum typically is composed of courses that faculty want to teach, rather than being the fruit of considered reflection on student learning and service. Even the economics of education tends to reinforce institutional practices and attitudes about what is important. Faculty spend a lot of money to get knowledge to teach students; students spend a lot of money to take courses in which that information is presented; and the administration spends a great deal of money sustaining systems that are not as effective as they should be. The notion of faculty as subject-matter specialists requires activities that can hinder their development as learning specialists—as those who facilitate learning.[8]

If we accept that cognition is more than the functions of a disembodied mind that operates by reason alone, and if we accept that responsible service is not optional, the next task is to deal with a theory-practice dichotomy. Though the notion of service within learning has an ancient pedigree and was grounded for most of history in knowledge, North American educators, at least, tend to equate service with simple practicality. The present dichotomy derives from the assumptions that theories and practices are separable, that they can be assigned to different departments (which are often in isolation from one another), that theory relates to real scholarship, and that practices are simply skills.

---

[8]Boyatzis et al. cite three factors that make the transition from being a teacher to being a facilitator of learning almost impossible: the expert status accorded to faculty, a reward system that does not recognize efforts in good teaching as diligently as efforts in research and writing, and faculty autonomy (Boyatzis et al. 1995, 6–7).

Factor 2. Reconceiving Practice to Put Theory in Proper Perspective

Almost every major book or article on the topic of renewal in theological education mentions the problem of a theory-practice dichotomy. In most cases, theory and practice are assumed to be two different things existing in linear relationship: theory is ordered knowledge, practices are skills or activities. Theory can remain aloof from practice. Practice is informed by theory, if not controlled by it. Practice does not inform theory, much less control it. Conrad Cherry observes that these assumptions are flawed products of the Enlightenment and the presumed autonomy of reason (Cherry 1995, 152).

Theological education generally conceives its task as the training of leaders for the church and other religious agencies. To accomplish this, the curriculum is divided into a theoretical division and a practical division—the theoretical disciplines consciously or unconsciously presumed to be the theory for the applied or practical disciplines. The belief that the theoretical disciplines could stand alone without some interaction with the applied disciplines has gone largely unquestioned. Charles Wood's example is apt: "Systematic theology, though it may try to anticipate the needs of practical theology in the way it shapes the presentation of its material, can remain essentially uninformed by practical theological inquiry.... It is assumed, in effect, that the question of the authenticity and truth of Christian witness can be settled apart from and prior to a consideration of its relation to its context" (Wood 1985, 51). Recently, however, the notion that a series of fragmented theoretical disciplines could provide some coherent theory for the practical disciplines is being criticized (see Ollenburger 1997; Jarvis 1999).

Perspectives on the Theory and Practice Relation

Several perspectives on theory and practice exist in the literature. Some argue that theory and practice exist in every discipline and that departmental distinctions should be abandoned. Others advocate a more reasonable distinction between theoretical and practical disciplines. Martin Marty argues that a rediscovery of practical theology is needed where "all theological reflection correlates with practice and all practice demands theological reflection" (Marty 1987, 126). For David Kelsey, learning to know God is to engage in practices—congregational practices. Craig Dykstra suggests that one of the tasks of theology is to study the assumptions and histories underlying practices. Richard Mouw counsels that theology is *not* the study of practices, theology is knowing God (see Mouw 1997).

The now extensive literature critiquing theological education includes much attention to the matter of practices. Dykstra, Kelsey, and Rebecca Chopp, following the writing of Alasdair MacIntyre, are typical of those who define practices as shared activities. Practices are learned by participation in a community, which assumes that there are appropriate patterns, contexts, and outcomes for its practices. MacIntyre defines practices as "any coherent and complex form of socially established cooperative human activity through which goods internal to that form of activity are realized in the course of trying to achieve those standards of excellence which are appropriate to, and partially definitive of, that form of activity" (MacIntyre 1984, 187). Decisions related to practices are seen in two dimensions: decisions that are made on the basis of factors external to the practice; and decisions that are consistent with the internal "good" of the practice. For example, in theological education, decisions about enrollment can be made on the basis of a need for more money (external) or on the basis of understanding what types of students are desired for what purpose (internal). MacIntyre concludes that practices derived from matters that are external to that practice will lead inevitably to unproductive ends.

MacIntyre's point is valid and fairly obvious but many times overlooked in organizations—especially in those struggling for survival. If the practices of the church are defined uncritically (i.e., without attention to the external and internal dimensions), and if people are trained to serve practices that are not central to the mission of the church and the kingdom, the end of that training will be unproductive. For example, as institutes proliferate in seminaries (and churches) to satisfy the demand of many churches for executive-style pastor-managers, vital matters related to the identity of the people of God and implications for leadership will not be addressed adequately. "Practices are often distorted by their modes of institutionalization, when irrelevant considerations relating to money, power and status are allowed to invade the practice" (MacIntyre 1994, 289). The institutions of the church and theological education are not immune to these distortions.

Joseph Hough identifies the practice of the church as the sharing of its faith and hope with the world—which involves more than simply speaking or writing about faith and hope. The practices peculiar to the church establish the tasks for theological education. "Theological education must go on wherever persons are gathered to claim the memory of Jesus Christ as their own internal history" (Hough 1984, 63). The conclusion of Hough's discussion is that *all* theological education is, therefore, practical. However, he is careful to note that practical theological education is not "only for practice *in* the church." "Quite the contrary...theological education is the attempt on the part of the church to understand how its being in the *world* is and can be a creative and redemptive work of God through Jesus Christ for the sake of the whole world. Theological education is thus the ongoing recollection of the memory of Jesus Christ by which the practice of the church in this world comes to express those virtues which define Christian holiness" (ibid., 63–64).

Reconceiving Practices

Efforts to reconceive the theory-practice relation almost always include a prior effort to redefine the meaning of practices. The effort is problematic because no matter how strong the stress that practices are not synonymous with functions or skills, and in spite of efforts to break down longstanding separations between practical and theoretical departments, faculty will hear the word *practices* and think "practical" or "functional."

The vital consideration is that Scripture reveals practices that are mandated by God for Christian development and service. These practices inhere in expectations of the worship of God, obedience or response to God's Word leading to a righteous life, and justice toward others. The context in which these biblically derived practices mature is the church, in the forms that support the people of God in engagement with the world and in relationship with God and one another.

If the life and behavior of the people of God are to be marked by these practices, habits of reflection and growth in understanding (wisdom) are necessary. Christians have long believed that the knowledge of God is mediated by the Holy Spirit and nurtured by a lifetime of spiritual discipline. Most Christians also believe that knowledge derived from human thought and research is valid. However, when human knowledge became a thing in itself and was relegated to school curricula, and when spiritual knowledge was either rejected as suspect or subordinated to propositional knowledge, the holism of spiritual knowledge, human thought, and response was undone. Other chapters in this book have described the severing of the one essence of theology and spirituality, the expulsion of theology from the university, the questioning of the validity of mystical knowing, and the uncoupling of knowledge and action. Thus theological education for the whole people of God has a unique opportunity to reverse decisions that have resulted in destructive polarities or dichotomies. For this, spiritual direction, the interaction of specialists from various disciplines (including theology and the social sciences), substantive involvement with congregations, and engagement with the larger society are essential. If the task is accomplished well, the Christian ethic may once again make a difference in an increasingly broken world.

In light of the above, should a seminary debate the reason for its existence based on theological categories (e.g., ecclesiology, mission, gospel) rather than practical categories (e.g., administration, sociology, homiletics, leadership) or vice versa? The ludicrousness of this question becomes more apparent when theory and practice are seen as parts of one whole. Should the focus shift to practices as the organizing principle for theological education? Chopp argues that "concentration on practices enables us to think about education in new ways. To identify practices as the sites of learning in theological education is to avoid some common 'divisions' in thinking about education and to require the development of new language to name the process of education" (Chopp 1995, 103). However, this assertion will not be convincing to those committed to the preeminence of the theoretical disciplines and concerned about the loss of important content if practices become the focus of the curriculum. Nor will those who understand practice as programs or as leadership skills be satisfied. At this point, a different way of envisioning practices is necessary.

Dykstra suggests that if practices are understood as cooperative human activities socially established over time, then theological study can be the study of how practices have been created and how they permeate theology and church life. Some disciplines study the history of practices; others examine their inner rationality and truth; others encourage and evaluate students' participation in practices (see Dykstra 1991b).[9] Drawing on the work of Hans-Georg Gadamer and revisiting Aristotle's view of the interconnectedness of understanding and practice, Don Browning suggests: "Rather than application to practice being an act that follows understanding, con-

---

[9]See also http://www.practicingourfaith.org/ (last accessed December 2005).

cern with practice, in subtle ways we often overlook, guides the hermeneutic process from the beginning" (Browning 1991, 299).[10]

Is practice, then, preeminent? This question is not helpful because it exacerbates an already problematic polarization. A more helpful direction is to envision a more holistic view of theory and practice—a view that blurs their distinctions to the point that they cannot be separated without mutual damage.

Toward a Reconceptualization of Theory and Practice

Proposing that processes of vision and discernment should replace the theory-practice dichotomy, Wood maintains that the goal of theological education is theological judgment, which is in turn the product of theological inquiry (Wood 1985b, 34). When Wood's and Kelsey's views are compared, a subtle distinction emerges that is no doubt representative of broader perspectives in the field. Kelsey asserts that theology is important for practice but that it is also necessary to see how the practice of Christian communities informs theology (Kelsey 1993, 202–20). Wood describes theology as an activity—a practice of theological education, if you will. Though the assertion that practice informs theology is needed, for Kelsey theology remains apart from practice—a subject in itself. However, Kelsey's linkage of theology and the practices of congregations should be considered in the search for a more holistic understanding of theory and practice (see below).

---

[10] Objecting to the assumption of a theory-to-practice linearity, Browning revisions the fourfold curriculum in four movements: "(1) descriptive theology understood as a 'thick description'...of present religious and cultural practices...(2) historical theology (guided by questions that emerge from movement one); (3) systematic theology (a search for generic features of the Christian message in relation to generic features of the present situation); and (4) strategic practical theology (studies about the norms and strategies of the concrete practices of the church...)" (Browning 1991, 309). Browning sees these four movements as part of the total practical theological task. Joseph Hough orients the theological curriculum around his conception of the minister as a "practical theologian" whose work is encompassed in four leadership tasks: (1) fostering the "church's memory of Jesus Christ for the sake of the continuing renewal of the identity of the Christian community," (2) giving "leadership in the reflective practice through which that identity can be given concrete, historical expression," (3) exercising institutional management, and (4) counseling (Hough 1984, 79–80).

Dykstra, too, is committed to the importance of the community in shaping theology, where the perspectives necessary for this task are derived from history and tradition. In his view, the theory-practice relation is inadequate for this task, because "theology and theological education are burdened by a picture of practice that is harmfully individualistic, technological, ahistorical, and abstract" (Dykstra 1991b, 35). Theological education tends to define practice as the work of an individual doing something to others or for the sake of others. Dykstra's corrective is not to deny that practice can be done by an individual but rather that "one person's action becomes practice only insofar as it is participation in the larger practice of a community and a tradition" (ibid., 37). He describes practice as cooperative: it involves people doing things *with* each other. Practice is "participation in a cooperatively formed pattern of activity that emerges out of a complex tradition of interactions among many people over a long period of time" (ibid., 43). Individuals who are involved in different activities thus "are not doing different things. Individual actions interrelate in such a way that they constitute engagement in a common practice" (ibid., 42). Dykstra is careful to point out that "common practice" does not simply involve a group of people's agreeing at a certain point to do something together. Practices are learned in the context of a community conscious of tradition, history, and identity. And it is at this point that a more productive understanding of practice begins to emerge.

Arguing that the "Berlin" model develops "not the person as an agent in a shared public world" but forms reason through the acquisition of disciplines (i.e., courses of study), Kelsey counters that the purpose of a theological school is to understand God truly. This understanding is "to come to have certain conceptual capacities...that is, dispositions and competencies to *act*, that enable us to apprehend God and refer all things including ourselves to God" (Kelsey 1992, 228). He identifies three senses of understanding God—contemplative understanding, discursive understanding, and affective judgment—and allows for a fourth: understanding in and through action (ibid., 72). "To grow in understanding something is to grow in a set of abilities in relation to what is being understood. *The growth comes through our engagement over a period of time in certain relevant practices*" (ibid., 126, emphasis added). Reasoning that practices are understood most clearly in relation to congregations, he takes the final step and asserts that because God cannot be understood directly, understanding of God "is accomplished from the vantage point of questions about congregations" (ibid., 131).

Similarly, for Miroslav Volf, "Christian beliefs *as beliefs* entail practical commitments. These commitments may need to be explicated so as to become clear, or they may need to be connected to specific issues in concrete situations. But they don't need to be *added* to the beliefs; they inhere in the beliefs" (Volf 2002, 254). For Volf, the fact that core beliefs are an integral part of Christian practices and vice versa means that "Christian beliefs normatively shape Christian practices, and engaging in practices can lead to acceptance and deeper understanding of these beliefs" (ibid., 258). For theologians, then, theology is concerned with more than how beliefs are related to practices as separable entities. Beliefs and practices together express truth and the nature of the relationship of God with the world. "Like Paul, we should resolutely place theology in the service of practices" (ibid., 263).

Susan Coakley, in her turn, draws on the long tradition of Christian spirituality, in which practices are integrally linked to the lifelong vocation of seeking God. She suggests a developmental process of disciplines that explicates the relation of beliefs and practices in the service of knowing God (Coakley 2002, 92–93).

Congregational Practices and Theological Education

Kelsey, Volf, and Coakley represent alternatives to a view of practices as merely skills, methods, or programs. Practices are inherent in beliefs and vice versa, they are inherent in one's spiritual journey toward knowing God, and they are congregational practices. It would seem that the congregational context—the communal nature of practices—is most significant. What are these congregational practices that are linked to belief and spirituality? Dykstra has offered his judgment about the more significant practices of the community of faith:

> (1) telling the Christian story to one another; (2) interpreting together the meaning of that story for our life in the world; (3) worshiping God together: praising God and giving thanks for God's redemptive work in the world and for our lives together; (4) praying together; (5) listening and talking attentively to one another; (6) confessing to one another, and forgiving and recon-

ciling with one another; (7) tolerating one another's failures and encouraging one another; (8) giving one another away, letting go of one another, freeing each other for the work each must do and the life each must live; (9) performing faithful acts of service and witness; (10) suffering for and with other people; (11) providing hospitality and care, not only to one another but also (perhaps especially) to strangers; and (12) criticizing and resisting all those powers and patterns (both within the church and in the world as a whole) which destroy human beings and corrode human community. (Dykstra 1985, 197)

He stresses the importance of involvement in these practices and growing in understanding of what they mean, and he says that growth in faith (belief and the nature of one's spiritual journey) is fostered as participation in the practices becomes more complex and varied (ibid., 199).

Kelsey shifts the focus to the responsibility of theological education, stressing that if theological education is irrevocably linked to the articulation and outworking of the practices of congregations, then the disciplines that inform learning experiences will be "mandated by the sorts of interests we have in congregations" (Kelsey 1992, 230). He suggests that among these disciplines are those of the intellectual historian and textual critic ("to grasp what the congregation says it is responding *to* in its worship and why"), the cultural anthropologist, ethnographer, and philosopher ("to grasp how the congregation shapes its social space by its uses of scripture, by its uses of traditions of worship and patterns of education and mutual nurture, and by the 'logic' of its discourse"), and the sociologist and social historian ("to grasp how the congregation's location in its host society and culture helps shape concretely its distinctive construal of the Christian thing" (ibid., 230–31).

Tasks appropriate to theological education, then, are to uphold the character of congregational practices, examine them against the long history of the church, and situate them in societies and cultures. Orienting theological education to the practices of congregations would seem more defensible than orienting it to some grand intellectual project. When we identify the practices of congregations with the theological quest to know God truly, matters of faith (theory) and practices are seen as one whole; both theology and the social sciences are mandated; inconsistency between belief and behavior is addressed in a prophetic voice; and concerns about organizational patterns and leadership style are not permitted to devolve to a pragmatic concern for what works.

Dykstra suggests that seminaries need to see themselves as part of a larger whole—larger than denominations and larger than the world of higher education. He identifies this larger whole as the "practice of Christian theological education" and names three fundamental elements of this broad practice: the academic study of theology, the education of the church and public in Christian faith and practice, and the equipping of church leadership. "What is important to notice in all this is that it is the *practices* that are perennial. They are institutionalized in different ways in different times and places—and the particular institutionalizations may come and go, or be transformed by taking on new practices. But whatever happens with particular institutions, the practices seem to endure—*because they are essential to the very existence of Christian faith!*" (Dykstra 1991a, 101, emphasis added). This understanding of practice is promising in that it frees us from identifying theological education with a particular institutional form (e.g., seminary or church).

One can hope that the concept of theological education for the whole people of God will be strengthened in coming years. Dykstra, among others, believes that seminaries are essential "for the perpetuation, enhancement, and enlargement of the practice of Christian theological education in our society." However, he insists that the education of clergy would be "more powerful and empowering were it to take more seriously the hunger and need for a theological education of the church and the public." The academic study of theology would be "enlarged and deepened as its practice is placed in the larger context of the actual public practice of faith" (ibid., 104).

Time will tell if seminaries are equal to this challenge. Clearly, financial anxiety and external pressures militate against the possibility that individual seminaries will examine seriously their capacity to participate in the practices of God. Yet this is just the time when such examination is needed.

Toward Praxis in Theological Education

In his day, Friedrich Schleiermacher's idea to orient the project of theology around church leadership and to orient the curriculum first around a notion of holism (expressed philosophically) and then around matters related to the development of the ministerial profession (as he understood it) was probably a good idea. However, the context of German academia could not support the development and refinement of his proposal. When the more visible and easily attainable elements of his approach made their way to North America, the potential for a praxis-based professional development dissipated into training for functional activities, and holism was lost in curricular compartmentalization.

In the early 1800s, the fourfold curriculum consisted essentially of biblical studies, theological studies, historical studies, and practical studies, a pattern that has persisted with slight modification to the present. To what extent can such a pattern, oriented to the development of a ministerial class and fragmented into disciplines of theory and practice, serve today's church and society?

The educational processes that serve *praxis,* foster reflective thinking and judgment and nurture the development of reflective practitioners (or scholar practitioners). The student is not simply equipped with a list of answers ready made for any circumstance, or a body of content ready to deliver, or a set of skills ready to apply. Educational processes oriented to *praxis* obligate a matrix of intellectual, affective, and volitional factors. *Praxis* is not the application of theories; it is what Donald Schön (1987) calls knowing-in-action. However, learning experiences developed from a *praxis* perspective are not simply a haphazard sharing of experiences but an intentional integration of knowledge and action.

The 1996 revised standards affirmed by the association of theological seminaries in North America include this goal:

> In a theological school, the over-arching goal is the development of theological understanding, that is, aptitude for theological reflection and wisdom pertaining to responsible life in faith. Comprehended in this over-arching goal are others such as deepening spiritual awareness, growing in moral sensibility and character, gaining an intellectual grasp of the tradition of a faith community, and acquiring the abilities requisite to the exercise of ministry in that community. These goals, and the processes and practices leading to their attainment, are normally intimately interwoven and should not be separated from one another. (Standards of Accreditation 1996, 4.1.1, 29)

This goal and other similar standards point to a future in which the flawed logic of the theory-practice dichotomy and the fragmented structure of disciplines will have to give way to a more *praxis*-oriented approach to theological education. The next ten-year review of all theological schools in ATS will *require* attention to curriculum design, assessment, and teaching consistent with such standards. It should be an interesting series of site visits!

Dan Aleshire, executive director of the Association of Theological Schools (ATS), in an address to a seminary faculty posed three questions that summarize the progression of emphasis in accreditation: Do you have the resources necessary to be a higher-education institution? Do you have the right resources to accomplish your educational purpose? Are you accomplishing educationally what you purport to accomplish? This third question, Aleshire indicates, was never asked before the 1980s. Though for good accreditation all three questions should be answered satisfactorily, it is the third question that raises, in Aleshire's words, the "squirreliest issues" for the next accreditation cycle. As ATS member schools face their ten-year review, how will they respond when asked to demonstrate that they have contributed to an aptitude for theological reflection and to the development of wisdom pertaining to responsible life and faith, that they possess a deepening spiritual awareness, evidence moral sensibility and character, have acquired an intellectual grasp of a tradition of a faith community, and the abilities requisite to the exercise of ministry in that community? Will they be accredited or not? Aleshire warns, "Nothing like this was in the ATS Standards prior to the 1996 Standards" (Aleshire 2000).

Ah well, there is always the regional accrediting associations.

Factor 3: The Community as the Proper Context for Learning

The ATS Standards describe the theological school as "a community of faith and learning that cultivates habits of theological reflection, nurtures wise and skilled ministerial practice, and contributes to the formation of spiritual awareness and moral sensitivity" (Association of Theological Schools 1998, 54). "Theological scholarship" is a central task in these communities, and the processes of learning are necessarily collaborative: "The collaborative nature of theological scholarship requires that people teach and learn from one another in communal settings; and that research is integral to the quality of both learning and teaching" (ibid.). Significantly, scholarship is understood in the Standards to include "the *interrelated activities* of learning, teaching, and research" (ibid., emphasis added). Further, collaborative efforts of faculty, librarians, and students that result in scholarly products should "extend beyond the theological school's immediate environment to relate it to the wider community of the church, the academy, and the society" (ibid., 56 [3.2.1.1, 3]).

Ernest Boyer suggests that the meaning of scholarship today is much more restricted than it was historically. He observes that scholarship is practiced in terms of "a hierarchy of functions. Basic research has come to be viewed as the first and most essential form of scholarly activity, with other functions flowing from it. Scholars are academics who conduct research, publish, and then perhaps convey their knowledge to students or apply what they have learned. The latter functions *grow out of* scholarship, they are not to be considered a part of it" (Boyer 1990b, 15). Consistent with the understanding of scholarship in the ATS Standards, Boyer proposes that scholarship include four elements: discovery (disciplined research and inquiry), integration (finding the connectedness of things), application (active service), and teaching (promoting understanding) (ibid., 17–25). Given the difficulty of realizing this vision in the modern academy, he also observes, "Faculty are expressing serious reservations about the enterprise to which they have committed their professional lives. This deeply rooted professional concern reflects, we believe, recognition that teaching is crucial, that integrative studies are increasingly consequential, and that, in addition to research, the work of the academy must relate to the world beyond the campus" (ibid., 75).

No doubt Boyer's observation is true for many faculty in theological schools as well. However, there are many who consider the phrase "learning community" or "learning in community" to denote soft learning or a loss of academic rigor. The standard encouragement to allow discussion, to form small groups, and to change from straight rows to sitting in a circle may help, but if there is little understanding of the relation of knowing to learning and limited grasp of the rich diversity of learning approaches, such format changes will be merely cosmetic. Simple changes in method will not accommodate the complex nature of learning and the facilitation of learning in community. Teachers who care about learning seek to foster critical reasoning, enable reflection on practice, nurture spirituality, and strengthen the capacities of decision-making, wise discernment, and judgment. Faculty responsibilities, then, include helping learners to acquire information, engage ideas, confront attitudes and values, examine beliefs and behavior, develop skills, interact meaningfully with others, and minister in a multicultural world. What remains is for the connection to be made that all of these capacities are developed most effectively in communities of learning, scholarship, and responsible service. Once this connection is accepted as valid, the next step is to confront the aspects of academic life and institutional structure that hinder the development of faculty as facilitators of learning and developers of others and that keep faculty and students from being coparticipants in the learning process.

Communities of Faith and Learning: A Persisting Concept

The concept of learning in community has long been important in the history and practice of education (Petrie 1992, 301–2). Robert Wilken observes that historically the great religious traditions were communities of faith that embodied traditions of learning (Wilken 1995, 17). When community is accepted as the proper context for learning and the social nature of learning is understood, faculty more readily acknowledge that they are not the sole providers of knowledge. Knowing this, they are more likely to employ a range of instructional approaches that contributes to and draws upon the strength of the learning community. Information acquisition, conceptual understanding, reflective practice, and other desirable outcomes are fostered through processes such as structured and unstructured dialogue, skillful questioning, shared problem solving, carefully designed shared projects, and individual responsibility coupled with mutual accountability. The teacher becomes a "highly knowledgeable member of the community.... Teachers and students together track the progress of the group's understanding...accept or refute proposed interpretations of others...propose interpretations of their own" (Leinhardt 1992, 24). In other words, each person in the community is potentially a teacher, and each person is a learner.

Critical Factors in Sustaining Communities of Learning

Faith Gabelnick et al. (1990) describe the formation of the Experimental College at the University of Wisconsin in 1927 by Alexander Meiklejohn.

His intention was to create a learning community by developing a curriculum based on the holistic study of subject matters, integration of disciplines, connections of faculty and students across the disciplines, and the requirement that

students connect their studies with the real world.[11] He believed that the curriculum had to be experiential, holistic, and problem based, and that faculty had a critical role to play in the way learning experiences were organized. However, the experiment was short lived (1927–1932). In reality, it is difficult to sustain such initiatives within the habitual structures of higher education. More importantly, it may not be possible to *create* community. In every educational venture where people gather some form of a community already exists. Understanding and assessing the epistemological and theological character of that community is a vital and ongoing task.

Though Meiklejohn's efforts demonstrated the importance of curricular integration and connections of faculty and students across the disciplines, restructuring curriculum and relationships will not in itself sustain learning communities. Two research studies of a Ph.D. learning community reveal a constellation of values and practices that energize and sustain the learning community.[12] Though improvement in all areas is sought, this Ph.D. learning community invites people from a variety of cultures and backgrounds who engage one another professionally, academically, and personally. They share resources and ideas, and consult one another concerning specific issues and situations related to their ministries. Learning experiences are collaborative rather than competitive, and mutual respect for colleagues and the diversity of perspectives is evident.

Such a community invites the Spirit of God to sustain the tension between the individual and the community and to discourage the human tendency to homogeneity. Learning is seen as lifelong, formal and nonfor-

---

[11]Gabelnick et al. identify five different formats that fostered efforts to learn in community: "(1) linked courses, (2) learning clusters, (3) freshman interest groups, (4) federated learning communities [thematically similar but autonomous seminars], and (5) coordinated studies" (Gabelnick et al. 1990, 19).

[12]Research by Laurie Bailey (1996) and Janyne Peek (1997) elicited perceptions of the values and practices that sustain the learning community of the Ph.D. in educational studies program at Trinity Evangelical Divinity School.

mal in context, linear and narrative in approach, and participatory. Processes of dialogue and disciplined inquiry and the integration of theology and the social sciences are viewed as normative. Participants are committed to a responsible and rigorous search for truth. Professional collaboration, a mentoring culture, and personal relationships continue beyond the formal boundaries of the program. Participants build and sustain networks of personal and professional relationship, and experiences within the programs assist with networking. Faculty commit themselves to the effective progress and completion of the participants and through the experiences of the program seek to foster sustainable habits in thought, spirit, relationship, and service. Evaluation and assessment are therefore ongoing, formative,, and collegial. Participants are conscious that the community does not exist for itself, that its values are communicated in a variety of ways to each new generation, and that each participant must accept personal responsibility for the continuing development of the community.

Educational Processes for Communities of Faith and Learning

The structures and reward systems of higher education almost exclusively support the solitary, often competitive learner. Room for individual learning is appropriate, but collaborative learning fosters intellectual and personal interdependence. It requires students to make a difficult transition to trusting the community and themselves as active co-participants in discovery, questioning, inquiry, and knowledge building. When learning is seen as both individual and collaborative, teachers are no longer the sole repositories and dispensers of knowledge and become facilitators of a complex learning process. Fear that they are not being responsible for delivering the content of their discipline is generally overcome as they gain expertise in selecting and developing suitable resources and providing the necessary conceptual frame of reference for dialogue, inquiry, and mutual research. Lectures and memorization are necessary, then, only as they contribute to the processes of inquiry and reflective practice.[13] In learning communities,

---

[13]Collaborative learning and reflection can take place with a partner, in a small group, in a large group. Collaborative learning makes use of portfolios, journals, case studies, professional reading and writing, peer interaction, study groups, cohort groups, professional dialogue groups, institutes, assessment centers, and so on.

students are forced to see the connections across disciplines and learn that it is important to have a perspective broader than isolated content areas—or contexts—provide. One of the tasks of theological education is to enable students to function more effectively in ethnically and socio-economically diverse communities. This broader perspective will challenge the notion that the only valid learning environment is the campus environment and that learning activities are necessarily campus based. Stephen Kemp argues that students are already in communities and that *these* communities have a role to play in the students' learning and development (Kemp 1999; see also Cannell 1999, 19).

Obviously, involvement in Internet-based or classroom-based education does not in itself guarantee community development or learning. Either environment can suffer from poor pedagogy and inattention to the importance of relationships and interaction in learning. The concern that educational technology will foster that which we care least about in education is certainly valid. However, recent literature affirms that advocates of distance learning affirm three elements: it must be interactive, it must promote higher order thinking, *and it must sustain learning in community, even at a distance.*

Curricular Issues for Communities of Faith and Learning

Labaree (1999) observes that one of the more obvious results of curriculum reform is that it tends to change the way we talk about curriculum, and about teaching and learning, without generating much substantive change. Kelsey describes the fourfold curriculum as the academic equivalent of the four major food groups, "daily selection from each of which is essential to a healthy theological diet" (Kelsey 1992, 235). Historically, the fourfold curriculum was oriented to the preparation of professional clergy (the clerical paradigm) and separated into discrete disciplines. The curriculum of theological education came to be seen in terms of two- to four-year programs culminating in a certificate or degree. Over time, more and more courses or skills were considered necessary for the preparation of leaders, who would complete their theological education in this period. Therefore, the curriculum is now crowded with subjects.

Is it necessary for curriculum to be seen as a sequence of courses, collected in departments, offered in a specified number of years, in classes taught by a teacher in a school or church or some other site? The course-based design was appropriate for an industrial-age education economy. However, in an information or knowledge age, the student will have access to knowledge sometimes beyond that of the teacher, and the learner may need to have access to particular aspects of knowledge that the faculty member has not designed into the course. Course design is typically based on the time constraints of faculty and institutions over those of the learner. Learners have little say in the determination of course time frames. Completion of a course is an artificial measure of learning. In reality, course units (seat time) were devised as a way to determine how much tuition to charge for a course (see Rowley, Lujan, and Dolence 1998, 170–72). Should a fourfold model expressed in disparate courses and bounded by artificially generated credit hours be continued? Is this way of structuring curriculum working for us?

Certainly, when translated into specific curricular practice, the fourfold structure exacerbates fragmentation and encourages specialization, which in turn contributes to departmental isolation and polarization. There is also a certain logical inconsistency within its organization. Subjects within the biblical field could equally well be part of the historical field or even the practical field, and vice versa. Further, the fourfold division of the curriculum can condition faculty, administrators, and students to focus only on the mastery of subjects. Faculty become specialists in subjects conveniently organized in categories or disciplines; and students can become recipients of those subjects without confronting the deeper concerns of culture and church that the subjects, taken together, should address. A structure formalized in the medieval period, modified to suit the theological shifts of the Reformation, influenced by the scientific methodology of the Enlightenment, shaped by the German research university, deeply affected by modernity, and assumed to define true theological education today is likely not adequate for the challenges of contemporary culture and the education of Christians who have been shaped by that culture.

Students entering our schools today are influenced by multiple perspectives, many views on what is true. In order to foster the capacities of wise judgment, reflection, and theological reasoning; in order to help people sustain healthy relationships, relate truly to God, judge clearly among ethical alternatives, and offer the kind of leadership needed by the church in this age, does the fourfold model need to be revised—or abandoned altogether and a new structure created?[14]

Rethinking the Structure of the Disciplines

Traditionally, curriculum development has been viewed as a linear process, including such tasks as needs assessment; formulation of purpose, goals, and objectives; organization of disciplines/subjects and methodology; and procedures for ongoing evaluation and assessment. Increasingly, however, the concept of curriculum design as a linear, scientific process is giving way to more fluid concepts.[15] Similarly, the conventional organization of disciplines whose subject matter is dispensed in independent classes structured by time and architecture is no longer the only acceptable approach to curriculum design and educational strategy.

The presumption of disciplines is at the heart of the curriculum. The common definition of a discipline is that it has its own literature, its own questions, and a particular subject matter. However, in reality, most disciplines are shaped by other disciplines and are in their very DNA interdisciplinary. For example, education is shaped by disciplines such as sociology, theology, anthropology, psychology, philosophy, and history. A

---

[14]This suggestion is not a radical new idea. In the late 1800s, William Rainey Harper advocated that only one-third to one-half of the theological curriculum be common to all students. "To divide the time of the theological student equally between four or five or six departments is, from the pedagogical point of view, absurd" (Harper 1899, 59–60). He believed that the fragmented model reinforced superficiality and suggested that the existing distinctions between departments were artificial and artificially maintained. He insisted that the amount of overlap was noticed more by students than by faculty but that students were powerless to effect change. He recommended that the seminar method be more widely adopted and that the seminary develop "theological clinics" to increase the faculty's proficiency in the kinds of learning experiences that were becoming increasingly common in other professional fields. Harper also advocated that the course of study "be directed to the study and investigation of great problems" (ibid., 65); that clinical experience be part of students' learning; that
students work with a pastor for a specified number of weeks; that small groups of students, with an instructor of their choice, be enabled to retreat from the activities of the seminary for a time of solitude and reflection; and that the theological curriculum should be organized in conjunction with a university. Finally, Harper suggested that seminaries should function in consortia so that greater breadth in resources would be available.

[15]See McTighe and Wiggins (1999 and 2000) and Slattery (1995).

specialist or scholar is one who is conversant with a particular discipline or specialty. However, we respect scholars who are able to make connections across several fields of study because their insights inform issues and practice in significant ways. For instance, because he recognizes that exclusive preoccupation with one field actually hinders knowledge development and discovery, George Whiteside, Mallinckrodt Professor of Chemistry at Harvard University, "believes that science is rapidly changing from separate studies of biology, chemistry, and physics to a new discipline that combines all three" (Duncan 2003, 22).

Given that disciplines are naturally interconnected, why do we persist in isolating them from one another in schools? Daniel James Rowley, Herman D. Lujan, and Michael G. Dolence suggest that "permanent departmental structures need to give way to learning teams of scholars, brought together by common interests and working with students as partners and aides" (Rowley, Lujan, and Dolence 1998, 181). Since a discipline creates a paradigmatic way of looking at reality, housing like faculty together prevents them from engaging broader arenas of knowledge that could inform their thinking and enrich their teaching. Surely, faculty from the same specialization could organize opportunities for conversation with one another even if they were not permanently sequestered in a specialized department.

Is combining or integrating disciplines the way forward? Certainly the proximity of disciplines—or of faculty from different disciplines—is no guarantee that integration is occurring. Still, since no one discipline has a monopoly on truth, some form of interdependence among fields of knowledge is desirable when learners are present. The fundamental principle is that learning communities, understanding the depth and variety of designs that are possible, can create a multitextured learning environment that will not, in its turn, become a curricular straitjacket for the next generation. Any modification of, or alternative to, the fourfold curriculum need not become yet another monolithic, rigid structure.

Clearly, the fragmentation of disciplines, or what Hugh Petrie terms the "ethnocentricity of disciplines" (Petrie 1992, 309), is problematic, as numerous writers concerned about the future of theological education have demonstrated. Those who advocate integration, or interdisciplinary education, often assume that integration is accomplished simply through some form of team teaching. Though the idea of team teaching is valid and in some cases is practiced effectively, the reality is that the problems that affect humankind do not easily fit the customary classroom patterns of the disciplines. It may be necessary to ground interdisciplinary experiences in something other than subject matter of the disciplines as we know them. In other words, the way forward may not be to attempt to integrate fields of knowledge or to have faculty members from different divisions in the same classroom speaking about their respective subject matter. It may be necessary to establish the curriculum on a different footing altogether. For example, if the curriculum were organized around church practices, or service, or problems, the faculty from the various disciplines would together become resources for learners who are working intensively with issues, problems, and well-considered tasks that constitute the curriculum. Contemporary society is not structured to benefit from a curriculum dispersed in isolated courses. Students, and faculty, then will benefit from learning experiences generated around the sorts of ill-structured problems that arise in society. Oon-Seng Tan (2003), among many others, asserts that the challenge of the twenty-first century is to develop a curriculum design conversant with real-world problems and structured to foster creativity and lifelong learning.

Integration of disciplines is difficult to manage, and the concept of integration may actually be founded on a curricular myth. The conventional assumption is that the four folds of the curriculum can be integrated because they are all concerned about the same thing—the same thing defined according to the perspective of particular faculty. Examples of the same thing include preparing leaders for the mission of the church, equipping the mind, promoting spiritual growth, and so on. "The literature rejects this view. Farley and others have produced convincing evidence that the pattern of studies and its divisions developed haphazardly. They were not devised to reach any one objective, and they are not parts of any larger whole. Therefore, contrary to the conventional wisdom, they are unlikely to be integrated, no matter how hard we struggle to do that" (Kelsey and Wheeler 1994, 79). Because any original intent to maintain coherence in the fourfold model has disappeared, leaving the four separate pieces of the curriculum to function on their own, integrative models may be undone by the strong tendency of each fold to establish a singular identity in relation to other folds. Besides, it is difficult to integrate things that are constantly changing and developing, and the powerful individualism of faculty and pervasive competitiveness among departments can politicize the effort to such an extent that integration at any level becomes impossible. When prestige is associated with one's own scholarly work, and when faculty have themselves been educated within competitive academic environments, collaboration and cooperation are even more difficult.

Petrie cites Richard Rorty's well-known saying that the problems of society are not contained in "discipline-shaped blocks" (in Petrie 1992, 305). Some might argue that the disciplines of the theological curriculum are, in fact, God-given because they reflect the structure of Scripture or Western Christianity. However, the disciplines are frameworks developed by people in time, to deal with questions in time. In the 1990s, ATS restructured the fourfold model to include the following: the tradition (the Bible, theology, history), culture, spirituality, and ministry practices. If these classifications are embraced by the seminaries, implications for curriculum structure, educational process, and assessment will emerge. Perhaps new groupings of scholars in newly constituted disciplinary structures are needed—oriented not around some notion of integrating disciplines but around enabling disciplines to work together in relation to a larger project or quest germane to the tasks of theology and ministry.

Decisions about curricular approaches and educational strategies are also decisions about learning experiences. Faculty tend to think that their material must be organized, packaged, and delivered in ways consistent with their own schooling. When faculty reflect on their own learning processes *since* their last degree, however, they often realize that their growing mastery of the subject is due to far richer and far more diverse learning experiences than those that were required in their degree programs. More effective learning may result through a curriculum designed to lead learners into the processes that reflect the more mature learning of the true scholar/practitioner.

Ted Ward and others suggest that all curriculum planning entails some vision for the future. Increasingly, the future of theological education is viewed as broader than schooling and encompassing both the nature of theology and the nature of education. Boyatzis, Cowen, and Kolb suggest that "managing change in the academic curriculum, in what is taught and how it is learned, must rank among the top twenty-first-century management challenges for higher education" (1995, 1). They note that it takes an average of five years to complete a curriculum revision and that resulting programs are seldom revised again for another five to twenty years. "This is too slow for the pace of the 21st century" (ibid.). The answer is not simply to shorten the revision cycle. Innovation within the entire learning process is necessary. The community as context for learning and the nature of learning as a holistic process of development will significantly affect course structure, teaching practices, and matters that reinforce learning. Effective instructional design requires time, thought, skilled leadership, and investment from wise donors and visionary foundations. Guidelines for curriculum development are readily available and numerous resources have been generated to serve curriculum planners in higher education. Educational planners are well-advised to make curriculum evaluation and design a ongoing process. To assist the process, a rotating coalition of stakeholders and educational specialists from several institutions would limit the tendency to reinvent the wheel and encourage sharing of ideas and findings.

The Assessment of Learning

Assessment for learning is part of curriculum design and educational strategy. Harris, a noted specialist in educational assessment, avers that higher education is packaged in ways that are not optimal for learning (see Harris 2003 and 2005). The silo structure of administrative and academic departments in reality serves the institution, not the learner. Similarly, course divisions often benefit the faculty and institution more than the student or the outcomes we desire. The world and ministry don't come packaged in the course divisions we have created. To strengthen its espoused purposes, theological education would be better served by changing the focus from eligibility for a degree to developing proficiencies in some area of endeavor or knowledge building.

Harris argues that the further away assessment is from the settings where learning is to be applied, the less acceptable or reliable it is. After many years of research and practice, he has determined that grades don't correlate with much of anything except other grades. Further, standardized tests have low validity in terms of what they purport to measure.[16] Assessment of little pieces of information is easy. Knowing that a student can answer a question or perform an action, however, is not sufficient. The more important issue is the extent to which a student can select and apply

---

[16] See Marzano (2000) for further information on the limitations of present modes of assessment.

knowledge when faced with a new situation. Unfortunately, faculty have thought relatively little about what constitutes assessment for learning and, he notes, that most faculty refuse to be evaluated by the measures they use for others.

The assignment of a grade on the basis of perceived performance on tests is recognized as one of the most flawed aspects of education. Gloria Stronks warns, "Too narrow a view of assessment will have a negative impact on instruction" (Stronks 1991, 98). Criticisms of testing practices include the following:

1. Teachers use testing to coerce certain behaviors from their students.

2. Grading may increase competition among students and may encourage learning that is focused on grades.

3. The system of grades does not really inform the student of weaknesses, strengths, and possible future directions.

4. Testing practices typically do not teach students how to evaluate their own performance—something they will have to do throughout life.

5. Grades are too subjective. Instructors are not consistent in their grading styles.

6. The system does not allow for evaluation of the professor's contribution to the student's learning (or lack of learning).

7. Improper testing can have serious effects on the student's morale, self-concept, and attitudes toward learning.

8. No course can be evaluated acceptably in a two-hour examination period.

In the 1980s, having carried out a national survey of testing practices in colleges and universities, Ohmer Milton, Howard Pollio, and James Eison concluded that there is little warrant for continuing the practice of grading, since "grades have come to influence educational practice in ways that are detrimental not only to the educational endeavor but to society as a whole" (Milton, Pollio, and Eison 1986, 224). Tests are seldom fair measures of student learning, and stories are legion of inequities and injustices in grading. Alternative forms of assessment are possible[17] but difficult to implement because parents, employers, and the gatekeepers of the next level of schooling believe that "good grades" are synonymous with competency and knowledge of the field.

Early in my teaching career I reasoned that it would be most helpful for the church if my students developed a high level of competency and understanding in a particular subject area. Why would I want students to go into a particular ministry with a C level of ability rather than an A level? I structured one course and its assessment procedures to allow students to evaluate their competency and understanding against criteria, to determine ways they could address their limitations, and to engage in many different learning experiences until the desired level of ability was reached. Needless to say, because academic policy required a letter grade for every student, the majority of students received an A. Later, the dean called me into his office and suggested that I stop the practice because it was interfering with the school's awards system! The awards system was based on the premise that a certain percentage of students would receive low grades and a certain percentage would fail. In response to this story, some would argue that grade inflation is a serious problem in higher education. It is. However, the problem is not that more faculty are giving more students higher grades but that the design of instruction in relation to assessment is inadequate and the practice of giving grades for student performance is itself flawed.

Ward argues that faculty perspectives on testing need to incorporate two fundamental elements: assessment of learning is the assessment of the products of *whole learning experiences* rather than isolated segments taken out of context, and assessment of a *program's* effectiveness is more important than assessment of a student. Milton, Pollio, and Eison offer five recommendations to address the problems of testing:

1. Clarify the purpose of testing. Does it promote learning and teaching, or does it simply rank order students?

---

[17]Resources are readily available under such search terms as assessment, evaluation, and quality improvement. The more important task is to organize teams of faculty, educational specialists, congregational leaders, and students to study current practices, examine options, and propose alternatives. No book can give the way forward or identify the definitive list of resources.

2. Improve the quality of test construction. "Many faculty know very little about how to measure learning or how to construct classroom tests" (Milton, Pollio, and Eison 1986, 215).

3. Supply more information than just the letter symbol to students. Provide information about their performance on tests and in other academic exercises.

4. Reduce the number of grade categories. Rankings of A+, A, A–, and so on give only an illusion of precision. The number of factors affecting grades renders their reliability and exactness doubtful.

5. Abolish the grade point average (GPA). For this misleading statistic to have meaning, it must have reference to the grading policies of every school represented in the student body, to the testing skill of every faculty member giving a grade in a similar course, and to each course for which a grade was given. Also, Milton, Pollio, and Eison note that it is less arithmetically defensible to go from a less differentiated metric (A, B, C, D) to a more differentiated metric (numbers).

These authors recommend that transcripts be redesigned to reveal patterns of personal, professional, and academic development across a student's academic career. Increasingly, as the focus of education shifts to learning, testing and assignment of grades for student performance as the inalienable right of faculty alone is being challenged. Learning can be transformative, even revolutionary. Perhaps one of the reasons so few students seem to be eager learners is that their *learning* is never assessed. It need not be so.

Factor 4: The Lifelong Learner—A Spiritual Vision for Theological Education

Lifelong theological learning is predicated on the understanding that two to four years of formal theological education is not sufficient for one to understand a field or develop competency in ministry. Yet the structures of formal theological education are based on the premise that the years involved in earning a degree are sufficient. Tragically, it is possible to complete a three- or four-year theology degree without having developed the habits of thinking theologically. Similarly, it is possible to complete two- or three-year degrees in some aspect of ministry leadership and not be able to function as a ministry leader. When preparation is the goal and the rationale for institutional structure and curriculum, and when the degree is considered a sufficient base for service, students will inevitably assume their learning is complete after the degree is attained.

The Cultivation of Sustainable Habits for a Lifetime

Habits of thoughtful reading, careful research, dialogue that is more than just talk, writing, critical thinking and analysis, reflective practice, conceptual reasoning, spiritual reflection, the ability to ground knowledge in a disciplined theory base, the ability to access and use resources, communication, social interaction, justice and reconciliation, and so on—these are the habits of a lifetime. The challenge for theological education in the twenty-first century is to foster these habits within degree programs, to provide graduates with opportunities for continued learning that are more than conventional continuing-education courses, and to create access to multiple modes of learning for the whole people of God. Roger Von Holzen (2000) observes that campus wide recognition of the need for a seamless interface between face-to-face, classroom-based modes and more flexible lifelong learning modes is necessary. When lifelong learning is accepted as the goal, schools are only one of many educational resources—and not necessarily the most significant. If a person is expected to learn through a lifetime, then schools are actually subordinate to other educational influences, since they normally occupy a lesser number of years in a person's life span. The familiar aphorism "Education is a process of living and not a preparation for future living" is apt.

In much of the world, and increasingly in North America, economic resources to support traditional schools are diminishing rapidly. It is becoming apparent that the only way forward is to seek productive relationships among formal and nonformal educational ventures so that individuals and communities have access to learning opportunities for all of life. In this way, the hopelessly crowded curricula of theological schools could be alleviated. It is no longer necessary for schools to teach all that is needed for a profession or an academic specialization in the brief years of a degree program. If schools partner with nonformal ventures in planning for and supporting lifelong learning opportunities, they can be much more selective and intentional about what to include in their curriculum; and use faculty with greater effectiveness. However, schools will have to be more creative in writing faculty contracts. The current practice in most schools, of contracting with faculty simply for a set number of credit hours or number of classes to be taught, militates against the sort of flexibility that will be needed in the future.

Lifelong Learning and the Desire to Know God

Embracing lifelong learning as normative for theological education is consistent with the deepest values and commitments of Christian faith. The desire to know God which has under girded higher education for most of its history could be rekindled and sustained as we embrace the value of lifelong learning. Discipleship is not optional. The church, as the people of God, is God's hidden mystery. Institutional churches, schools, and other agencies are human creations that, at their best, serve God's purposes for the world. This purpose includes a future hope, the eschaton, and the "not yet" of human experience. Christians are pilgrims, learning is best imaged as a shared journey, and lifelong learning is compatible with the Christian mandate of a lifetime of obedience. The culture of learning communities, whether formal or nonformal, is such that each one helps the other to be more like Christ. The late Henri Nouwen once observed that the culture of the academy tends upward, toward pride, arrogance, and elitism, whereas the gospel points one to humility, service, and obedience. Learning, virtue, and service are lifelong endeavors, and the academy has a vital role to play in a new ecology of formal and nonformal modes of education.

Many current academic habits are artifacts of the forces of institutionalization, rationalism, and professionalism, not the values of Christ and the gospel. Conventional curricula, educational forms, assessment processes, and credentialing are largely inadequate to serve the mission of the church in the world. Schooling tends to compartmentalize knowledge and life. Time is at such a premium in school programs that the inner life is seldom touched, and relationships that could have characterized the pilgrim journey remain unborn.[18]

At present, the development of skills and attitudes necessary for lifelong learning are not a priority in conventional theological education. Because of this lack, efforts at cultivating the desire for God are hindered. We expect leaders to be learning constantly; however, the identity of the church suggests that the whole people of God are to be learning and growing. Simi-

---

[18]For an eloquent treatment of this theme, see Palmer (2004).

larly, professional development is expected of Christian leaders. However, if lifelong learning is, in fact, consistent with the desire for God, professional development cannot simply copy the practices of other professions without also considering the ongoing development and service of the whole people of God.

If Christians embraced the life of the disciple, with its attendant obligation of a life of learning, the educational enterprise would be transformed. If lifelong learning is also a theological value, then the God of grace offers hope that even if we stumble, we can get up and move on; failure does not have to be the end of the course. Theological education can no longer simply be a fragmented course of studies in a school. The future of theological education in its several modes is found in a commitment to lifelong learning for the whole people of God.

CHAPTER 10

Toward an International 21ˢᵗ Century Theological Education

To what extent can typically Euro-American institutional models of theological education serve today's Christian communities?—Ted Ward

"What constitutes a valid theological education in Manila, or Tokyo, or rural Nigeria? What does the student need to learn, to know, to do, to be? How can learning experiences be structured which will achieve these goals?" (Ward and Rowen 1972, 19). These questions are important today because of growing concerns about the implicit or explicit assumptions that characterize much theological education: courses exist to deliver necessary content to students; faculty are the determiners and organizers of that which is delivered, and evaluators of how well it is received; seminaries and congregations seldom collaborate in the development and assessment of those being trained or prepared for the ministry; accreditation procedures are governed by the academy, with little input from congregations. Theology and spirituality have not yet rediscovered a unity that would provide wholeness and accountability for study and service. The parts of the curriculum represented by theory and practice continue to drift apart as courses proliferate in each area and as language and concepts become increasingly arcane to faculty and students not of that area. Faculty who function as independent contractors relate mainly to their respective guilds and professional commitments and tend to be unwilling to invest much time and energy in reform of the system.

The familiar curricular and institutional relationships of Western theological schools were shaped by an emerging institutionalism and rationalism and a demand for professional church leaders. Western forms of theological education have been copied in other countries, but more recently these forms are being reconsidered as non-Western personnel assume leadership in international theological education. It is no longer a matter of debate that conventional approaches to theological education are deficient. Even in the West, alternative approaches are emerging at a rapid rate, but often without the benefit of informed reflection from the rest of the world. For example, how many North American schools have consulted with Brazilian, Nigerian, Indian, or Argentinian educators, to name a few? How many North American schools have sent their administrators to the Philippines, Indonesia, South Africa, or Hong Kong to learn from them what issues will affect the future? Until we develop equitable partnerships or consortia of schools internationally, with curricula that offer reciprocity in what constitutes experience and knowledge, we will make little headway in addressing the challenges of leadership development for the church.

Many years ago, the president of a leading American university asserted that since knowledge is everywhere the same, education can be everywhere the same. Whether our primary association is with the church or within the various expressions of theological education, dare we assume that there is one world norm for theological education?[1] Read the brochures from the increasing number of conferences on international education or intercultural dialogue. What insight do they provide for those leading curriculum and program change? For example, among the seminars offered at a recent conference were topics such as these:

- developing alternatives to polarization on divisive issues
- understanding cross-cultural conflict
- experiential learning strategies for intercultural training
- forming a vocabulary for intercultural interaction

---

[1]Though their racial and ethnic diversity has increased in the past ten years, almost all of the 244 member schools of the North American Association of Theological Schools (ATS) remain predominantly white in racial and ethnic composition. The racial and ethnic mix of the faculty is slowly increasing, from 9.4 percent in 1993 to 14.3 percent in 2002, in member schools, and though the racial/ethnic composition of students is far from that occurring in the general population, the increase in minority-group representation among students is still significant: from 4 percent in 1977 to 21 percent in 2002 (Association of Theological Schools 2002–2003). As of fall 2005, the proportion of racial and ethnic students was 22% of the head count enrollment, and the racial and ethnic proportion of faculty was 13%. See www.ats.edu for updated figures.

- building bridges across cultures
- diversity training in ecclesiastical contexts

Duane Elmer (1994 and 2002) asserts that three major issues must be understood in international relationships: shame (losing versus saving face), collectivism (one's duty is to help those in the group), and harmony (trust in relationship takes precedence over a task). The respective ways in which these issues are practiced will affect arrangements in areas such as administration, communication, assessment and instruction. Check out the websites of institutes and university programs in intercultural relations, intercultural communication, international leadership, intercultural development, international consulting, expatriate assessment, living overseas, multicultural education, multicultural counseling, and so on. Study these initiatives and begin to learn what it will mean to interact effectively with educational and church leaders in other cultures as we move through the early years of the twenty-first century.

Two problems will hinder this development: the West still tends to control development through disbursing wealth, and Western schools tend not to encourage internationals to look critically at the content and context of their Western education. A South African pastor once said that the West has to stop sending money to Africa. "It isn't helping. What we need is intellectual and ministry partnership." A church in the United States has taken this view seriously and thus enters into partnership with churches in Africa only when there is reciprocity. All churches in the relationship are both giving and receiving help and support. Another leader, while valuing his educational experience, observed that his Ph.D. from a Western school has been virtually useless for the work he has to do in his home country. Significantly, theological schools are exploring the feasibility of international consortia in theological education—without the presumption of Western dominance and credentialing.

Perspectives on the Nature of Theological Dialogue

Different traditions—evangelical, liberal, Protestant, Catholic—may use different language and approach theological issues from different perspectives, but the concern is the same: What understanding of the role of theology will be at the heart of theological education for the twenty-first century? Philip Jenkins casts this question against a larger and more significant intercultural reality. "Because of the long Western dominance of Christianity, debates over faith and culture often focus on attitudes toward specifically European matters. When a Christian group acclimatizes to a new society, the common assumption holds that what is traditionally done in Europe or North America is correct and authentic, and provides the reliable standard by which to assess local adaptations" (Jenkins 2002, 109).

A key question that emerges from this observation is how to distinguish core beliefs of Christianity from "cultural accidents" (ibid., 109). In his study of international patterns of Christianity, Jenkins discusses issues that ought to be posed as learning experiences for those who serve the church. For example, how do Christians understand differing cultural perspectives on Christian practices? Jenkins recounts how the language of faith emerged in Western contexts to produce images ("white as snow" is a simple example) that are often incomprehensible in other contexts. The vitality of the non-Western church is overtaking the churches of the North. Inevitably, images that are used to describe Jesus, the nature of liturgy, the practices of the faith, the meaning of the gospel, and so on, will change to accommodate the cultures in which the gospel is flourishing. The default response for some in the West is to brand these changes as heresy. Nonetheless, barring a worldwide catastrophe, such changes are gaining momentum.

As the church in the majority world grows more vibrant, what might change in the way leaders are developed? In the way new believers are taught? What will become of theological education internationally when these churches achieve a global impact? Christians will need to engage productively in international dialogue in order to deal with questions about the "acceptable limits of accommodation. At what point does enculturation end, to be replaced by the submergence of Christianity into some other religion?" (ibid., 119). As these and other questions become more urgent, it is likely that some elements that have been assumed to be core beliefs in Western Christianity will be challenged, nuanced, or purged. Theological institutions that learn how to engage in authentic collaboration, allowing their students to experience learning in other contexts and cultures, will have a better chance to assist the international church to deal with matters that affect belief and practice.

Though concerns about justice, spirituality, power, and the role of theology are not unique to this age, perhaps the most notable distinctive of the current discussions is the breadth of involvement. While not agreeing in every particular, theologians, faculty from different disciplines, and church leaders are interacting. More important, the dialogue is increasingly multinational and multicultural. The way theology is understood and practiced will be of increasing importance in coming discussions. Ronald Thiemann (1987) describes theology as a communal, formative, and critical activity capable of integrating seminary teaching and serving as a link to the rest of the university and society. As a communal activity, it must include more than the typically academic sectors of society and must represent well the international nature of the church. The communities that form the context for theological discussions will be of necessity less cohesive and more diverse. The inclusion of Europeans and North Americans in a more global dialogue is a positive trend as centers for evangelism, leadership development, and ecclesial vitality are relocating to Africa, Latin America, and some parts of Asia. As new or renewed thinking and writing emerge from the international dialogue, implications for theological education will become more focused. Even at the slow pace of change in higher education, the evidence of the past fifteen hundred years is that educational structures do change and will continue to change.

No doubt, the breadth of perspective needed in the dialogue will be unsettling for those who believe that theological orthodoxy is compromised by cultural relativism and unfamiliar questions. Given that academic theology has a relatively recent history, that God claims to have a purpose for the church, that God is involved with the world, and that therefore no one voice can speak for Christian belief, the formulation of mutually agreed-upon principles and definitions to guide conversations about the nature and role of theology would be helpful. It is beyond the scope of this book and the capability of this author to suggest such, but some suggestions are being offered.

Interestingly, Western theologians are recognizing the need to offer something of worth to such a dialogue. Perspectives differ on the role of theology. For example, Ingolf Dalferth suggests that it is of foremost importance that theology has to do with God—especially as the veracity of other voices is acknowledged, as questions about the nature and role of theology are explored, and as the existing Euro-American hegemony in theology is challenged.

> . . . theology becomes realistic only when it searches for criteria allowing it to decide concerning the truth, validity, and reasonableness of a particular faith, *and* when it does not consider these criteria adequately justified by the function of this faith in the life of the corresponding community of faith, but rather first and foremost grounds those criteria in God's reality, which itself precedes and grounds the community. Its efforts must be directed toward the critical knowledge of God focusing on the distinction between *God* and *notions of God*, and not merely toward a knowledge of the various understandings of God entertained by various communities. (Dalferth 1996, 137–38)

Suggesting that the search for new theological methodologies is essentially irrelevant in a pluralistic age, Jeffry Stout proposes that any "theology that hopes to converse on moral and other topics in a pluralistic setting like ours had better dispense with the quest for a method. There is no method for good argument and conversation save being conversant—that is, being well-versed in one's own tradition and on speaking terms with others" (Stout 1988, 165). Stout's perspective implies that any good conversation is more than just talk, more than voices in a blender. One enters the conversation with knowledge and intentionality, able to exercise effectively the skills of listening and dialogue.

Regardless of perspective, multiple sectors of an international society and church are raising questions about suffering, injustice, the meaning of life and personhood, sources of hope and of value, and the role of the church in society. In light of these questions, theology approached exclusively as the application of propositions is an unfitting exaltation of reason and will not help us deal with contemporary challenges and complexities. Theological method that includes conversation, or engagement, is necessary if the full resources of the Holy Spirit in the midst of God's people, historically and currently, and the complexity of possible interpretations are to be apprehended and assessed.

Theological Education and the Growing International Church

Paul Pierson is one of several asserting that the church is being reshaped in ways unprecedented since the sixteenth century. The traditional institutional churches in the West are in decline, while in Africa, Asia, and Latin

America they are still growing. In the midst of the decline of traditional (institutionalized) churches of the West, newer churches are emerging. Pierson summarizes studies of these newer churches that reveal certain common factors about church development:

- "Most evangelism and nurture of believers takes place in cells of five or ten persons who meet weekly in homes." Pierson observes that these groups are similar to Puritan conventicles, Pietist *ecclesiolae*, Moravian choirs, and Wesleyan class meetings. He notes that the modern Protestant missionary movement was birthed from these movements and that such small groups played a key role in every major revival.

- Most of the newer churches are not "classically Pentecostal" but are open to all the gifts of the Spirit. There is greater focus on the ministry of the laity.

- "Normally, there is an extended time of praise and prayer. A worship team, using contemporary music, sometimes composed by the group, leads the praise."

- "Often these churches have their own training programs, but they are for those already in some form of ministry. That is, ministry comes first, then sometimes more formal training."

- "Along with the emphasis on praise and prayer, there is strong emphasis on the exposition of Scripture."

- "Often these churches are remarkably holistic in their ministries."

- These churches seek to remove elements that they believe alienate the younger generation (e.g., hymnbooks, organs; Pierson 2003, 19–21).

These "characteristics in common" are of interest as we seek to describe the growing church. However, to have "characteristics in common" is neither an accurate reflection nor a predictor of church health. Sociological analysis is important but insufficient if corresponding consideration of the identity and purpose of the church as God sees it is lacking. Pierson does proceed to delineate several issues to be faced by these newer churches:

- Since most of them were started by charismatic leaders, transition to a new generation of leaders will be difficult. Since most of the leaders in the growing churches are from the grassroots, leadership development strategies are needed that will avoid fostering a ministerial elite.

- Substantive theological reflection is difficult when growth is so rapid and growth issues so numerous. Churches in much of the world face the challenge of developing structures to maintain growth without degenerating into stifling bureaucracies. Along with this comes the challenge to adapt communication methods and institutional forms to the next generation.

- Growing churches will face the question of how a high level of commitment can be maintained into the third and fourth generations.

- As most of the world's population is found in urban centers, growing churches face the challenge of ministry in the most crucial missionary frontiers—the cities of the world.

- "Finally, as we confront the opportunities and challenges in mission today, we need to realize that mission has always come out of renewal, both personal and corporate" (Pierson 2003, 26–27).

The desire to train leaders for the rapidly growing churches in much of the world is increasing in urgency. Parachurch agencies and coalitions of wealthy entrepreneurs seek to make a difference in leadership development. However, many of these efforts are driven by money from the West, which is counterproductive, and tend to be characterized by Western perspectives on what constitutes leadership for the church. Certainly leadership development for an exploding church is needed, but seminaries and Bible colleges cannot train leaders fast enough. Most of the leaders in the majority world, and increasing numbers in the West, will be developed in nonformal ventures established by concerned national leaders. These leaders are learning to resist pressures to import training materials and methods from the West. In the non-Western world, one might hope that there will be a shift from valuing the prestige of degrees and academic attainment toward creatively assessing one's culture to determine what modes of educational development are needed in that context. As these ventures develop, men and women from the West may be of help as they share experiences, discussing what has been helpful and what has proved limiting in the development of leaders for the Western church. As mutual understanding emerges, the Western church may likewise be helped.

In Jenkins's words, "We are currently living through one of the transforming moments in the history of religion worldwide" (Jenkins 2002, 1–2). The story that was once written with culturally Western nations at the center is now being rewritten to accommodate the new major players: Asia, Africa, and Latin America.

> This global perspective should make us think carefully before asserting 'what Christians believe' or 'how the church is changing.' All too often, statements about what 'modern Christians accept' or what 'Catholics today believe' refer only to what that ever-shrinking remnant of what *Western* Christians and Catholics believe. Such assertions are outrageous today, and as time goes by they will become ever further removed from reality. The era of Western Christianity has passed within our lifetimes, and the day of Southern Christianity is dawning. (Jenkins 2002, 3)

There is little doubt that the centers of Christianity have shifted to Africa, Latin America, and Asia. However, Christian churches in the majority world could suffer the same fate as Western churches—especially as presumed successful examples of leadership and organization are copied from churches in the West. Export of procedures has been a common practice in the history of the West, and because Westerners often take politeness as acceptance, North American church leaders will feel that their export has improved matters. However, in many cases, when a conference is over, church leaders will return to their own cultural context and face the same problems—problems that were unrecognized and not included in a Western dominated agenda. We learn how to partner in the ministry of the gospel by participation in the social reality rather than by delivering Western forms into a culture.

International Theological Education

What cultural assumptions inform our decisions about curriculum and structure? "What does it mean to teach students for ministries in communities that differ theologically and culturally from those to which we as individual faculty members or to which the school gives allegiance? Does everyone have constructive critique of what we teach and how?" (Foster 2002, 24). As he asks whose knowledge, values and skills shape educational process, Charles Foster reviews the historical patterns of dealing with diversity: alienation, subjugation, assimilation, and accommodation. He notes that accommodation gives the appearance of equity, but power is often retained by the dominant group, and educational processes serve to protect that dominance (ibid., 25). A commitment to embrace difference and to listen out of a posture of mutual respect will require considerable educational readjustment. Educational settings that are ecologies "of language processes, cultural patterns, and world views or faith commitments" increasingly require strategies that emphasize interaction and mutual critique (ibid., 35)

The more we learn about international initiatives, the more we realize the fallacy of trying to create a standardized education for all the world. Similarly, as leaders in other countries attempt to find indigenous expressions of Christian faith, numerous voices are calling for multinational, intercultural partnerships among churches, schools, mission enterprises, and development work. Regardless of the sending country, the temptation to send faculty to another country with little expectation that they will actually engage the culture and learn something from that engagement is to be resisted. Similarly, establishing programs in direct competition with national efforts is inappropriate.

The twenty-first-century paradigm involves learning how to connect and share resources. Rather than competition, consider partnerships that give students the option of not having to leave their home country for advanced degree work, that provide opportunity for faculty and students to become more competent interculturally, that allow international dialogue about critical issues. There is no reason today that the movement of international students and the flow of resources cannot be a two-way stream. Leaders in every country are learning how to be financially independent, or better, interdependent. Theological educators are seeking a new vision for theological education that takes seriously issues of injustice and violence—especially in countries that claim to be 80–90 percent Christian!

One-way patterns of dependency are neither desirable nor necessary. Western patterns adopted wholesale have left churches with limited capacity to understand their indigenous cultural patterns of leadership. Harvie Conn observes that wholesale adoption of Western forms has hindered biblical critique of existing patterns of leadership and authority. In many cases, ethnic tendencies toward all-powerful, authoritative leadership models have combined with Western missionary models to make clericalism even more rigid. The prophet orientation of many African communities, the Indian guru as the authority regarding truth, the Confucian respect for the teacher, the Western advocacy of the CEO, are imposed without thinking on pastor-leaders and encourage an elitist notion of Christian ministry. In every culture, practices can and should be critiqued not in light of cultural tradition but in light of the gospel.

What is an appropriate standard of excellence for the church in the world and for the variety of educational patterns that serve this church? To what extent should churches worldwide accept gifts of training in ways envisioned by a previously dominating Christian culture? To what extent are Western-style approaches to theological education, church practices, and Christian faith really what is needed?

In a work as challenging today as when it was first published, Roland Allen asserts that the methods of the West are not compatible with St. Paul's methods.

> We modern teachers from the West are by nature and by training persons of restless activity and boundless self-confidence. We are accustomed to assume an attitude of superiority…and to point to our material progress as the justification of our attitude. We are accustomed to do things ourselves for ourselves, to find our own way, to rely upon our own exertions, and we naturally tend to be impatient with others who are less restless and less self-assertive than we are. We are accustomed by long usage to an elaborate system of church organization, and a peculiar code of morality. We cannot imagine any Christianity worthy of the name existing without the elaborate machinery which we have invented…. We desire to impart not only the Gospel, but the Law and the Customs…. St. Paul distrusted elaborate systems of religious ceremonial, and grasped fundamental principles with an unhesitating faith in the power of the Holy Ghost to apply them to his hearers and to work out their appropriate external expressions in them. It was inevitable that methods which were the natural outcome of the mind of St. Paul should appear as dangerous to us as they appeared to the Jewish Christians of his own day. (Allen 1962, 6–7)

Significantly, at the end of his polemic Allen observed, "But that day is passing." Let's hope he was right.

CONCLUSION

What *Does* It Mean to be Theologically Educated?

Seems like old times just got new again. —George Gershwin

Movies set in the era when the horse and buggy were giving way to the automobile often show these modes of transportation coexisting. For a time, the symbols of two different eras traveled together on the same roads—not without mutual annoyance. It seems we are in another time of transition, in which the educational forms of one era coexist with initiatives that forecast the new. Interestingly, in theological education at least, many current initiatives reflect the values and practices of much earlier times. Nonformal education has been the pattern for most of history. For centuries the church was the center of theological education. Apprenticeship models were common in ancient times. Learning in ministry is a longstanding tradition. Interacting across disciplines of knowledge was taken for granted until it was determined that it would be more efficient to organize the curriculum in broad subject areas. Current efforts to reform theological education could be seen, then, as flawed efforts to recover approaches that were proven inadequate and cast aside in favor of today's more familiar academic models.[1] Or the educational practices of most conventional theological schools around the world gradually emerged from a series of decisions made across time and should be reformed.

The premise of this book is that any promise for the academy has been seriously hampered by decisions related to institutionalism, professionalism, academic rationalism, and even by ways in which the desire to know God

---

[1] The apprenticeship model faltered when the limitations of the master were replicated in the apprentice. The master-apprentice model could be rendered ineffectual by an inadequate master. On-the-job training (or what theological education would term fieldwork or internship) has been criticized on the same basis: the trainee can be shaped adversely by an inadequate work environment.

was expressed. Further, economic pressures and grassroots movements, protest or otherwise, are threatening the survival of all but the most well-endowed of conventional theological schools. Significantly, many of the voices calling for reform are no longer from outside the academy and are therefore not as easily dismissed.

> Perhaps the most striking formal feature of the last decade of activity has been the participant: most of the writers and discussants have been faculty members. Such broad faculty participation in national debates about theological education is a new development. Until this decade, almost all the public discussion was conducted by presidents and deans. Even within schools, as we noted before, substantial numbers of faculty members had resisted administrative attempts to involve them in discussion about their common educational tasks.... If faculty members continue to become engaged in national discussion in significant numbers, perhaps they will bring back to their home institutions some of the excitement, critical self-consciousness, and rigor in thinking about theological education that have marked the larger discussions, but that the school based debates have frequently lacked. (Kelsey and Wheeler 1994, 73)

It also seems that an increasing number of men and women, most between thirty-five and forty-five years of age, and most with a Ph.D. in any of a variety of disciplines, are less interested in progressing through an academic career in conventional programs. Their vision for education and leadership development is not easily accommodated in traditional structures. Unfortunately, vision is often held captive by the need to eat! But, perhaps, one or more foundations, several courageous and skilled academic administrators, insistent and collegial faculty, persistent and discerning students, and a host of committed congregational leaders will one day work together to reshape theological education for the whole people of God.

"I Skate Where the Puck Will Be, Not Where It Is."
—Wayne Gretzky

Decisions made across centuries led to what we know today as theological education.[2] Throughout the twenty-first century, we will continue to confront the need for wise decisions. The following are among several of the more important matters that provide opportunity for informed decision making.

Not anti-institution, but not serving the institution for the institution's sake. The more important matter is the extent to which institutional forms are accomplishing essential purposes and allowing for the inevitable processes of change. Edward Farley observes that the "history of theological schools is a history of constant reform" (Farley 1983a, 3). It may be more accurate to say, given the persistence of change and its generally slow progress in academic institutions, that schools are in a state of constant *adjustment*. Unfortunately, contemporary adjustments are too often in response to a crisis, a market demand, the whim of a committee, or the need to renew what is often perceived as the accreditation "license" for another five or ten years. Well-considered institutional in-course modifications should be a constant process. An accreditation agency should be able to show up announced at any time and see evidence of ongoing institutional assessment and well-considered adjustment.

Not anti-technology, but not letting technology drive education. Educational institutions are rightly incorporating technology, but much of the educational design is being driven by technologists (and bottom-line administrators who mistakenly see in technology a way to make money) rather than by educators, no matter what their discipline. Tool- or market-driven change is not serving well the task of developing men and women in ministry. At present, the more effective uses of technology are found in schools and nonformal ventures that have competent support staff, who know how to secure grant money for the right things (though equipment is needed, money for development and design is often the more important priority) and who have developed a design that obligates face-to-face interaction in different ways and places *supplemented* by technology.

---

[2]Dallas Willard once observed that it is important to remember that these were decisions, not doctrines.

To assist development, competent educational specialists and colleagues concerned about learning and development can work together to test alternative approaches to course design for adult learners. Faculty from different disciplines could come together in a retreat-style setting for enough time to build trust, to name criteria that they instinctively know are indicators of good practice, to experience different learning approaches (e.g., problem-based learning, research and inquiry models, simulation), and to practice facilitation skills.

Not antiknowledge, but not knowledge for knowledge's sake. Mere rationalism is not sufficient for the challenges that confront the mission of the church in the world. A sense of the holism of learning, a less restrictive view of the roles of formal and nonformal modes of education, and accreditation and assessment in the service of learning are essential as theological education evolves. As Rick Dunn envisions a fitting seminary model for the twenty-first century, he names six transforming values: "an emphasis on reflective learning, the metaphor of ecology as descriptive of learning (as opposed to the 'factory model'), interdependent community as the context for learning, church-seminary partnerships as the environment for pastoral formation, cultural engagement and exegesis, and a 're-formed' educational design for facilitating learning" (Dunn 1998, 4–5). In her turn, Mary Pazdan (1998) uses the term "wisdom community" to describe an alternative model of theological education, noting that the current traditions and structures of theological education hinder the development of such communities. Predetermined curricular patterns, lock-step timetables, and large classes do not allow the extended reflective and relational time needed for the cultivation of wisdom. Preoccupation with content obscures the important learning to be found in dialogue, debate, reflection on experience, and critical inquiry. If Dunn and Pazdan indicate a useful direction for theological education, it will not be achieved through the conventional curriculum and academic structures. It is time to launch and fund research projects that help us find and gather data on alternative practices developed by theological educators in churches, schools, and nonformal initiatives internationally.

Not anti-theology, but not theology for theology's sake. Charles Wood has suggested that theological education is "that process through which persons become...com-petent participants in theological inquiry. It is the fostering in a person of an aptitude for theology" (Wood 1994, 3–4). Richard Muller suggests that theology as a discipline is suffering a crisis of credibility, noting that

> virtually all of the writers who have examined the study of theology in recent times—most notably Gerhard Ebeling, Edward Farley, and Wolfhart Pannenberg—have remarked on the diversity and general disarray of the subject. And virtually all have recognized that this diversity and disarray both undermine the credibility of theology in our time and render exceedingly difficult, if not impossible the task of reintegrating the theological disciplines in such a way that they support a cohesive and cogent ministry of the gospel. (Muller 1991, 26)

Though suggestions as to what theology might become if not defined by a cluster of often disconnected subjects are few, there seems little objection to the notion that theology is somehow responsible to the church and society. As the role of theology in relation to the church and the public is explored, the poverty of existing structures and the need for new ways to "do theology" become apparent. Arguing for a church theology that is more than church dogmatics, John Cobb suggests that theology take "its problems, not from the intellectual and scholarly tradition, but from the life of the church. The disciplinization of theology has meant that most members of theological faculties do little of their work in this way" (Cobb 1996, 199; see also Tracy 1981, 16). Is this another form of anti-intellectualism? Since Cobb refers to intellectually demanding work within the academic disciplines, it seems unlikely that he is dismissing the need for critical scholarly work. However, it can be argued that academic theology, preoccupied with its own scholarly work, has not given enough attention to the need for a "church theology."

Why do ministers need to know theology? Why is it important for the whole people of God to be able to assess life and experience theologically? Does theology, in the forms that are common in many seminaries, contribute to the development of a church that is qualitatively different from any other organization in society? Since theology as we know it today was constructed out of the experience of humankind, what difference would it make to Western theology if it truly encountered the rest of the world? What difference would it make if voices that are not traditionally heard (the disadvantaged, the oppressed, those without power or authority in congregations, children and youth) were included?

Simply crafting a different way to organize the theological disciplines will not help us. All that we currently know as disciplines, including theology, must be enabled to interact in relation to a project that is larger than simply learning the stuff of isolated disciplines. The decision that learning should be organized in disciplines rather than around that which is critical to the mission of the people of God in the world has been one of theological education's greatest misjudgments.

Not against ordered learning, but not organizing learning in relation to specialized disciplines. The decision to organize knowledge by knowledge categories, rather than to view knowledge as an important resource for purposeful and responsible action, created academies that are now objects of persisting critique. Assuming that it is valid to bring together scholars with differing areas of expertise in local settings, what role will these scholars play? Surely the expectation that scholars will, one by one, transmit their particular pieces of information to groups of receivers is now seen as counterproductive and wasteful of scholarly resources. Perhaps the seminary will learn how to foster genuine communities of scholars who serve as a resource for agencies now emerging as the primary venues for the development of leaders—teaching churches, nonformal initiatives, and the variety of church-based efforts. Jeffrey Cantor argues "that the future of higher education in America will include significant partnerships and joint ventures with the private sector business community [in order to] maximize their resources and attract the kinds of resources and capabilities from outside that bring new opportunities for the student body and faculty" (Cantor 2000, 78). Various sorts of partnership are emerging in theological education. However, the nature and purpose of these partnerships is still evolving.

Not against theological education, but not equating theological education with formal schooling. In many instances, those who are rightly critical of schooling have only a limited repertoire of ways to promote and assess *learning* and a limited understanding of the variety of contexts that enhance learning. The solution is not necessarily to do away with schools but to understand the nature of learning, to develop a better sense of when, where, why, and how to use various approaches that foster learning, and to take context more seriously. Once we accept that theological education is not simply about school-like activities, then two areas of decision- making become important. First, what is the nature of church-based theological education, and why does it exist? Simply transferring school-like courses, curricula, and manuals to a church basement or creating school-like institutes attached to churches suggests that the concern that spawned the church-based movement is as yet unclear. Healthy church-based movements have several growing edges:

- to embed leadership development in a community of faith and learning,
- to develop a range of strategies conducive to learning and assessment for learning,
- to change the notion of leader development from the creation of a specialized class to the equipping of those who are able to equip others also (see 2 Tim. 2:2),
- to develop strategies for learning that recognize the holism of knowledge building, critical thinking, problem solving, and reflection,
- to broaden perspectives beyond one's group and way of thinking,
- to provide time for trust to develop in interpersonal and intercultural encounters,
- to create opportunities to test and refine skills.

The second area of decision-making relates to the relationship of formal and nonformal modes of education. Two questions most often raised in conversations about alternative approaches to theological education are: What do we do about accreditation? How do we deal with the felt need for a credential or degree? If accreditation is better understood as involving standards of assessment generated by an association of schools (who vote) rather than as laws imposed on schools by an external committee, and if accreditation is primarily a process of peer review rather than a flurry of report writing that leads to renewal of what an institution may perceive as a license, then conversations about the relationship of formal and nonformal modes of education are less difficult. Where academic accreditation is viewed as a political act or as the work of an agency that assumes only one standardized form of school is valid, then those concerned about learning and leader development in contexts different from conventional schooling may need to develop an association with accreditation standards that fit the outcomes they desire.

Credentialing is a different sort of problem. If employers require a certain type of credential, nonformal initiatives will have to negotiate relationships with each employer, or group of employers, probably on a case-by-case basis. There is no reason why nonformal initiatives cannot provide a certificate. But if the credential becomes an artifact sought for reasons of prestige or membership in an elite class, then any learning process must challenge the false pride, arrogance, and sense of superiority that such credentials too often generate.

Varieties of nonformal theological education are emerging in many countries. Many of these ventures will fail because the designers simply attempt to replicate courses, tests, and curriculum designs from the schools they criticize, or because for financial, prestige, or perceived credentialing needs, they connect with a school and are absorbed by that school, or because, driven by the agenda of one person or narrowly focused group, they are unable to respond to the complex challenges of this age. Still, since there will never be enough seminaries to complete the task of leader development for the church, productive interaction between formal and nonformal agencies of education are essential.

Becoming Theologically Educated

In how many ways can we answer the question of what it means to be educated theologically? Ernest Boyer (1990a) once said that to be truly educated requires going beyond isolated facts; it means putting learning in a larger context, it means discovering the connectedness of things.[3] Surely, to be educated theologically is to be able to make judgments and authentic connections at critical junctures in pastoral and other ministries. Surely, to

---

[3]Boyer, who until his death was president of the Carnegie Foundation and one of the more influential leaders in American education, proposed eight core commonalities for the curriculum. He suggested it was time to do away with the "Carnegie unit" (*x* number of hours of seat time, or what in higher education would be considered required credit hours) and think of education as discovering the connectedness of things in relation to the life cycle, production and the meaning of work, understanding our heritage, understanding the meaning and purpose of life, the aesthetic, communication and the use of symbols for communicating, understanding our relationship to the planet, and understanding the nature of institutions and the structures that shape our lives and thought (Boyer 1990a).

be educated theologically means that all members of the educational community are learning to set their minds on divine things. To be educated theologically means we are learning that in the most intimate, profound and moving experiences of our lives we turn to the aesthetic to express feelings and ideas that words could never convey. Surely, to be educated theologically means that all members of the learning community are learning to value each other and those outside our communities in all their diversity. Surely to be educated theologically means that we are becoming obedient disciples of God, committed to virtue and works of service.

We are long past the day when the seminary could do all that was expected of it. The curriculum is glutted with programs, littered with degrees, stuck in an instructional paradigm. Conversations today about theological education increasingly tackle such questions as, Should theological education be considered preparatory (ignoring the experience and background of students) or developmental (presuming that theological education is part of a long process of lifelong learning)? Is theological education primarily about knowledge for knowledge's sake, or is some notion of *praxis* important? Should theological education continue to reinforce competitive modes of learning or foster an active and diverse learning community? To what extent can formal and nonformal modes of learning support and inform one another? How do we serve the continuing professional development needs of alumni and other ministry professionals? How defensible is it to maintain disciplines in isolation from one another? At a time when theological institutions are playing off theological education accrediting agencies against government accrediting agencies, to whom is theological education accountable and how? Who are the stakeholders in decisions that are made in relation to curriculum, learning experiences, and assessment?

It is likely that pressure from congregations, nonformal initiatives, and developments in distance learning will force the shift from an instructional paradigm to a learning paradigm and sensitize us to the need for internationalization of the curriculum. Harris once asked a group of Bible college administrators: "If assessment revealed that your educational programs are not meeting their goals, are your faculty ready to rebuild them?" If faculty are prepared to tackle this challenge, different notions of what constitutes a faculty contract will be necessary. Others believe that faculty enclaves have developed too many protective behaviors and that as long as the power brokers are academics, the future is bleak. Before substantial change is possible, the academy may require a managed curriculum that challenges the right of faculty to have *exclusive* control over curriculum development. Similarly, as the focus shifts from instruction to learning, from preparation to development, from passive students to adult learners, the nature of admissions criteria will become a significant area of discussion. Dan Aleshire notes that the acceptance rate for applicants to seminaries is about 90 percent. The fact that most evangelical seminaries are tuition-driven likely contributes to this inflated statistic. He suggests that more productive admissions criteria will require evidence of a range of aptitude (e.g., intellectual ability, evaluated work history, financial indebtedness at time of application, evaluated in-ministry capacity, openness to diversity and different perspectives).

It seems inevitable that the understanding of theological education as that which takes place in a college or seminary in a specified period of years, and in classroom formats, will change significantly. It seems inevitable that commitment to justice and dialogue will be the future coinage of theological education as we confront power issues, the nature of knowledge, ways of knowing, and the relationship of the individual to the larger web of humankind. It seems inevitable that theological education has to be both centralized and decentralized. It seems inevitable that, in the development of theological education broadly conceived, discussion of what the Christian faith entails, and collaboration among many agencies that serve the mission of the people of God in the world will become necessary.

Perhaps the way forward is to discern where *God* is working. How would you answer Craig Dykstra's three basic questions: What is God doing in the world? What do churches have to be like that are responding to what God is doing in the world? What is theological education doing to equip leaders for the church that is responding to what God is doing in the world?

REFERENCES

After Communism. (no author identified). 1994. *Economist* 333, no. 7892 (December 3): 23–27.

Aleshire, Dan. 2000. Evangelical Theological Education in 2000 Decade. Audiotape of faculty workshop presented at Trinity Evangelical Divinity School, Deerfield, Ill.

Allen, Diogenes. 1997. *Spiritual Theology: The Theology of Yesterday for Spiritual Help Today.* Cambridge, Mass.: Cowley.

Allen, Roland. 1962. *Missionary Methods: St. Paul's or Ours?* Grand Rapids, Mich.: Eerdmans.

Alston, Wallace. 2000a. The Ministry of Christian Theology. In *Theology in the Service of the Church: Essays in Honor of Thomas W. Gillespie*, ed. Wallace Alston. Grand Rapids, Mich.: Eerdmans.

⸻, ed. 2000b. *Theology in the Service of the Church: Essays in Honor of Thomas W. Gillespie.* Grand Rapids, Mich.: Eerdmans.

Anderson, Lorin, David Krathwohl, and Benjamin Samuel. 2000. *Taxonomy for Learning, Teaching, and Assessing: A Revision of Bloom's Taxonomy of Educational Objectives.* New York: Longman.

Anderson, Philip. 1997. Education and Piety in an Immigrant Evangelical Tradition: North Park and the Challenge of Fundamentalism. Paper presented at the Aims and Purposes of Theological Education Consultation, Pasadena, Calif.

Anderson, R., K. N. Cissa, and R. C. Arnett, eds. 1994. *The Reach of Dialogue: Confirmation, Voice, and Community.* Cresskill, N.J.: Hampton.

Angelo, Thomas. 1997. The Campus as Learning Community: Seven Promising Shifts and Seven Powerful Levers. *AAHE Bulletin* 49, no. 9 (May): 36.

Angelo, Thomas, and K. Patricia Cross. 1993. *Classroom Assessment Techniques.* San Francisco: Jossey-Bass.

Argyris, Chris. 1993. *Knowledge for Action: A Guide to Overcoming Barriers to Organizational Change.* San Francisco: Jossey-Bass.

Argyris, Chris, and Donald Schön. 1974. *Theory in Practice: Increasing Professional Effectiveness*. San Francisco: Jossey-Bass.

Ashby, Eric. 1976. Reconciliation of Tradition and Modernity in Universities. In *On the Meaning of the University*, ed. Sterling McMurrin. Salt Lake City: University of Utah Press.

Association of Theological Schools. 1998. *Bulletin* 43, pt. 1. (Available from ATS, 10 Summit Park Drive, Pittsburgh, PA 15275-1103.)

_____. 2002–2003. *Fact Book on Theological Education*. Pittsburgh: Association of Theological Schools (available from ATS, 10 Summit Park Drive, Pittsburgh, PA 15275-1103).

Astley, Jeff, Leslie Francis, and Colin Chowder, eds. 1996. *Theological Perspectives on Christian Formation*. Grand Rapids, Mich.: Eerdmans.

Bailey, Laurie. 1996. Meaningful Learning and Perspective Transformation in Adult Theological Students. Ph.D. diss., Trinity Evangelical Divinity School, Deerfield, Ill.

Bainton, Roland. 1957. *Yale and the Ministry: A History of Education for the Christian Ministry at Yale from the Founding in 1701*. New York: Harper and Brothers.

Bandy, Thomas. 1998. *Moving off the Map*. Nashville: Abingdon.

_____. 1999. *Christian Chaos*. Nashville: Abingdon.

Banks, Robert. 1999. *Revisioning Theological Education: Exploring a Missional Alternative to Current Models*. Grand Rapids, Mich.: Eerdmans.

Barclay, William. 1959. *Educational Ideals in the Ancient World*. Grand Rapids, Mich.: Baker.

Barna, George. 1998. *The Second Coming of the Church*. New York: Thomas Nelson.

_____. 2002. The Third Coming of George Barna. *Christianity Today*, August 5 (www.christianitytoday.com/ct/2002/009/1.32.html). Last accessed in October 2005.

Barr, Robert, and John Tagg. 1995. From Teaching to Learning: A New Paradigm for Undergraduate Education. *Change* 27, no. 6: 12–25.

Bass, Dorothy, ed. 1997. *Practicing Our Faith: A Way of Life for a Searching People*. San Francisco: Jossey-Bass.

Bender, Ross. 1997. *Education for Peoplehood: Essays on the Teaching Ministry of the Church*. Text Reader Series 8. Elkhart, Ind.: Institute of Mennonite Studies.

Benne, Robert. 2004. Crisis of Identity: A Clash over Faith and Learning. *Christian Century* 121, no. 2 (January 27): 22–26.

Bennison, Charles. 1999. *In Praise of Congregations*. Boston: Cowley.

Bledstein, Burton. 1976. *The Culture of Professionalism: The Middle Class and the Development of Higher Education*. New York: W. W. Norton.

Bloom, Allen. 1987. *The Closing of the American Mind*. New York: Simon and Schuster.

Bloom, Benjamin, ed. 1956. *Taxonomy of Educational Objectives*. Handbook 1, *Cognitive Domain*. New York: David McKay.

Bloomer, Tom. 1997. A Research Inquiry into Greek and Hebrew Worldviews. Manuscript, Trinity Evangelical Divinity School, Deerfield, Ill.

Bouwsma, William. 1987. Humanism: The Spirituality of Renaissance Humanism. In *Christian Spirituality: High Middle Ages and Reformation*, ed. Jill Raitt. New York: Crossroad.

Bouyer, Louis. 1990. *The Christian Mystery: From Pagan Myth to Christian Mysticism*. Trans. Illtyd Trethowan. Edinburgh: T & T Clark.

Boyatzis, Richard, Scott Cowen, David Kolb, and associates. 1995. *Innovation in Professional Education: Steps on a Journey from Teaching to Learning*. San Francisco: Jossey-Bass.

Boyer, Ernest. 1990a. Making the Connections: The Search for Our Common Humanity. In *Rethinking the Curriculum*, ed. Mary Clark and Sandra Wawrytko. New York: Greenwood.

―――. 1990b. *Scholarship Reconsidered: Priorities of the Professorate*. Princeton, N.J.: Carnegie Foundation for the Advancement of Learning.

―――. 1993. What Is an Educated Person? Address to the Association for Supervision and Curriculum Development, Washington, D.C., March 27 (transcribed and used with permission).

Braaten, Carl. 1982. The Contextual Factor in Theological Education. *Dialog* 21, no. 3: 169–74.

Bradbeer, James. 1998. *Imagining Curriculum: Practical Intelligence in Teaching*. New York: Teachers College, Columbia University.

Bradley, James. 1996. The Nineteenth Century. In *Theological Education in the Evangelical Tradition*, ed. Daryl Hart and Albert Mohler. Grand Rapids, Mich.: Baker.

Bridston, Keith and Dwight Culver. 1965. *Pre-Seminary Education*. Minneapolis, Minn.: Augsburg.

Brody, Celeste, and Neil Davidson, eds. 1998. *Professional Development for Collaborative Learning: Issues and Approaches*. New York: State University of New York Press.

Brown, Andrew. 1995. *Popular Piety in Late Medieval England: The Diocese of Salisbury*. Oxford: Clarendon.

Brown, Colin. 1971. *Philosophy and the Christian Faith*. Downers Grove, Ill.: Inter-Varsity Press.

_____. 1990. *Christianity and Western Thought: A History of Philosophers, Ideas and Movements*. Vol. 1. Downers Grove, Ill.: InterVarsity Press.

Brown, William. 1996. *Character in Crisis: A Fresh Approach to the Wisdom Literature of the Old Testament*. Grand Rapids, Mich.: Eerdmans.

Browning, Don, ed. 1983. *Practical Theology, the Emerging Field in Theology, Church, and World*. San Francisco: Harper and Row.

_____. 1991. Toward a Fundamental and Strategic Practical Theology. In *Shifting Boundaries: Contextual Approaches to the Structure of Theological Education*, ed. Barbara Wheeler and Edward Farley. Louisville, Ky.: Westminster John Knox.

Brubacher, John, and Willis Rudy. 1968. *Higher Education in Transition: A History of American Colleges and Universities, 1636–1968*. New York: Harper and Row.

Brueggemann, Walter. 1982. *The Creative Word: The Canon as a Model for Biblical Education*. Philadelphia: Fortress.

Bruffee, Kenneth. 1993. *Collaborative Learning: Higher Education, Interdependence, and the Authority of Knowledge*. Baltimore: Johns Hopkins University Press.

Bunge, Marcia. ed. *The Child in Christian Thought*. Grand Rapids, Mich.: Eerdmans.

Burkhart, John. 1983. Schleiermacher's Vision for Theology. In *Practical Theology, the Emerging Field in Theology, Church, and World*, ed. Don Browning. New York: Harper and Row.

Burtchaell, James. 1998. *The Dying of the Light: The Disengagement of Colleges and Universities from Their Christian Churches*. Grand Rapids, Mich.: Eerdmans.

Calhoun, Daniel. 1965. *Professional Lives in America: Structure and Aspiration, 1750–1850.* Cambridge, Mass.: Harvard University Press.

Calhoun, David B. 1994–1996. *Princeton Seminary.* 2 vols. Carlisle, Pa: Banner of Truth Trust.

Callahan, Kennon. 2000. *Small, Strong Congregations.* San Francisco: Jossey-Bass.

Canham, Elizabeth. 1999. *Heart Whispers: Benedictine Wisdom for Today.* Nashville: Upper Room.

Cannell, Linda. 1996. Selective Amnesia: A Church in Transition. In *Studies in Canadian Evangelical Renewal: Essays in Honour of Ian S. Rennie*, ed. Kevin Quast and John Vissers. Toronto: FT Publications.

_____. 1999. A Review of Literature on Distance Education. *Theological Education* 36, no. 1 (Autumn): 1–72.

Cannon, William. 1983. *History of Christianity in the Middle Ages.* Grand Rapids, Mich.: Baker.

Cantor, Jeffrey. 2000. *Higher Education outside of the Academy.* San Francisco: Jossey-Bass.

Cantor, Norman. 1969. *Medieval History.* Toronto: Macmillan.

Carmody, Denise, and John Carmody. 1996. *Mysticism: Holiness East and West.* Oxford: Oxford University Press.

Carroll, Jackson. 1971. Structural Effects of Professional Schools on Professional Socialization: The Case of Protestant Clergymen. *Social Forces* 50: 61–74.

_____. 1985. The Professional Model of Ministry–Is It Worth Saving? *Theological Education* 21, no. 2 (Spring): 7–48.

Carson, Don. 1984. Church, Authority in. In *Evangelical Dictionary of Theology*, ed. Walter Elwell. Grand Rapids, Mich.: Baker.

Cervero, Ronald. 1988. *Effective Continuing Education for Professionals.* San Francisco: Jossey-Bass.

Chapman, Tasha. 2004. The Nature of Educating for the Professions in Higher Education. Manuscript, Trinity Evangelical Divinity School, Deerfield, Ill.

Charry, Ellen. 1997. *By the Renewing of Your Minds: The Pastoral Function of Christian Doctrine.* Oxford: Oxford University Press.

———. 2000. To What End Knowledge? The Academic Captivity of the Church. In *Theology in the Service of the Church: Essays in Honor of Thomas W. Gillespie*, ed. Wallace Alston. Grand Rapids, Mich.: Eerdmans.

Chawla, Sarita, and John Renesch, eds. 1995. *Learning Organizations: Developing Cultures for Tomorrow's Workplace*. Portland, Ore.: Productivity.

Cherry, Conrad. 1995. *Hurrying toward Zion: Universities, Divinity Schools, and American Protestantism*. Bloomington: Indiana University Press.

Chong, Calvin. 2003. From Archaeology to Architecture: Exploring Systemic Structure Reforms for Theological Institutions Situated in Re-made, Post-conservative Singapore. Manuscript, Trinity Evangelical Divinity School, Deerfield, Ill.

Chopp, Rebecca. 1995. *Saving Work: Feminist Practices of Theological Education*. Louisville, Ky.: Westminster John Knox.

Clarke, Andrew. 2000. *Serve the Community of the Church: Christians as Leaders and Ministers*. Grand Rapids, Mich.: Eerdmans.

Clarke, James. 2001. Johann Gottlieb Fichte. In *Fifty Major Thinkers on Education: From Confucius to Dewey*, ed. Joy Palmer. New York: Routledge.

Clowney, Edmund. 1995. *The Church*. Downers Grove, Ill.: InterVarsity Press.

Coakley, Susan. 2002. Deepening Practices: Perspectives from Ascetical and Mystical Theology. In *Practicing Theology: Beliefs and Practices in Christian Life*, ed. Miroslav Volf and Dorothy Bass. Grand Rapids, Mich.: Eerdmans.

Cobb, John. 1991. Theology against the Disciplines. In *Shifting Boundaries: Contextual Approaches to the Structure of Theological Education*, ed. Barbara Wheeler and Edward Farley. Louisville, Ky.: Westminster John Knox.

———. 1996. The Multifaceted Future of Theology. In *The Future of Theology: Essays in Honor of Jürgen Moltmann*, ed. Miroslav Volf, Carmen Krieg, and Thomas Kucharz. Grand Rapids, Mich.: Eerdmans.

———. 1998. *Reclaiming the Church*. 2nd ed. Louisville, Ky.: Westminster John Knox.

Cohen, Joel, and Mark Castner. 2000. Technology and Classroom Design: A Faculty Perspective. In *Teaching with Technology: Rethinking Tradition*, ed. Les Lloyd. Medford, N.J.: Information Today.

Colish, Marcia. 1998. *Medieval Foundations of the Western Intellectual Tradition, 400–1400*. New Haven, Conn.: Yale University Press.

Conant, James Bryan. 1956. *The Citadel of Learning*. New Haven, Conn.: Yale University Press.

Conn, Harvie. 1984. *Eternal Word and Changing Worlds: Theology, Anthropology, and Mission in Trialogue*. Grand Rapids, Mich.: Zondervan.

Cornell, Marguerite Louise. 1982. The University of Kuwait: An Historical-Comparative Study of Purposes in a New University in a Developing Nation. Ph.D. diss., McGill University, Montreal.

Courtenay, William. 1987. Spirituality and Late Scholasticism. In *Christian Spirituality: High Middle Ages and Reformation*, ed. Jill Raitt. New York: Crossroad.

Cranton, Patricia. 1994. *Understanding and Promoting Transformative Learning: A Guide for Educators of Adults*. San Francisco: Jossey-Bass.

Crenshaw, James. 1985. Education in Ancient Israel. *Journal of Biblical Literature* 104, no. 4 (December): 601–15.

Cross, George. 1911. *The Theology of Schleiermacher*. Chicago: University of Chicago Press.

Cross, K. Patricia. 1998. Why Learning Communities? Why Now? *About Campus* 3, no. 3 (July-August): 4–11.

Cuninggim, Merrimon. 1994. *Uneasy Partners: The College and the Church*. Nashville: Abingdon.

Cunningham, Mary Kathleen. 1995. *What Is Theological Exegesis? Interpretation and the Use of Scripture in Barth's Doctrine of Election*. Valley Forge, Penn.: Trinity Press International.

Cymbala, Jim, and Merrill Dean. 1997. *Fresh Wind, Fresh Fire*. Grand Rapids, Mich.: Zondervan.

Dabney, D. Lyle. 1996. Otherwise Engaged in the Spirit: A First Theology for a Twenty-first Century. In *The Future of Theology: Essays in Honor of Jürgen Moltmann*, ed. Miroslav Volf, Carmen Krieg, and Thomas Kucharz. Grand Rapids, Mich.: Eerdmans.

Dalferth, Ingolf. 1996. Time for God's Presence. In *The Future of Theology: Essays in Honor of Jürgen Moltmann*, ed. Miroslav Volf, Carmen Krieg, and Thomas Kucharz. Grand Rapids, Mich.: Eerdmans.

Davies, David. 1998. Lifelong Learning Competency in the Twenty-first Century: A Prospectus. In *The Virtual University: An Action Paradigm and Process for Workplace Learning*, ed. Richard Teare, David Davies, and Eric Sandelands. London: Cassell.

Dawson, Christopher. 1991. *Religion and the Rise of Western Culture*. New York: Doubleday.

Dentan, Robert. 1968. *The Knowledge of God in Ancient Israel*. New York: Seabury.

De Ridder-Symoens, Hilde. 1992. *A History of the University in Europe*. Vol. 1, *Universities in the Middle Ages*. Cambridge: Cambridge University Press.

DeVries, Dawn. 2001. "Be Converted and Become as Little Children": Friedrich Schleiermacher on the Religious Significance of Childhood. In *The Child in Christian Thought*, ed. Marcia Bunge. Grand Rapids, Mich.: Eerdmans.

Dickens, A. G. 1964. *The English Reformation*. New York: Schocken.

_____. 1966. *Reformation and Society in Sixteenth-century Europe*. London: Harcourt, Brace and World.

_____. 1994. *Late Monasticism and the Reformation*. London: Hambledon.

Dixon, Nancy. 1994. *The Organizational Learning Cycle: How We Can Learn Collectively*. McGraw-Hill Developing Organizations Series. Berkshire, U.K.: McGraw-Hill.

_____. 1996. *Perspectives on Dialogue*. Colorado Springs, Colo.: Center for Creative Leadership.

Dockery, David, ed. 1995. *The Challenge of Postmodernism: An Evangelical Engagement*. Wheaton, Ill.: Bridgepoint.

Doll, William, Jr. 1993. *A Post-modern Perspective on Curriculum*. New York: Teachers College, Columbia University.

Donald, Janet. 1997. *Improving the Environment for Learning: Academic Leaders Talk about What Works*. San Francisco: Jossey-Bass.

Duncan, David Ewing. 2003. The New Biochemist. *Discover* 24, no. 12 (December): 22–24.

Dunn, Rick. 1994. Theological Education: Presuppositions Regarding Learning and the Tasks of Ministry. Ph.D. diss., Trinity Evangelical Divinity School, Deerfield, Ill.

———. 1998. Learning for Ministry: Six Transforming Values and One Alternative Model. Paper presented at Evangelical Theological Society meeting, Orlando, Fla., November 18.

Dykstra, Craig. 1985. No Longer Strangers. *Princeton Seminary Bulletin* 6, no. 3 (November): 188–200.

———. 1991a. Looking Ahead at Theological Education. *Theological Education* 28, no. 1 (Autumn): 95–105.

———. 1991b. Reconceiving Practice. In *Shifting Boundaries: Contextual Approaches to the Structure of Theological Education*, ed. Barbara Wheeler and Edward Farley. Louisville, Ky.: Westminster John Knox.

Dykstra, Craig, and Dorothy Bass. 2002. A Theological Understanding of Christian Practices. In *Practicing Theology: Beliefs and Practices in Christian Life*, ed. Miroslav Volf and Dorothy Bass. Grand Rapids, Mich.: Eerdmans.

Eisner, Elliot. 1994. *Cognition and Curriculum Reconsidered*. 2nd ed. New York: Teachers College, Columbia University

Eisner, Elliot, and Elizabeth Vallance. 1974. *Conflicting Conceptions of the Curriculum*. Berkeley, Calif.: McCutchan.

Elmer, Duane. 1994. *Cross-Cultural Conflict: Building Relationships for Effective Ministry*. Downers Grove, Ill.: InterVarsity Press.

———. 2002. *Cross-Cultural Connections: Stepping Out and Fitting In around the World*. Downers Grove, Ill.: InterVarsity Press.

Elmer, Duane, and Lois McKinney, eds. 1996. *With an Eye on the Future: Development and Mission in the Twenty-first Century*. Monrovia, Calif.: MARC.

Engel, Arthur. 1983. The English Universities and Professional Education. In *The Transformation of Higher Learning, 1860–1930*, ed. Konrad Jarausch. Chicago: University of Chicago Press.

Enns, Marlene. 2000a. The "Devotio Moderna" Movement: Towards Restoration and Integration through *Praxis Pietatis*. Manuscript, Trinity Evangelical Divinity School, Deerfield, Ill.

———. 2000b. An Ecclesial Paradigm Approach to Theological Education. Manuscript, Trinity Evangelical Divinity School, Deerfield, Ill.

Erb, Peter, ed. 1983. Introduction. In *Pietists: Selected Writings*. New York: Paulist.

Evdokimov, Paul. 1998. *Ages of the Spiritual Life*. Crestwood, N.Y.: St. Vladimir's Seminary Press.

Eyler, Janet, and Dwight Giles. 1999. *Where's the Learning in Service-Learning?* San Francisco: Jossey-Bass.

Fallon, Daniel. 1980. *The German University: A Heroic Ideal in Conflict with the Modern World*. Boulder: Colorado Associated University Press.

Farley, Edward. 1983a. *Theologia: The Fragmentation and Unity of Theological Education*. Philadelphia: Fortress.

———. 1983b. Theology and Practice outside the Clerical Paradigm. In *Practical Theology, the Emerging Field in Theology, Church, and World*, ed. Don Browning. San Francisco: Harper and Row.

———. 2003. *Practicing Gospel: Unconventional Thoughts on the Church's Ministry*. Louisville, Ky.: Westminster John Knox Press.

Fee, Gordon. 1987. *The First Epistle to the Corinthians*. Grand Rapids, Mich.: Eerdmans.

———. 1989. *Laos* and Leadership under the New Covenant. *Crux* 25, no. 4: 3–13.

Feilding, Charles. 1966. *Education for Ministry*. Dayton, Ohio: American Association of Theological Schools.

Ferguson, Everett. 1987. *Backgrounds of Early Christianity*. Grand Rapids, Mich.: Eerdmans.

Ferré, Nels. 1954. *Christian Faith and Higher Education*. New York: Harper and Brothers.

Finke, Roger, and Rodney Stark. 1992. *The Churching of America: Winners and Losers in Our Religious Economy*. New Brunswick, N.J.: Rutgers University Press.

Fletcher, John. 1983. *The Futures of Protestant Seminaries*. Washington, D.C.: Alban Institute.

Flexner, Abraham. 1910. *Medical Education in the United States and Canada: A Report to the Carnegie Foundation for the Advancement of Teaching. Bulletin* no. 4. Boston: D. B. Updike, Merrymount.

Flowers, Steve, and Steve Reeve. 2000. Positioning Web-Based Learning in the Higher Education Portfolio: Too Much, Too Soon? In *Teaching with Technology: Rethinking Tradition*, ed. Les Lloyd. Medford, N.J.: Information Today.

Foster, Charles. 2002. Diversity in Theological Education. *Theological Education* 38, no. 2: 15–37.

Fouché, H. L., and D. J. Smit. 1996. Inviting a Dialogue on "Dialogue." *Scriptura*, no. 57: 79–102.

Fowl, Stephen. 1998. *Engaging Scripture*. Oxford: Blackwell.

Frank, Thomas. 2000. *The Soul of the Congregation: An Invitation to Congregational Reflection*. Nashville: Abingdon.

Freire, Paulo. 1970. *Pedagogy of the Oppressed*. New York: Continuum.

———. 1992. *Pedagogy of Hope*. New York: Continuum.

———. 1994. There Is No True Word That Is Not at the Same Time a Praxis. In *The Reach of Dialogue: Confirmation, Voice, and Community*, ed. R. Anderson, K. N. Cissa, and R. C. Arnett. Cresskill, N.J.: Hampton.

———. 1997. *Pedagogy of the Heart*. New York: Continuum.

———. 1998. *Pedagogy of Freedom: Ethics, Democracy, and Civic Courage*. New York: Rowman and Littlefield.

French, Robert, and John Bazalgette. 1996. From "Learning Organization" to "Teaching-Learning Organization"? *Management Learning* 27, no. 1: 113–28.

Gabelnick, Faith, Jean McGregor, Roberta Matthews, and Barbara Smith. 1990. *Learning Communities: Creating Connections among Students, Faculty, and Disciplines*. San Francisco: Jossey-Bass.

Gambrell, Mary Latimer. 1937. *Ministerial Training in Eighteenth Century New England*. New York: Columbia University Press.

Garrison, D. R., and Terry Anderson. 2003. *E-Learning in the Twenty-first Century: A Framework for Research and Practice*. New York: Routledge Farmer.

Gawronski, Raymond. 1995. *Word and Silence: Hans Urs von Balthasar and the Spiritual Encounter between East and West*. Grand Rapids, Mich.: Eerdmans.

Gellert, C. 1992. Faculty Research. In *Encyclopedia of Higher Education*, ed. Burton Clarke and Guy Neave, 3:1634–41. Oxford: Pergamon.

Giles, Kevin. 1995. *What on Earth is the Church? An Exploration in New Testament Theology*. Downers Grove, Ill.: InterVarsity Press.

Gill, David. 1989. *The Opening of the Christian Mind: Taking Every Thought Captive to Christ*. Downers Grove, Ill.: InterVarsity Press.

———, ed. 1997. *Should God Get Tenure? Essays on Religion and Higher Education*. Grand Rapids, Mich.: Eerdmans.

Goldman, Israel. 1975. *Lifelong Learning among Jews: Adult Education in Judaism from Biblical Times to the Twentieth Century*. New York: KTAV.

Goodchild, L. F. 1992. Religious Vocations (Theological Seminaries). In *Encyclopedia of Higher Education*, ed. Burton Clark and Guy Neave, 2:1200–1217. Oxford: Pergamon.

Goodwin, Wayne. 1989. Theological Education and the Reorganization of Consciousness. Ph.D. diss., University of Kentucky, Lexington.

Grant, Gerald, ed. 1992. *Review of Research in Education* 18. Washington, D.C.: American Educational Research Association.

Grant, Robert. 1986. Theological Education at Alexandria. In *The Roots of Egyptian Christianity*, ed. Birger Pearson and James Goehring. Philadelphia: Fortress.

Greaves, Richard. 1969. *The Puritan Revolution and Educational Thought*. New Brunswick, N.J.: Rutgers University Press.

Green, Madeleine, ed. 1997. *Transforming Higher Education: Views from Leaders from around the World*. Phoenix: American Council in Education, Oryx.

Green, Madeleine, and Fred Hayward. 1997. Forces for Change. In *Transforming Higher Education: Views from Leaders from around the World*, ed. Madeleine Green. Phoenix: American Council in Education, Oryx.

Greenleaf, Robert. 1996a. The Need for a Theology of Institutions. In *Seeker and Servant: Reflections on Religious Leadership*, ed. Larry Spears and Anne Fraker. San Francisco: Jossey-Bass.

———. 1996b. Religious Leadership for These Times. In *Seeker and Servant: Reflections on Religious Leadership*, ed. Larry Spears and Anne Fraker. San Francisco: Jossey-Bass.

———. 1996c. The Seminary as Institution. In *Seeker and Servant: Reflections on Religious Leadership*, ed. Larry Spears and Anne Fraker. San Francisco: Jossey-Bass.

———. 1996d. Theology: A Concern for the Conditions under Which the Human Spirit Flowers. In *Seeker and Servant: Reflections on Religious Leadership*, ed. Larry Spears and Anne Fraker. San Francisco: Jossey-Bass.

Greer, Robert. 2003. *Mapping Postmodernism: A Survey of Christian Options*. Downers Grove, Ill.: InterVarsity Press.

Greer, Rowan. 1986. *Broken Lights and Mended Lives: Theology and Common Life in the Early Church*. University Park: Pennsylvania State University Press.

Grendler, Paul. 1989. *Schooling in Renaissance Italy: Literacy and Learning, 1300–1600*. Baltimore: Johns Hopkins University Press.

Grenz, Stanley, and Roger Olson. 1992. *Twentieth-century Theology: God and the World in a Transitional Age*. Downers Grove, Ill.: InterVarsity Press.

Gründler, Otto. 1987. Devotio Moderna. In *Christian Spirituality: High Middle Ages and Reformation*, ed. Jill Raitt. New York: Crossroad.

Guinness, Os. 1993. *Dining with the Devil: The Megachurch Movement Flirts with Modernity*. Grand Rapids, Mich.: Baker.

Gustafson, James. 1981. *Ethics from a Theocentric Perspective: Theology and Ethics*. Chicago: University of Chicago Press.

———. 1987. Priorities in Theological Education. *Theological Education* 23, supp., 69–87.

———. 1988. Reflections on the Literature of Theological Education Published between 1955 and 1985. *Theological Education* 24, supp. 2, 9–73.

Gutek, Gerald. 1972. *A History of the Western Educational Experience*. New York: Random House.

Habermas, Jürgen. 1971. *Knowledge and Human Interests*. Boston: Beacon.

Halstead, Kenneth. 1998. *From Stuck to Unstuck*. Bethesda, Md.: Alban Institute.

Handy, Charles. 1995. Managing the Dream. In *Learning Organizations: Developing Cultures for Tomorrow's Workplace*, ed. Sarita Chawla and John Renesch. Portland, Ore.: Productivity.

———. 1998. The *Hungry Spirit: Beyond Capitalism; A Quest for Purpose in the Modern World*. New York: Broadway.

Handy, Robert. 1982. Trends in Canadian and American Theological Education, 1880–1980: Some Comparisons. *Theological Education* 18, no. 2 (Spring): 175–218.

Happold, F. C. 1970. *Mysticism: A Study and an Anthology*. Rev. ed. New York: Penguin.

Harpaz, Yoram, and Adam Lefstein. 2000. Communities of Thinking. *Educational Leadership* 58. no. 3 (November): 54–57.

Harper, William Rainey. 1899. Shall the Theological Curriculum Be Modified, and How? *American Journal of Theology 3*, 45–66.

Harris, John. 2003. Assessment of Ministry Preparation to Increase Understanding. *Theological Education* 39, no. 2: 117–36.

Harris, John, John Tagg, and Mike Howell. 2005. Organize to Optimize: Organizational Change and Higher Education. *The Observatory on Borderless Higher Education*. June Report. The full text is available to subscribers at: http://www.obhe.ac.uk/products/reports/ Last accessed in October 2005.

Harris, Maria. 1989. *Fashion Me a People: Curriculum in the Church*. Louisville, Ky.: Westminster John Knox.

Harrisville, Roy, and Walter Sundberg. 1995. *The Bible in Modern Culture*. Grand Rapids, Mich.: Eerdmans.

Hart, Ann Weaver. 1990. Effective Administration through Reflective Practice. *Education and Urban Society* 22, no. 2 (February): 153–67.

Hart, Daryl G.. 1999. *The University Gets Religion: Religious Studies in American Higher Education*. Baltimore: Johns Hopkins University Press.

_____. 1992a. American Learning and the Problem of Religious Studies. In *The Secularization of the Academy*, ed. George Marsden and Bradley Longfield. New York: Oxford University Press.

_____. 1992b. Faith and Learning in the Age of the University: The Academic Ministry of Daniel Coit Gilman. In *The Secularization of the Academy*, ed. George Marsden and Bradley Longfield. New York: Oxford University Press.

Hart, Daryl, and Albert Mohler, eds. 1996. *Theological Education in the Evangelical Tradition*. Grand Rapids, Mich.: Baker.

Hartshorne, Hugh and Milton Froyd. 1945. *Theological Education in the Northern Baptist Convention: A Survey*. Philadelphia, PA: Judson Press.

Haskins, Charles. 1957. *The Rise of Universities*. Ithaca, N.Y.: Cornell University Press.

Hatch, Nathan. 1989. *The Democratization of American Christianity*. New Haven, Conn.: Yale University Press.

Hauerwas, Stanley. 1999. *Prayers Plainly Spoken*. Downers Grove, Ill.: InterVarsity Press.

Hawkins, D. J. B. 1947. *A Sketch of Medieval History*. New York: Sheed and Ward.

Hawkins, Thomas. 1997. *The Learning Congregation: A New Vision of Leadership*. Louisville, Ky.: Westminster John Knox.

Hayes, Charles. 1995. *Proving You're Qualified: Strategies for Competent People without College Degrees*. Wasilla, Alaska: Autodidactic.

Healy, Nicholas. 2000. *Church, World, and the Christian Life*. Cambridge: Cambridge University Press.

Hebblethwaite, Brian, and Stewart Sutherland, eds. 1982. *The Philosophical Frontiers of Christian Theology*. London: Cambridge University Press.

Heisey, Nancy, and Daniel Schipani, eds. 1997. *Theological Education on Five Continents: Anabaptist Perspectives*. Strasbourg, France: Mennonite World Conference.

Hengel, Martin. 1974. *Judaism and Hellenism*. Vol. 1. Philadelphia: Fortress.

Henry, Patrick, ed. 1984. *Schools of Thought in the Christian Tradition*. Philadelphia: Fortress.

Hesselbein, Frances, Marshall Goldsmith, and Richard Beckhard, eds. 1997. *The Organization of the Future*. San Francisco: Jossey-Bass.

Hibbert, Richard. 2004. Nurturing Vitality in the Church through Appropriate Structure: A Challenge for Facilitators of Church Planting Movements. Manuscript, Trinity Evangelical Divinity School, Deerfield, Ill.

Hiebert, Paul. 1985. Epistemological Foundations for Science and Theology. *TSF Bulletin*, March-April, 5–10.

———. 1999. *Missiological Implications of Epistemological Shifts*. Harrisburg, Penn.: Trinity Press International.

Hinson, E. Glenn. 1986. Puritan Spirituality. In *Protestant Spiritual Traditions*, ed. Frank Senn. New York: Paulist.

Hoffecker, W. Andrew. 1981. *Piety and the Princeton Theologians: Archibald Alexander, Charles Hodge, Benjamin Warfield*. Grand Rapids, Mich.: Baker.

Honan, James P., and Cheryl Sternman Rule. 2002. *Using Cases in Higher Education*. San Francisco: Jossey-Bass, Harvard Institutes for Higher Education.

Hopewell, James. 1984. A Congregational Paradigm for Theological Education. *Theological Education* 21 (Autumn): 60–70.

Horton, John, and Susan Mendus, eds.1994. *After MacIntyre: Critical Perspectives on the Work of Alasdair MacIntyre*. Notre Dame, Ind.: University of Notre Dame Press.

Hostetter, D. Ray. 1994. Universitas: The Case for a New University. *Faculty Dialogue*, no. 22 (Fall): 19–41.

Hough, Joseph. 1981. The Politics of Theological Education. *Occasional Papers, United Methodist Board of Higher Education and Ministry*, no. 37 (September 7): 2–12.

———. 1984. The Education of Practical Theologians. *Theological Education* 20, no. 2 (Spring): 55–84.

Hough, Joseph, and John Cobb. 1985. *Christian Identity and Theological Education*. Atlanta: Scholars.

Hough, Joseph, and Barbara Wheeler, eds. 1988. *Beyond Clericalism: The Congregation as a Focus for Theological Education*. Atlanta: Scholars.

Hudson, Jill. 2004. *When Better Isn't Enough*. Herndon, Va.: Alban Institute

Hutchins, Robert M. 1953. *The University of Utopia*. Chicago: University of Chicago Press.

Hütter, Reinhard. 1997. *Suffering Divine Things: Theology as Church Practice*. Grand Rapids, Mich.: Eerdmans.

Hyma, Albert. 1950. *The Brethren of the Common Life*. Grand Rapids, Mich.: Eerdmans.

Hyman, Ronald. 1973. *Approaches in Curriculum*. Englewood Cliffs, N.J.: Prentice-Hall.

Jackson, Lewis, and Rosemary Caffarella. eds. 1994. *Experiential Learning: A New Approach*. Series: New Directions for Adult and Continuing Education: no. 62. San Francisco, CA: Jossey-Bass Publishers.

Jaeger, Werner. 1939. *Paideia: The Ideals of Greek Culture.* Trans. Gilbert Highet. 3 vols. London: Oxford University Press.

———. 1985. *Early Christianity and the Greek Paideia.* Cambridge, Mass.: Harvard University Press. Orig. pub. 1961.

Jarausch, Konrad H., ed. 1983. *The Transformation of Higher Learning, 1860–1930.* Chicago: University of Chicago Press.

Jarvis, Peter. 1999. *The Practitioner-Researcher: Developing Theory from Practice.* San Francisco: Jossey-Bass.

Jaspers, Karl. 1959. *The Idea of the University.* Trans. H. A. T. Reiche and H. F. Vanderschmidt. Boston: Beacon.

Jenkins, John. 1997. *Knowledge and Faith in Thomas Aquinas.* Cambridge: Cambridge University Press.

Jenkins, Philip. 2002. *The Next Christendom: The Coming of Global Christianity.* New York: Oxford University Press.

Johns, Cheryl. 1997. To Know God Truly: The Community of Faith Model in Theological Education. Paper presented at the Aims and Purposes of Theological Education Consultation, Pasadena, Calif.

Jones, Alison. 1999. The Limits of Cross-Cultural Dialogue: Pedagogy, Desire, and Absolution in the Classroom. *Educational Theory* 49, no. 3 (Summer): 299–316.

Jones, David, Jeffrey Greenman, and Christine Pohl. 2000. The Public Character of Theological Education: An Evangelical Perspective. *Theological Education* 37, no. 1: 1–15.

Jones, L. Gregory. 2002. Beliefs, Desires, Practices, and the Ends of Theological Education. In *Practicing Theology: Beliefs and Practices in Christian Life,* ed. Miroslav Volf and Dorothy Bass. Grand Rapids, Mich.: Eerdmans.

Jones, L. Gregory, and Stephanie Paulsell, eds. 2002. *The Scope of Our Art: The Vocation of the Theological Teacher.* Grand Rapids, Mich.: Eerdmans.

Joyce, Bruce, and Marsha Weil. 1986. *Models of Teaching.* 3rd ed. Englewood Cliffs, N.J.: Prentice-Hall.

Judge, E. A. 1983a. The Interaction of Biblical and Classical Education in the Fourth Century. *Journal of Christian Education,* paper 77 (July): 31–37.

———. 1983b. The Reaction against Classical Education in the New Testament. *Journal of Christian Education,* paper 77 (July): 7–14.

Kallistos of Diokleia. 1986. The Human Person as an Icon of the Trinity. *Sobornost* 8, no. 2: 6–23.

Kelly, Robert. 1924. *Theological Education in America*. New York: George H. Doran.

Kelsey, David. 1992. *To Understand God Truly: What's Theological about a Theological School?* Louisville, Ky.: Westminster John Knox.

————. 1993. *Between Athens and Berlin: The Theological Education Debate*. Grand Rapids, Mich.: Eerdmans.

Kelsey, David, and Barbara Wheeler. 1991. Thinking about Theological Education: The Implications of "Issues Research" for Criteria of Faculty Excellence. *Theological Education*, Autumn, 11–26.

————. 1994. The ATS Basic Issues Research Project: Thinking about Theological Education. *Theological Education* 30, no. 2: 71–80.

Kemp, Stephen. 1999. Being Where? Culture and Formation in Ministry Training: A Response to *Being There*. Paper presented to the ACCESS conference, Orlando, Florida, January 22.

Kenneson, Philip, and James Street. 1997. *Selling Out the Church*. Nashville: Abingdon.

Kieckhefer, Richard. 1987. Major Currents in Late Medieval Devotion. In *Christian Spirituality: High Middle Ages and Reformation*, ed. Jill Raitt. New York: Crossroad.

Kling, David. 1996. New Divinity Schools of the Prophets. In *Theological Education in the Evangelical Tradition*, ed. Daryl Hart and R. Albert Mohler. Grand Rapids, Mich.: Baker.

Kolb, David. 1984. *Experiential Learning*. New York: Prentice-Hall.

Krathwohl, David, Benjamin Bloom, and Bertram Masia. 1964. *Taxonomy of Educational Objectives*. Handbook 2, *Affective Domain*. New York: David McKay.

Kuklick, Bruce. 1985. *Churchmen and Philosophers*. New Haven, Conn.: Yale University Press.

Küng, Hans. 1967. *The Church*. New York: Sheed and Ward.

————. 1994. *Great Christian Thinkers*. New York: Continuum.

Kuyper, Abraham. 1954. *Principles of Sacred Theology*. Trans. Hendrik De Vries. Grand Rapids, Mich.: Eerdmans.

Labaree, David. 1999. The Chronic Failure of Curriculum Reform. *Education Week*, May 19, 42–44.

Latchem, Colin, and Donald Hanna. 2001. *Leadership for Twenty-first Century Learning: Global Perspectives from Educational Innovators (Open and Distance Learning)*. New York: Routledge Farmer.

Lawler, Edwina. 1991. Neohumanistic-Idealistic Concepts of a University. In *Friedrich Schleiermacher and the Founding of the University of Berlin*, ed. Herbert Richardson. Lewiston, N.Y.: Edwin Mellen.

Lawson, John. 1967. *Medieval Education and the Reformation*. London: Routledge and Kegan Paul.

LeClercq, Jean. 1982. *The Love of Learning and the Desire for God: A Study of Monastic Culture*. New York: Fordham University Press.

―――. 1985. Western Christianity. In *Christian Spirituality: Origins to the Twelfth Century*, ed. Bernard McGinn and John Meyendorf. New York: Crossroad.

Leinhardt, Gaea. 1992. What Research on Learning Tells Us about Teaching. *Educational Leadership* 49, no. 7 (April): 20–25.

Lewis, Linda, and Carol Williams. 1994. Experiential Learning: Past and Present. In *Experiential Learning: A New Approach*, ed. Lewis Jackson and Rosemary Caffarella. Series: New Directions for Adult and Continuing Education: no. 62. San Francisco, CA: Jossey-Bass Publishers.

Lieberman, Myron. 1956. *Education as a Profession*. Englewood Cliffs, N.J.: Prentice-Hall.

Liefeld, Walter, and Linda Cannell. 1991. The Contemporary Context of Theological Education: A Consideration of the Multiple Demands on Theological Educators. *Crux* 27, no. 4 (December): 19–27.

―――. 1992. Spiritual Formation and Theological Education. In *Alive to God: Studies in Spirituality*, ed. J. I. Packer and Lorne Wilkinson. Downers Grove, Ill.: InterVarsity Press.

Light, Donald. 1983. The Development of Professional Schools in America. In *The Transformation of Higher Learning, 1860–1930*, ed. Konrad Jarausch. Chicago: University of Chicago Press.

Lilge, Frederic. 1948. *The Abuse of Learning: The Failure of the German University*. New York: Macmillan.

Lindbeck, George. 1996. Spiritual Formation and Theological Education. In *Theological Perspectives on Christian Formation: A Reader on Theology and Christian Education*, ed. Jeff Astley, Leslie Francis, and Colin Crowder. Grand Rapids, Mich.: Eerdmans.

Lippy, Charles, and Peter Williams, eds. *Encyclopedia of American Religious Experience: Studies of Traditions and Movements.* Vol. 3. New York: Charles Scribner's Sons.

Lloyd, Les, ed. *Teaching with Technology: Rethinking Tradition.* Medford, N.J.: Information Today.

Lodahl, Thomas M., and Stephen M. Mitchell. 1980. Drift in the Development of Innovative Organizations. In *The Organizational Life Cycle: Issues in the Creation, Transformation, and Decline of Organizations,* ed. John R. Kimberley, Robert H. Miles, and associates, 184–207. San Francisco: Jossey-Bass.

Longfield, Bradley. 1992. "For God, for Country, and for Yale": Yale, Religion, and Higher Education. In *The Secularization of the Academy,* ed. George Marsden and Bradley Longfield. New York: Oxford University Press.

Lotz, David, ed. 1989. *Altered Landscapes: Christianity in America, 1935–1985.* Grand Rapids, Mich.: Eerdmans.

Louth, Andrew. 1981. *The Origins of the Christian Mystical Tradition: From Plato to Denys.* Oxford: Clarendon.

———. 1983. *Discerning the Mystery: An Essay on the Nature of Theology.* Oxford: Clarendon.

Lovin, Robin, and Richard Mouw. 2000. Theme Introduction: The Public Character of Theological Education. *Theological Education* 37, no. 1: ix-xvii.

Lynn, Elizabeth, and Barbara Wheeler. 1999. Missing Connections: Public Perceptions of Theological Education and Religious Leadership. *Auburn Studies Bulletin,* no. 6 (September): 1–16.

Ma, Wonsuk, and Julie C. Ma, eds. *Asian Church and God's Mission.* West Caldwell, N.J.: OMF Literature.

Maas, Robin, and Gabriel O'Donnel, eds. *Spiritual Traditions for the Contemporary Church.* Nashville: Abingdon.

MacDonald, Gordon. 1977. Some Questions Seminaries Must Face. *Evangelical Newsletter* 4, no. 12 (June 17).

MacIntyre, Alasdair. 1984. *After Virtue: A Study in Moral Theory.* Notre Dame, Ind.: University of Notre Dame Press.

———. 1994. A Partial Response to My Critics. In *After MacIntyre: Critical Perspectives on the Work of Alasdair MacIntyre*, ed. John Horton and Susan Mendus. Notre Dame, Ind.: University of Notre Dame Press.

Malik, Charles. 1982. *A Critique of the Christian University*. Downers Grove, Ill.: InterVarsity Press.

Manchester, William. 1992. *A World Lit Only by Fire: The Medieval Mind and the Renaissance*. Toronto: Little, Brown.

Marrou, Henri. 1956. *A History of Education in Antiquity*. New York: Sheed and Ward. Reprint 1982 by University of Wisconsin Press, 1982.

Marsden, George. 1980. *Fundamentalism and Modern Culture: The Shaping of American Evangelicalism, 1870–1925*. New York: Oxford University Press.

———. 1991. The Soul of the American University. Reprint. *Faculty Dialogue*, no. 15 (Fall): 83–118.

———. 1992. The Soul of the American University: An Historical Overview. In *The Secularization of the Academy*, ed. George Marsden and Bradley Longfield. New York: Oxford University Press.

———. 1994. *The Soul of the American University: From Protestant Establishment to Established Unbelief*. New York: Oxford University Press.

———. 1997. *The Outrageous Idea of Christian Scholarship*. Oxford: Oxford University Press.

Marsden, George, and Bradley Longfield, eds. 1992. *The Secularization of the Academy*. New York: Oxford University Press.

Marshall, Stephanie Pace. 1997. Creating Sustainable Learning Communities for the Twenty-first Century. In *The Organization of the Future*, ed. Frances Hesselbein, Marshall Goldsmith, and Richard Beckhard. San Francisco: Jossey-Bass.

Martin, James, and James Samels. 1997a. First among Equals: The Current Roles of the Chief Academic Officer. In *First among Equals: The Role of the Chief Academic Officer*, ed. James Martin and James Samuels. Baltimore: Johns Hopkins University Press.

———, eds. 1997b. *First among Equals: The Role of the Chief Academic Officer*. Baltimore, Maryland: Johns Hopkins University Press.

Marty, Martin. 1987. The New Church and the Seminaries. *Dialog* 26:124–27.

Marzano, Robert. 2000. *Transforming Classroom Grading.* Alexandria, Va.: Association for Supervision and Curriculum Development.

———. 2001. *Designing a New Taxonomy of Educational Objectives.* Thousand Oaks, Calif.: Corwin.

May, Mark, with William Adams Brown, Charlotte Feeney, R. B. Montgomery, and Frank Shuttleworth. 1934. *The Education of American Ministers.* Vol. 3, *The Institutions That Train Ministers.* New York: Institute of Social and Religious Research.

McClellan, B. Edward. 1999. *Moral Education in America: Schools and the Shaping of Character from Colonial Times to the Present.* New York: Teachers College, Columbia University.

McClelland, Charles. 1983. Professionalization and Higher Education in Germany. In *The Transformation of Higher Learning, 1860–1930,* ed. Konrad Jarausch. Chicago: University of Chicago Press.

McCord, James. 1978. The Understanding of Purpose in a Seminary Closely Related to the Church. *Theological Education* 14, no. 2 (Spring): 59–66.

McGinn, Bernard. 1991. *The Presence of God: A History of Western Christian Mysticism.* Vol. 1, *The Foundations of Mysticism.* New York: Crossroad.

———. 1994. *The Presence of God: A History of Western Christian Mysticism.* Vol. 2, *The Growth of Mysticism.* New York: Crossroad.

McGinn, Bernard, and John Meyendorf, eds. 1985. *Christian Spirituality: Origins to the Twelfth Century.* New York: Crossroad.

McIntosh, Mark. 1998. *Mystical Theology.* Oxford: Blackwell.

McMurrin, Sterling, ed. 1976. *On the Meaning of the University.* Salt Lake City: University of Utah Press.

McTighe, Jay, and Grant Wiggins. 1999. *The Understanding by Design Handbook.* Alexandria, Va.: Association for Supervision and Curriculum Development.

———. 2000. *Understanding by Design.* Englewood Cliffs, N.J.: Prentice-Hall.

Mead, Sidney. 1956. The Rise of the Evangelical Concept of the Ministry in America, 1607–1850. In *The Ministry in Historical Perspectives,* ed. Richard H. Niebuhr and Daniel D. Williams. San Francisco: Harper and Row.

Meeks, Wayne. 1990. Seminary Education: A Philosophical Paradigm Shift in Process. *Faculty Dialogue* 3 (Winter): 21–34.

Meister, Jeanne. 1998. *Corporate Universities: Lessons in Building a World-Class Work Force.* New York: McGraw-Hill.

Meyendorf, John. 1979. *Byzantine Theology: Historical Trends and Doctrinal Themes.* New York: Fordham University Press.

Mezirow, Jack. 1990. *Fostering Critical Reflection in Adulthood: A Guide to Transformative and Emancipatory Learning.* San Francisco: Jossey-Bass.

———. 1991. *Transformative Dimensions of Adult Learning.* San Francisco: Jossey-Bass.

Miller, Glenn. 1989. Professionals and Pedagogues: A Survey of Theological Education. In *Altered Landscapes: Christianity in America, 1935–1985*, ed. David Lotz. Grand Rapids, Mich.: Eerdmans.

———. 1991. The Virtuous Leader: Teaching Leadership in Theological Schools. *Faith and Mission* 9, no. 1 (Fall): 19–35.

Miller, Glenn, and Robert Lynn. 1988. Christian Theological Education. In *Encyclopedia of American Religious Experience: Studies of Traditions and Movements*, ed. Charles Lippy and Peter Williams, 3:1627–52. New York: Charles Scribner's Sons.

Milton, Ohmer, Howard Pollio, and James Eison. 1986. *Making Sense of College Grades: Why the Grading System Doesn't Work and What Can Be Done about It.* San Francisco: Jossey-Bass.

Morse, Mary Kate. 1995. Henri J. M. Nouwen: A Pastoral Voice for the Reformation of Theological Education. *Faculty Dialogue*, no. 23 (Winter): 33–40.

Mouw, Richard. 1997. The "Ontology" of the Theological School. Paper presented at the Aims and Purposes of Theological Education Consultation, Pasadena, Calif.

———. 1999. What Is Our Business? *Auburn Studies Bulletin*, no. 6 (September): 17–19.

———. 2001. *He Shines in All That's Fair: Culture and Common Grace.* Grand Rapids, Mich.: Eerdmans.

Muller, Richard. 1991. *The Study of Theology.* Vol. 7. Grand Rapids, Mich.: Zondervan.

Myers, Edward. 1960. *Education in the Perspective of History.* New York: Harper and Brothers.

Myklebust, Olav Guttorm. 1955. *The Study of Missions in Theological Education*. Vol. 1, *To 1910*. Studies of the Egede Instituttet. Oslo: O. C. Olsen.

Nassif, Bradley, ed. 1996. *New Perspectives in Historical Theo-logy*. Grand Rapids, Mich.: Eerdmans.

Neuhaus, Richard John. 1984. *The Naked Public Square: Reli-gion and Democracy in America*. Grand Rapids, Mich.: Eerdmans.

———, ed. 1988. *The Believable Futures of American Protestantism*. Grand Rapids, Mich.: Eerdmans.

Niebuhr, H. Richard. 1956. *The Purpose of the Church and Its Ministry: Reflections on the Aims of Theological Education*. New York: Harper and Brothers.

———. 1960. *Radical Monotheism and Western Culture*. New York: Harper and Brothers.

Niebuhr, H. Richard, and Daniel D. Williams, eds. 1956. *The Ministry in Historical Perspectives*. San Francisco: Harper and Row.

Niebuhr, H. Richard, Daniel Williams, and James Gustafson. 1957. *The Advancement of Theological Education*. New York: Harper and Brothers.

Niebuhr, Richard R. 1962. Schleiermacher: Theology as Human Reflection. *Harvard Theological Review* 60, no. 1 (January): 21–49.

Nisbet, Robert. 1971. *The Degradation of the Academic Dogma: The University in America, 1945–1970*. New York: Basic Books.

———. 1980. *History of the Idea of Progress*. New York: Basic Books.

Nisbett, Richard, Kaiping Peng, Incheol Choi, and Ara Norenzyan. 2001. Culture and Systems of Thought: Holistic versus Analytic Cognition. *Psychological Review* 108, no. 2: 291–310.

Noll, Mark. 1979. The Founding of Princeton Seminary. *Westminster Theological Journal* 42, no. 1 (Fall): 72–110.

Noll, Mark, David Bebbington, and George Rawlyk, eds. 1994. *Evangelicalism: Comparative Studies of Popular Protestantism in North America, the British Isles, and Beyond, 1700–1990*. New York: Oxford University Press.

Nouwen, Henri J. M. 1989. *In the Name of Jesus: Reflections on Christian Leadership*. New York: Crossroad.

Novak, Michael. 1965. *Belief and Unbelief: A Philosophy of Self-Knowledge*. New York: New American Library.

Nowlen, Philip M. 1988. *A New Approach to Continuing Education for Business and the Professions*. Old Tappan, N.J.: Macmillan.

Oberman, Heiko Augustinus. 1981. *Masters of the Reformation: The Emergence of a New Intellectual Climate in Europe*. Cambridge: Cambridge University Press.

⸺. 1992. *The Dawn of the Reformation*. Grand Rapids, Mich.: Eerdmans.

⸺. 1994. *The Reformation: Roots and Ramifications*. Grand Rapids, Mich.: Eerdmans.

O'Dea, Thomas. 1961. Five Dilemmas in the Institutionalization of Religion. *Journal for the Scientific Study of Religion* 1, no. 1: 30–39.

Oden, Thomas. 1995a. *Requiem: A Lament in Three Movements*. Nashville: Abingdon.

⸺. 1995b. So What Happens after Modernity? A Postmodern Agenda for Evangelical Theology. In *The Challenge of Postmodernism: An Evangelical Engagement*, ed. David Dockery. Wheaton, Ill.: Bridgepoint.

Oleson, Alexandra, and John Voss, eds. 1979. *The Organization of Knowledge in Modern America, 1860–1920*. Baltimore: Johns Hopkins University Press.

Ollenburger, Ben. 1997. Theory and Practice in Theological Education. Paper presented at the Aims and Purposes of Theological Education Consultation, Pasadena, Calif.

Ortiz, Manuel. 1996. *One New People: Models for Developing a Multiethnic Church*. Downers Grove, Ill.: InterVarsity Press.

Oswald, Roy. 1980. Crossing the Boundary between Seminary and Parish. Research Report. Bethesda, Md.: Alban Institute.

Ozment, Steven. 1980. *The Age of Reform, 1250–1550: An Intellectual and Religious History of Late Medieval and Reformation Europe*. New Haven, Conn.: Yale University Press.

Palmer, Parker. 1998. *The Courage to Teach*. San Francisco: Jossey-Bass.

⸺. 2004. *A Hidden Wholeness: The Journey toward an Undivided Life*. San Francisco: Jossey-Bass.

Parks, Sharon Daloz. 2000. *Big Questions, Worthy Dreams: Mentoring Young Adults in Their Search for Meaning, Purpose, and Faith*. San Francisco: Jossey-Bass.

Pazdan, Mary. 1998. Wisdom Communities: Models for Christian Formation and Pedagogy, *Theological Education* 34, no. 2 (Spring): 25–30.

Pazmiño, Robert. 1997. *Foundational Issues in Christian Education: An Introduction in Evangelical Perspective.* 2nd ed. Grand Rapids, Mich.: Baker.

Pearson, Birger, and James Goehring, eds. 1986. *The Roots of Egyptian Christianity.* Philadelphia: Fortress.

Peek, Janyne. 1997. Transforming Learning, Transformational Leadership: The Relationship between Meaningful Learning in Higher Education and Visionary Leadership. Ph.D. diss., Trinity Evangelical Divinity School, Deerfield, Ill.

Pelikan, Jaroslav. 1992. *The Idea of the University: A Reexamination.* New Haven, Conn.: Yale University Press.

Peng, Kaiping, and Richard Nisbett. 1999. Culture, Dialectics, and Reasoning about Contradiction. *American Psychologist* 54, no. 9 (September): 741–54.

Peterson, Eugene. 1987. *Working the Angles: The Shape of Pastoral Integrity.* Grand Rapids, Mich.: Eerdmans.

Petrie, Hugh. 1992. Interdisciplinary Education: Are We Faced with Insurmountable Opportunities? In *Review of Research in Education* 18, ed. Gerald Grant, 299–330. Washington, D.C.: American Educational Research Association.

Pierson, Paul. 2003. The New Context of Christian Mission: Challenges and Opportunities for the Asian Church. In *Asian Church and God's Mission*, ed. Wonsuk Ma and Julie C. Ma. West Caldwell, N.J.: OMF Literature.

Porter, Noah. 1868. *The Human Intellect with an Introduction Upon Psychology and the Soul*. New York: Charles Scribner's Sons.

Posterski, Donald, and Irwin Barker. 1993. *Where's a Good Church?* Winfield, B.C.: Wood Lake.

Posterski, Donald, and Gary Nelson. 1997. *Future Faith Churches.* Winfield, B.C.: Wood Lake.

Prozeky, Martin. 1981. The Young Schleiermacher: Advocating Religion to an Age of Reason. *Journal of Theology for Southern Africa* 37:50–75.

The Public Character of Theological Education. 2000. Special issue of *Theological Education* 37, no. 1.

Quast, Kevin, and John Vissers, eds. 1996. *Studies in Canadian Evangelical Renewal: Essays in Honour of Ian S. Rennie.* Toronto, Ontario: FT Publications.

Raitt, Jill, ed. 1987. *Christian Spirituality: High Middle Ages and Reformation.* New York: Crossroad.

Ramsey, Boniface. 1985. *Beginning to Read the Fathers.* New York: Paulist.

Rashdall, Hastings. 1936a. *The Universities of Europe in the Middle Ages*, ed. F. M. Powicke and A. B. Emden. Vol. 1. London: Oxford University Press.

———. 1936b. *The Universities of Europe in the Middle Ages*, ed. F. M. Powicke and A. B. Emden. Vol. 3. London: Oxford University Press.

Rasmussen, Larry. 1997. Shaping Communities. In *Practicing Our Faith: A Way of Life for a Searching People*, ed. Dorothy Bass. San Francisco: Jossey-Bass.

Rawlyk, George, and Mark Noll, eds. 1993. *Amazing Grace: Evangelicalism in Australia, Britain, Canada, and the United States.* Grand Rapids, Mich.: Baker.

Readings, Bill. 1996. *The University in Ruins.* Cambridge, Mass.: Harvard University Press.

Reed, Jeff. 1992. Church-Based Theological Education: Creating a New Paradigm. In *The Paradigm Papers.* Ames, Iowa: Learncorp.

———. 2001. Church Based Ministry Training That Is Truly Church-Based. Paper presented to ACCESS Thirtieth Annual Conference, Chicago, Illinois, January 19.

Rendle, Gil, and Alice Mann. 2003. *Holy Conversations: Strategic Planning as a Spiritual Practice for Congregations.* Herndon, Va.: Alban Institute.

Retallick, John. 1999. Transforming Schools into Learning Communities: Beginning the Journey. In John Retallick, Barry Cocklin, and Kennece Coombe, *Learning Communities in Education: Issues, Strategies and Contexts.* New York: Routledge.

Retallick, John, Barry Cocklin, and Kennece Coombe. 1999. *Learning Communities in Education: Issues, Strategies, and Contexts.* New York: Routledge.

Richardson, Herbert, ed. 1991. *Friedrich Schleiermacher and the Founding of the University of Berlin*. Lewiston, N.Y.: Edwin Mellen.

Richey, Russell. 1996. The Early Methodist Episcopal Experience. In *Theological Education in the Evangelical Tradition*, ed. Daryl Hart and Albert Mohler. Grand Rapids, Mich.: Baker.

Ringenberg, William. 1990. Education, Protestant Theological. In *Dictionary of Christianity in America*, ed. Daniel G. Reid. Downers Grove, Ill.: InterVarsity Press.

Ringer, Fritz. 1979. The German Academic Community. In *The Organization of Knowledge in Modern America, 1860–1920*, ed. Alexandra Oleson and John Voss. Baltimore: Johns Hopkins University Press.

Ritschl, Dietrich. 1996. Is There Anything "New" in Theology? Reflections on an Old Theme. In *The Future of Theology: Essays in Honor of Jürgen Moltmann*, ed. Miroslav Volf, Carmen Krieg, and Thomas Kucharz. Grand Rapids: Eerdmans.

Roberts, Frank C. 1981. *To All Generations: A Study of Church History*. Grand Rapids, Mich.: Board of Publications of the Christian Reformed Church.

Roberts, Jon, and James Turner. 2000. *The Sacred and the Secular University*. Princeton, N.J.: Princeton University Press.

Rorty, Amélie Oksenberg, ed. 1998. *Philosophers on Education*. New York: Routledge

Rowen, Samuel. 1996. Missiology and the Coherence of Theological Education. In *With an Eye on the Future: Development and Mission in the Twenty-first Century*, ed. Duane Elmer and Lois McKinney. Monrovia, Calif.: MARC.

Rowley, Daniel James, Herman D. Lujan, and Michael G. Dolence. 1998. *Strategic Choices for the Academy: How Demand for Lifelong Learning Will Re-create Higher Education*. San Francisco: Jossey-Bass.

Rüegg, Walter. 1992. Themes. In *A History of the University in Europe*, vol. 1, *Universities in the Middle Ages*, ed. Hilde De Ridder-Symoens. Cambridge: Cambridge University Press.

Ryan, Alan. 1998. Deweyan Pragmatism and American Education. In *Philosophers on Education*, ed. Amélie Oksenberg Rorty. New York: Routledge.

Sandvig, Steven. n.d. The Shape of Theological Education. Manuscript, Trinity Evangelical Divinity School, Deerfield, Ill.

Scales, Peter, and Donna Koppleman. 1997. Service Learning in Teacher Preparation. In *Service Learning: Ninety-sixth Yearbook of the National Society for the Study of Education*, ed. Joan Schine. Chicago: University of Chicago Press.

Schine, Joan, ed. 1997. *Service Learning. Ninety-sixth Yearbook of the National Society for the Study of Education*. Chicago: University of Chicago Press.

Schipani, Daniel. 1997. The Church and Its Theological Education: A Vision.. In *Theological Education on Five Continents: Anabaptist Perspectives*, ed. Nancy Heisey and Daniel Schipani. Strasbourg, France: Mennonite World Conference.

Schleiermacher, Friedrich. 1966. *Brief Outline on the Study of Theology*. Trans. Terrence N. Tice. Richmond, Va.: John Knox. Orig. pub. 1830.

⸻. 1996. *Dialectic, or, the Art of Doing Philosophy: A Study Edition of the 1811 Notes*. Trans. Terrence N. Tice. Atlanta: Scholars.

Schneider, Alison. 1999. When Revising a Curriculum, Strategy May Trump Pedagogy. *Chronicle of Higher Education*, February 19: A14–16.

Schön, Donald. 1987. *Educating the Reflective Practitioner: Toward a New Design for Teaching and Learning in the Professions*. San Francisco: Jossey-Bass.

Schreiber, Leanne. 2004. Keith Black: Determined to Enter the Brain in a Friendly Way. *Discover* 25, no. 4: 66–73.

Schuller, David. 1981. Editorial. *Theological Education* 17 (Spring): 1–10.

Schwehn, Mark. 1993. *Exiles from Eden: Religion and the Academic Vocation in America*. New York: Oxford University Press.

⸻. 2002. Where are the Universities of Tomorrow? In *Religion, Scholarship, and Higher Education*, ed. Andrea Sterk. Notre Dame, Ind.: University of Notre Dame Press.

Scott, Donald. 1978. *From Office to Profession: The New England Ministry, 1750–1850*. Philadelphia: University of Pennsylvania Press.

Seitz, Christopher, and Kathryn Green-McCreight, eds. 1999. *Theological Exegesis: Essays in Honor of Brevard S. Childs*. Grand Rapids, Mich.: Eerdmans.

Senge, Peter M. 1990. *The Fifth Discipline: The Art and Practice of the Learning Organization*. New York: Doubleday Currency.

Senior, Donald, and Timothy Weber. 1994. What Is the Character of Curriculum, Formation, and Cultivation of Ministerial Leadership in the Good Theological School? *Theological Education* 30, no. 2: 17–33.

Senn, Frank, ed. 1986. *Protestant Spiritual Traditions.* New York: Paulist.

Sheckley, Barry, and Morris Keeton. 1997. Service Learning: A Theoretical Model. In *Service Learning. Ninety-sixth Yearbook of the National Society for the Study of Education*, ed. Joan Schine. Chicago: University of Chicago Press.

Sheldrake, Philip. 1998. *Spirituality and Theology: Christian Living and the Doctrine of God.* Maryknoll, N.Y.: Orbis.

Slattery, Patrick. 1995. *Curriculum Development in the Postmodern Era.* New York: Garland.

Sloan, Douglas. 1971. *The Scottish Enlightenment and the American College Ideal.* New York: Teachers College Press, Columbia University.

Smith, Gary Scott. 1996. Presbyterian and Methodist Education. In *Theological Education in the Evangelical Tradition*, ed. Daryl Hart and Albert Mohler. Grand Rapids, Mich.: Baker.

Smith, L. Glenn, et. al. 1984. *Lives in Education: People and Ideas in the Development of Teaching.* Ames, Iowa: Educational Studies.

Spears, Larry, and Anne Fraker, eds. 1996. *Seeker and Servant: Reflections on Religious Leadership.* San Francisco: Jossey-Bass.

Spener, Philip Jacob. 1964. *Pia Desideria.* Trans. Theodore Tappert. Philadelphia: Fortress.

Springsted, Eric. 1988. *Who Will Make Us Wise? How Churches Are Failing Higher Education.* Cambridge, Mass.: Cowley.

Stackhouse, John, Jr., ed. 2000. *Evangelical Futures: A Conversation on Theological Method.* Grand Rapids, Mich.: Baker.

Stackhouse, Max. 1988. *Apologia: Contextualization, Globalization, and Mission in Theological Education.* Grand Rapids, Mich.: Eerdmans.

Stafford, Tim. 2002. The Third Coming of George Barna. *Christianity Today*, August 5 (available at www.christianitytoday.com/ct/2002/009/1.32.html).

Standards of Accreditation. 1996. *Theological Education* 32, no. 2 (Spring).

Stanton, Timothy, Dwight Giles, and Nadinna Cruz. 1999. *Service-Learning: A Movement's Pioneers Reflect on Its Origins, Practice, and Future.* San Francisco: Jossey-Bass.

Sterk, Andrea, ed. 2002. *Religion, Scholarship, and Higher Education*. Notre Dame, Ind.: University of Notre Dame Press.

Stevens, Paul, and Brian Stelck. 1993. Equipping Equippers Cross-Culturally: An Experiment in the Appropriate Globalization of Theological Education. *Missiology: An International Review* 21, no. 1 (January): 31–40.

Stevenson, Louise. 1986. *Scholarly Means to Evangelical Ends: The New Haven Scholars and the Transformation of Higher Learning in America, 1830–1890*. Baltimore: Johns Hopkins University Press.

Stewart, Bruce. 1990. Tensions in North American Theological Education. *Evangelical Review of Theology* 14, no. 1 (January): 42–49.

Stoeffler, F. Ernest, ed. 1976. *Continental Pietism and Early American Christianity*. Grand Rapids: Mich.: Eerdmans.

———. 1983. Preface to *Pietists: Selected Writings*, ed. Peter Erb. New York: Paulist.

Storr, Richard. 1966. *Harper's University: The Beginnings*. Chicago: University of Chicago Press.

Stout, Jeffrey. 1988. *Ethics after Babel: The Languages of Morals and Their Discontents*. Boston: Beacon.

Stronks, Gloria. 1991. Assessing Outcomes in Higher Education. *Faculty Dialogue* 14 (Spring): 91–105.

Stroup, John. 1984. The Idea of Theological Education at the University of Berlin: From Schleiermacher to Harnack. In *Schools of Thought in the Christian Tradition*, ed. Patrick Henry. Philadelphia: Fortress.

Sullivan, William. 2005. *Work and Integrity: The Crisis and Promise of Professionalism in America*. San Francisco: Jossey-Bass

Sweeney, James, and Stephen Fortosis. 1994. Seminary and Church: Allies for Change. *Christian Education Journal* 14, no. 3 (Spring): 74–85.

Sykes, S. W. 1982. Theological Study: The Nineteenth Century and After. In *The Philosophical Frontiers of Christian Theology*, ed. Brian Hebblethwaite and Stewart Sutherland. London: Cambridge University Press.

Tan, Oon-Seng. 2003. *Problem-Based Learning Innovation: Using Problems to Power Learning in the Twenty-first Century*. Singapore: Thomson Learning.

Tanis, James. 1976. Reformed Pietism in Colonial America. In *Continental Pietism and Early American Christianity*, ed. F. Ernest Stoeffler. Grand Rapids: Mich.: Eerdmans.

Tarnas, Richard. 1991. *The Passion of the Western Mind: Understanding the Ideas That Have Shaped Our World View.* New York: Ballantine.

Taylor, Mark. 1994. Unsettling Issues. *Journal of the American Academy of Religion* 62, no. 4 (Winter): 949–63.

Teare, Richard, David Davies and Eric Sandelands, eds. 1998. *The Virtual University: An Action Paradigm and Process for Workplace Learning.* London: Cassell.

Thangaraj, M. Thomas. 1992. Theological Education in the United States: A View from the Periphery. *Theological Education* 28, no. 1 (Spring): 8–20.

Thiemann, Ronald. 1987. Making Theology Central in Theological Education. *Christian Century* 104, no. 4 (February 4–11): 106–8.

Toulmin, Stephen. 1990. Theology in the Context of the University. *Theological Education* 26, no. 2 (Spring): 5–65.

Tracy, David. 1981. *The Analogical Imagination: Christian Theology and the Culture of Pluralism.* New York: Crossroad.

Treier, Dan. 1999. Theology as the Acquisition of Wisdom: Reorienting Theological Education. *Christian Education Journal*, n.s., 3, no. 1: 127–39.

Tucker, Ruth, and Walter Liefeld. 1987. *Daughters of the Church*. Grand Rapids, Mich.: Zondervan.

Tugwell, Simon. 1985. *Ways of Imperfection: An Exploration of Christian Spirituality.* Springfield, Ill.: Templegate.

A Twenty-first Century Seminary Faculty Model. 1998. Report of a survey commissioned by the Murdoch Foundation, Portland, Ore.

Ulich, Robert. 1968. *A History of Religious Education*. New York: New York University Press.

⸻, ed. 1971. *Three Thousand Years of Educational Wisdom: Selections from Great Documents.* 2nd ed. Cambridge, Mass.: Harvard University Press.

Van Der Ven, Johannes A. 1996. *Ecclesiology in Context.* Grand Rapids, Mich.: Eerdmans.

Van Engen, Charles. 1994. Shifting Paradigms in Ministry Formation. *Perspectives*, October, 15–17.

Van Engen, John, ed. and trans. 1988. *Devotio Moderna: Basic Writings*. New York: Paulist.

Vanhoozer, Kevin. 1998. *Is There a Meaning in This Text? The Bible, the Reader, and the Morality of Literary Knowledge*. Grand Rapids, Mich.: Zondervan.

―――――. 2000. The Voice and the Actor: A Dramatic Proposal about the Ministry and Minstrels of Theology. In *Evangelical Futures: A Conversation on Theological Method*, ed. John G. Stackhouse Jr. Grand Rapids, Mich.: Baker.

Vest, Norvene. 2000. *Desiring Life: Benedict on Wisdom and the Good Life*. Cambridge, Mass.: Cowley.

Volf, Miroslav. 1996. Theology, Meaning, and Power. In *The Future of Theology: Essays in Honor of Jürgen Moltmann*, ed. Miroslav Volf, Carmen Krieg, and Thomas Kucharz. Grand Rapids, Mich.: Eerdmans.

―――――. 2002. Theology for a Way of Life. In *Practicing Theology: Beliefs and Practices in Christian Life*, ed. Miroslav Volf and Dorothy Bass. Grand Rapids, Mich.: Eerdmans.

Volf, Miroslav, and Dorothy Bass, eds. 2002. *Practicing Theology: Beliefs and Practices in Christian Life*. Grand Rapids, Mich.: Eerdmans.

Volf, Miroslav, Carmen Krieg, and Thomas Kucharz, eds. 1996. *The Future of Theology: Essays in Honor of Jürgen Moltmann*. Grand Rapids, Mich.: Eerdmans.

Von Holzen, Roger. 2000. A Look at the Future of Higher Education. *Syllabus* 14, no. 4: 56–57, 65.

Waits, James. 2000. Looking Forward, Looking Backward: A View of Theological Education at the Beginning of a New Millennium. *Theological Education* 36, no. 2: 47–54.

Ward, Ted. 1982. Metaphors of Spiritual Reality, Part 3: Evaluating Metaphors of Education. *Bibliotheca Sacra* 139, no. 556 (October-December): 291–301.

―――――. 1985. Service: An Endangered Value. *Faculty Dialogue* 4:1–6.

―――――. 1989. The Lines People Draw. *Faculty Dialogue* 11 (Spring): 7–22.

―――――. 1996. Servants, Leaders, and Tyrants. In *With an Eye on the Future: Development and Mission in the Twenty-first Century*, ed. Duane Elmer and Lois McKinney. Monrovia, Calif.: MARC.

Ward, Ted, and Linda Cannell. 1999. Theological Education and the Church. *Christian Education Journal*, n.s., 3:29–47.

Ward, Ted, and Sam Rowen. 1972. The Significance of the Extension Seminary. *Evangelical Missions Quarterly* 9, no. 1 (Fall): 17–27.

Watkins, Karen, and Robert Golembiewski. 1995. Rethinking Organizational Development for the Learning Organization. *International Journal of Organizational Analysis* 3, no. 1 (January): 86–101.

Watson, Francis. 1994. *Text, Church, and World: Biblical Interpretation in Theological Perspective*. Grand Rapids, Mich.: Eerdmans.

———. 1997. *Text and Truth: Redefining Biblical Theology*. Grand Rapids, Mich.: Eerdmans.

Weborg, C. John. 1978. A Study of Schleiermacher's Concept of Faith. *Covenant Quarterly* 36, no. 1 (February): 39–49.

———. 1986. Pietism: "The Fire of God Which Flames in the Heart of Germany." In *Protestant Spiritual Traditions*, ed. Frank Senn. New York: Paulist.

Webster, Douglas. 1992. *Selling Jesus: What's Wrong with Marketing the Church*. Downers Grove, Ill.: InterVarsity Press.

Welch, Claude. 1971. *Graduate Education in Religion: A Critical Appraisal*. Missoula: University of Montana Press.

Welker, Michael. 1996. Christian Theology: What Direction at the End of the Second Millennium? In *The Future of Theology: Essays in Honor of Jürgen Moltmann*, ed. Miroslav Volf, Carmen Krieg, and Thomas Kucharz. Grand Rapids, Mich.: Eerdmans.

Westerhoff, John. 1982. Theological Education and Models for Ministry. *St. Luke's Journal of Theology* 25, no. 2 (March): 153–69.

Westphal, Merold. 1997. Academic Excellence: Cliché or Humanizing Vision? In *Should God Get Tenure? Essays on Religion and Higher Education*, ed. David Gill. Grand Rapids, Mich.: Eerdmans.

Wheeler, Barbara. 1999. The Heart of Things. *Auburn Studies Bulletin*, no. 6 (September): 20–23.

Wheeler, Barbara, and Edward Farley, eds. 1991. *Shifting Boundaries: Contextual Approaches to the Structure of Theological Education*. Louisville, Ky.: Westminster John Knox.

Wilburn, Ralph G. 1962. The Role of Tradition in Schleiermacher's Theology. *Encounter*, no. 23 (Summer): 300–315.

Wilken, Robert. 1995. *Remembering the Christian Past*. Grand Rapid, Mich.: Eerdmans.

———. 1996. Grace and the Knowledge of God. In *New Perspectives in Historical Theology*, ed. Bradley Nassif. Grand Rapids, Mich.: Eerdmans.

Wilkes, Paul. 1990. The Hands That Would Shape Our Souls. *Atlantic* 266, no. 6 (December): 59–88.

Willard, Dallas. 2000a. "Twenty-first Century Realities and Choices for the Christian University." Presentation to the *Ward Consultation*, at Trinity Evangelical Divinity School, Deerfield, Ill., November 13–14. (see www.wardconsultation.org) Last accessed in October 2005.

Willard, Dallas. 2000b. Discipleship to Jesus Christ as Basis for Fellowship, Session 4.

Transcription of presentation at Leadership Conference, "The Unnecessary Leader: Leadership for the Whole People of God," Regent College, Vancouver, B.C., May 19–20.

Willimon, William, and Thomas Taylor. 1995. *The Abandoned Generation: Rethinking Higher Education*. Grand Rapids, Mich.: Eerdmans.

Wilshire, Bruce. 1990. *The Moral Collapse of the University: Professionalism, Purity, and Alienation*. Albany: State University of New York Press.

Wilson, Arthur. 2001. Professionalization: A Politics of Identity. *New Directions for Adult and Continuing Education*, no. 91 (Fall): 73–83.

Wilson, Marvin. 1989. *Our Father Abraham: Jewish Roots of the Christian Faith*. Grand Rapids, Mich.: Eerdmans.

Wind, James. 1987. *The Bible and the University: The Messianic Vision of William Rainey Harper*. Atlanta: Scholars.

Wind, James, and James Lewis. 1994. *American Congregations: New Perspectives in the Study of Congregations*. Vol. 2. Chicago: University of Chicago Press.

Wolterstorff, Nicholas. 1995. Does Truth Still Matter? Reflections on the Crisis of the Postmodern University. *Crux* 31, no. 3 (September): 17–28.

———. 1996. The Travail of Theology in the Modern Academy. In *The Future of Theology: Essays in Honor of Jürgen Moltmann*, ed. Miroslav Volf, Carmen Krieg, and Thomas Kucharz. Grand Rapids, Mich.: Eerdmans.

———. 2002. Scholarship Grounded in Religion. In *Religion, Scholarship, and Higher Education*, ed. Andrea Sterk. Notre Dame, Ind.: University of Notre Dame Press.

———. 2004. *Educating for Shalom: Essays on Christian Higher Education*. Ed. Clarence W. Joldersma and Gloria Goris Stronks. Grand Rapids, Mich.: Eerdmans.

Wolverston, Mimi, and Walter Gmelch. 2002. *College Deans: Leading from Within*. Series on Higher Education. Westport, Conn.: American Council on Education, Oryx.

Wood, Charles. 1985a. Theological Inquiry and Theological Education. *Theological Education* 21, no. 2 (Spring): 73–93.

———. 1985b. *Vision and Discernment*. Atlanta: Scholars Press.

———. 1993. *The Formation of Christian Understanding: Theological Hermeneutics*. 2nd ed. Valley Forge, Penn.: Trinity Press International.

———. 1994. *An Invitation to Theological Study*. Valley Forge, Penn.: Trinity Press International.

———. 1996. Theological Education and Education for Church Leadership. In *Theological Perspectives on Christian Formation*, ed. Jeff Astley, Leslie Francis, and Colin Chowder. Grand Rapids, Mich.: Eerdmans.

Woods, Leonard. 1885. *History of the Andover Theological Seminary*. Boston: James R. Osgood.

Woodward, Kenneth. 2001. The Changing Face of the Church. *Newsweek*, April 16, 46–52.

Wright, N. T. 1992. *The New Testament and the People of God*. Minneapolis: Fortress.

Wyman, Walter. 1991. The Historical Consciousness and the Study of Theology. In *Shifting Boundaries: Contextual Approaches to the Structure of Theological Education*, ed. Barbara Wheeler and Edward Farley. Louisville, Ky.: Westminster John Knox.

Yeide, Harry. 1997. *Studies in Classical Pietism: The Flowering of the Ecclesiola*. Studies in Church History 6. New York: Peter Lang.

Yoduf, Mark. 2004. What If the Yankees Were Run like a Public University? *Chronicle of Higher Education*, March 12, B7–9.

Zizioulas, John. 1985. The Early Christian Community. In *Christian Spirituality: Origins to the Twelfth Century*, ed. Bernard McGinn and John Meyendorf. New York: Crossroad.

INDEX

A

Academic Rationalism, 44, 58, 62, 70, 88, 97, 116, 317
Academic Theology, 21, 44, 58, 60, 61, 62, 70, 72, 73, 79, 91, 92, 93, 165, 184, 214, 217, 236, 310, 321
Accreditation, 14, 15, 17, 52, 84, 109, 112, 114, 124, 152, 266, 288, 306, 319, 320, 323
Aleshire, Dan, 19, 20, 105, 107, 244, 288, 325, 327
American Revolution, 138, 183, 184
Andover Theological Seminary, 141, 183, 362
Apprentice, 140, 190, 200, 317
Apprenticeship, 41, 82, 83, 139, 190, 200, 208, 258, 259, 317
Aquinas, Thomas, 166, 167, 168, 169, 171, 225, 343
Aristotle, 128, 145, 164, 165, 167, 169, 171, 181, 282
Assessment, 10, 32, 40, 76, 84, 104, 107, 108, 109, 114, 115, 117, 123, 131, 152, 155, 169, 199, 203, 230, 271, 288, 292, 293, 295, 298, 299, 300, 301, 304, 306, 308, 319, 320, 323, 325
Association of Theological Schools, 17, 52, 83, 109, 153, 162, 201, 207, 244, 267, 288, 289, 307, 328, 336
Augustine, 99, 127, 164, 167, 168, 169, 171, 214, 225

B

Banks, Robert, 35, 36, 96, 257, 328
Bloom, Benjamin, 148, 209, 274, 327, 329, 344
Brethren and Sisters of the Common Life, 6, 132, 227, 228, 229, 230, 231
Brethren of the Common Life, 126, 227, 230, 342

C

Cathedral School, 128, 190
Church-based Theological Education, 33, 244, 256, 258, 322
Clerical Paradigm, 22, 38, 77, 108, 110, 119, 175, 191, 263, 293
Cognition, 37, 88, 221, 235, 274, 276, 278
Collaborative, 15, 16, 26, 258, 264, 289, 291, 292
Collegia Pietatis, 232
Colonial, 78
Communities of Faith and Learning, 18, 32, 40, 277
Communities of Learning, 52, 290

376

Community, 9, 14, 16, 18, 21, 29, 33, 39, 41, 45, 46, 49, 50, 56, 61, 65, 70, 75, 79, 81, 94, 97, 100, 114, 115, 116, 121, 139, 143, 156, 162, 176, 179, 180, 191, 198, 208, 209, 210, 221, 227, 230, 239, 240, 242, 244, 245, 246, 247, 248, 249, 250, 251, 253, 254, 257, 259, 260, 261, 263, 264, 265, 268, 271, 276, 279, 282, 283, 285, 288, 289, 290, 291, 292, 293, 298, 310, 320, 322, 323, 324, 325

Congregational, 25, 79, 83, 107, 108, 120, 122, 143, 196, 201, 205, 247, 249, 254, 258, 261, 262, 263, 264, 265, 279, 285, 286, 300, 318

Conventional Theological Education, 17, 274, 304

Credentialing, 32, 113, 265, 266, 304, 308, 324

Curriculum, 18, 19, 21, 22, 23, 29, 30, 31, 32, 33, 35, 36, 37, 38, 42, 49, 51, 56, 58, 61, 71, 76, 77, 79, 80, 81, 82, 84, 85, 87, 91, 93, 94, 95, 104, 105, 109, 110, 113, 116, 117, 118, 120, 121, 128, 131, 136, 137, 139, 140, 142, 143, 144, 145, 146, 148, 149, 150, 151, 152, 153, 154, 156, 157, 158, 160, 161, 164, 165, 166, 171, 172, 178, 181, 185, 186, 187, 188, 190, 192, 193, 194, 195, 196, 197, 198, 201, 203, 204, 205, 206, 208, 209, 211, 212, 220, 229, 237, 251, 252, 254, 258, 259, 261, 262, 264, 270, 274, 276, 277, 278, 279, 282, 287, 288, 291, 293, 294, 295, 296, 297, 298, 299, 302, 303, 306, 307, 314, 317, 320, 324, 325

D

Dag Hammarskjöld Citation, 25

Disciplines, 21, 23, 30, 31, 35, 36, 37, 38, 40, 51, 53, 56, 58, 59, 60, 61, 62, 63, 71, 72, 73, 74, 75, 76, 77, 86, 90, 91, 93, 94, 95, 98, 102, 104, 105, 106, 109, 115, 117, 118, 119, 120, 136, 147, 148, 149, 150, 154, 156, 157, 165, 173, 176, 178, 179, 186, 188, 190, 194, 196, 201, 204, 205, 209, 212, 215, 221, 236, 258, 267, 270, 276, 277, 279, 281, 282, 284, 285, 287, 288, 291, 293, 294, 295, 296, 297, 298, 309, 317, 318, 320, 321, 322, 325

Divinity Schools, 9, 24, 48, 76, 78, 79, 104, 123, 136, 141, 142, 146, 148, 149, 150, 161, 170, 184, 187, 206, 210, 211

E

Ecclesial Paradigm, 264, 265

Education, 8, 9, 12, 14, 15, 17, 18, 19, 20, 21, 22, 23, 24, 25, 26, 27, 28, 29, 30, 31, 32, 33, 35, 36, 37, 38, 39, 40, 42, 44, 48, 49, 50, 51, 53, 54, 55, 56, 57, 58, 59, 61, 62, 63, 64, 65, 66, 67, 68, 69, 70, 71, 72, 76, 77, 79, 80, 81, 82, 83, 84, 85, 86, 87, 88, 89, 90, 91, 93, 95, 96, 97, 98, 99, 101, 102, 103, 104, 105, 106, 107, 108, 109, 110, 111, 112, 113, 114, 115, 116, 117, 118, 119, 120, 121, 122, 123, 124, 126, 127, 128, 131, 132, 134, 135, 136,

137, 139, 141, 143, 144, 145, 147, 148, 149, 150, 151, 152, 153, 154, 156, 157, 158, 159, 160, 161, 163, 164, 165, 166, 168, 169, 170, 172, 174, 177, 179, 180, 182, 183, 185, 186, 189, 190, 191, 192, 194, 195, 196, 197, 198, 199, 200, 201, 202, 203, 204, 205, 206, 207, 208, 209, 210, 211, 212, 213, 216, 218, 219, 221, 222, 225, 226, 228, 230, 231, 232, 233, 236, 237, 240, 242, 243, 244, 248, 250, 254, 255, 256, 257, 258, 259, 260, 261, 262, 263, 264, 265, 266, 267, 268, 269, 270, 271, 272, 273, 274, 276, 277, 278, 279, 280, 281, 282, 283, 285, 286, 288, 290, 291, 292, 293, 294, 296, 298, 299, 300, 301, 302, 303, 304, 306, 307, 308, 309, 310, 314, 315, 317, 318, 319, 320, 322, 323, 324, 325, 326

Enlightenment, 92, 134, 176

Epistemology, 24, 62, 64, 65, 67, 69, 75, 117, 179, 181, 264

Evagrius Ponticus, 217

F

Farley, Edward, 4, 21, 36, 37, 38, 40, 41, 42, 86, 87, 88, 89, 90, 93, 108, 110, 119, 136, 175, 191, 193, 225, 297, 319, 320, 330, 332, 335, 336, 360, 362

Flexner Report, 5, 199

Formal Education, 25, 54, 55, 62, 72, 122, 143, 274

foundations, 48, 52, 67, 123, 124, 201, 223, 265, 299, 318

Fourfold Model, 21, 136, 192, 195, 221, 294, 295, 297, 298

Francke, August, 231, 232

Freire, Paulo, 67, 337

G

Grading, 274, 300, 302

Greek, 15, 62, 63, 64, 65, 67, 68, 69, 70, 90, 97, 128, 139, 164, 168, 216, 217, 221, 226, 255, 329, 343

Greenleaf, Robert, 45, 46, 47, 48, 55, 124, 338

Groote, Geert, 227, 228, 229, 230

H

Habitus, 36, 37, 40, 87, 191, 225

Harper, William Rainey, 78, 146, 211, 295, 328, 330, 336, 340, 348, 349, 350, 357, 361

Harris, John, 104, 106, 115, 119, 299, 325, 340

Harvard University, 14, 51, 296, 331, 343, 353, 358

Hebrew, 62, 63, 64, 65, 67, 70, 96, 139, 329

Humboldt, 103, 134, 135, 136, 137, 188, 197

Humboldt University, 103

Hutchins, Robert, 51, 111, 112, 113, 145, 147, 342

I

Institutionalization, 22, 53, 69, 280, 304

Institutions, 9, 10, 11, 12, 14, 15, 16, 24, 28, 36, 45, 46, 47, 50, 51, 52,

54, 57, 62, 106, 114, 115, 130, 152, 153, 154, 156, 182, 183, 209, 243, 246, 249, 250, 257, 261, 262, 263, 269, 288, 299, 319, 323
Instructional Paradigm, 31, 270, 325
Integration, 8, 30, 35, 38, 72, 91, 97, 119, 123, 128, 142, 149, 158, 161, 168, 175, 193, 196, 209, 232, 236, 249, 276, 277, 287, 289, 291, 292, 296, 297
International Education, 14, 307

J

Johns Hopkins University, 209, 330, 339, 340, 347, 351, 354, 357

K

Kelly, Robert, 151, 152, 158, 202, 207, 344
Kelsey, David, 36, 61, 83, 87, 88, 95, 96, 105, 109, 151, 155, 177, 194, 195, 202, 203, 204, 225, 279, 283, 284, 285, 293, 297, 318, 344
Kuyper, Abraham, 344

L

Land Grant, 25, 74, 210
Learning, 10, 14, 15, 16, 17, 18, 19, 20, 23, 24, 25, 26, 29, 30, 31, 32, 33, 39, 45, 50, 51, 52, 53, 54, 55, 58, 59, 61, 66, 67, 69, 71, 74, 76, 77, 78, 79, 82, 88, 90, 91, 95, 99, 104, 106, 107, 108, 109, 111, 112, 115, 116, 117, 118, 119, 121, 122, 123, 126, 127, 128, 129, 131, 132, 135, 136, 137, 138, 139, 140, 142, 145, 147, 148, 149, 151, 152, 153, 160, 164, 165, 171, 172, 178, 179, 180, 181, 183, 186, 187, 197, 199, 209, 211, 212, 214, 224, 226, 228, 229, 232, 235, 240, 250, 257, 258, 263, 266, 268, 269, 270, 271, 272, 273, 274, 276, 277, 278, 279, 282, 285, 287, 289, 290, 291, 292, 293, 294, 295, 296, 297, 298, 299, 300, 301, 302, 303, 304, 306, 307, 309, 313, 315, 319, 320, 321, 322, 323, 324, 325
Learning Community, 69, 117, 271, 289, 290, 291, 324, 325
Learning Paradigm, 31, 270, 274, 325
Liberal Arts, 80, 83, 108, 127, 128, 136, 137, 159, 165, 207, 209, 224, 226, 254
Liberal Education, 111, 145
Liefeld, Walt, 8, 41, 42, 253, 345, 358
Lifelong Learning, 52, 58, 82, 117, 118, 160, 232, 267, 268, 270, 271, 297, 303, 304, 325

M

M.Div., 80, 108, 109, 254
Marsden, George, 71, 73, 141, 142, 145, 146, 178, 185, 186, 187, 197, 198, 209, 210, 340, 346, 347
May and Brown Survey, 203
McGinn, Bernard, 91, 92, 93, 98, 127, 128, 164, 216, 217, 218, 221, 222, 223, 224, 345, 348, 363
Medical Education, 199, 200, 201
Medicine, 78, 82, 118, 135, 140, 148, 153, 165, 172, 188, 200
Medieval, 86, 87, 88, 127, 130, 131,

133, 164, 165, 166, 168, 169, 170, 171, 172, 188, 189, 194, 195, 213, 215, 219, 220, 221, 222, 224, 225, 226, 227, 228, 230, 231, 236, 294
Methodist Education, 142, 143, 144, 149, 183, 342, 354, 356
Middle Ages, 74, 88, 90, 98, 127, 128, 129, 130, 131, 133, 164, 165, 167, 170, 188, 194, 216, 224, 329, 331, 333, 334, 339, 344, 353, 354
Ministry Education, 22, 109, 212, 277
Monasteries, 5, 126
Monastic, 49, 98, 127, 132, 165, 167, 169, 170, 213, 216, 217, 218, 222, 223, 225, 226, 228, 230
Monasticism, 126, 223, 334
Morrill Act, 209
Mystical Theology, 98, 215, 217, 224, 225

N

Niebuhr, Reinold or H. Richard, 72, 154, 155, 156, 157, 158, 159, 176, 202, 204, 205, 206, 207, 272, 348, 350
Nonformal Education, 53, 54, 55, 115, 126, 190, 244, 273, 303

P

Path of Love, 96, 121, 170, 225, 227, 231, 234, 237, 242
Path of Reason, 96, 121, 170, 225, 227, 231, 234, 237
Patristic, 22, 23, 59, 86, 87, 88, 90, 91, 100, 127, 168, 171, 172, 213, 214, 215, 216, 218, 220, 221, 224, 227

Pietism, 175, 180, 181
Postmodern, 24, 71, 74, 100
Postmodernism, 24
Practical Theology, 61, 78, 139, 151, 191, 193, 194, 196, 233, 279, 282
Praxis, 23, 36, 38, 65, 67, 216, 271, 287, 288, 325
Princeton Seminary, 141, 142, 331, 335, 350
Professional Model, 84, 109, 158, 179
Professional School, 80, 81, 83, 84, 85, 103, 107, 119, 140, 162, 191, 197, 199, 200, 203, 208, 209, 263, 264, 268
Professionalism, 38, 44, 77, 78, 80, 81, 83, 85, 86, 88, 95, 103, 114, 119, 120, 159, 171, 187, 198, 203, 208, 254, 271, 304, 317
Puritan Education, 139, 180, 181, 234, 311, 338, 341

Q

Quality Improvement, 300
Quality Management, 45

R

Rationalism, 22, 44, 58, 62, 64, 67, 69, 70, 72, 73, 86, 88, 97, 100, 103, 114, 116, 117, 175, 176, 213, 220, 226, 233, 234, 237, 242, 271, 276, 304, 306, 317, 320
Reformation, 5, 88, 89, 130, 132, 147, 171, 172, 176, 181, 190, 192, 194, 195, 226, 227, 228, 230, 236, 294, 329, 333, 334, 339, 344, 345, 351, 353
Reformers, 133, 172, 181, 190, 195,

236
Renaissance, 5, 74, 87, 130, 131, 132, 133, 171, 172, 192, 227, 329, 339, 347
Research University, 95, 102, 103, 137, 138, 153, 177, 183, 184, 186, 191, 197, 200, 203, 209, 294
Rockefeller, John D., 124, 152, 153, 207

S

Sapientia, 87, 195, 214, 224, 227, 230, 236
Schleiermacher, Friedrich, 5, 6, 21, 60, 134, 135, 136, 174, 175, 176, 177, 179, 185, 188, 191, 192, 193, 194, 195, 196, 197, 202, 208, 234, 235, 287, 330, 333, 334, 345, 350, 352, 354, 355, 357, 360
Schola Exterior, 127, 128
Schola Interior, 127
Scholastic, 79, 131, 139, 171, 181, 189, 224, 226, 256
Scholasticism, 89, 90, 128, 169
Schooling, 11, 12, 23, 25, 46, 53, 55, 56, 68, 69, 90, 104, 106, 126, 131, 191, 203, 274, 276, 298, 301, 322, 323
Scientia, 74, 87, 195, 214, 224, 227, 230, 236
Service Learning, 276, 277
Silos of Theological Education, 30, 31, 115, 118, 136
Spener, Philip Jacob, 231, 232, 233, 356
Spirituality, 22, 32, 38, 40, 42, 55, 58, 61, 72, 83, 88, 90, 91, 92, 93, 95,
96, 98, 99, 100, 104, 121, 152, 165, 168, 169, 170, 171, 180, 181, 213, 214, 216, 217, 218, 220, 222, 223, 224, 225, 227, 229, 235, 236, 237, 242, 245, 248, 264, 275, 277, 281, 284, 285, 290, 298, 306, 309
standards, 17, 52, 80, 81, 109, 112, 143, 153, 162, 198, 201, 202, 205, 207, 209, 266, 267, 279, 287, 288, 323
Standards, 17, 52, 80, 81, 109, 112, 143, 153, 162, 198, 201, 202, 205, 207, 209, 266, 267, 279, 287, 288, 323
Surveys, 50, 142, 150, 158, 160, 162, 202, 203, 204, 207, 272
Synagogue, 11, 65, 66

T

Taxonomy, 274
Testing, 10, 54, 122, 177, 265, 271, 274, 300, 301, 302
Theologia, 37, 40, 86, 87, 88, 166, 168, 169, 194, 213, 219, 220, 221, 222, 225, 226, 237
Theological Education, 17, 18, 19, 20, 21, 22, 23, 24, 25, 27, 28, 29, 30, 31, 32, 33, 35, 36, 37, 38, 40, 42, 44, 48, 50, 51, 53, 55, 56, 57, 58, 59, 61, 63, 67, 69, 76, 77, 79, 80, 81, 83, 85, 86, 87, 88, 89, 90, 93, 95, 96, 97, 98, 99, 101, 102, 103, 105, 106, 107, 109, 110, 113, 115, 118, 119, 120, 121, 122, 123, 124, 139, 143, 144, 149, 150, 151, 152, 154, 156, 157, 158, 159, 160, 161, 162, 166, 168, 169, 172, 177, 185,

191, 192, 194, 195, 198, 200, 202, 204, 205, 206, 207, 212, 213, 216, 219, 221, 223, 225, 226, 231, 232, 236, 237, 242, 243, 244, 250, 254, 255, 256, 257, 258, 260, 261, 262, 263, 264, 265, 266, 267, 268, 269, 271, 272, 273, 274, 277, 278, 279, 280, 281, 282, 283, 285, 286, 288, 293, 294, 296, 298, 299, 302, 303, 304, 305, 306, 307, 308, 309, 310, 315, 317, 318, 319, 320, 322, 323, 324, 325, 326

Theology and Spirituality, 21, 87, 90, 91, 93, 96, 98, 100, 104, 168, 169, 213, 216, 217, 220, 235, 236, 281

Theory and Practice, 18, 23, 35, 82, 109, 148, 150, 153, 154, 160, 211, 243, 271, 278, 279, 282, 283, 287, 306

Threat Matrix, 22, 23, 43

U

Universities, 11, 15, 22, 25, 48, 49, 56, 57, 59, 71, 72, 74, 77, 78, 79, 93, 98, 103, 106, 111, 115, 118, 122, 128, 129, 130, 131, 133, 134, 135, 136, 138, 144, 145, 146, 147, 150, 152, 153, 161, 162, 164, 165, 170, 171, 172, 173, 174, 178, 179, 180, 182, 183, 185, 186, 187, 188, 189, 197, 199, 200, 201, 207, 208, 209, 210, 212, 215, 227, 231, 236, 300

University, 5, 6, 14, 16, 25, 44, 51, 59, 72, 78, 103, 111, 112, 129, 133, 134, 135, 137, 138, 145, 146, 149, 166, 173, 174, 175, 178, 183, 184, 189, 190, 191, 192, 193, 197, 199, 200, 201, 202, 207, 209, 211, 229, 232, 234, 291, 296, 328, 329, 330, 331, 332, 333, 334, 335, 336, 337, 338, 339, 340, 341, 342, 343, 344, 345, 346, 347, 348, 349, 350, 351, 352, 353, 354, 355, 356, 357, 358, 360, 361, 362, 363

University of Berlin, 5, 135, 174, 183, 191, 192, 193, 197, 202, 234, 345, 354, 357

University of Chicago, 78, 111, 145, 146, 211, 333, 335, 339, 342, 343, 345, 348, 355, 356, 357, 361

University of Halle, 175, 232, 234

University of Utopia, 113

V

Vanhoozer, Kevin, 24, 40, 42, 359

Volf, Miroslav, 57, 58, 60, 73, 284, 285, 332, 333, 334, 335, 343, 354, 359, 360, 362

W

Ward, Ted, 4, 8, 16, 21, 25, 27, 28, 46, 54, 64, 67, 76, 97, 242, 256, 257, 258, 266, 298, 301, 306, 341, 344, 347, 359, 360, 361

Weber, Max, 104, 177, 178, 179, 356

Welch, Claude, 160, 161, 162, 360

Wheeler, Barbara, 36, 48, 49, 105, 109, 261, 265, 297, 318, 330, 332, 335, 342, 344, 346, 360, 362

Willard, Dallas, 50, 76, 137, 243, 245, 246, 247, 251, 254, 255, 319, 361

Wisdom, 20, 22, 24, 36, 37, 40, 41, 42, 63, 65, 68, 86, 87, 93, 95, 100,

106, 107, 112, 113, 117, 135, 145, 165, 166, 169, 182, 188, 195, 214, 219, 224, 225, 226, 230, 239, 265, 273, 281, 288, 297, 320

Wissenschaft, 103, 134, 177, 178, 202

Wolterstorff, Nicholas, 70, 71, 73, 74, 75, 177, 178, 260, 361

Y

Yale University, 184, 333, 341, 344, 351, 352

Made in the USA
Lexington, KY
05 September 2013